THE A. W. MELLON LECTURES IN THE FINE ARTS

DELIVERED AT THE NATIONAL GALLERY OF ART,
WASHINGTON, D. C.

BOLLINGEN SERIES XXXV · 4

Black Bull. *Lascaux Cave, Dordogne, France*
Aurignacian period (about 60,000–40,000 B.C.)

Etienne Gilson

PAINTING AND REALITY

THE A. W. MELLON LECTURES
IN THE FINE ARTS
1955
NATIONAL GALLERY OF ART
WASHINGTON

BOLLINGEN SERIES XXXV · 4

PANTHEON BOOKS

750, 4
G42p

THIS IS THE FOURTH VOLUME
OF THE A. W. MELLON LECTURES IN THE FINE ARTS,
WHICH ARE DELIVERED ANNUALLY
AT THE NATIONAL GALLERY OF ART, WASHINGTON.
THE VOLUMES OF LECTURES CONSTITUTE NUMBER XXXV
IN BOLLINGEN SERIES, SPONSORED BY AND PUBLISHED FOR
BOLLINGEN FOUNDATION

49, 402
Mar., 1965

Library of Congress Catalogue Card No. 57–11125

MANUFACTURED IN THE U. S. A.
BY KINGSPORT PRESS, INC., KINGSPORT, TENNESSEE

Designed by Andor Braun

To J. G.

WHO TAUGHT ME TO UNDERSTAND WHAT I LOVED

Preface

THE literature about painting has become so abundant that one feels somewhat guilty for adding one more volume to its already impressive bulk. Whether there was any justification for doing so is a question whose answer will ultimately hang on the free judgment of every reader. My only intention in writing this introduction is to dispel one of the misunderstandings that this book is likely to create in many minds.

There is only one justifiable approach to painting, and it is neither archaeology, nor history, nor science, nor art criticism, nor philosophy; it is paintings. Far from being a precautionary statement, this is one of the main conclusions that I hope to establish. Painters are fully qualified to say what their own art is, and a philosopher would simply make himself ridiculous if he undertook to tell them how to paint.

I hope to avoid this mistake. In my intention, at least, this is not a philosophical approach to painting, but, rather, a pictorial approach to philosophy. My own problem exactly is: what has a philosopher to learn from painting? This book, therefore, is the work of a philosopher asking himself philosophical questions on what he happens to know about a certain art. Just as we can philosophize about science, about history, or about religion, so also we can philosophize about art. The first chapter of this book will make clear, I hope, the reason it has seemed advisable to confine this inquiry to what philosophy can learn only from the art of painting.

Such preliminary remarks are not likely to create an atmosphere of good will and of mutual understanding between artists and philosophers. If a philosopher says anything about their art, painters find it hard to believe that he is talking about philosophy, not about painting. This is an evil to which I know no remedy. At any rate, painters will perhaps notice how careful I have been to listen to what they themselves had to say concerning the nature of their own work, its essence and its end.

Assuredly, when they write about painting, painters themselves become philosophers, and their own statements suffer from the difficulty of applying words to any one of the silent arts. Yet, when all is said and done, a fundamental difference remains between artists and philosophers, even when works of art are the common object of their reflections. Philosophers start from art in the hope that its study will open new vistas on philosophical problems to them, whereas artists, when they philosophize, do so in the hope of clearing up for themselves difficulties inherent in their art. In consulting artists about the nature of painting, I did not expect philosophical conclusions from them that art cannot possibly provide, but I wanted to make at least reasonably sure that my own conclusions were not wholly irrelevant to what painters themselves call the art of painting. In his first lecture at the Royal Institution, May 26, 1836, John Constable declared himself "anxious that the world should be inclined to look to painters for information on painting." I hope that, from this point of view at least, this book would have given John Constable some measure of satisfaction.

Such as they are, my conclusions will be found to arise at the meeting point of two entirely different disciplines: metaphysics and the concrete reality of the painted works of art. My first publication concerning the philosophy of art was written in November–December, 1915, and published the next year, in the *Revue de métaphysique et de morale*, under the title "Art et métaphysique." That was forty years ago, and during this long space of time, many things have happened to art as well as to my own metaphysics.

In art, we have witnessed the boldest creative experiment ever attempted during the whole evolution of the art of painting. With admirable and penetrating lucidity, the artists themselves have done their utmost to explain to their public the meaning of initiatives by which, not feeling their inner necessity, even the onlookers of good will could not help being puzzled. In metaphysics, a purely personal evolution led the author of the 1915 article to the rediscovery of the solid, down-to-earth realism of the classical metaphysics of being as interpreted by St. Thomas Aquinas.

This book would not have been written without the invitation extended to me by the Trustees of the A. W. Mellon Lectures in the Fine Arts at the National Gallery of Art, Washington. I wish to avail myself of this opportunity to express to them my heartfelt gratitude for inviting me to reconsider, in a new light, a problem that had never ceased to haunt my mind for forty years. In accepting the invitation, I was committing myself to the task of interpreting the evolution of the art of painting, especially that of its most recent phase, in the light of the classical metaphysics of being.

On this point, however, it will not be amiss to dispel a widespread illusion. Because they know the first principles in whose light all the rest becomes intelligible, metaphysicians sometimes imagine that the knowledge of the principles enables them to *deduce* from these principles the knowledge of all the rest. No attempt will be found in this book to achieve any such deduction. The only persons who know anything about painting as a creative art are the painters themselves; metaphysicians as such know nothing about it. Only, since modern painters have begun to worry about the nature of their art as well as about its relationship to the world of visible realities, they themselves have raised "metapictorial" problems to which the art of painting itself can give no answer. In such cases, the metaphysician must learn from the painters the data of the problems, after which he can feel justified in trying to see whether the light of the first principles does not facilitate their solution. Metaphysics essentially is a wisdom. Its proper function is not to do away with art, but, rather, to develop from art, in order to reveal it to art itself, the fullness of its own intelligibility.

In his Introduction to *Aesthetics and History,* Bernard Berenson has rightly observed that "no little of the sterility of art theory, and the unsatisfactoriness of art history, from late antiquity to our own day, is due to the failure to state at the outset whether one is thinking from the point of view of the producer of the work of art, or of the consumer." This is a very sensible challenge indeed. My own answer to it is that, in so far as I am aware of its place, the center of perspective in this book will be found to be neither the producer nor the consumer, but, rather, the work of art taken in itself as well as in its relationship to the world of natural reality.

For reasons that will be given in the book itself, the plates do not pretend to place real paintings under the eyes of the readers. Their strictly functional role is to substantiate, or, at least, to exemplify statements made in our text about certain paintings. The real paintings are not here, not even under the form of "reproductions." Real works of art can be found only in the seclusion of private homes, on the walls of certain public buildings, or in those galleries of art wherein, when these are allowed to fulfill their essential function, art lovers find a place of felicity, of light, and of peace.

ETIENNE GILSON

Toronto, December 5, 1955

ACKNOWLEDGMENTS

I DESIRE to acknowledge my indebtedness to the following persons who greatly helped me when, in the spring of 1955, I gave at the National Gallery of Art, Washington, the six A. W. Mellon Lectures out of which this book has grown: Huntington Cairns, without whom this book would not have been written; Macgill James, assistant director of the National Gallery of Art, who assembled the slides and always was of excellent advice; Richard S. Zeisler, New York, who found for me the writings of several modern painters; and Lionel Trilling, professor of English at Columbia University, who helped me out of a semantic difficulty.

Acknowledgments are due to Professor Lane Cooper, Ithaca, for giving permission to use the pages we have quoted from his translation of Plato's *Republic;* to D.-H. Kahnweiler for a hard-to-find photograph of a painting by Juan Gris and for permission to quote from his book on Juan Gris published by Curt Valentin; to the painter Alfred Reth, Paris, for photographs of two of his works; to Mr. and Mrs. A. S. J. Zacks, Toronto, for a photograph of a painting by Derain in their collection; to Martin Baldwin, Director of the Art Gallery of Toronto, for a photograph of the Gleizes painting; to Hayward Cirker, president of Dover Publications, for his gracious permission to quote material from Ozenfant, *Foundations of Modern Art;* and also to the following publishing firms for permission to quote from the works indicated: *Art News,* for James Johnson Sweeney's essay on Miró; Jonathan Cape, for Eric Gill's *Letters* and Edward MacCurdy's *Notebooks of Leonardo da Vinci;* Cassel and Co., for Gill's *Art-Nonsense and Other Essays;* Phaidon Press, for Delacroix's *Journal,* Eugène Fromentin's *The Masters of Past Time,* and the Mayne edition of Leslie's *Memoirs;* Wittenborn, Schultz, for Hans Arp's *On My Way;* and Harold Holtzman, for Mondrian's *Plastic Art etc.* Various other institutions and individuals who co-operated in making photographs available are detailed in the List of Plates, and to all of these my thanks.

E. G.

CONTENTS

FRONTISPIECE. Black Bull. *Lascaux Cave, Dordogne, France. Aurignacian period (about 60,000–40,000 B.C.).*
P: Windels, Montignac.

following page 24

1. MATTEO GIOVANETTI. Christ on the Cross. *About 1345. Fresco. St. Martial Chapel, Palace of the Popes, Avignon.*
P: Service Commercial Monuments Historiques, Paris.

2. JACQUES-LOUIS DAVID. Bonaparte Crossing the St. Bernard. *1800. Versailles.*
P: Giraudon.

1. The responsibility for the choice of the plates is entirely mine, but the responsibility for the captions has been largely assumed by scholars to whose judgments I was the more willing to defer as, not being myself an art historian, I could not have brought them to the same degree of precision. Two or three minor discrepancies between the captions and my own text will perhaps be noted. These are not oversights. Here are the points on which I would have expressed myself in a slightly different way.

Pl. 17a, b. These two portraits are fragments, not only of an originally larger composition, but of one and the same composition. The fact has a direct bearing upon the problem of "individuality" in paintings, for, indeed, its knowledge enables one to give their full meaning to the attitudes of the two personages. Despite what the catalogues say, Delacroix has not painted two portraits, one of George Sand, the other of Frédéric Chopin. He has painted a single composition representing Chopin playing for George Sand and George Sand listening to Chopin. Even separated by what looks like an act of vandalism, this is what they still are doing. There is no obligation, for catalogues, to ratify the consequences of such an act. My own captions would be: *Frédéric Chopin Playing for George Sand,* and *George Sand Listening to Frédéric Chopin.*

Pl. 41. The caption should be read as meaning: engraving from a pen drawing by Pieter Brueghel. See the relevant note by Elizabeth Mongan, *Selections from the Rosenwald Collection* (Washington: National Gallery of Art, 1943), p. 61.

Pl. 74. The caption says: *The Marriage of Giovanni Arnolfini and Giovanna Cenami.* The first word, at least, is not correct. What an unusual marriage, celebrated by a man and a woman in what seems to be their own bedroom, with no other witness than their dog! Moreover, for very strong reasons developed by Maurice W. Brockwell (see my bibliography), it seems certain that the man represents the painter himself. The title should be: *The Double Portrait of Jan Van Eyck and His Wife Margaret.* When an error has been printed in a catalogue, only a supernatural power could dislodge it.

To repeat, such details have their importance for art history, but they are of secondary importance for painting taken precisely qua art.

E. G.

70. PABLO PICASSO. Still Life. *1908.*
Solomon R. Guggenheim Museum, New York. P: Solomon R. Guggenheim Museum.

71. PABLO PICASSO. Mandolin and Guitar. *1924. Oil with sand on canvas.*
Solomon R. Guggenheim Museum, New York. P: Solomon R. Guggenheim Museum.

72. PIET MONDRIAN. Composition in White, Black, and Red. *1936.*
Museum of Modern Art, New York. P: Soichi Sunami, Museum of Modern Art.

73. PIET MONDRIAN. Victory Boogie Woogie. *1944. Paint and paper. Unfinished.*
Miller Company Collection, Meriden, Connecticut. P: Soichi Sunami, Museum of Modern Art, New York.

74. JAN VAN EYCK. The Marriage of Giovanni Arnolfini and Giovanna Cenami. *1434.*
National Gallery, London. P: National Gallery.

75a. ERNEST MEISSONIER. The Flutist. *1858.*
Louvre. P: Giraudon.

75b. ÉDOUARD MANET. The Fifer. *1866.*
Louvre. P: Braun.

76. ÉMILE RENOUF. The Helping Hand. *1881.*
Corcoran Gallery of Art, Washington. P: Woltz, Washington.

77. MARY CASSATT. The Boating Party. *1893/94.*
Chester Dale Collection, National Gallery of Art, Washington. P: National Gallery of Art.

78a. NORMAN ROCKWELL. Thanksgiving, 1951.
The Saturday Evening Post Collection, Philadelphia. P: *The Saturday Evening Post,* © Curtis Publishing Co., Philadelphia.

78b. J.-B.-S. CHARDIN. Grace. *1740.*
Louvre. P: Braun.

79. ALFRED MANESSIER. Crown of Thorns. *1954.*
Carnegie Institute, Pittsburgh. P: Carnegie Institute.

80a. JACQUELINE GILSON. Sketch for a Pietà.
P: The artist.

80b. JACQUELINE GILSON. Pietà. *1952.*
In the possession of the artist. P: Nelson C. Hitchinson, Toronto.

following page 296

81. JACQUELINE GILSON. Red and Green. *1945.*
Hart House, Toronto. P: Marc Vaux, Paris.

82. ALFRED RETH. Harmonie de matières. *1951.*
Musée national d'art moderne, Paris. P: Studio Yves Hervochon, Paris.

83. MAURICE DENIS. Petrach and Laura.
Private collection. P: Vizzavona, Paris.

84. PAUL GAUGUIN. The Yellow Christ. *1889.*
Albright Art Gallery, Buffalo. P: Albright Art Gallery.

85. GEORGES ROUAULT. Crucifixion. *1925. Lithograph.*
From Marcel Brion, *Georges Rouault, Collection des Maîtres* (Paris: Editions Braun, 1950). P: Marc Vaux, Paris.

PAINTING AND REALITY

If one attempted to belittle the arts by saying that,
in creating, they imitate nature, the answer should
be that . . . the arts create many things by themselves. Where something is lacking, they supply it,
because they own beauty.

—PLOTINUS, *Enneads* v, viii, 1

CHAPTER ONE

PHYSICAL EXISTENCE

THE first question a philosopher should ask about paintings is related to their mode of existence. About what does not exist, there is nothing to say. About what does actually exist, the first point to be considered is the nature, or modality, of its existence.

Strictly speaking, the word *being* should be used only in connection with that which enjoys the fullness of being, without any restriction or qualification. Philosophers usually agree that, if there is a God, his nature precisely consists in enjoying the permanent possession of absolute being or, better still, in *being* it. Thus understood, the notion of being excludes those of change, of beginning and of end. Being *is*, and that is about all there is to say about it.

Even though we may have reasons to affirm its reality, no such being is given in human experience. All the things we see and touch are particular and qualified beings. They are so many entities that endure in time between the moment each of them comes to be and the moment each of them finally passes away. The type of reality that characterizes such entities is less that of being, properly so called, than that of becoming. This time-honored distinction goes back at least as far as Plato, but it still is familiar to our own contemporaries. Most of us would agree that the kind of entity proper to things given in human experience is "existence" rather than "being." To exist is to have the kind of being proper to things enduring in time between their coming to be and their passing away. No deduction is required to establish the fact that paintings belong in the category of those things which have existence. Each of them has come to be at a certain date, and, as will be seen later on, each of them is fated to cease to be in a more or less distant future. While they are enduring in time, pictures, or paintings, are so many "existents." For this reason, we shall feel justified in speaking of the existence of paintings, in asking about their mode, or modes, of existence; in short, we shall everywhere consider existence as the type of being that it is fitting to attribute to this particular class of works of art.

1. Physical Existence

THE ontological nature of this approach to the study of painted works of art entails limitations to which philosophers and art critics rarely consent to submit. They are fond of talking about art in general, itself considered as an expression of what they call "poetry," that is, in the universal sense of this word, the primary process that is "the secret of each and of all arts." [1] From this lofty point of view, there is no reason not to consider reflections about plastic arts as directly relevant to "poetry" understood in the universal sense that has just been defined.[2] Not so in our own inquiry. Starting as we do from the fact that paintings are, or exist, we have no right to assume that their mode of existence has anything in common with that of other works of art. We do not even know a priori if there is such a thing as a universal "poetry" whose study would lead to conclusions equally valid for painting, for music, and for literature. Granting that there is an a priori probability in favor of this supposition, it should remain for us a

1. Jacques Maritain, *Creative Intuition in Art and Poetry*, p. 3. According to Maritain, poetry is "another name for what Plato called *mousikè*." Poetry therefore exceeds, or transcends, the more limited notion of art, which is the only one we intend to deal with in this book. This limitation of our own subject implies no judgment, explicit or implicit, on the notions that lie beyond its boundaries. The distinction between poetry and art in Maritain's book is best understood from pp. 167–71. See especially the remarks about the "free creativity of the spirit, essential to poetry," but not essential to either science or art, in which "the creativity of the spirit is *subordinate* to an *object*" (p. 169). Cf. "Poetry, as distinct from art, has no object" (p. 169). In this book, on the contrary, everything will revolve around the notion of a certain art; if anything is said in it concerning poetry, the remarks in question will only apply to the kind of poetry that is, if not subordinate to the object of art, at least intentionally related to it. [For full bibliographical references, see the Bibliography.]

2. Ibid., p. 4, art. 2.

supposition so long as separate inquiries have not confirmed it for each one of the various arts under consideration. In fact, if we consider the various kinds of works of art from the point of view of their specific natures as well as of the specific type of existence they enjoy, it becomes at once apparent that no common conclusion can apply to them all.

In order to simplify the problem, let us first examine separately what can be called the physical mode of existence of a work of art. By its "physical mode of existence" we intend to point out the mode of existence that belongs to it inasmuch as it is a physical object characterized by the same properties as any other object belonging in the same natural class. In the case of paintings, for instance, their physical mode of existence is practically identical with that of the very stuff of which they are made. In this sense, the mode of existence of a decorated wall is practically the same as that of any wall covered with a plain coat of paint, and this is true whether the painter be Botticelli, Michelangelo, or a modest house painter. In other words, the physical mode of existence of a painted wall, of a painted canvas, or of a painted wood panel is the same as that of the plaster, of the canvas, and of the wood on whose surfaces a certain coat of paint has been applied and continues to exist.

This is no place to analyze the mode of physical existence that belongs to works of art other than pictures. We must, however, give summary indications concerning some of them, be it only to invite further investigation and to make clearer what we have to say about the kind of existence that belongs to paintings. Let us consider, for instance, the kind of existence proper to poetry. In what sense can it be said of the *Ode on a Grecian Urn* that it is, or exists? In other words, in what sense can any poem be said to be an actually existing being?

To answer this seemingly simple question is, in fact, an exceedingly difficult task. Anybody who attempts to unravel this modest mystery soon understands for what reasons so few people have dared to approach it. In the beginning, everything is simple: a poem exists while somebody reads it or hears it being read. Its physical existence then is that of its reader, or that of the people who make up the audience to which it is being read. But while it is not being actually read, or heard, in what sense can it still be said to exist? What then remains of it is exactly what is left of *Hamlet* between any two of its private readings or of its public performances—that is to say, a certain number of letters printed in a certain order on some sheets of paper. The analysis of this ghostlike mode of existence would never end. It requires the existence of a poet inventing a poem in a certain language; the existence of a system of conventional signs standing for the various sounds and words constituting that language; the existence of a reader who, because he knows the language and can read, is able to reproduce, within his own mind, the same poem that first existed within the mind of the poet. Now, there is no necessary relationship between the conventionally adopted letters and the sounds for which they stand. Nor is there any necessary relationship between these articulate sounds, or words, and the things, or notions, they signify. Let us suppose a poem written in a language that scholars have not yet been able to decipher: the engraved stone or the parchment does indeed exist, and so does the would-be reader, but in what sense does the poem itself exist? There is no contradiction in imagining far-away times when stray copies of Shakespeare's plays will have survived all their possible readers; in what sense will Shakespeare's poetry then still exist? To this question the answer is: in the same sense as it does now exist for men who cannot read English. In short, it will not exist at all.

This is tantamount to saying that poetry has perhaps no physical existence of its own. But what about music? This time we are dealing with works of art whose physical existence is certain, but only within strangely narrow limits. The physical being of a musical piece, that which we could call its body, consists of sounds, that is, of vibrations in the gaseous mixture that envelops the earth, namely, air. The mode of existence of these vibrations is a physical one; yet it is very different from that of a solid body. Here again we cannot undertake the complete analysis of the mode of physical existence proper to music, but it will not be amiss to consider at least its first moments, to provide a point of comparison between music and painting.

In what sense can it be said of a musical piece that it is, or exists? In a first sense music exists, in the same way as poetry, under the form of con-

ventionally acceptable signs, written or printed on sheets of paper and signifying, for those who know how to read them, certain sounds or combinations of sounds. These signs or musical symbols, printed in black on white
paper, enjoy a physical existence, but they are not music.[3] Music has no
other actual existence than that of the actually existing sounds, and because
sounds exist only while they are being actually produced, music exists only,
precisely qua music, while it is being actually performed.

This entails the immediate consequence that musical pieces have a discontinuous mode of existence. A sonata, a symphony, or an opera endures
as long as the time of its performance. As soon as an orchestral mass and
the choirs it supports have sounded the last chord of Beethoven's Ninth
Symphony, the whole structure vanishes into nothingness. Nothing of it is
left except grateful memories and the hope to hear the same masterpiece
again, or, rather, another rendering of it. But one never knows with absolute
certitude that there ever will be another one. Countless ancient musical
scores have been destroyed during the past centuries; the reading of those
which have survived is full of problems whose answers are uncertain; many
musical instruments once in use have now ceased to exist, or, at any rate, we
no longer know how to play them. Apart from all such accidental difficulties, it is a fact that, between any two of its performances, a musical piece
has no physical existence of its own, and the interval between two performances can be a very long one. Bach's *Passion According to St. Matthew* completely ceased to exist qua music during the time between Bach's death and its
revival, largely owing to Mendelssohn's efforts, in 1829. Monteverdi's *Orfeo*
had to wait a still longer time. In short, the mode of physical existence proper
to music is discontinuous because it consists of sounds that have no subsistence of their own except while they are actually being produced.[4]

3. See the next note.

4. On musical existence in general, see Étienne Souriau, "L'Insertion temporelle de
l'œuvre d'art," in Charles Lalo *et al.*, *Formes de l'art, Formes de l'esprit*, pp. 42–45. These
excellent pages convey a just impression of the complexity of the problem. The phenomenology of musical existence is still more complex than that of pictorial existence, at
least if the physical mode of existence alone, irrespective of the aesthetic mode of existence, is taken into account. — A slightly different approach to the problem is to be found
in Harold Osborne, *Theory of Beauty: An Introduction to Aesthetics*, pp. 101–10. This
book favors a phenomenological interpretation of art. On painting, see pp. 110–12.

This character of music entails another one. Precisely because sounds lack the kind of substantiality proper to solid bodies, a musical piece has no simultaneous existence. It never enjoys the kind of total presence that naturally belongs to paintings. The remark is an old one. St. Augustine made it, many centuries ago, in the famous passage of his *Confessions* that deals with the paradoxical nature of time.[5] His analysis of the mode of existence that belongs to a poem is directly applicable to a song, to a sonata, to a symphony. The fragmentary character of their existence is obvious. What do we actually hear of a sonata? Not the sonata as a whole. Not even one of its movements, its themes, or its bars; all that we actually hear of it at a time is one of its chords. While this one is actually sounding, the next one has not yet come and the preceding one has already ceased to be. Taken as a whole, a musical piece has no actual existence except in the mind, owing to our memory of the past and to our expectation of the future. Were we to express this ontological condition in the language of traditional philosophy, we would not refuse existence to music; on the contrary, we would describe music as the very type of that which, because it never is but ceaselessly becomes, is much less a being than an existent striving to be without ever quite doing it.

Whatever else it may be called, then, a musical piece cannot be said to be, in the full sense of the term, a thing. A painting, on the contrary, is typically a thing. In dealing with such primary notions as "being" and "thing," one cannot help feeling tempted to define them; but their definition is impossible precisely because these are the very first notions that occur to our intellect. Whatever we may say about them, they themselves are inevitably included in their attempted description. But actually existing things have at least certain well-known properties that make it possible for us to ascertain their presence.

5. St. Augustine, *Confessions*, bk. XI, ch. 27, art. 34, up to ch. 28, art. 38 (ed. M. Skutella, pp. 288–92). English translations of the *Confessions* are easy to find, even the classic one of E. B. Pusey. Augustine carries his analysis up to the mode of existence that belongs to a syllable. Long or short, a syllable endures in time; it does not exist whole in any single instant of its duration.

The most striking one among these properties is well expressed by the German word that points out actual existence: *Dasein.*[6] A thing is recognizable by the fact that *it is there*. The two notions of thing and of place are inseparable in our minds because, indeed, an actually existing thing is always somewhere. To the question, where is the "Kreutzer" Sonata? there is no answer. Its score is to be found in many places, because it is a thing; the sonata itself does not exist anywhere else than, ideally, in the minds of the music lovers who hear it or remember it after hearing it. Strictly speaking, it is nowhere. On the contrary, we can say with precision where a painting is to be found, and its location is the only place where it can really be seen. Because it is a thing, the *Death of Procris,* by Piero di Cosimo, occupies a certain place, and only one. If we want to see it, we must go to the National Gallery in London, for this is where it is and it can be seen nowhere else. But where is *Parsifal?* To the extent that music can ever be said to be, *Parsifal* exists nowhere in particular, unless we prefer to say that it exists everywhere it is being actually performed. Only, if we say so, we must remember that the only reason there can be two or three *Parsifal*s existing at one and the same time in various parts of the world is that there is no such thing as a *Parsifal* subsisting somewhere, itself in itself, after the manner of a physical substance. On the contrary, each and every picture has its own *Dasein,* which cannot be duplicated. To the question, where is Veronese's *Marriage Feast at Cana?* the precise answer is, it is, at least for the present, in the Louvre, Paris, France. Similar answers could be given to all similar questions. When an art historian cannot answer one of them, he simply says that the picture in question is "lost." We shall have to come back later on to the consideration of this curious notion. Just now, let it

[49]

---

6. Endless commentaries have been written concerning the allegedly untranslatable meaning of the German *Dasein.* In a way, it is a mysterious term, in this sense at least, that it points out a mystery—namely, that it is impossible to define actual being. But its own meaning is not at all mysterious. It simply stresses the fact that "to be somewhere" is the simplest and most manifest of all marks of actual existence. The English *there is* has the same meaning. Other indirect formulas (German, *es gibt;* French, *il y a,* etc.) serve the same purpose. Such expressions do not attempt to say what being is; they simply point out so many signs of actual existence. Etienne Gilson, *Being and Some Philosophers,* ch. III, "Essence and Existence."

suffice to say that even a "lost" picture is supposed to be somewhere, in an unknown place where it is peacefully continuing to exist.[7]

Let us consider more closely the implications of this doctrine. The more immediate and the more fundamental of these implications is that, strictly speaking, the mode of existence proper to pictures is practically the same as that of all material objects. This is so true that, in many cities whose artistic collections are still young, the same building can indifferently shelter a few paintings, some pieces of furniture, and even geological specimens or stuffed animals. All these are material objects, subsisting in definite places where each of them enjoys a continuous existence so long as no accident happens to destroy it. The perfectly obvious nature of this evidence should not render it trivial in our sight. On the contrary, to keep in mind such fundamental certitudes is the best way to protect ourselves against many confusions in art criticism and even in art history. All comparisons between painting and music should first take into account the radical difference there is between their respective modes of physical existence.[8] They *are* not in the same way.

This is the reason many questions can be asked about paintings that cannot be asked about music. For instance, we shall have to discuss the kind of relationship that obtains between an original painting and its copies. And indeed such a question makes sense, for all painted copies can be compared with some actually existing original. Not so with music. True enough, there can be an indefinite number of performances of the Ninth Symphony, but there is no original prototype of that symphony with which each one of these performances can be compared and, by comparison with it, be judged. All that Beethoven has left us is a musical score; he has not left us a symphony in the same sense in which Michelangelo has left us the *Moses* of San Pietro in Vincoli, or, to confine ourselves to paintings, in the same sense in which

7. We call "lost" a picture whose place is unknown to us. Art historians consider a picture "lost" when they themselves do not know where it is. For instance, if an art lover owns a picture and cherishes it so much that he does not even want other people to know that he owns it, the picture in question is "lost" for the history of art and therefore for its historians.

8. On certain objections against this position, see below, sec. 2, "Aesthetic Existence," p. 12.

Veronese has left us the *Marriage Feast at Cana.* Still another way to point out the same difference would be to say that it is possible to own a painting, be it even a Rembrandt or a Vermeer, but it is not possible to own a Beethoven sonata, or a symphony, except, of course, under the form of musical scores that are neither sonatas nor symphonies. To own the original manuscript score of one of Haydn's quartets is in no way to own an original quartet, for the simple reason that there is no such thing. Even the first performance of such a quartet, in Haydn's own lifetime and under his personal supervision, was but the first one of an indefinite series of possible performances, each of which was an original, and none of which could be considered *the* quartet at stake. The modern technique of recording performances and of multiplying such records does not modify the data of our problem. We can listen to one of the recordings of one of the possible interpretations of any musical score, but since the original of its ideally perfect interpretation does not exist in nature, we cannot point out the features whereby any such performance either keeps faith with this ideal original or betrays it.[9] On the contrary, any painter can set side by side an original and one of its copies and show in what they differ, in what they are alike. All these facts (and many others that we shall have to discuss later on) necessarily follow from the physical mode of existence that belongs to paintings. To sum up, a painting is a solid, material thing, enduring in a certain place and enjoying a continuous mode of existence so long as it lasts. The whole ontology of painting rests upon this fundamental fact, which also accounts for the specific nature of our relations with painted works of art. These relations are not the same as those we have with the products of the other arts, precisely because, not having the same kind of being, poems, musical compositions, and paintings do not exist in the same way.

2. *Aesthetic Existence*

IN WHAT precedes, the words "physical existence" signify the existence of paintings conceived as simple material objects. To simplify the problem,

9. This does not prevent conductors, virtuosos, and even "connoisseurs" from entertaining pretty definite ideas concerning the proper interpretations that alone permit one to hear the "true" *Don Giovanni,* etc. The arbitrariness of such convictions is as complete as their dogmatism.

we can consider each painting as constituting a single physical unit made up of a support (plaster, wood, plywood, canvas, cardboard, paper, etc.), its underpainting, and a coat of colors. But it can be objected that thus to consider a painting as any other material object is not to consider it as a painting at all. And, indeed, each and every material object that we can see and handle is likewise a solid, located in space and enjoying a continuous existence in time. From this point of view, there does not seem to be any difference between a painting and the brush of the painter or his easel. Hence the conclusion that, although the physical mode of existence of paintings may well differ from that of music, their artistic and their aesthetic modes of existence can nevertheless be the same. Like a poem or a musical piece, a painting has actual existence only during those moments that it is being actually experienced as a work of art.

This position has recently been maintained with great force by excellent aestheticians. In order to understand it, one must first remember the modern distinction introduced by philosophers between ontology and phenomenology. Ontology deals with being, or beings, such as they are in themselves, irrespective of the fact that they are apprehended or not as well as of the particular way in which they may happen to be apprehended. From this point of view, it is true to say that, like every other solid body, a painting continues to be that which it is, irrespective of the fact that it is being seen or not. Even artistic existence belongs to paintings irrespective of the fact that they are being experienced or not. The modern preponderance attributed to the point of view of the onlooker has finally led the aestheticians to reason as though to experience a painting as a work of art was to cause its existence as a work of art.[10] In fact, just as a work of nature is such because it owes its

10. The contrary position is perfectly expressed in John Dewey, *Art as Experience*. "A work of art, no matter how old and classic, is actually, not just potentially, a work of art only when it lives in some individualized experience. As a piece of parchment, of marble, of canvas, it remains (subject to the ravages of time) self-identical throughout the ages. But as a work of art it is re-created every time it is esthetically experienced" (*Intelligence in the Modern World: John Dewey's Philosophy*, ed. J. Ratner, p. 983). The example of the Parthenon, quoted by Dewey himself, clearly shows where the error lies. The Parthenon is in no way re-created by art every time it is actually experienced as a work of art. It is a work of art because it has been produced by the art of an artist. It always subsists as a permanent possibility of aesthetic experience, as long as it lasts (Souriau, "L'Insertion temporelle de l'œuvre d'art," in Lalo *et al.*, p. 41), but unless

existence to the efficacy of natural forces, so also a work of art is such because it is the work of a certain artist who has caused it to be by means of
his own art. Up to what point our awareness of their artistic existence is
implied in our aesthetic experience of paintings is a point to be discussed
later. For the present, the point at stake is that the consideration of the
artistic mode of existence of a painting, since it hangs on that of its efficient cause, belongs in ontology.

Phenomenology rests upon the assumption that, as it has been established
by Kant's *Critique of Pure Reason,* we cannot speculate about what things
are in themselves, since this would entail an attempt to know things such as
they are while they are not being known. To avoid this contradiction,
phenomenology substitutes, for the knowledge of things in themselves, the
knowledge of things such as they are in human experience. In other words,
what philosophers call a "phenomenon" is "being" as an object of experience. In the light of this distinction, it is commonly said that the only being
of a painting in which we should take an interest is not its so-called physical
being, but rather the phenomenological being that it has as an actually experienced work of art.

This is a good occasion to remember the great saying of Leibniz, that
systems are true in what they affirm and false in what they deny. For, indeed, phenomenology is a very important discovery and it is here to stay.
Even if its arrival should not prevent the survival of ontology, the fecund
investigation of the manifold modes of phenomenological existence deserves
to be carried on, as it has been ever since the time of Hegel, with increased

we identify artistic existence (existence of that which has been produced by art) with
aesthetic existence (existence of that which is actually experienced as a work of art)
works of art remain such *in themselves* whether they are being experienced as such or
not. — Against our own position, see Osborne, pp. 95–96. Starting from a distinction
introduced by H. S. Goodhart-Rendel (in *Fine Art*) between the *material* of any work of
art and its *vehicle,* Osborne defines the *vehicle* of a work of art as "that which, persisting
unchanged through time and outside perception or apprehension, enables (more or less)
the same *organization of material* to enter the experience of different persons at different times." Whence his conclusion (p. 96): "The vehicle of a work of plastic art is what
is commonly called the picture, an arrangement of pigments upon canvas, wood, plaster
or what not." Again: "If a beautiful picture is painted, all that is further needed for its
actualization as a work of art is that a competent observer should look at it." We simply prefer to say that if a beautiful picture is painted nothing is further needed for its
actualization as a work of art. The work of an artist's art is, by definition, a work of art.

care, but the aesthetic implications of this new philosophical attitude are not so simple as they seem to be in the eyes of some contemporary aestheticians.

Let us first observe that, from a strictly phenomenological point of view, the distinction should not simply be between a painting taken as a physical being and the same painting taken as an object of aesthetic experience. Philosophers are mainly concerned with knowing. Consequently, the type of phenomenological existence in which they are interested is the one that belongs to things inasmuch as they are being known. Now, the distressing fecundity of the notion of phenomenon is such that the analysis of no phenomenological being ever comes to an end. Because any object can enter human experience in a practically infinite number of different ways, the investigation of its various modes of existence—that is, its "phenomenology" —can be indefinitely pursued without ever exhausting the object in question.

This, which is both the greatness and the misery of phenomenology, can be verified in the case of paintings. Apart from having its physical existence, a painting has the being of that which is known and seen; but it can also exist as an object of aesthetic experience, which is a mode of being distinct from the two preceding ones. To the painter himself, a painting is first something to be done, but it also is something to be sold, and very great painters, such as van Gogh, have known the distance from a completed picture to a sold picture.[11] Nor is this all, for the mode of existence of the painting we intend to buy is not the same as that of the same painting the art dealer is trying to make us buy. Still more modest modes of existence should be listed, even in the case of the greatest masterpieces. Paintings are things to be stored, or to be exhibited, or to be packed and carted or shipped; they are things to be dusted, repaired, restored, or more simply protected by guardians. As a mere suggestion, let us try to imagine what a world-famous masterpiece really would mean to us if we were in charge of seeing to it, eight hours a day, that no one should touch it, scratch it, or steal it.[12] From the point of

11. The only painting ever sold by van Gogh was *The Red Vineyard*. Cf. Charles Terrasse, "Vie de Vincent van Gogh," in *Lettres . . . à son frère Théo*, p. 16.

12. Ingres once sent for a messenger to take the portrait of Cherubini from his studio. The story continues as follows. The man calmly takes the painting down from the easel,

view of phenomenological existence, all these are so many different modes of being. Considering these various modalities of their existence, it is at least doubtful that all works of art can be said to exist in the same way. Many problems arise, in connection with paintings, that do not arise, at least under the same form, in connection with poetry or music. To mention only one of them, the problem of selling art is not at all the same for the art dealer as it is for the bookseller to sell art books. Our present problem is to ascertain the common origin of these differences, and our tentative answer is that we should look for it in the fundamental mode of physical existence that is proper to each specifically distinct type of work of art.[13]

Let us call aesthetic existence the mode of existence that belongs to paintings inasmuch as they are being actually perceived as works of art and as objects of aesthetic experience. It then becomes obvious that, like music or poetry, paintings enjoy only a discontinuous mode of existence, which lasts as long as aesthetic experience itself and varies together with it. Everyone will grant that there is such a mode of existence, but some philosophers maintain that works of art, taken precisely as such, have no other one. Their reason for upholding this thesis is both subtle and simple; it is that, so long as it is not being perceived as a work of art, an object is not a work of art. In other words, what is not a work of art for somebody is not a work of art at all.

There is something to be said in favor of this philosophical position. In Europe at least, small forests of seventeenth- and eighteenth-century furniture have been used to keep stoves burning; to those who were using it that way, such furniture was just fuel. Quite recently (July, 1954), a Milan newspaper announced that a large-sized Tintoretto had just been discovered

wraps it up, ties it carefully, and carries it away without further ado. "The imbecile," remarked Ingres; "he did not say a word." Quoted from Jules Laurens, *La Légende des ateliers,* by Amaury-Duval, *L'Atelier d'Ingres,* p. 203. Obviously, the phenomenological being of the portrait was not the same for the "imbecile" and for the painter.

13. On the various modes of phenomenological existence attributable to works of art, see Souriau, *La Correspondance des arts,* pp. 70–71. — On the allegedly "univocal" nature of aesthetic existence, "whatever its specification according to the different genres of art," see Souriau, "L'Insertion temporelle de l'œuvre d'art," in Lalo *et al.,* p. 41. The word "existence" would apply to all works of art univocally if the nature of aesthetic experience was not diversified by the physical nature of its objects.

in the basement of the Cathedral. Up to that day it had been used to cover a pile of junk. The question then is, To those who had been using it that way what was it? Was it a Tintoretto or was it a covering? But the problem can be generalized. What is a cathedral, while nobody is looking at it, if not a heap of stones? In the same way, while nobody is looking at them and enjoying them precisely as paintings, these are nothing more than colored pieces of canvas, cardboard, or wood. It seems therefore that, like musical pieces, paintings exist only while they actually *are* being perceived.[14]

These remarks are justified to the extent that aesthetic existence is at stake, but they do not apply to the artistic existence of the experienced works of art. Taken in itself, aesthetic experience involves time. It is only one among many psychological events that all have a beginning and an end and whose nature is such that they can be more or less exactly repeated. From this point of view—that is, considered as an object of actual aesthetic experience—the existence of a painting, and even that of a statue or of a monument, is just as fleeting and discontinuous as that of music. We all know this from bitter experience. Being abroad and in one of the rooms of some art gallery to which his chances of ever returning are remote, does not an art lover experience a feeling of distress at the thought that, after crossing the next door, he will never again find himself face to face with one of the world's masterpieces? Especially if he is advanced in years, an art pilgrim cannot leave even certain art cities without thinking that this time is perhaps the last time. At any rate, there is no doubt that for each of us, whatever his age, the mode of existence that belongs to objects of aesthetic experience is discontinuous and fragmentary.

Let us go further still. There are, on the part of paintings themselves, subjective causes for this discontinuity. One of these causes, at least, is familiar to all, namely, the presence or the absence of light. However long

14. The fact that there are many correspondences among the various fine arts cannot be denied. What is less certain is that the fine arts can be organized into anything like a "system of the fine arts." The interrelations among the various arts should neither be denied nor stressed to the point of obliterating the specific characters proper to each one of the fine arts considered in itself. On this problem, see Souriau, *La Correspondance des arts*; and Thomas Munro, *The Arts and Their Interrelations*, for philosophical classifications of the arts, pp. 157–208 (on Souriau's doctrine, pp. 202–6).

they try to stay open, a moment comes every day when art galleries have to close their doors. Darkness then sets in, and, from the point of view of possible aesthetic experience, all the paintings cease provisorily to exist. Is not this another feeling familiar to most of us? At the time the guardians of art first begin surreptitiously to look at their wrist watches, and then, politely but firmly, escort us from room to room until they finally march us out of some art gallery, do we not sometimes wonder what kind of existence those masterpieces are still enjoying during the long hours that their colors are blacked out and can no longer be seen? Nor is this all. For, indeed, works of art can disappear for years, sometimes even for centuries, with the result that, as did happen in the case of cave paintings, some of them ceased to be actually experienced for some fifteen thousand years. Moreover, even after being thus rediscovered, they were not recognized at once as works of art, much less as the kind of works of art that they are.

The radical contingency of aesthetic existence is strikingly symbolized by the story of the discovery of the rock paintings of Altamira. In 1879, the Spanish archaeologist, Marcelino de Sautuola, was exploring a cave near Santander, in Spain. While he was at work, his little daughter, who was playing around him, suddenly told him that she saw a beast on the rock. De Sautuola looked at it and saw several animal forms painted on the walls of the gallery he was in as well as of the following ones. Thus and in this way did works of art buried in darkness for many thousands of years relive for the first time in the eyes of a child wholly unaware of having made a momentous archaeological discovery. At the time, however, nobody paid attention to it. It was going to take a few more years before, being at last recognized for what it was, the prehistoric cave art of Altamira achieved the fullness of its aesthetic existence.[15] The more recent, but equally accidental, discovery of the Lascaux murals bears witness to the same truth. Far from being identical, ontological existence and phenomenological existence are not always compatible. Unseen, the Lascaux [front.] murals have victoriously stood the strain of many millenniums. Exposed to

15. A. Laming and J. Emperaire, *L'Art préhistorique: peintures, gravures et sculptures rupestres*, introduction.

[1] the natural vandalism of crowds, the crucifixion of Avignon is now ending an agony of five hundred years.

The same conclusion can be directly obtained by considering the problem from the point of view of aesthetic experience itself. In the case of painting as well as of music, there are an experiencing subject and an experienced object. In both cases, the experiencing subject is a human consciousness that endures in time and whose fluidity communicates itself to the very being of aesthetic experience. A certain painting may not have perceptibly changed during fifty or sixty years, but the man who sees it at the age of sixty is very different from the young boy of ten or from the man of thirty who had seen it before. Let us leave aside the tricky problem of artistic tastes and of the way they have of changing with age; the same painting, even if it is as much admired as it ever was, is not seen in the same way by the child, by the same child now become a mature man, and by the same man now entering a ripe old age. It is the same painting; it is the same human being; it is by no means the same being of aesthetic experience in one and the same person.

Nor is this all. Let us consider ourselves while we are looking at a certain painting in some art gallery. It takes time for us to see it. However long or short this time is, our inspection of the painting has a beginning, a middle, and an end.[16] We see it better and better; at any rate, we see it

16. This discontinuity has invited several aestheticians, including painters, to question the received distinction between arts of time (poetry, music) and arts of space (sculpture, painting, and, generally speaking, the "arts of design"). See, for instance, the remarks of Paul Klee in his "Creative Credo" (*Schöpferische Konfession*): "Movement is the source of all growth. In Lessing's *Laokoon*, the subject of so much mental exercise in our younger years, there is much ado about the difference between time and space in art. Once we examine it more closely, this is really just a bit of erudite hair-splitting; for space, too, implies the concept of time." (In Will Grohmann, *Paul Klee*, p. 98.) Klee then observes that it takes time for a dot to become a line, for a line to form a surface, for a surface to form a solid, for an artist to construct his work, and for the beholder to see it. To which he adds: "It was Feuerbach, I think, who said that a picture cannot be appreciated without a chair. Why the chair? So that your tired legs won't distract your mind. Legs get fatigued from standing for so long. What is needed is leisure-time once more." All this is true, but it is true of the genesis of the work of art and of its apprehension by a beholder only. On the contrary, from the point of view of the work of art itself, the distinction between space and time seems to remain valid. On the one hand, music is always performed and heard somewhere; so music, too, is in space; but the very substance of a musical piece is quite different from that of a sculpture or a painting. On the other hand, a painting endures in time, but it does so as a complete whole whose parts are simultaneously given in space, which is not the case with music.

otherwise, so that its aesthetic mode of existence never ceases to change even while we are looking at it. The same remark applies to the various modes of existence of one and the same painting in the consciousness of five or six different persons looking at it at one and the same time. They do not all see it under the same angle or in the same light. Even if they did, they still would not be the same person, so that there still would be five or six different modes of aesthetic existence, each of them continually changing, for one and the same painting.

It is therefore true to say that, because all human experience is subjective and takes place in time, the aesthetic mode of existence of painting is somewhat similar to that of music. And yet, when all is said and done, even this is not wholly true, because the difference between their respective modes of physical existence is confusedly perceived in aesthetic experience, and this is enough to render the aesthetic existence of a painting specifically different from that of a musical piece. In the case of music, we have a fleeting apprehension of a fleeting and always incompletely existing thing; in the case of painting, we have a changing, fleeting, and always incomplete experience of a stable, complete, and enduring entity. This is enough to account for the fact that we do not expect the same kind of emotion from paintings and from music. Some of us are tone-deaf to music, others are color-blind, and while many men are fortunate in being able to enjoy both painting and music, very few, if any, are equally sensitive to both. At any rate, personal experience, to which one often appeals in the last resort, seems to confirm the fact that the physical difference there is between their respective relations to space and time remains perceptible in our different ways of apprehending the existence of music and the existence of painting.

The easiest way to realize this difference is perhaps to compare the two kinds of places where music and painting are to be found. Musical scores exist in libraries where they can be consulted; only, as has already been said, musical scores are not in themselves music. In order to hear music, we have to go to appointed places, such as theaters and concert halls, and it is necessary for us to be there at certain appointed times that are the only ones during which some music will exist in those places. During the interval between two performances or two rehearsals, an opera house or a concert hall is totally empty of music. There is nothing there. On the contrary, museums and art galleries are permanently inhabited by a multitude of man-made things whose unseen presence is perceptible to us even when, having something else to do, we must content ourselves with passing by. Every time we can enter one of these buildings, and especially one of the rooms in which some world-famous painting is exhibited, our impression of being admitted to an awesome presence becomes irresistible. One enters the room of the Brera, in Milan, where the sole painting exhibited is Raphael's *Marriage of the Virgin,* as he would enter the hall in which some sovereign is sitting in state, waiting for the homage of his visitors.

This solid physical presence is part and parcel of the aesthetic existence of paintings, and it renders their aesthetic experience specifically different from that of music, which, far from being focused upon a whole completely given at once in an intuition of the present, consists of a succession of instants each of which is full of memories of the past as well as of expectations of the future. To experience music is to communicate with the kind of order, and therefore of unity, of which becoming is capable. Sonorous structures have their own forms, without which they would not exist as works of art, but here again we can apply to music what St. Augustine once said about poetry; [17] all the rhythms, numbers, proportions, and, generally speaking, all the rules to which poets or musicians resort in order to turn the words of common language into poetry, or the sounds of human voices and of instruments into music, have no other effect than to impart to a fleeting multiplicity the only kind of unity, order, and stability of which it is capable. It is no mediocre achievement, for a musician, to fill up the emptiness of silence with sounds whose intelligible structure is perceived by man's ears as endowed with a unity of its own and, consequently, with a certain degree of entity. But painters have no such problems to solve. The difficulty for them is not to impart to becoming enough unity to turn it into some sort of being. Precisely because they are

17. Because order is the only kind of unity that multiplicity is able to receive. On this doctrine: E. Gilson, *Introduction à l'étude de saint Augustin,* pp. 159–60.

material solids, paintings enjoy the same kind of concrete existence, the same sort of actually complete being, that belongs to things of nature. The painter's own problem rather is to obtain from the solid and immobile objects produced by his art an expression of movement, of becoming, and, in short, of life.

All painters are aware of the problem, but some of them give in to the desire of obtaining from their art results that it is not in its nature to yield. In the case of great artists, the result is always interesting, yet it never wholly fulfills the ambitions of the painter. In such pictures as the *Bonaparte Crossing the St. Bernard*, by David, the eternally rearing horse [2] whose forelegs never touch the ground offers a rather disturbing contrast between the immobility of the painting and the frantic intensity of the action it attempts to represent. In his famous *Epsom Derby*, Géricault has [3] cleverly avoided attributing to his galloping horses any one of the many positions in which a snapshot would catch them in reality. His intention has certainly been to suggest motion rather than to represent it. Yet, when all is said and done, there remains a puzzling ambiguity in the sight of these horses that always fly and never move. Many pictures of battles, fighting animals, and hunting scenes call for similar remarks. In them, whirls of apparently frantic motions stay frozen solid in an everlasting immobility.

There are ways of palliating the difficulty. One of them consists in representing a scene implying motion at the very moment that the forces at play are reaching a point of equilibrium. This is what Manet has done in his *Tumblers* (*Les Saltimbanques*). We all know the moment of sus- [4a] pense during which, having at last achieved a precarious poise, an acrobat keeps us breathless; this is also the moment for a painter to get us interested in a combination of lines that represents an interval of rest between two motions. In his *Horses Fighting*, Delacroix has achieved a similar result by [4b] means of another triangular composition whose summit, irresistibly attracting the eye, is the head of the tall dark horse. As will presently be seen, the static equilibrium of the figure interests the painter much more than his apparent intention of representing movements. Another, and a hardly less perfect, an- swer to the same problem is exemplified by Seurat's *Circus*. An important [5] part of it is in motion, but our eyes cannot possibly follow its lines without going full circle and, by the same token, without achieving some sort of immobility.

Not so, however, in the many cases in which painters obviously lose sight of the problem. When they are not mere feats of skill to be enjoyed as such, their unconvincing renderings of motion by means of cleverly combined immobilities achieve no other result than to mislead us as to the true pictorial meaning of the works in question. Seen as a snapshot, *The Sabine Women* of David is hardly bearable. After a first glance at it, which immediately reveals the accomplished mastery of the classical traditions typical of David's art, most of us consider that we are done with this gigantic canvas. But it may happen that a painter knowing his craft invites us to spend a few more moments in the contemplation of this cumbersome structure and points out for us the true result that David intended to achieve. Our painter friend first warns us to forget any idea of motion and even any desire, on the part of the artist, to convey to us any impression of mobility. Only one thing interests him, as it should interest us, namely, the visual pattern formed by the intricate lines indicating the supposed motions of the painted figures. As soon as we look at it, not as suggesting motion in time but as a visual pattern in space, the work of David becomes highly interesting. Without attempting one of those endless analyses which mean little to anybody except their own authors, let us briefly observe the striking horizontal line that divides the picture from the extremity of the spear leveled by the warrior on the right up to the crest on the helmet of the opposite warrior on the left. Let us also observe the dominating rectangle determined by these two opposite figures between which, in point of fact, the whole subject is depicted: a Sabine woman attempting to separate a Roman warrior from a Sabine warrior. But, above all, let us note the triangular structure of the middle group formed at its base by the central figure of the Sabine woman with extended arms and descending to the apex formed by the playing children. On the right, it follows the line that goes from the hand of the standing figure to the head of the older woman, then of the younger woman; the line continues

[6a]

following the arm of the younger woman to her own right hand, but at the very point where it reaches the tip of her fingers this descending line begins to reascend through the raised hand of the child on the left, then through the drapery of the gown, then through the left leg of the standing woman who shows a child to the warriors, until it reaches again the fingers of the other extended arm of the central figure. Other similar patterns will easily be detected by any careful observer of this complex composition. Its true pictural meaning then clearly appears. We would achieve nothing by giving these frozen figures a mental push in order to set them in motion. They cannot move without wrecking the composition. But we shall be amply rewarded if, forgetting everything about motion, we concentrate upon the structured interplay and the arabesque of the lines.

The static nature of paintings is therefore included in our aesthetic experience of them. This conclusion can be verified by comparing the effect produced by *The Sabine Women* of David with our immediate impression of any other similar composition in which, because no suggestion of motion is intended, the geometrical pattern is immediately discernible. David's *Distribution of the Eagles* [18] cleverly picks up the moment that, for a split second, all the movements are supposed to stop; there is perfect harmony between the static nature of the art of painting and the equally static nature of the subject. But the contrast is still more fully perceptible if we compare *The Sabine Women* with Velázquez's *Surrender of Breda*.   [6b] In this masterpiece, there is hardly a trace of motion left. Time seems to have come to a standstill. Human beings themselves, however well painted they may be, are only second in importance to the pattern of the lines and to the balance of the masses. Nor is it without reason that this world-renowned picture is often called *The Lances*. Most of those who admire it do not know with perfect precision where Breda is, nor by whom it was taken, nor at what date; but they all perceive at once the impressive hedge of verticals that, while dividing its surface according to the "golden section," establishes communication between the verticals of the lower part and the horizontals of the higher part of the painting. For, indeed, the powerful

18. A drawing (1808), in the Louvre.

effect produced by these vertical lances is largely owing to the fact that the horizontal landscape in the background still remains visible behind them.[19]

This, of course, does not mean that a painter is wrong when he tries to represent action. Few pictures are completely free from action, and some very great painters have often taken pleasure in representing it. The reason for this is not hard to find: the more action there is in a subject, the more opportunity it affords to achieve complex patterns of lines and combinations of forms in whose apprehension, as will be seen, the cause of our pleasure chiefly resides. If the artist is a master in his art, the effect of the represented action is precisely to lead our eyes along lines whose pattern we might otherwise fail to discern. As has been seen, such was the case in *The Sabine Women* of David; but such had already been the case with [7a] *The Rape of the Sabine Women* by Nicolas Poussin, in which, provided only it follows the lines of the represented action, the eye spontaneously perceives the general distribution of the masses and the main lines of the composition. The point we are enforcing is that, whether or not it harbors the secret ambition to represent action, a painting first is a static pattern of colors, forms, and, in the last analysis, lines. Moreover, a painting is experienced as being such a static pattern, and this fact accounts for the feeling of incongruity that, after a short moment of full satisfaction, most people experience at the sight of the static representation of some intensely dynamic action. If we compare the two versions of Poussin's *Rape of the Sabine Women* with either his *Baptism of Christ* or his [7b, 8a] [8b] *Funeral of Phocion,* the two latter works, in which the maximum of composition combines with the minimum of action, convey an impression of solid and harmonious stability more in keeping with the physical mode of existence that belongs to paintings.[20]

19. See the commentary written on *Las Lanzas* by Thomas Bodkin, *The Approach to Painting,* ch. XX, pp. 131–34. Compare, *op. cit.,* pl. XVI, the lopsided composition of José Leonardo's treatment of the same subject.

20. Bodkin, p. 128, attributes to Nicolas Poussin the following principle: "Without action, neither drawing nor colour in a picture influences the mind." (No reference is given.) In the same book, opposite p. 128, pl. XV reproduces Poussin's *Rape of the Sabine Women* as a perfect illustration of this theory. Let us observe, however, that action is not

MATTEO GIOVANETTI. Christ on the Cross
About 1345. Fresco. St. Martial Chapel, Palace of the Popes, Avignon

JACQUES-LOUIS DAVID. Bonaparte Crossing the St. Bernard
1800. Versailles

THÉODORE GÉRICAULT. Epsom Derby
1821. Louvre

a. ÉDOUARD MANET. The Tumblers
About 1861. Black lead pencil and sepia wash.
Bibliothèque Nationale, Paris

b. EUGÈNE DELACROIX. Arab Horses Fighting in a Stable
1860. Louvre

4

GEORGES SEURAT. The Circus
1890/91. Unfinished. Louvre

a. JACQUES-LOUIS DAVID. The Sabine Women
1799. Louvre

b. DIEGO VELÁZQUEZ. The Surrender of Breda
1634/35. Prado, Madrid

a. Nicolas Poussin. The Rape of the Sabine Women
Before 1637. Metropolitan Museum of Art, New York

b. Nicolas Poussin. The Baptism of Christ
1646/47. Collection of the Earl of Ellesmere, Mertoun, Scotland

a. NICOLAS POUSSIN. The Rape of the Sabine Women
About 1630. Louvre

b. NICOLAS POUSSIN. The Funeral of Phocion
1648. Louvre

FRANCISCO GOYA. The Forge
About 1815. Frick Collection, New York

PIETER JANSSENS. Woman Reading
About 1760. Haus der Kunst, Munich

a. HENDRIK VAN DER VLIET.
Interior of a Church
Mid 17th century. Private collection

b. PIETER SAENREDAM.
Interior of St. John's Church, Utrecht
1645. Centraal Museum, Utrecht

JAN VERMEER. A Street in Delft
About 1658. Rijksmuseum, Amsterdam

a. JAN VERMEER. View of Delft
About 1658. Mauritshuis, The Hague

b. PIETER SAENREDAM. View of St. Mary's Church, Utrecht
1663. Boymans Museum, Rotterdam

13

a. BAUGIN. Wafers and Wine
About 1630. Louvre

b. J.-B.-S. CHARDIN. The Silver Cup
About 1776. Louvre

GEORGES SEURAT. La Parade
1887/88. Stephen C. Clark Collection, New York

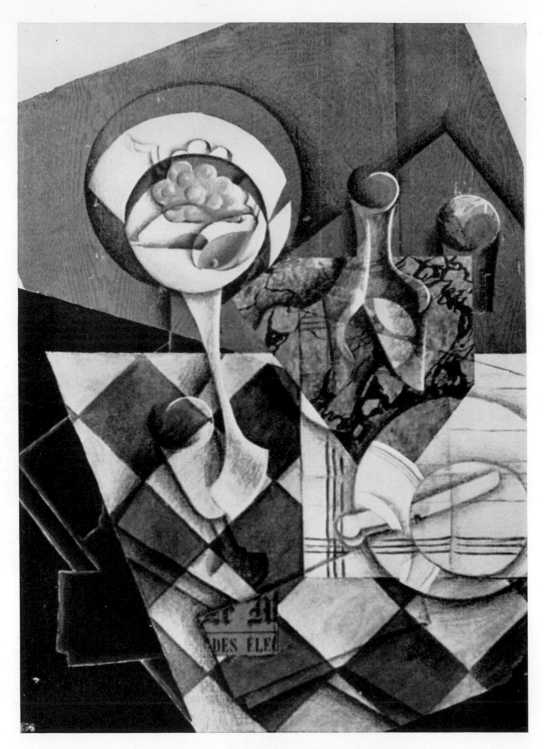

JUAN GRIS. Fruit Dish with Water Bottle
1914. Collage. Rijksmuseum Kröller-Müller, Otterlo

As it is not easy to dissociate the two notions of suggested motion and of represented motion, a simple experience can help in realizing the distinction. It consists, while looking at the painting of some animated scene, in trying to imagine what would happen to the composition if the figures depicted in it really began to move. Most of the time the composition would be wrecked without being replaced by a new one. Pictorial composition requires immobility. In the words of Baudelaire: "Je hais le mouvement qui déplace les lignes."[21] While looking at *The Forge*, by Goya, some visitors to the Frick Collection express misgivings about what would happen to the skull of the person who holds the iron on the anvil in case the blacksmith wielding the hammer really should strike. One prefers not to think of it. But, precisely, this has nothing to do with the quality of the painting. A certain pyramidal structure, and the trace left in space by a possible movement, not actual movement, is what the painter was interested in. To sum up, the aesthetic mode of existence of a painting includes an awareness of the static mode of existence of its object just as, on the contrary, the aesthetic mode of existence of music includes the awareness of the discontinuous and fleeting existence of its object. And no wonder. It is as difficult for painting to move as it is for music to stand still.

This specificity of the physical mode of existence proper to paintings accounts for the growing importance attributed to still life in the history of art. On the one hand, most of the aestheticians and painters who insist that there is a hierarchy of genres of painting seem to agree that still life is the humblest of these genres. There is nothing particularly noble about representing fruit, loaves of bread, forks, knives, cups, and other such ob-

[9]

identical with movement. It resides in the subject rather than in the painting itself. A subject calling for the representation of some action helps in imparting to a picture a quality that Delacroix regretted not finding in the compositions of Titian: "Have I always felt a lack of enthusiasm for Titian because he almost invariably ignores the . . . charm of line?" (*The Journal of Eugène Delacroix*, p. 71 [March 7, 1847].) What Delacroix means to say is that, because they lack action, the works of Titian are often deprived of the charm that goes with ingenious arabesques. Naturally, this is a criticism of a kind that is quite frequent among creators. Delacroix resented the relative inactivity of Titian's figures because he himself was fond of the complex patterns of lines that normally go with action.

21. "I hate movement which disarranges lines" (*Beauty*).

jects whose sight evokes nothing more than the most modest aspects of everyday life.[22] On the other hand, one cannot look at one of the best Chardins,
or, for that matter, at any good still life of any school and any period,
without feeling that this is indeed a genre in which painting reveals its
very essence and reaches one of its points of perfection. A still life does
not inspire us with the same kind of admiration as the frescoes of Michelangelo in the Sistine Chapel, but we derive from it a different and, in a
sense, a fuller feeling of contentment. However great the artist, he cannot convince us that his immobile puppets are really running, talking, and
acting. Not so in a still life, which, by definition, is a picture consisting
of inanimate objects. It may comprise animals, provided these animals be
dead. In a still life nothing acts, nothing gesticulates, nothing does anything else than to be. Now, precisely, this is what painting is best equipped
to depict. The kind of plenary satisfaction we experience while looking at
a still life is due to the perfect adequacy that obtains, in this case, between
the substance of the work of art and the reality that it represents. Such
pictures are solid and inanimate objects enjoying a continuous mode of
physical existence; the cups, the forks, or the books they represent are
beings of the same sort, and they enjoy the kind of continuous existence
that belongs to inanimate solids situated in space. In this case, the artist
is not attempting to make his art say more than it can say. The specific
pleasure given by the best still lifes clearly reveals the radical difference
there is between the aesthetic mode of existence of paintings and that of
music.

22. In the passage where he refuses to reduce painting to imitation, Reynolds says:
"In the same rank [as Watteau or Claude] and perhaps of not so great merit is the cold
painter of portraits. But his correct and just imitation of his object has its merit. Even
the painter of still life, whose highest ambition is to give a minute representation of every
part of those low objects which he sets before him, deserves praise in proportion to his
attainment; because no part of this excellent Art, so much the ornament of polished life,
is destitute of value and use." (*The Discourses of Sir Joshua Reynolds*, ed. John Burnet,
p. 50.) Better inspired, Eugène Fromentin has rightly observed that "just as there are
in the most practical of lives motives and influences that ennoble the behaviour, so in this
art, held to be so positive, among these painters, held for the most part to be mere copiers
of detail we feel a loftiness and a goodness of heart, an affection for the true, a love for
the real, that give their works a value the things do not seem to possess" (*The Masters
of Past Time: Dutch and Flemish Painting from Van Eyck to Rembrandt*, p. 101).

The notion of "still life" does not apply only to the pictures representing dead animals or inanimate household objects. It is surely not by chance that the seventeenth-century Dutch painters, who were the first to handle still life as a distinct genre and brought it to its point of perfection, were also the first to find fitting subjects in many other man-made objects, or things, whose only common quality precisely is their stillness. The old belief, expressed by Reynolds, that a still-life painter simply aims to imitate the visual appearance of the lowest kinds of objects befits a large number of still lifes whose authors never imagined that another conception of their art was possible. But when the still-life style extended itself from household objects to houses themselves; then to churches, which are the houses of God; then to cities, which are made up of houses and of churches, it became obvious that the aim and scope of a still life was something far beyond the mere imitation of inanimate objects.[22a]

There is magic in the art of the great Dutch painters. The same intense feeling of reality and of enduring stability suggested by their fruit bowls and their loaves of bread remains perceptible in the interiors painted by Pieter de Hooch before, yielding to a temptation fatal to so many painters of still lifes, he began to turn out mere genre pictures. Generally speaking, the best Dutch interiors invite the spectator to partake of a life that is not his own,   [10] but with which he communicates without disturbing it in the least. Their quiet housewives do not mind us; they are not even aware of our presence; as to themselves, even if they pretend to be doing something, all that they really have to do is to be. Many Dutch pictures of church interiors proceed from the same spirit. The small personages that people the churches painted by H. van der Vliet do not prevent them from remaining so many still lifes. This   [11a] is still truer of the churches painted with a unique blending of finish and sensibility by Pieter Saenredam. But there is a short distance, if any, from   [11b] an interior by Jan Vermeer to his justly celebrated *Street in Delft*, whose life   [12] is no less still than that of his own interior scenes. Even his equally famous *View of Delft* shares in the same qualities of quiet presence and actionless   [13a]

22a. "Also avoid motion in a pose. Each of your figures ought to be in a static position" (Paul Gauguin, *Intimate Journals*, p. 32).

existentiality that characterize his little street. A similar extension is observable in the works of Saenredam when he passes from the inside of his
churches to their external appearance. There is something of the stillness of
[13b]   Vermeer's *View of Delft* in the portrait of a Utrecht public place by
Saenredam. One might feel tempted to include some landscapes in the
same class, but even when they are peaceful, Dutch landscapes and seascapes are not still. An intense life quickens their skies as well as their
seas. The spirit of still life is no longer there. But we find it again every
time we turn our attention to one of the masterpieces anterior to the time,
when, even in Holland, still life deteriorated into plain imagery. And since
the corruption of the best brings about the worst, we should not feel surprised to find in the most mediocre of modern genre pictures the posterity
of such perfect masterpieces.

There is a sort of metaphysical equity in the fact that this humblest
genre is also the most revealing of all concerning the essence of the art of
painting. If, by the word "subject" we mean the description of some scene or
some action, then it can rightly be said that a still life has no subject.
[14a, b]   Whether its origin be Dutch or French, the things that a still life represents
exercise only one single act, but it is the simplest and most primitive
of all acts, namely, to be. Without this deep-seated, quiet, and immobile
energy from which spontaneously follow all the operations and all the
movements performed by each and every being, nothing in the world would
move, nothing would operate, nothing would exist. Always present to that
which is, this act of being usually lies hidden, and unrevealed, behind
what the thing signifies, says, does, or makes. Only two men reach an awareness of its mysterious presence: the philosopher, if, raising his speculation
up to the metaphysical notion of being, he finally arrives at this most secret
and most fecund of all acts; and the creator of plastic forms, if, purifying
the work of his hands from all that is not the immediate self-revelation of
the act of being, he provides us with a visible image of it that corresponds,
in the order of sensible appearances, to what its intuition is in the mind
of the metaphysician.

3. Existence and Operation

PAINTINGS are experienced as solid bodies enjoying the mode of duration proper to all such beings, and the awareness of this fact specifies their aesthetic existence as distinct from that of either poetry or music. But the same remark applies to the artistic mode of existence of paintings. Produced as it is by the art of some painter, a painting is usually experienced as a man-made thing. The art of the artist is perceived in his work in the same way as the efficient cause is perceived in any one of its effects. The fact is easily confirmed by personal experience. Just as a real landscape is spontaneously seen as a work of nature, so also is a painted landscape, or a musical composition, seen or heard with the full awareness of the fact that its origin lies in the creative power of an artist. Rembrandt, Veronese, and Delacroix are really present in our art galleries through the presence of their art embodied in their works. So also are Bach, Mozart, and Beethoven present in every concert hall in which one of their masterpieces happens to be performed. In short, both the author and his art are included in our aesthetic experience of any work of art. Yet, because the relationship between painters and their works is different from the relationship between a musician and his compositions, our experience of paintings is deeply different from our aesthetic experience of music. Here again, phenomenology has a great deal to gain from an attentive study of its ontological conditions.

Paintings are not only man-made, as all works of art are; they also are handmade. It is the hand of the painter that embodies in actually existing physical objects the conceptions of his mind. This fact entails important consequences concerning the very art of the painters even before affecting our aesthetic experience of their works. The first of these consequences is that painters are craftsmen, doing handwork in more or less comfortable workshops, whose artistic activity consists in making things. If we visit his studio, a painter will be able to exhibit his works exactly as a watchmaker can show his watches stored in drawers or hanging on walls. As often as not, a painter has to don working clothes in the same way as a mechanic or any other artisan. He does not resent dirtying his hands with paint, just as wall painters have almost unavoidably to do in their own work. Among those who specialize in painting portraits of socialites, some artists seem to resent this servitude. They do their utmost to make their studios look like drawing rooms, but when all is said and done, painters (and sculptors) are related to manual laborers by a deep-seated affinity that nothing can eliminate. Poets, playwrights, and novelists all belong in the category of those who hold white-collar jobs. Even a music composer is a writer using ink, paper, and pen to draw symbols signifying a work of art that, unlike a picture or a statue, has no actual existence of its own outside the mind of the artist.

The fact that painting is manual work has visibly influenced the course of its history. Ever since the Renaissance, painters have struggled to ensure the recognition of their art as one of the "liberal arts" and its distinction from merely "servile" work.[23] This accounts for the insistence of some painters, in their writings, on stressing the all-importance of the part played by the mind, by the intellect, and even by what they call science in the composition and execution of paintings. This same preoccupation is like-wise apparent in their criticism of purely imitational painting. We are not here alluding to the modern opposition between imitational and nonimita-tional art. Within imitational art itself, representatives of the purest tradition of academic art have insisted that painting must not be considered a "mechanical art," because the object of the painter's art is not simply

---

23. Art was so clearly understood to be manual work that it has long been considered a servile avocation. "The boy [Michelangelo] devoted all the time he could to drawing secretly, for which his father and seniors scolded and sometimes beat him, thinking that such things were base and unworthy of their noble house" (Giorgio Vasari, *The Lives of the Painters*, IV, 109). — "You have set painting among the mechanical arts! Truly were painters as ready equipped as you are to praise their own works in writing, I doubt whether it would endure the reproach of so vile a name . . ." (*The Notebooks of Leonardo da Vinci*, tr. and ed. E. MacCurdy, II, 228). — "The value and rank of every art is in proportion to the mental labour employed in it, or the mental pleasure produced by it. As this principle is observed or neglected, our profession becomes either a liberal art, or a mechanical trade." (*The Discourses of Sir Joshua Reynolds*, p. 52.)

to copy nature, but to interpret it in some original way, which is an act of the mind. All this is true, but intellectual speculation alone is unable to make anything. It cannot move matter. It is in the nature of things that the maker of a solid physical body has to use his hands in order to make it. However much he may have to use his brains, a painter's work is also manual work, and this is a point that, obvious as it is, seems to have been overlooked by some of those who have philosophized about art.

The contrary illusion arises from the ancient social distinction between masters and slaves, in consequence of which all manual labor was considered slave work. It even presupposes a state of society in which the authority of masters over slaves was an unchallenged despotism. An echo of this state of mind can still be perceived in the passage of his *Summa theologiae* (I–II, 57, 3) where Thomas Aquinas distinguishes the "liberal arts," which are ordained to purely speculative works, from "those arts that are ordained to works done by the body; for these arts are, in a fashion, servile, inasmuch as the body is in servile subjection to the soul, and man, as regards his soul, is free." No painter would describe the relationship between his hand and his mind as one of servile subjection. A painter's hand is a progressively educated hand, which it takes infinite patience to turn into a reliable collaborator and whose co-operation will never be an entirely passive one. Man does not think *with* his hands, but the intellect of a painter certainly thinks *in* his hands, so much so that, in moments of manual inspiration, an artist can sometimes let the hand do its job without bothering too much about what it does. At any rate, unless we call servile all manual work—and what can a man do, or make, without using his hands?—it cannot be doubted that the art of a painter resides in his hands, in his fingers, and probably still more in his wrist, at the same time that it resides in his intellect. The art of the painter is an art of the whole man.

Aristotle himself never said anything to the contrary. His own definition of art is "a reasoned state of capacity to make," or else "a state of capacity to make involving a true course of reasoning."[24] As it stands, the

---

24. *Nicomachean Ethics*, VI, 4, 1140a, 7–10 (tr. W. D. Ross). It has been suggested that "state of possession" would be a better rendering of *habitus* (Greek: *exis*) than

definition of Aristotle is both correct and complete. Art is not concerned with things that come to be in virtue of the laws of nature: such things fall under the competency of science. Art is exclusively concerned with things that come to be because there is, in their maker, an acquired capacity to make them. Philosophers would never have thought differently if, instead of contenting themselves with thinking, they had attempted to make something that they could consider the work of their own hands.

It is a curious fact that, so many centuries after his death, Aristotle should have been made responsible for the "mentalism" that has placed art entirely on the side of the mind. One of the most frequent objections directed by Aristotle against the Ideas of Plato is that, even though they did exist, the Ideas would be wholly useless as principles of explanation because, of themselves, Ideas are unable to act upon matter and to produce physical effects. Plato himself knew this so well that, in his *Timaeus,* he did not represent the formation of the cosmos as the work of any Ideas, but, rather, as that of a god working after the pattern of the Ideas. Before anything else, the Demiurge of Plato has to take the three elements in order to shape up the world: the Demiurge is an artist. Being a self-thinking thought, the god of Aristotle has no hands; the result is that he does not create. On the contrary, Yahweh is most eminently a creator, and this is why, using a metaphor borrowed from the observation of human nature, Scripture says that "the heavens shew forth the glory of God, and the firmament declareth the work of his hands" (Ps. 18 : 2). If it is a question of making things by means of art, where there are no hands, there is no art. The art is in the operation of the hand as the soul is in the body.

This is the truth that some artists intend to stress in identifying the two notions of art and of skill.[25] To do so is to follow a traditional usage of

"state of capacity" used by Ross (Maritain, p. 49, n. 3). Ross' choice seems to be justified in the light of the context, for, indeed, even in art, *habitus* remains a possession, or a "state," but it then is the possession of a capacity to make—that is, a "state of capacity to make." The text of Aristotle (*Nicomachean Ethics*, VI, 4, 1140a, 3–5) cannot be translated differently; a "state of possession to make" would still signify, in more awkward terms, an acquired capacity to make.

25. "By the word Art I understand simply skill" (Eric Gill, *Work and Property*, p. 39). This definition agrees with the English usage, and although it differs from that of Thomas Aquinas, there is no real contradiction between them. Conceived as an "ac-

the word "skill." The root of this word signified "distinction," "discernment." Today, it first signifies a "reason or ground for doing or saying" something; then, by extension, "the ability to use one's knowledge effectively; technical proficiency" (*Webster's* [25a]). However we understand its notion, skill expressly includes the knowledge that is needed for the performing of a certain operation. Skill always is a "know-how." If the notion at stake were that of art in general, or that of certain arts, like the art of writing, in which nothing more is required from the hand than the ability to use a pen or a typewriter, it could be maintained, with some probability, that the acquired ability called "skill" entirely resides in the mind. Not so in the case of painting. If skill includes the ability to use acquired knowledge, then art itself is found in the hand as well as in the mind.

Nor would it suffice to object that, even in the case of painting, all the skill in the hand has first to be, under the form of art, in the mind. On the contrary, one of the main reasons painters find it so hard to make themselves understood when they speak of their art is that their hearers listen with their minds only, not with their hands. If it is a question of painting, the artist himself can form no clear notion of his own art without including in it manual skill. True enough, there are cases in which an artist knows beforehand all he is going to do or to make. This particularly applies to artisans making such simple artifacts as chests or chairs. Everywhere there is a blueprint, the very detail of a certain operation can be foreseen. The same remark applies to the skill of real painters, and sometimes of truly great ones, every time they undertake to do a replica of one of their

quired facility in doing something," skill implies the knowledge of the proper way to make something that Thomas Aquinas attributes to the practical intellect and that he calls art. There is little or no difference between the Thomistic notion of "art" and the usual notion of skill if skill includes the knowledge of its own rule and if art includes skillfulness in its own operation. Cf. Gill, *Beauty Looks After Herself*, p. 11. Note, p. 12, "Skill in making and skill in doing are both loosely called art," and pp. 180–83, "Art is skill"; "Art is deliberate skill"; "Nevertheless, the *word* art means, first of all, *skill*. Skill in *making* (poiesis)." There is something pathetic about the plight of a competent craftsman, so keenly aware of the true nature of his own art, worrying because philosophers assure him that "Art abides always on the side of the mind," p. 11. Cf. Gill, *Art-Nonsense*, p. 289; refers to Maritain, *The Philosophy of Art*, p. 17 of the English translation. This formula is not Thomas Aquinas', but John of St. Thomas'.

25a. All of the *Webster's* citations are to *Webster's Collegiate Dictionary*, 5th edn. (1936).

own works. Facility is not creative. On the contrary, "limited means [of execution] beget new forms, they invite creation, they make style." [25b] As will be seen in connection with another problem, there even is for painters a constant danger of falling victims to the perfection of their acquired technique: a painter knows beforehand all he is about to do, when no element of novelty is included in his work. If, on the contrary, creative work is at stake, many other factors than intellectual knowledge become involved in the process. The hand is one of them, and the hand of a painter is for him full of surprises. Even when his hand does exactly what he wanted it to do, the knowledge that an artist has of his own art is not an abstract notion of lines, surfaces, and colors to be seen on a piece of canvas; it is the concrete cognition of the very acts and motions whereby a certain pattern of lines, surfaces, and colors can actually be produced. In painting, it is impossible to distinguish between art itself and execution, as if art were wholly in the mind and execution wholly in the hand. Art here is *in* execution, and if it is true to say that the intellect of the painter is engaged in all the motions of the hand, it is equally true to say that a painter could entertain no thought about his own art if his hand were not there to give to the word "art" a concrete meaning. If, what is very doubtful, the Aristotelian definition of art really implies that the art of the painter, taken precisely qua art, entirely stands on the side of the mind, it seems to call for correction. [26]

25b. Georges Braque, *Le Jour et la nuit*, p. 16.

26. It is legitimate to seek in St. Thomas for the principles of a philosophy of art. He himself, however, does not seem to have been interested in the problem. There is no doctrine of art in his own writings. Most of the texts borrowed from his works on this question are concerned, not with art as art, but, rather, with art as distinct from ethics. The antithesis *recta ratio factibilium—recta ratio agibilium* is no definition of art; it simply aims at distinguishing between the two orders of making and doing. Moreover, as will presently be seen, it is far from certain that the oft-quoted formula, *recta ratio factibilium*, justifies the conclusion with which Gill seems to have found it so hard to reconcile his own creative experience. A good antidote for the mentalism endemic in philosophical minds can be found in the assiduous reading of the writings left us by painters. For instance, Fromentin on Rubens' *Miraculous Draught of Fishes* at Malines (Belgium): "It is a beautiful canvas, smooth, clean, and exact, worked by a hand of magnificent skill, adroitness, sensitiveness, and balance. The hastiness one reads into it is rather a manner of feeling than a disorder in the manner of painting. The brush is as calm as the mind is heated, and the genius ready to burst forth . . ." (*The Masters of Past Time*, p. 34). Cf. the rules prescribed by Delacroix for the painting of leaves: "The fist-

Such an error would not be too surprising. One of the shortcomings of philosophers is that, because they think rather than make, they have few opportunities to realize how clever the body of an intelligent being actually is. As he was visiting Matisse, a painter friend found him in his studio surrounded with a litter of drawings. Wondering how Matisse could make a choice among them, he asked him: "How do you know the really good ones?" To this question, a philosopher, or a theologian, would have answered with considerations about beauty, order, splendor of the true, and suchlike, applied to the drawings under discussion. But Matisse's answer was a different one. "How one knows the really good ones?" Matisse answered. "Well, one feels that in the hand." The knowledge by the intellect of the proper way of making something here jointly resides in the intellect that knows and in the hand that makes. Only in God, a perfect knowledge of the things to be made precedes, so to speak, their actual making.

Even the most resolute supporters of a purely "mental" conception of art betray some embarrassment when it comes to defining, or describing, the relationship between the knowledge of the work to be made and the power of execution without which nothing would ever come out of the mind. Some of them seem to consider skill a certain faculty, "made" by art and from which the operation of the artist proceeds.[27] Even Thomas

alone moving the brush, not the fingers, as for flourishes in handwriting. The hand serves only to hold the thing that draws or that paints; it remains stiff, pliantly yielding to the motions of the fist; it remains immobile in all the displacements to which the fist has to submit it in order to follow the contours of the leaves and of the stems" (Louis de Planet, *Souvenirs de travaux de peinture avec M. Delacroix*, p. 53). These precepts are not art; rather, they are the knowledge of the reality that art is in the hand of the painter. — Similar remarks about Japanese art in Henri Focillon, *Hokousai*, p. 13. In Hokusai's own art "it is not the fist that is moving; it is the forearm, or the shoulder, while the fingers, clenched on the brush, which sometimes is solidly clutched with the hand, do nothing more than hold it."

27. The Thomistic notion of art seems to include two notions, both distinct and inseparable: (1) art properly so called, which is the knowledge of what an artist wants to make and of the correct way to make it ("recta ratio factibilium"—Thomas Aquinas, commentary on Aristotle's *Nichomachean Ethics*, nn. 8, 282, 1496); and (2) practiced ability—that is to say, the habit, acquired by the training of natural dispositions, of performing the visual and manual operations required for the making of a work of art. So "art" is a knowledge entirely related to the making of certain material objects: it directs the operation ("ars est factiva generationis, quia est recta ratio factibilium . . . non est autem factiva operationis, sed potentiae alicujus ex qua procedit operatio," n. 1496). The Aristotelian definition of art, taken up by St. Thomas, "habitus operativus" (*Summa*

Aquinas, when he lets himself go for a moment, speaks of art as of an acquired disposition that enables man to know how to operate, and even to operate, so as to produce a work of art. And indeed, what kind of art would be an acquired disposition with respect to things to be made, if it implied no practical ability to make them? The question is not to know if an act of abstract cognition permits us to conceive art apart from any operation conducive to the actual production of works of art. There is nothing that man cannot conceive apart. He can conceive a nose apart from any face; he even can conceive snubness apart from any nose. Yet, when all is said and done, there is no such thing in the world as a nose in itself, or snubness in itself. Nor is there any such thing as an art of painting conceivable apart from its operation. Thomas Aquinas himself seems to suggest a similar notion of art when he says of it that art perfects man as to both knowledge and power in operating.[28]

Such abstract discussions would be pointless were it not for the fact that some artists feel inclined to take what philosophers say about art more seriously than philosophers deserve to be taken in matters of which they have little or no personal experience. As it exists in the minds of metaphysicians, art is eminently conceivable apart from its operation, for the simple reason that abstractions do not operate. Only man operates, through his

---

theologiae, I–II, q. 57, art. 3, answer), includes art, its operation, and even the product of this operation. Cf. "idem est ars quod habitus factivus cum vera ratione" (bk. VI, ch. 4, lecture 3, nn. 1153 and 1159). These two definitions mean the same thing in the mind of Thomas Aquinas (compare n. 8 with n. 1153). Thus understood ("ars est habitus cum ratione factivus," n. 1166), the notion of art cannot be separated from that of its proper operation. It then includes: (1) a speculation as to the best way to do the work; (2) a set of considerations concerning the choice and the preparation of the matter of the work; and (3) the skill required for the making of the work under the guidance of practical reason (n. 1154). Let us not forget that, like all forms, art is there in view of its operation, and, in the case of painting, the skill by which alone art can operate is in the hand. This is the reason we are saying that, concretely speaking, the "aptitude to operate" includes manual skill. Nobody knows the proper way to make a thing unless he himself can make it. The proof of the art is in the making.

28. Thomas Aquinas, *De virtutibus in communi*, art. 7, answer to the question. Here again, Thomas Aquinas is not interested in the notion of art qua art; he only wants to establish that there are virtues in the practical intellect; and what he says is that the effect of art is not to inspire man with the desire to operate well according to art, but, simply. to give him the knowledge of how to operate and the aptitude thus to operate.

art.[29] In the case of painting, whose proper effect it is to make material objects that occupy definite places in space, art cannot possibly be conceived apart from its operation.

4. *Existence and Execution*

T H I S first consequence of the material nature of paintings entails a second one, namely, that the painter is to himself his own executant. Eugène Delacroix, who was acquainted with several musicians of the stature of Liszt and Chopin, was well aware of the fact that, in such cases, the musician happened to be, at one and the same time, both a composer and a performer; but he also knew that it was not necessarily so. A musician can write music for an instrument that he cannot play, or that he plays only badly. If what he writes is the score of a duet, a quartet, a symphony, or an opera, he cannot possibly be the performer of his own work; nor is it always enough to put an orchestra at the disposal of a musician, since as often as not the music composer turns out to be an indifferent conductor of his own music, sometimes even a decidedly poor one. Johannes Brahms is a case in point. The famous German conductor, Hans von Bülow, is said to have broken relations with Brahms, at least for a time, not at all because he did not like his music, but, on the contrary, because he could not endure the way Brahms, as a conductor, was ruining his own symphonies. These facts, and similar ones that everyone will no doubt remember, are enough to explain the meaning of the remark made by Delacroix: "The craft of the painter is the most difficult of all and it takes longest to learn. Like composing, painting requires erudition, but it also requires execution, like playing the violin."[30]

Since a painter is to himself his own virtuoso, there is no hope for anyone to become an artist worthy of the name before he has mastered the

29. "Art is simply the well making of what needs making" (Gill, *Art-Nonsense*, p. v). This artist has clearly seen why his own interpretation of such elementary notions could hardly please purely speculative minds. It is that "few who are trained in philosophy and few who have the cure of souls seem to have any understanding of the job of the artist or a just appreciation of his work."

30. *Journal*, p. 81 (September 18, 1847). Cf. pp. 162–63 (Tuesday, October 12, 1852).

technique of his art. A painter does not deserve the name until he has reached both intellectual maturity and the full mastery of his craft. In an age such as our own, when children's drawings and children's paintings receive a degree of attention amounting to a superstitious cult, it should be remembered that, undeniable as they sometimes are, the natural gifts of these young painters are not even an inchoation of what is perhaps later on going to be their art; for, indeed, art, or craftsmanship, is essentially technique, and technique requires time before being assimilated. In John Constable's terse words: "There has never been a boy painter, nor can there be. The art requires a long apprenticeship, being *mechanical*, as well as intellectual."[31]

This fact accounts for the feeling, common among painters, that their relationship to their own works is a peculiar one. They are conscious of being the causes of their works much more completely and absolutely than musicians can pretend to be. The very being and existence of pictures is directly caused by painters. To the extent that it fulfills the ambition of the artist, a painting not only owes him its existence, it is also indebted to him, and to him alone, for being what it is. In other words, a painter is the sole and total cause of his work. Hence his feeling of superiority in comparison with the restricted role played by artists in some other branches of art—for instance, poetry and music. To limit ourselves to the particularly clear case of music, it cannot be said that a composer, let us say Wagner writing *Parsifal*, is the sole cause of its actual existence, nor that he causes it to be exactly such as he wants it to be. Many executants will be required before any opera succeeds in achieving actual existence as the sonorous structure that it is; and not only many executants working through many rehearsals,

---

31. C. R. Leslie, *Memoirs of the Life of John Constable*, p. 276. — Cf. the remarkable page in which Daniel-Henry Kahnweiler explains why "There is every reason severely to exclude from art children's drawing, from which the formative factor is absent" (*Juan Gris*, p. 170). See the English translation of this work by Douglas Cooper, p. 85 (we have brought the translation nearer the French original). — The main reason alleged by Kahnweiler (who quotes Matisse in support of his position) is that the kind of drawing practiced by children, and sometimes abusively called "child art," is a kind of handwriting, ideographic rather than pictorial, and therefore foreign to art. Children do not draw forms; they describe concepts. Incidentally, Kahnweiler rightly warns his readers against the mistake made by certain critics when they reproached Paul Klee with returning to child drawing. Nothing is more calculated than the drawings in which Klee has extracted from the ideographic handwriting of children the truly pictorial elements it contains.

but also conductors, no two of whom will cause *Parsifal* to exist in identically the same way. Taken precisely as composer, the musician is powerless to impart to his own work the actual existence that any painter imparts to his paintings. And this again is a point that Delacroix has expressed in a particularly felicitous way.[32] The relationship of the painter to his work is specifically other than that of the poet to his poems or of the musician to his music.

For the very same reason, our own relationship to painting is different from the one that obtains between us and the works of the poets or of the musicians. Delacroix has subtly analyzed the difference between the physical realities that painters place under our own eyes and the books in which writers speak to us, explain things to us, and try to convince us. Not so with painters. Having done his work, the artist simply puts it before our eyes, after which he disappears without explanations or commentaries. In Delacroix's own words, painting is one of those "silent arts" for which, like Poussin, he professed a preference. The author of a book, Delacroix says, "seems to wrestle against criticism. He argues, and one can argue with him in return. The works of painters and sculptors, on the other hand, are all of one piece, like the works of nature. The author does not appear in them, is not in touch with us like the writer or orator. He offers, as it were, a tangible reality, yet one that is full of mystery."[33] Let us keep in mind these remarks concerning the naturalness of the physical bodies made by the particular class of artists whom we call painters. What Delacroix was trying to say is, perhaps, still more tangible in the case of sculpture. The works of Arp, made of "stone formed by human hand,"[34] seem to be the perfect fulfillment of this high ambition of the plastic arts.

The same remarks apply to our experience of music. As has already

32. "What I have been saying about the *power of painting* now becomes clear. If it has to record but a single moment it is capable of concentrating the *effect* of that moment. The painter is far more master of what he wants to express than the poet or musician who are in the hands of interpreters; even though his memory may have a smaller range to work on, he produces an effect that is a perfect unity and one which is capable of giving complete satisfaction." (*Journal*, p. 201 [Thursday, October 20, 1853].)

33. *Journal*, p. 259 (September 23, 1854). The title of this entry is: "On silence and the silent arts."

34. Hans Arp, *On My Way*, p. 6.

been noted, it takes a sort of conjurer to give music actual existence. We are not more in contact with Beethoven himself, while listening to one of his quartets, than we are in contact with Rembrandt while looking at one of his paintings. Yet, in listening to music, we are always in personal contact with an artist whose presence between the musician and ourselves cannot possibly be ignored. As often as not, there first is a conductor. His functions are, besides directing his orchestra, to perform a sort of pantomime, or interpretative dance, whose purpose it is to keep his musicians interested in what they are playing and to make his public see what, without this visual help, they would perhaps fail to hear. Moreover, the conductor of an orchestra is responsible for his own interpretation of the works performed under his direction. This is so important, especially in our own day, that it does not sound ridiculous to speak of the Ninth Symphony of such and such a conductor, as if its author were anybody else than Ludwig van Beethoven. The virtuosos are no less necessary intermediaries between written music and our ears, and it is today permitted to include certain great orchestras in the class of the virtuosos. In short, hosts of intermediaries are required to ensure the performance of musical compositions whose physical existence would be impossible without these interpreters, performers, or executants.

The importance of these mediators cannot be denied. Unless it is actually performed, music simply does not exist. It is therefore natural that our immediate gratitude should go to those men to whom we feel indebted for the very existence of the music we love. Without overlooking the ludicrous side of this sometimes misdirected veneration,[35] one must recognize that, up

35. It is not rare to hear music critics compare the "Eroica" of Weingartner with the "Eroica" of Bruno Walter, Furtwängler, or Toscanini. They seem to forget the name of its true author. But they are excusable because, indeed, conductors are efficient causes of the actual existence of musical works. As an example among many of the dithyrambic praises bestowed by journalists upon conductors, we beg to borrow the following ones from the first 1954 program of a well-known American symphonic society: "Mr. X, for whose art we have exhausted every possible praise," "one of the greatest musicians of our time," etc. It would be difficult to say more in praise of the greatest music composers of the past as well as of the present, since this musical hero is simply called "A PHENOMENON OF ALL TIME" and "A VERITABLE PROMETHEUS." Let us note that the conductor in question is undoubtedly one of the best. His merit is not here in question. We are simply wondering if, after these glorious epithets, there are any left for Bach, Mozart, Haydn, Beethoven, and Wagner.

to a point, it is founded in the nature of things. Nay, the very freedom enjoyed by conductors and virtuosos of every denomination is likewise founded in the nature of things. Since musical compositions have no physical existence of their own, it is for conductors, virtuosos, singers, and, generally speaking, all executants an absolute necessity to decide upon one of the countless possible interpretations of an original whose idea has died with the composer himself. Like a Platonic idea, the ideal original of a musical composition is nothing more than a notion of the mind. Strictly speaking, it does not exist.[36]

This ontological difference between painting and music entails many more consequences whose detailed study would be endless. One of them at least should be added to the preceding ones because of its impact on practical life. It may happen that music is enjoyed by a solitary music lover playing to himself the kind of music he prefers. Most of the time, however, musical performances are collective undertakings that require the co-operation of many executants, plus the no less necessary co-operation of a more or less large public. Let us forget all the material side of musical life, not, however, without remembering that it takes money, and a very great deal of it, to "revive," as they aptly say, such works as the great oratorios of Bach or certain operas that, despite their artistic value, or perhaps even because of it, cannot be expected to be financial successes. The least that can be said on this point is that, in many cases, the production of music and its enjoyment are a social and collective business. Without pretending that the experience of paintings is necessarily a solitary one, it seems at least true to

36. The virtuoso or the conductor is freer than the copyist who strives to duplicate a given picture. For, indeed, in the case of the painter, the model exists, and it is easy to compare the copy with it, whereas one cannot prove to a musician that his interpretation betrays the original. On the other hand, the musician cannot help comparing his own interpretation with a mental ideal that, precisely because it has no substance of its own, it is impossible to duplicate. As the pianist Artur Schnabel is reported to have said to one of his pupils, music, especially that of Beethoven, is "always better than it could be played." This is why, with deep insight, the same pianist would not call himself an "interpreter" of Beethoven. Still, it would have been interesting to hear Schnabel's comments on the performance by Beethoven of one of the famous sonatas on which his interpreter spent so much more time than the musician himself ever did. He might well have felt sorely disappointed at Beethoven's own interpretation. — On the trouble caused by the intervention of executants in the plastic arts, see Redon, *À soi-même*, pp. 123–24.

say that it is not a normally collective one. There is a sort of satisfaction in the sight of a well-filled concert hall in which one thousand listeners or more can hear together the same symphony. On the contrary, it seems doubtful that the best day to visit an art gallery is the one on which the place is so full of visitors that there are always several persons between ourselves and the paintings we desperately try to see. From time to time, small groups of friends go from painting to painting, exchanging a few remarks and communing admiringly; but we never see the fifty visitors of some room in an art gallery stop before the same picture and, after ten minutes of silent contemplation, suddenly burst into applause.[37] An audience attending the performance of a musical piece witnesses the quasi miracle of its re-creation by its performers. We then see the very men to whom we are indebted for the actual existence of the masterpiece, and they themselves are there to receive in person the expression of our gratitude. But there are no painters in art galleries, or, if some of them happen to be there, their presence adds nothing to the cause of our gratitude. Art galleries contain only paintings. Paintings, that is to say, things. One does not speak to things.

A still deeper consequence of the same fact affects the very structure of the works of art themselves. The powerful shock, sometimes amounting to a blow, inflicted by certain paintings upon our sensibilities is due to the fact that, being solid bodies, they are totally given at once. Because total presence is impossible for music, musicians have resorted to various artifices to help memory keep the fleeting musical chords and phrases more or less simultaneously present in the mind. The most fundamental of these expedients is repetition. To be sure, there is a measure of repetition in painting, too, be it only under the form of rhythm.[38] Many painters resort to rhythm,

37. Applause is a complex collective reaction whose analysis would include physiological, psychological, sociological, and aesthetic elements. Its study should perhaps take into account the fact that, at the end of an exceptional performance, the audience is saying farewell to something infinitely precious, which will never again exist under identically the same form or with identically the same kind of perfection. "That strain again! it had a dying fall." All music has it.

38. Remarkable observations on the musical rhythm of colors in Delacroix and Cimabue, as well as on "the musical part that, henceforward, color is going to perform in modern paintings," in *Lettres de Gauguin*, pp. 287–88. On the attempts of "dynamic futurism" (Boccioni) to represent movement in pictures, see Kahnweiler, *The Rise of*

but they do not all understand it in the same way. Rhythm can arise from the calculated repetition of certain forms, certain patterns, or certain colors. It can also arise from a distribution of the light values whose regularity divides space as musical rhythm divides time. Seurat would provide striking illustrations of pictorial rhythm—for instance, his *Parade.* Yet, in the last analysis, even a picture without much rhythm can be apprehended as a whole by the eyes of any onlooker. On the contrary, repetition is of the very essence of symphonic music, and this probably is the reason some painters have objected to what appeared to them as an excess of it on the part of even very great composers.[39] The use of subjects and countersubjects in fugues; the constantly recurring method of musical development by mode of "theme and variation"; the extension of this method from symphonic music to dramatic music by Richard Wagner when he completely transformed the notion of theme; in fine, the extension of this dramatic notion of theme to symphonic music again, when César Franck and his school decided to achieve "cyclical" composition[40]—all these facts are so many con-

[15]

Cubism, p. 21. On the suggestions made by Picasso to the same effect, p. 22. Those among the painters who have emphasized the notion of rhythm have been naturally led to stress the similarities between painting and music. On this point, see Wassily Kandinsky, *Concerning the Spiritual in Art,* p. 40, how a painter "seeks to apply the means of music to his own art"; p. 76, how to distinguish between melodic and symphonic composition in painting, and how melodic composition ("which is regulated according to an obvious and simple form") gives rise to what Cézanne called "rhythmic" composition. "Complex rhythmical composition, with a strong symphonic cast, is to be seen in many paintings, woodcuts, miniatures, and so on, of the past" (p. 76). This timeless rhythm, which is proper to plastic arts, only deserves this title owing to the fact that, after its first instantaneous apprehension, a picture requires time to be seen in its structure and properly understood. Painting becomes an art of time to the extent that aesthetic experience is concerned.

39. Delacroix was so thoroughly a painter that, even while listening to music, he sometimes felt impatient with its essential lack of simultaneity. After admiring the "divine 'Pastoral' Symphony," Delacroix observes: "I ventured to say that Beethoven's pieces are usually too long, in spite of the astonishing variety with which he reintroduces the same themes. I do not remember noticing this defect when I heard the symphony before, but however that may be, it is clear to me that an artist spoils his effect when he claims one's attention for too long at a time. Painting, among other advantages, is more discreet than music; the most gigantic picture can be seen in an instant. If its qualities, or certain portions of it, hold one's attention that is all to the good; one can enjoy it even longer than a piece of music. But if the painting seems mediocre, one has only to turn one's head away to escape boredom." (*Journal,* pp. 91–92 [Sunday, March 11, 1849].)

40. Without entering into the problems of musical composition, we beg leave to observe that the significance of the Wagnerian leitmotiv precisely consists in its aptitude to be

sequences of a first one, namely, the fleeting mode of existence proper to music on the one hand and the permanent solidity of pictures on the other hand. These two kinds of works of art *are* not in the same way.

When painters resort to the essentially musical notion of rhythm in order to define what they consider one of the necessary elements of their own art, it is a sure sign that this art itself is trying to overstep its natural limits. Nor are painters themselves unaware of the fact. The arts of space, from architecture to sculpture and painting, have always included among their fundamental notions that of composition. To compose is to arrange the parts of a picture in such a way that the proportions between their respective sizes, shapes, colors, and degrees of luminosity are pleasing to perceive. The reason modern painters, especially since the time of Picasso, Braque, and Juan Gris, have added the notion of rhythm to that of composition is not mysterious. For, indeed, rhythm implies composition, but it adds to it a regularly recurring pattern in the duration of sounds. This is to say that, as soon as pictorial composition in space assumes the form of patterns of lines and colors successively perceived in time, composition becomes for us a rhythm.

Classical painters were quite familiar with this notion, especially such colorists as Rubens and Delacroix, whose paintings often repeat hues and light values so as to lead the eye from place to place, following a perceptible pattern. Lines, of course, always can answer to one another, as they have regularly done in classical compositions, including those of purely academic style. But the need for such line and color patterns was more and more forcibly felt as, caring less and less for the imitation of natural appearances, painters had finally to rely upon pure formal elements. These patterns and their composition provide in modern paintings the equivalent of the intelligible content that used to be provided by imitation in most of

---

reproduced whole, and practically self-identical, without ceasing to provide matter for an infinity of variations. The Wagnerian theme imparts to music an amount of simultaneous presence that it is not in its nature to have. The Wagnerian reform was the more genial as it was brought to bear upon theatrical music, in which the presence of action made it less necessary to impart to the work the kind of unity so important in symphonic compositions. The nearest approach to total presence in an opera is represented by such works as *Tristan* and *Parsifal*, whose end is in their beginning.

the works produced between the Renaissance and our own times. Precisely because of their nonimitational nature, such rythmical motives act upon our sight in a way similar to that in which musical sounds act upon our ears.[41] Again, it seems that nonrepresentational paintings require from us a more protracted effort of attention, be it only because to "understand" such paintings can no longer consist in recognizing the subject—figure, face, or story—which traditional pictures represent. Even in such works as those of Juan Gris, in which the imitational element remains immediately percepti- [16] ble, the structure of the composition so engages the attention that it is some- times practically impossible to stop the eye in its investigation of the rhyth- mical interplay of lines.[42] Painting then feels tempted to describe itself in terms of music. If the phenomenology of aesthetic existence were more ad- vanced than it is, the interaction of our experience of paintings in time and of their substantial stability in space could be analyzed with more precision than can now be done. Higher literary and art criticism has long held it lawful artistically to look for musical analogies in poetry, for poetic analo- gies in painting, and for pictorial analogies in both poetry and music. Artists and art critics do not need philosophers to realize that such lofty speculations are possible; it is, however, to be hoped that philosophy will someday discover the reasons why, in their own order, these speculations are not only legitimate, but sources of the highest among the joys accessible to understanding.

41. See the developments of Kahnweiler on these analogies between painting and music, in his *Juan Gris*, pp. 119–24. The following pages extend the comparison to poetry.

42. See the pencil drawing of Juan Gris, *Girl Seated* (1922); pl. 48 in Kahnweiler's text (*Juan Gris*, p. 121). Even in his lithograph illustration for Salacrou's *Le Casseur d'assiettes* (pl. 49, p. 124), dated 1924, we find it difficult to keep our eyes on any one of the three main volumes: the head, the top of the table, or the cap-holding hand. But, of course, there is no standard way of perceiving a work of art.

CHAPTER TWO

INDIVIDUALITY

[17a, b]

AS ACTUALLY existing substances, paintings are individuals—that is to say, beings that cannot be divided into parts without ceasing to be the particular beings they are. When a painter is not pleased with the over-all effect of one of his works, he may cut out of it one or two of the parts he prefers and throw away the rest. If he does so, each part becomes a new individual.[1] As for the primitive painting—that is, the primitive individual —it ceases at once to exist. To say that paintings are individuals is therefore to say that, considered as the very being it is, each of them enjoys the privilege of indivisibility.

The indivisibility of a physical substance is one and the same thing as its individuality. The primitive meaning of "individual" exactly is: "not divisible." An "individual" is an entity that cannot be divided without ceasing to be that which it is. Now, the notion of individuality itself is inseparable from that of singularity. Strictly speaking, an indivisible entity cannot be duplicated. Leibniz was fond of saying that no two identical tree leaves could be found in any garden, nor, for that matter, two identical beings in

1. Delacroix's portraits of George Sand and Chopin used to form a single picture representing "Chopin improvising at the piano, George Sand behind him listening." See the *Journal*, pls. 20, 21, and the notes on p. 485. They have been separated; some say by Delacroix himself, others, as late as 1889. Degas had made a study of Manet and Mme Manet; he gave it to Manet, who, not liking the effect produced by Mme Manet in the picture, simply cut her face out of it. Vollard wonders if Manet would have hesitated to cut a painting by Ingres or Delacroix. On this anecdote, and on the dissection, by Manet's family, of one of his versions of the *Execution of Maximilian* (National Gallery, London), see Ambroise Vollard, *En écoutant Cézanne, Degas, Renoir*, pp. 125–26.

the whole universe. And, indeed, it is one and the same thing for any being to be one and to be the very being it is.

Individuality and singularity belong to every being taken as a whole. In other words, in any given being, individuality belongs to the whole as such. In applying these notions to paintings, we shall say that each and every one of them is a distinct entity, which cannot be duplicated, even by its own author. However carefully he may copy himself, a painter can turn out only another painting. Now, the fundamental cause assigned by philosophers to this character of physical substances lies in the very matter that enters their composition. The classical formula—matter is the principle of individuation—means something quite simple. It merely expresses the fact that each definite portion of matter, delimited by certain dimensions, exists only once. A man, or even a machine, can turn out any number of similar chairs made out of the same kind of wood, but the same kind of wood is not the same piece of wood. The number of similar chairs it is possible to make depends only on the available quantity of wood, but the particular piece of wood that goes into the making of one particular chair cannot enter the structure of another one. This is what the philosophers give us to understand in saying that, on account of its fundamental incommunicability, matter is the principle of individuation.[2]

These notions apply to paintings inasmuch as these are material objects. In view of the considerations that are to follow, any painting should be considered as a single material unit consisting of its solid support (plaster, wood, cardboard, etc.), together with the successive coats of color and varnishes that cover it. Although our analysis will have to examine these various elements separately, they can be considered as making up, taken to-

2. Many discussions have taken place among the Scholastics themselves on the cause of individuation. The generally received answer to the problem can be summed up as follows. Supposing that there are species (for instance, the species "man"), the notion of the species itself applies in the same sense to all its individuals. All men are men in the same sense, and one man cannot be more or less man than another one (although he can be man in a better or in a less good way). Individuals can be multiplied as distinct entities, within their respective species, by their bodies only; this, of course, does not mean that corporeal matter constitutes their "individuality," but it is the cause of their individuation.

gether, a single material unit endowed with all the properties that physical beings derive from their materiality.

A similar remark applies to the philosophical notions of matter and form. They, too, must be examined apart without being conceived as separate in reality. Even in our own day, very few art critics, and still fewer aestheticians, have been able to do away with these two classical notions. At the same time, they seem to have felt reluctant to resort to them, because these two notions strongly smack of their scholastic origin and, by the same token, of the discredited philosophy of Aristotle. In other words, the notions of matter and form, so often ridiculed ever since the time of Descartes and his school, suffer a regrettable lack of modernity.

There is no reason this should prevent anybody from resorting to them. In the first place, even if the philosophy of Aristotle were rightly discredited, these two notions should still be considered valid, for the simple reason that the arts did not borrow them from Aristotle's philosophy; on the contrary, the philosophy of Aristotle borrowed them both from art. It is enough for anyone to consider any kind of artifact in order to realize that it is made up of a matter either informed or worked into shape by the skill of some artisan. This is true of all handmade products, from painted vases to statues and paintings. In returning to the fundamental distinction of matter and form, art borrows nothing from any philosophy; it is simply reclaiming what has always been its own property.[3]

1. Invention of the Material

THE treatment of color as the very stuff of which pictures are made implies a strong temptation to try what has often been called the "scientific approach" to painting. And, indeed, colors are physical facts; they are part and parcel of the subject matter of optics; especially since the time of

3. Focillon (*Vie des formes*, p. 47) has forcefully stressed the fact that, in art, form remains a mere view of the mind, an abstract speculation about geometrical extension, as long as it does not live in matter. This, which is absolutely true, has far-reaching consequences. In plastic arts at least, as long as matter is not there, it can be a question of philosophy, aesthetics, art history, or art criticism. It can even be, in the mind of the artist himself, a question of dreaming about art. But there is no art.

Newton, it is not easy to imagine a painter wholly indifferent to what science says about the nature and properties of colors; at a more recent date, the research work of Chevreul in that field has provided the neoimpressionists with food for thought.[4] There is no contradiction between being a painter and being a scientist or, at least, a man interested in science, especially in those parts of it which deal with the very material out of which works of art are made. Generally speaking, there is no such thing as useless knowledge. Nevertheless, complete scientific ignorance would be better than the slightest confusion between the respective domains of optics and painting, or, in other words, of science and art.

Art is much older than science. We cannot imagine the kinds of notions present in the minds of the men who, millenniums ago, decorated the caves of Lascaux and Altamira; it is at least certain that modern physics would have meant nothing to them. Even at the time of the Italian Renaissance, few artists were comparable in learning to Leonardo da Vinci, and some of them knew very little indeed. Speaking of Luca della Robbia, Vasari observes as the most natural thing in the world that "he was carefully brought up, so that not only was he able to read and write, but, like most Florentines, he could do such arithmetic as he needed."[5] In our own day, even leaving aside the primitive masters of African art, comparatively few painters are worrying about the last discoveries of physiology concerning sight and of physics concerning colors. Even though they could understand them, artists would find these discoveries practically irrelevant to their own problems, for the simple reason that the colors of the physicist have little in common with those used by painters in their work.[6]

4. Paul Signac, *D'Eugène Delacroix au néo-impressionnisme*, p. 80. — On account of what follows concerning the radical difference between the optical mixtures of light-colors and the pigmentary mixtures, or mixtures of material pigments, it may prove useful to read of Signac's remarks (he is a neoimpressionist) on the fundamental analogy that subsists between their respective laws; Signac even attempts to prove that, in the last analysis, a pigmentary mixture can be made to look like an optical mixture (p. 66, n. 1). In fact, this was the very essence of neoimpressionism.

5. *Lives*, I, 224.

6. For an introduction to the general theory of color, see Arthur Pope, *The Language of Drawing and Painting* (it includes a bibliography). — For the background of the problem, see Goethe's celebrated contribution, *Zur Farbenlehre*, in *Sämtliche Werke*, vol. 28, especially the first part, pp. 20–284. Also, Goethe's *Theory of Colours*, tr. Charles Lock

Even considered under its simplest form, that is, in the optics of Newton, the scientific notion of color is practically irrelevant to painting. The so-called seven primitive colors of the spectrum are not primitive; nor are they seven in number. The reasons Newton counted seven of them have little to do even with science. After decomposing white light into a spectrum by means of a prism, Newton observed a certain correspondence between the proportions of the spaces occupied by the main colors on the spectrum and the ratios of the notes in the diatonic musical scale. So the only reason there are seven primitive colors in the spectrum is that there are seven notes in the diatonic scale. In fact, painters refuse to recognize at least one of them as a distinct color; it does not even take a painter's eye to see that "indigo" is a variety of blue. Moreover, since spectral colors are physically distinct on account of their wave lengths, the spectrum really is continuous. True enough, the number of hues that the average human eye can distinguish and identify to the point of giving them fixed names is small enough, but this simply means that we take a discontinuous view of a continuous reality. Last but not least, the very title of the first memoir of Newton on the question, *New Theory about Light and Colours* (1672), is for us a reminder of the fact that the spectral colors arise from the decomposition of light, whereas no painter, precisely qua painter, is called upon to handle anything like the white light of the sun or the colors arising from its decomposition.[7]

Eastlake. This translation includes the first part of Goethe's work, besides a series of notes that have been mainly borrowed from the historical part of the *Farbenlehre*. — Newton and Goethe made the same error in looking for a theory that could account for both psychophysiological colors (i.e., qualitative) and physical colors (i.e., quantitative). If he had let Newton alone, Goethe would have largely been right. Most of Newton's optics is irrelevant to painting; most of Goethe's *Farbenlehre* is irrelevant to optics, but it is highly relevant to painting. See, particularly, Didactic Part, sec. VI, arts. 758–919, pp. 194–230, on the moral connotations of color perceptions.

7. Light and the spectrum colors would provide material for an art entirely different from painting. The French Jesuit Louis Castel conceived it as a combination of sound and color and imagined what was called an "ocular harpsichord." The idea has never been entirely forgotten, but the present trend seems to be to eliminate the element of sound in order to preserve the color element only. The "clavilux" of Thomas Wilfred (1919) is a color projector that enables a trained artist to give color recitals. On the question: A. W. Rimington, *Colour Music: The Art of Mobile Colour*; A. B. Klein, *Colour-Music: The Art of Light*; and art. "Colour-Music," *The Encyclopædia Britannica*, 14th edn., vol. 6, pp. 64–65. — Klein observes that the analogy between color and sound is misleading. One of the main obstacles to the success of an art of light is that, if it uses

Painters use only specially prepared pigments, that is, colored bodies, whose surfaces appear to be differently colored according to the wave lengths of the light radiations they absorb or reject. Absolutely pure colors are practically impossible to obtain. A blue object usually reflects some violet and some green together with the blue; a similar phenomenon takes place in the case of a yellow object, or of a green one; and because the possible combinations and proportions of these overtones are practically infinite in number, countless hues are at the disposal of the painter. Some prefer to produce them on their own palette by means of the three colors painters consider primitive, yellow, red, and blue; but there are illustrious examples to the contrary.[8] In any case, the matter that enters the structure of modern paintings ultimately comes from vulgar tubes prosaically bought at some paint dealer's. The history of their production is part of the general history of chemistry; factories are busy providing painters with an always increasing number of different hues; just as musicians write music for instruments that have had to be invented, so also the creation of colors precedes the

nothing else than light-color, it is purely qualitative. Now, it is a curious fact that without a quantitative element (such as intervals and rhythms in music) there is no art. In painting, design and composition provide this quantitative element that colors alone would not provide. As to their intervals, which are no less real than those of sounds, it is difficult to say if our eyes could be trained to perceive them and to locate them at fixed places on color scales similar to the musical ones. There is much relativity in sensory habits (remember how hard it is for Western ears to perceive any music in the sounds made by African or Asiatic musicians), so that to deny the intrinsic possibilities of color music would be to take a gratuitous risk. Certain color sequences in some cartoons of Walt Disney suggest what such an art could be. We cannot help feeling that, handled by him, nonimitational color films could be successful experiments.

8. See the scene between Émile Bernard and Cézanne. Bernard was using a very sparingly loaded palette: flake white, chrome yellow, ultramarine, blue, vermilion, plus a madder red (*laque de garance*) that he obviously needed to get his scale of reds. Cézanne indignantly asked him: "Are these all the colors with which you paint?"— "Yes."—"But where is your Naples yellow? Where is your peach black? Where are your raw sienna, your cobalt blue, your burnt lake? . . . One cannot paint without these colors!" (Émile Bernard, *Souvenirs sur Paul Cézanne, et lettres*, p. 35.) — Absolutely speaking, Bernard was right; with his four colors and his white, he could produce all the other colors either on his palette or on the canvas. But Cézanne used to paint differently. For instance, he would obtain a certain gray by the juxtaposition, on the canvas, of three slightly overlapping spots of blue, ocher, and green whose blending takes place in the eye of the spectator. He needed an extended scale of pure hues in order to create the scale of grays he wanted without multiplying his operations to infinity. The often-made remark that, under close inspection, the works of Cézanne reveal an incredible number of color spots illustrates in part what has just been said.

creation of the paintings whose matter they provide. Artistic invention extends to the very matter of the works of art.

The importance of the part played by chemical industries in the development of modern painting should not be underestimated. Art lovers do not think of it, because they are interested only in the finished product, but there is at least one aspect of this product in which they should feel interested, namely, its preservation. Durability is a fundamental quality in a pigment. Some paints do not age well, and however great an artistic genius he may be, a painter is powerless to preserve his works from partial or total destruction if he uses exceptionally perishable pigments. All paintings are ultimately doomed to perish, but there are degrees in this risk of impermanence, and the color solidity of a pigment is of primary importance in this respect.[9]

In comparing hues with musical sounds we have just said that even the material element of a picture results from an invention. Let us add that, although produced in laboratories, colors and hues also result from an effort of artistic creation.

One of the fundamental facts to whose consideration it is often necessary to return is the aptitude of human sensibility to experience pleasure at the mere sight of certain colors or, inversely, the aptitude of certain colors to please the eye. This is not true of the human eye alone. Darwin has shown that the perception of colors plays a decisive part in the sexual life of many animal species, and, to some extent, the same remark also applies to the

9. This is a point on which, far from being a threat to art, science and industry are of vital importance for the survival of its works. When artists themselves start experimenting with colors, anything may happen. As a symbol of a long series of disasters owing to the poor quality of the material used by painters, let us recall the incident of Leonardo da Vinci's *Battle of Anghiari:* "Thinking that he could paint on the wall in oils, he made a composition so thick for laying on the wall that when he continued his painting it began to run and spoil what had been begun, so that in a short time he was forced to abandon it" (Vasari, *The Lives of the Painters,* II, 166). Leonardo also painted a *Virgin and Child* "with infinite diligence and art, but today it is much spoiled either by neglect or because of his numerous fanciful mixtures and the colouring" (II, 166). — Nearer to our own times: "It must be admitted that the names of some of the pigments —*momie, vert-chou* and *laque de gaude* for example—leave one aghast at the risk of impermanence he [Delacroix] was willing to accept. One no longer wonders at the ruin of so many canvases." (*The Journal of Eugène Delacroix,* Introduction by Hubert Wellington, p. xxiii.) The conditions for the possibility of the very existence of paintings is what is at stake in these considerations.

botanic species, the colors of whose flowers probably attract the attention of insects. But art is for us human art, and its very existence rests upon the fact that certain musical sounds, certain forms, and certain colors are pleasing to perceive in themselves and by themselves. Since sense perception is the common act of the sensible quality and of the perceiving subject, the very possibility of the pleasure that, in Aristotle's own words, accompanies an act as "an end which supervenes as the bloom of youth does on those in the flower of their age" hangs on the presence of a certain harmony between the perceiving subject and the structure of its object.[10]

If this be true, one cannot deny that the subjective dispositions of the onlooker play a decisive part in the aesthetic experience of the kind of pleasure given by the perception of colors. This is so true that most of us cannot help envying such artists as Delacroix to whom the sight of certain colors was enough to cause joys whose intensity remains unknown to us. At the same time, and precisely for the same reason, the invention of a certain color, or even of a certain shade of red, yellow, or green, by a chemist working in a laboratory compares in importance with the creation of the musical sounds produced by the bass tuba, the bass clarinet, or the Mustel celesta. From this point of view, there is an artistic creation of colors as there is one for sounds. Some painters are fond of using colors exactly as they buy them. Others appreciate the same colors in the light of what they become when various proportions of flake white or zinc white are added to them. A chemical formula thus results in a certain color pigment, sold by a paint dealer in a tube, that appeals more or less to the eye of the painter according to his personal taste and his own visual sensibility. The names given to colors by their makers are largely arbitrary, for the simple reason that the colors themselves depend on the makers' free choice. What is advertised as a pure Naples yellow by a certain firm may be identical with what

10. *Nicomachean Ethics*, X, 4, 1174b, 31–33. — This sets a limit to the possibility of universalizing aesthetic experience. Delacroix does not seem to have entertained too many illusions as to the number of people qualified by nature to experience the beauty of colors: "They speak of *having an ear* for music: not every eye is fit to taste the subtle joys of painting. The eyes of many people are dull or false; they see objects literally, of the exquisite they see nothing." (*Journal*, p. 414 [June 22, 1863], the last entry.)

is represented by another firm as Naples yellow tinted with zinc white. These facts are being mentioned here as so many tokens of this general truth, that artistic creation begins at the level of the fabrication of its material element, that is, colored pigments.

Expressed in terms of classical philosophy, this means that even colors, which are the "material cause" of paintings, have first to be invented. Painters do not create out of nothing; they must resort to some sort of given material to be formed later on by their art. Since there is no painting without this material element, the matter out of which a picture is made can rightly be considered one of the causes for its existence. But this is not the whole truth. It will presently be seen that, when it is applied to art, the very notion of matter, and the kind of causality proper to it, exhibit an extreme complexity.

2. *Material Causality*

SUCH as it was understood in classical metaphysics, the word "matter" pointed out, in its first acceptation, "primary matter," that is to say, matter as such, taken in itself and without any formal specification. Thus understood, matter was common to all material beings, in this sense at least that, according to its very notion, it was complete and absolute indetermination. Conceived as a mere aptitude to receive further determinations, this receptacle was, in Plato's own words, a near nothingness, so much so that it could not even be conceived in itself and apart from some determining form.

This absolute meaning of the term, however, was reserved to its metaphysical use. In sense experience, and consequently in given reality, this notion of primary matter never applies. In the infinite chain of determining and determined beings we observe that all that is being determined, shaped, or molded, in any way, is considered as standing on the side of matter, whereas all that is determining, shaping, or molding stands on the side of form. According to this empirical interpretation, what is matter in a certain relation can be form in another one. More important still, since there is no such thing as pure and absolute indetermination in reality, each and every given matter includes a certain amount and a certain kind of formal determination. In fact, the physical unit made up of a solid support and of the colored pigments applied to it by the painter constitutes, so to speak, the body of the painting.

A general remark must be made concerning the meaning of the term "matter" or "material" when it applies to works of art. Whatever its origin, its physicochemical structure, and even though it already is in itself a manufactured object, that which an artist assumes in order to use it as a material in the making of a work of art ceases thereby to be a natural element or an industrial product. It becomes at once an artistic material. When the prehistoric artists who decorated the Lascaux caves first collected various earths with a view to turning them into colors, these "natural" earth pigments, along with the animal grease they probably used as a medium, ceased at once to be "natural" materials. They became artistic materials, whose function was henceforth entirely foreign to those they were fulfilling before their introduction into the new world in which they now belonged. An earth pigment may be a "natural" product, or it may have been artificially produced in a chemical plant; in both cases, the pigment at stake will not be used by the painter as a natural or as a chemical product, but as one of the various elements that can enter the structure of a work of art and be made subservient to its ends.

This truth accounts for the recent attempts made by several painters to use paper, leather, sand, metallic objects, and practically anything as a painting material. The fact that it is possible to do so is not in itself a sufficient justification for the method. The only judge of the method is its final success or failure. But this at least is certain: since everything that enters the structure of a work of art assumes an artistic significance, there is no a priori reason to disqualify any kind of material. Everything hangs on what Focillon has so admirably called the "formal vocation" of each and every kind of material at the disposal of the artist.[11] His creative imagination

[10]
[82]

11. *Vie des formes*, pp. 48–51. — On the paper collages used by Picasso, Braque, Juan Gris, and Reth, see Michel Seuphor, "Matière à discussion," *La Matière et le temps dans les arts plastiques*, pp. 9–14. One of the most certain successes in this field is Reth's *Still Life before a Window*, formerly in the Musée d'art moderne, Paris (see Pl. 18). Picabia's use of sardine tins, combs, matches, and bits of string had perhaps chiefly the value of bravado. On the contrary, plaster, sawdust, sand, gravel, sea shells, and piled eggshells

alone is judge of the possibilities of any material available. No abstract precept is of any value to determine what it is "lawful" or "unlawful" to use in order to reach the ends of art.

This first truth contains within itself the principle of its own limitation. Any material can be assumed by a painter to the ends of his own art, but the formal vocation of matter entails the consequence that, once selected by the painter and integrated with his work, each kind of material will have to be used according to its own nature. Anything can be used by the artist, but the choice that he freely makes of a certain material will determine to a large extent the nature of his future work. To be sure, the painter is the sole judge of the possibilities latent in the material he has decided to use. Still, when all is said and done, the formal vocation of a painting material has both its possibilities and its limits. This is the moment the causality attributable to their matter becomes a determining factor in the genesis of the works of art.

One cannot do much more, to make precise the nature of this causality, than to illustrate it by means of selected examples. For instance, its consideration should help to curb an unsound ambition that has literally wrecked the career of several promising artists.

Some painters are so deeply impressed with the masterpieces of the Italian Renaissance exhibited in art galleries that they dream of reviving the art of the masters of the past. Ever since the time of Delacroix, and certainly not without good reason, the conviction has been spreading among painters that the secret traditions of the great techniques of the Renaissance were "mysteriously lost" about the beginning of the eighteenth century. Hence the efforts made by some modern artists to "rediscover the methods of such masters as Titian, Rubens, Rembrandt, Velázquez," as well as of some of their predecessors, such as Jan van Eyck, Memling, and Giovanni Bellini.[12]

seem to have become part and parcel of the media normally used by certain painters. Some walls painted by Utrillo owe much of their quality to the fact that the painter used real plaster in painting them instead of the usual pigments.

12. Jacques Maroger, *The Secret Formulas and Techniques of the Masters*, p. 7. Following the example of Louis Anquetin (the "French Michelangelo"!), Maroger finally gave up creative work in order to dedicate himself to the quest for the discovery of "the *secret material* known to the old masters but lost to us." — This seems to be a

a. Eugène Delacroix. George Sand
1838. Fragment of originally larger composition. Hansen Collection, Ordrupgaard Museum, Copenhagen

b. Eugène Delacroix. Frédéric Chopin
1838. Fragment of originally larger composition. Louvre

ALFRED RETH. Still Life Before a Window
1912. Paint and paper collage. Musée national d'art moderne, Paris

a. J.-A.-D. Ingres. Mme Destouches
1816. Black lead pencil. Louvre

b. J.-A.-D. Ingres. Mme Ingres
1814. Black lead pencil and wash.
Musée Ingres, Montauban

c. J.-A.-D. Ingres. Mme Rivière
1805. Louvre

ÉDOUARD MANET. A Bar at the Folies-Bergère
1881. National Gallery, London

ÉDOUARD MANET. The Model for "A Bar at the Folies-Bergère"
1881. Pastel. Musée, Dijon

21

The Annunciation
Fifth century. Mosaic. Santa Maria Maggiore, Rome

JEAN LURÇAT. The Virgin and the Dragon
1928. Tapestry. Notre-Dame de Toute Grâce, Assy, France

Fernand Léger. The Instruments of the Passion
Installed 1951. Stained glass. Sacré-Cœur, Audincourt, France

There is something pathetic in the thought that, in our own times, such painters as Louis Anquetin and Émile Bernard either wholly renounced the art of painting in order to hunt for its lost secrets or else exhausted themselves in obstinate efforts to achieve works similar in general effect to those of the Venetians. Assuredly, this kind of investigation is most interesting in itself. It can even prove helpful to painters, since it calls to their attention painting techniques that once flourished, then died out, and could perhaps be revived with profit. The long-lost art of encaustic painting, the ancient tempera technique, even the primitive oil technique used by Jan van Eyck, certainly deserve to be investigated. The very fact that modern art almost entirely depends, in its rise and development, upon the discovery of oil painting clearly shows how deeply the very material of which paintings are made affects their nature as works of art. But this also is the fundamental reason, even though modern painters could rediscover the lost secrets of the ancient painters, they still could not duplicate their works in our own times. This truth has been clearly stated by J. L. F. Mérimée (the father of Prosper), in his book *De la Peinture à l'huile* (1830), when he said that "although a pupil of the École des Beaux-Arts, who had won the Grand Prix de Rome, might well be capable of copying correctly a work done by his own master, he could never successfully attempt the reproduction of any work of the earlier periods *because he did not possess the exact medium used in those times.*"[13]

The same truth has been formulated in a still deeper way by the painter André Lhote, when he said that since our own oils, essences, gums, and

widely generalized obsession: "The tradition entirely lost in modern painting." (*The Journal of Eugène Delacroix*, p. 331 [January 11, 1857].) — "We might say that for a long time the art of painting has been a lost secret, and that the last masters of great experience who practiced it took the key away with them. We need it, we ask for it, and it cannot be found." (Fromentin, *The Masters of Past Time*, p. 132.) — André Lhote (*La Peinture, le cœur et l'esprit*, p. 290) accounts for the return of many modern painters to primitive techniques by the fact that they have lost the tradition of the classics; they pass before the *Venus of Urbino*, or before the *Entombment* (Titian), as they would pass "before the doors of a lost paradise."

13. Maroger, p. 12. — Note, same page, the sad remark: "Mérimée's researches have given us the formula for four varnishes. Unfortunately, the use of some of these proved disastrous in actual practice. Prud'hon used one of them on his *Christ on the Cross*, in the Louvre Museum, and in view of its present state we cannot but confirm the failure of this particular formula."

colors are wholly different from what they still were in the eighteenth century, even a modern painter of genius could not achieve today "the equivalent of that art (of Titian and Veronese) whose expressive power *wholly resides in its painting material.*"[14] This statement should be understood in its full force, for indeed, despite its paradoxical appearance, it is literally true. A very great amount of literature can be written about the genius of such painters as van Eyck, Veronese, Vermeer of Delft, or Titian; aesthetic and technical studies can go a long way to help us understand the nature of their works, but to the extent that these act upon sight by their very color, all attempts to achieve the same effects have been doomed to fail ever since the same color material ceased to be available.

The fact that the material elements included in paintings are determined by forms of their own brings about a second series of still more important consequences. Many ancient philosophers expressed the opinion that there is in matter, not only an absence of form, but a sort of obscure craving for it. To the extent that matter is already determined by a certain type of form, this aspiration seems to be directed toward further determinations of a definite type. In more simple terms, the medium chosen by the artist in which to express himself partly determines the general nature of what he will say.

This remark rests upon the fact that, in reality, matter and form are inseparable. They are always given together. Modern aesthetic has forcibly stressed the part played by matter in the "life of forms." On the one hand, form strives to liberate itself from matter; on the other hand, without its matter, form could not possibly subsist. In one of the deepest remarks he ever made, Focillon said that, without matter, art would neither be "nor be such as it wishes to be." [15] Whereupon, seized by a curious scruple, he pres-

14. *La Peinture*, p. 289. Lhote quotes (p. 290) as an example of a painting material whose progressive corruption is observable in our own times the "Haarlem siccative" used by Ingres and Cézanne. To which he presently adds: "Besides, if we still had this precious material, we would not know how to use it. It is in the presence of this mystery that those among the moderns who still were somewhat honest and aware of the situation, renouncing the lost art of glazing, adopted the ancient, primitive technique of the flat tints."

15. *Vie des formes*, p. 47. "The old antinomies, spirit-matter, matter-form, still obsess our mind with as much force as the time-honored opposition between the matter and

ently added that, although they still obsess our minds, the "ancient antinomies," such as spirit versus matter, matter versus form, manner versus matter, should be left behind and this, precisely, for the reason that, in fact, both terms of these antinomies are always given together, reacting upon one another and mutually determining one another. But these alleged "antinomies" have really never existed. Only prime matter, could it exist apart, would be absolute indetermination. But it does not and cannot exist apart. In concrete experience, all relations are of act to potency, and inversely, that is, they are relations between that which determines and that which is being determined. In such relations, that which stands on the side of act and fulfills a determining function is called form, while that which stands on the side of potency and of determinability is called matter. Since a particular material is always specified by its form, it is through its form that the matter of a work of art finally exercises its own formal vocation.

As has already been said, the integration of a certain material with a work of art introduces it into a new order of reality. Its physical qualities may well remain the same, but they become the qualities of an artistic material. This is to say that, in a work of art, everything is determined to an artistic mode of existence. When it is pasted on a canvas by a painter, a piece of newspaper loses its newspaperly nature; physically the same, it no longer exists as a piece of newspaper, but as part of a painting. It is painting. On the other hand, since each particular kind of material is determined by its own natural form, no two of them are interchangeable. The same form will not be able to pass from a certain matter to another one without undergoing some modification. In fact, it will not remain *the same*.

Henri Focillon has so forcibly made this truth his very own that it cannot be better expressed than in his own language. "In passing from a given mat-

the manner. Even though some shadow of meaning or usefulness may still remain attached to these antitheses in pure logic, anybody wishing to gain some understanding of the life of forms must first get rid of them." As will presently be seen, the admirable master is here at grips with historical phantoms. Incidentally, let us recall that, according to Focillon himself (p. 47): "Every science of observation, especially if it studies the activities and the creations of the human mind, is, before anything else, a phenomenology, in the strictest sense of the word." As is the case with every phenomenology, this one would fare better if it were supported by a correct ontology, without which, *even as a phenomenology*, it cannot be completely right. — On matter and form, see pp. 106 ff.

ter to another one, a form undergoes a metamorphosis." [16] This is the deepest reason why the same aesthetician has so often considered the two notions of matter and of technique practically equivalent. Each kind of material requires a mode of treatment adapted to its own nature, and, in turn, this technique itself largely conditions the form and substance of the work. Assuredly, the formal qualities of a pencil drawing by Ingres are akin to those of his oil paintings, yet, in the last analysis, a drawing and a painting of the same model, or of similar ones, done by the same painter, are two specifically distinct works of art.[17]

It is easy to verify the truth of this remark by comparing works done by the same artist when, as was the case with Ingres, he happened to be both a great portrait painter and an unsurpassed master in the art of drawing. He himself knew the difference between these two media so well that he once refused to exhibit some of his drawings together with oil portraits. He felt afraid for the oils, not for the drawings. "People," he said, "would look at nothing else than the drawings." Leaving aside all problems of preferences, this at least is certain, that neither the end nor the means are [19a] the same in a lead drawing, like the portrait of Mme Destouches, in which a few lines suffice to circumscribe a space that is hardly occupied; in the [19b] portrait of Ingres' first wife, in which wash comes to the rescue in order to ensure an effective occupation of space; and in any one of his oil portraits [19c] —for instance, that of Mme Rivière, which entirely submits space, lines, and forms to the controlling will of the artist. In this case, oil enables the painter to achieve a work that, rather than a rendering of reality, is in itself a subsisting reality.

The importance of the material causality exercised by the various species of colors becomes manifest when one attempts more or less arbitrarily to classify the various branches of the art whose means of expression is color.

16. Ibid., p. 52.

17. Ibid., p. 51. — A primary introduction to the basic knowledge of the material used by painters can be found, among many other ones, in the charming yet extremely precise little book of Norman Colquhoun, *Paint Your Own Pictures*, especially ch. 5, "Paints and Pigments"; ch. 6, "Oil Painting"; ch. 7, "Water-Colour and Other Media"; ch. 8, "Colour" (including the color circle, p. 161). The book is completed by a useful Glossary of Technical Terms.

A first class would include, under the name of painting properly so called, all the works executed by means of colored pigments diluted in some liquid and applied with a brush or otherwise, such as oil, tempera, water, etc. The two main classes of paintings, properly so called, are those in oils and those in water color. But there are other techniques, and the point we are now enforcing is that, taken in its very materiality, the same red is different, depending on whether it is painted in water color, in oil, in tempera, or in fresco. It is the same color as the same note is the same sound when produced by a piano, a violin, an oboe, or a horn. All the wash drawings, sepias, etc., are included in this class.

A second class should comprise the various kinds of drawings—that is to say, media of design in all their forms. Lead pencil, conté crayon, charcoal, chalks (white, black, or colored), pastel colors, etc., constitute so many materials whose influence on the formal structure of the work is decisive. As has been said, these matters are not interchangeable;[18] their physicochemical structure determines the way in which each of them must be handled as well as the general effect that can be expected from their use. Since their combinations, and even the way to handle them, can be indefinitely diversified, no exhaustive enumeration of such materials is possible. No two artists use the same color material in identically the same way. Even the touch of the painter changes the color effect, just as the "hand" of the artist changes the material qualities of a line. Form is here beginning to react upon its matter. In fact, the very choice an artist makes of a certain material is conditioned by the effect this artist intends to achieve. Matter is there in view of its form. Yet, the fact that their causality is [20, 21]

18. "Ink, wash drawing, lead pencil, charcoal, red chalk, white chalk, either separated or united, represent so many different properties, so many different languages. To convince himself of this, let one try to figure out this impossibility: a red chalk by Watteau, for instance, copied by Ingres in lead pencil" (Focillon, *Vie des formes*, p. 51). More simply, let us imagine Ingres himself copying in pencil one of his own oil portraits. The results would be altogether different. — As an example of the modifications to which artists can subject their materials, see the treatment of pastels by Degas, in Vollard, p. 120. Degas used to wash his pastels, let them dry, then wash them again. The result was the mat and solid appearance of some of his drawings, especially of ballet girls, so puzzling if one remembers the effect of unsubstantial fluffiness that normally goes with the use of pastels.

reciprocal implies that matter itself acts as a cause on the structure of such works of art.[19]

Whatever their materials, all the preceding techniques have this in common, that they let the painter free himself to produce the colors or the light values included in his work. This is true of all paintings properly so called, including Chinese inks painted on silk, with or without addition of faint colors; Japanese sepias on paper screens; painted potteries of all denominations, from the black-figure and red-figure Greek potteries, with all the brushwork required for their painting, to the Urbino painted dishes and the incredible variety of decorated vases, cups, and vessels dating from so many centuries and coming from practically all the explored parts of the earth. In these techniques, the painter is more or less master of the colors he uses, and they all are destined to be seen, on a plane surface, under reflected light.

Other color materials are used by certain arts that, although intimately related to painting, cannot be identified with it. Such is, for instance, the case of mosaic. Nothing more closely resembles a painting than a mosaic. A mosaicist has to face the same problems as a painter: composition, tone values, light values, and so on; the only difference is that he is no complete master of his colors. A mosaic is a surface decoration made up of small pieces of colored stone, marble, glass, or any other such material; its author has therefore to make use of the colored fragments at his disposal, and he must use them such as they are. The influence exercised by the material on the whole work is nowhere more evident than it is here. The mode of decadence proper to the art of mosaic has consisted in its attempting to achieve [22] the effects proper to the art of painting. This art seems to have yielded its most perfect masterpieces in the Greco-Roman antiquity, and in early Christian art. Giotto is rightly credited with having liberated painting from the Byzantine tradition, and indeed he was among the very first artists to paint pictures that did not look like Byzantine mosaics; but what then was the

19. Compare the head of the barmaid in Manet's *Bar at the Folies-Bergère* (National Gallery, London) with Manet's pastel portrait of the model, now in the Museum of Dijon (Pls. 20 and 21). Incidentally, to use plates to show the difference between the material texture of two paintings is self-defeating. We can only hope that some of the differences between a pastel and an oil rendering of the same model, by the same painter, will remain perceptible even in their printed condition.

beginning of a rebirth of the art of painting was also for mosaic the beginning of a long decadence. Despite its merits, Giotto's famous *Navicella*[20] has initiated the interminable series of modern mosaics whose ambition it is to be mistaken for so many pictures. Many churches bear witness to the fact that this time-honored error, already familiar to the Romans, has not ceased to dominate an art that, in antiquity, produced admirable masterpieces.

For similar reasons, tapestry should be set aside as distinct from the art of painting. The tapestry maker works with woolen threads of different colors. His choice is a limited one. Even in modern tapestries, which make use of an enormous number of different hues, the artist has to use the ready-made colors set at his disposal. He can only place side by side threads of different colors whose juxtaposition cannot achieve the continuity so easily obtained by painters. Like mosaic, tapestry has undergone a decadence on account of its ambition to ape the effects proper to painting. The contemporary renaissance of this art is due to the decision made by certain painters to liberate tapestry from its submission to painting and to restore it to its own independence. The basis for this reformation is precisely provided by the "formal vocation" of its material cause: the colored woolen thread.[21] The same problem arises in connection with silk embroidery, the only difference being that the temptation to make an embroidery as indiscernible from a picture as possible will probably always remain an irresistible one. Only true artists are clear-sighted enough to discern the particular kind of form that can fulfill the potentialities proper to a certain kind of matter. Among those who perceive the different formal requirements of the different matters, few succeed, during their own lifetime, in obtaining the recognition of these requirements by the public.

[23]

20. In the atrium of St. Peter's, Rome. This mosaic will have to be considered from the point of view of the art of painting itself. See below, pp. 242 f.

21. Marc Saint-Saëns ("Le Carton et la création dans la tapisserie," in Lalo *et al.*, pp. 176–84) shows how tapestry has lost its own technique by attempting to imitate painting and how modern painting is trying to bring back tapestry to its own traditional technique. As can be seen from this remarkable study, the difficulty does not lie on the side of painters, but, rather, on the side of the artisans who have lost the traditional knowledge of their own means of execution.

[24]

Twice removed from painting, despite contrary appearances, is the art of stained glass. Taken in the purity of its style, stained glass is more like a mosaic than a painting. Nevertheless, unlike the mosaics properly so called, it is made up of colored fragments of glass through which light shines instead of being reflected by it. Naturally, stained glass has followed the same evolution as mosaic and tapestry. It has progressively degenerated into an imitation of painting. Recent efforts to rediscover the formal vocation of this kind of matter are beginning to yield promising results.[22]

3. Originals and Reproductions

PASSIVE as it is, the kind of causality exercised by matter produces a number of positive effects. If what precedes is true, it entails the consequence that, strictly speaking, no picture can be duplicated. We thus find ourselves confronted, for the first time, with one of the many problems that arise from the constant interfering of aesthetics with education.

There is no more common expression than the formula: *reproduction of works of art*. The manufacturing, distributing, and selling of so-called "reproductions" of works of art in our own day is a rather thriving business. As is often the case, financial, cultural, ethical, and even religious interests are involved in one and the same process. Some benefactors of mankind seem to feel convinced that it is their solemn duty to spread artistic culture among the masses by multiplying mechanical "reproductions" of famous paintings, either in black and white or in colors. They hope to render many people so art-conscious that they will want to own at least duplicates of originals out of their reach.

It would be hypocritical to take a scandalized attitude toward this industrial exploitation of art and of artistic feeling. The fact is so intimately tied up with the structure of modern society that it cannot possibly be avoided. Be it religion, love under all its forms, literature, or art, there is not a single spiritual force that does not become an object of commercial exploitation. Besides, all the consequences of this fact are not necessarily

22. The recent stained glass designed by Léger for the church of Audincourt is by itself a sufficient proof that the resurrection of this long-lost art is possible.

bad. On the contrary, some of them are undeniably good, so that here again, as is often the case in matters related to art, a wholesale condemnation of such practices would not do justice to the complexity of the problem.

On the other hand, and for the very same reasons, a wholesale approval of the commercial utilization of art also raises certain objections, some of which are of direct interest to us because they are rooted in the very being of painted works of art. Without denying in the least that much good can be achieved along the lines of artistic propaganda, one thing at least should be made clear from the very beginning—be it only for purely physical reasons, no painting can possibly be duplicated. As has been said, there is a contradiction in conceiving a painting as identical with another one. Even if they are not always easy to detect, their individuating differences do nevertheless exist. First of all, since they are two in number, the material out of which one of them is made cannot be the material included in the other one. Secondly, since it has been seen that, in works of art, matter always is specified by its own form, it is hardly possible to imagine two paintings in which the quality of the canvas, of the colors, and of the execution could be said to be really alike in all respects. Strictly speaking, then, a picture can be "imitated"; it cannot be "reproduced." To reproduce a picture is to produce another one. To speak of the "reproduction of works of art" has become so common that there would be no point in refusing to use this now received expression. Provided only we remember that, in this case, reproduction means "imitation," no harm is done. As to the good public, on which it seems clear that some sort of deception is very consciously practiced,[23] this represents only one more case in which men buy

---

23. The standard technique is a well-known one. First, the advertisement presents itself as mainly concerned with art itself and with the artistic education of the people (the Great Art Treasures of the World in every home). Secondly, it builds up the romantic figure of the painter whose works are supposed to be "reproduced" (he always happens to be the most important painter of the day, and, perhaps, the greatest painter of all time). Thirdly, it invites the public to buy, at a nominal price, a batch of "paintings by X, faithfully reproduced in full color." The last moment of the operation is also its triumph. Having persuaded some people that they now can own masterpieces at practically no cost, it remains to invite them to subscribe to a course in art appreciation based upon the "paintings" they now own. The cycle then is complete. Art appreciation is being taught on the basis of industrial products imitated from works of art, which are not works of art.

something else than what they are supposed to be sold. It is both naïve and vain to object to such practices, so long at least as fraud does not present itself as a method of education.

To this remark, the ready objection is that it is a purely theoretical one. So long as the differences between an original and its reproduction are indiscernible, the fact that the two works remain materially distinct is of no importance. To all practical purposes, and educational purposes certainly are practical ones, the distinction between the notions of imitation and of reproduction seems to be irrelevant.

In fact, everything proceeds as if it were irrelevant indeed. Nay, we shall have ample proof that, in many cases, this distinction is intentionally disregarded. But it should not be, for the simple reason that there always are perceptible differences between a painting and any one of its so-called reproductions.

Even leaving aside the formal differences that occur when the reproducing process is not a mechanical one (no man signs his own name twice in identically the same way), the fact that matter itself always exhibits some formal differentiations makes it impossible to do two identical paintings. Even if, as sometimes happens, a replica is the work of the same painter who did the original, the finished product will really be another original, and the more inventive the painter, the freer he will feel to introduce minor variants in either the conception or the execution of the replica. But even if a copyist undertakes to duplicate as perfectly as possible an original painting, the result is bound to be a different one, because he will not use the same canvas, the same brushes, the same colors, or the same varnishes. At any rate, even though all the rest were indiscernible, he would not use the same hand.

The experiment has been made at least once, under circumstances so peculiar, and so unusually favorable, that there is little hope ever to perform a more convincing one. It is related to Ingres' famous portrait of M. Bertin. Bertin had two sons. After his death, the elder inherited the famous portrait, and since it was impossible for the younger son to have it too, he thought of having a copy of it made by Amaury-Duval. Now, this Amaury-

Duval, who tells the story in his memoirs, had been a pupil of Ingres for years. If it was a question of painting *à la* Ingres, nobody could touch him, not only because he knew all the workshop recipes and all the tricks, but also because, after applying them for years and years under the supervision of the master, he achieved a result *à la* Ingres. Still, there was nothing in it that could make it pass for an authentic work of the master. Ingres knew it, his pupil knew it, and we ourselves still can see it by looking at Amaury-Duval's portrait of the Countess of Circé that is now preserved in the art gallery of Poitiers. This picture cannot have been painted by anyone else than a pupil of Ingres; it is the work of a perfectly trained artisan; its craftsmanship is flawless, and still, even if we did not know its author, nobody would mistake it for a work of Ingres.

In the case under discussion, however, the problem was different. It was only a question of copying a portrait already done by Ingres, and since the work was to be that of a pupil perfectly conversant with the technique of the master, the result should have been an exact duplicate of the original. Remarkably enough, to all external appearances, it was. Ingres was a frightening judge; he had no illusions as to the genius of his pupil, and the cruelty of his judgments could sometimes be appalling. In this case, his favorable verdict was the more surprising, as one of his own works was at stake. After carefully examining the copy, Ingres simply concluded: "I would willingly sign it." Here is, as it seems, a perfect experiment, whose success is wholly guaranteed by the most competent authority. Yet, we also know from the same Amaury-Duval that when, several years later, he saw again his own copy, he found it darkened. Let us not investigate the reasons he quotes in explanation of the fact,[24] for the fact itself is what now matters, and it is that, to use the same colors as the painter a second time, and to

24. *L'Atelier d'Ingres*, pp. 162–65. Ingres had used violet hues in the hope that, after darkening, they would yield the equivalent of warm dark browns. When Amaury-Duval did his copy, this effect had already taken place, so that in "reproducing" the painting he started, not from any violet, but from a dark brown that, in turn, became still darker with time. — Incidentally, let us note the curious fact that, had he not been held in check by the respect he felt for his model, Amaury-Duval would have painted the background in greenish tones. After extending to him his warm felicitations, Ingres suddenly asked Duval: "Why didn't you try another background . . . a greenish background?"

use them twice in identically the same way, is a practical impossibility.

The real problem is not there. It rather consists in knowing if imitations, or reproductions of paintings that nobody could mistake for originals, can be used, to any practical purpose, as so many substitutes for the originals they represent. This point deserves careful consideration, because many different interests, each of them respectable in its own order, are involved in it. Big business is naturally concerned with serving civic communities and, by the same token, with promoting artistic culture in the masses. If it could succeed in placing three or four color prints of world-famous masterpieces in each and every home, big business would, at one and the same time, serve a lofty cause and promote its own interests.

The same remark applies to the colossal multiplication of art books, folders, postcards, color slides, and illustrated art histories, whose avowed ambition it is to introduce school children and, generally speaking, the public of art galleries to the mysteries of art appreciation. These so-called albums of famous masterpieces are a constantly rising tide or, rather, a flood that progressively invades bookstores, private and public libraries, newspapers, and weeklies; so much so that at the same time that Cézanne, van Gogh, and Utrillo are being used to decorate the walls of schools and colleges, they meet us in every hotel room and even assail us through our mail. This pictorial inflation parallels the musical persecution we have to resist in order not to let radio sets pour the "Eroica" upon us ten times a month, particularly at breakfast time, or while we wash, dust, or sweep.[25]

Whatever their ultimate motives, commercial, artistic, educational, or otherwise, those who devote themselves to this pictorial propaganda act as if, to all practical purposes, there were no specific difference between looking at a painting and looking at one of its mechanically produced imitations. This conviction is not without justification. There are at least four extremely useful things that the image of a painting can do for us: it shows

---

25. It has been said that reproducing a work of art is analogous to recording a musical piece (Mikel Dufrenne, *Phénoménologie de l'expérience esthétique*, I, 73). But the two problems are very different. Even an exactly recorded performance of one of his own piano sonatas played by Beethoven himself would still not be an original. It would simply represent that sonata as Beethoven was able to play it, on the instrument then at his disposal, and as he happened to play it on the day it was recorded.

the subject of the picture; it shows its composition; it helps us to remember it after a more or less long time has elapsed since we last saw it; it prevents a painting from relapsing into absolute nothingness when the original has been destroyed. The third and fourth points need no commentary, but it may prove profitable to make some remarks concerning the first two.

Subject and composition are inseparable, and although the importance of subject can be exaggerated, that of composition is beyond doubt. From these two points of view, photographic documents are strictly irreplaceable, and everybody knows it from bitter experience. In reading ancient art histories or critical studies written when nothing but words were available as a means of conveying some idea of the paintings at stake, we feel slightly discouraged at the endless descriptions of objects that, because we have not seen them, we feel powerless to imagine. The most modest drawing then appears a priceless help. And, indeed, a sketch belongs in the same class of objects as the paintings it represents. It makes us see something intended to be seen, whereas literary descriptions consist of written symbols, each of which contributes to the formation of a verbal sign that evokes a certain image in us. Now, mental images are more or less indeterminate, and not all men enjoy the imaginative power required in order to organize them into definite structures comparable, in intensity and in coherence, with the perceptions of sight. When an art critic or an art historian attempts to describe a painting, he has us at a disadvantage. He has seen the picture he describes; he probably has kept a written record of what he has seen; in some cases, he is describing a picture he actually has before his eyes; in all these cases, the writer goes from actually seen objects to the words by which he is trying to make us form certain images, whereas we are invited to go from written words to the images of sense perceptions we have never had.[26] The poorest photograph of a painting is incomparably preferable

26. Our remarks do not apply to the many instances in which plates are used for other ends than the communication of paintings. For instance, iconography is incomparably better equipped when it uses plates than when it has to rely on the direct inspection of the original works. The same applies to "art culture" as well as to the kind of dialectical speculation about art that André Malraux has popularized. In short, our remarks apply to all that, in the art of painting, is directly relevant to painting as such. Painting can exist, subsist, and thrive without iconography, art history, art criticism, or

to the most eloquent of literary descriptions. One of the great services rendered by the introduction of plates has been to rid art histories of an infinite number of practically useless descriptions.

Incidentally, let us remark that the same conclusions hold good for all the cases in which the direct inspection of a painting is difficult or impossible. Inaccessible murals, pictures placed in such a bad light that they are permanently invisible, high painted ceilings, details that escape our sight on account of their small size or the distance at which they are seen—all these and many other similar instances of hardly visible paintings wholly justify the use of photographs, plates, and slides as so many helps to our sight. To sum up, it is always advisable to substitute for language any kind of graphic document. A visible object is always better represented by its own image than it can possibly be by any combination of words. This being said, the fact remains that a painting and any one of its mechanically made images are two *specifically* distinct things.

On this point, attention should be called to the problem raised by the present vogue of color plates and by their diffusion in school circles as well as among the book-buying public. Color plates give satisfaction to the natural taste of men for colored images of recognizable objects. Even children delight in such pictures; yet, however perfect the reproducing process, even the best color plates never exactly duplicate the originals. To stand in front of a painting and to compare it with even a good plate of it is enough to reveal how different they are. A more costly experiment consists in collecting different color plates of the same painting, or to compare the plates printed in several different books dealing with the same work of art; no two of them agree on the most fundamental tones either between themselves or with the original. But a supreme indifference seems to prevail in this matter. Not only publishers, booksellers, and art shops, but even art galleries, in Europe as well as in America, offer for sale illustrated books on painters and on the history of painting, color plates of all sizes and,

aesthetics. It particularly stands in no need of any phenomenology or ontology of art. All these disciplines are legitimate in themselves, and most of them can put plates to good use. But their conclusions can be valid with respect to plates without being valid with respect to art.

unfortunately, of any color too, plus collections of color slides, vignettes, and miniatures, including even postage stamps, all of which constitute so many betrayals of the paintings they are supposed to represent.

To try to substantiate such statements by means of concrete examples is obviously impossible. The operation would imply a vicious circle. The color plates of one and the same painting are not perfectly identical even within the same edition of one and the same book. Any attempt to show, by reproducing them side by side, how different the color plates of a certain painting can be in several different reproductions of the same work would simply lead to printing new color plates themselves different from their own originals.[27]

Even if an objective demonstration of this truth were possible, there would be no point in giving it. Most of those who favor the diffusion of color plates content themselves with observing that many of them are "pretty good." They do not wonder what the painter himself would think of certain minor differences that, to him, are simply destructive of his work. Those who manufacture these so-called reproductions sometimes think that the difference in price more than compensates for the artistic difference there certainly is between the originals and their approximative imitations. Or else they feel that color plates are better than nothing at all. Generally speaking, all the differences in colors and value that put a painting "out of tune" are considered unimportant by those who do not see them with a painter's eye. Moreover, all these problems are often obscured in the minds of the popularizers of the great masterpieces of painting by the nobility of the motives that prompt them to act. Fortunes have been spent in subsidizing such "educational" ventures, and they have often been spent in a most disinterested way.

27. It would not be fair to judge color plates on their regular failure to "reproduce" the colors of Cézanne. But it does not seem unfair to compare different color plates representing simpler works, such as Matisse's *Le Piano* (Museum of Modern Art, New York) or Rousseau's *The Dream* (same museum). Naturally, it can be objected that color plates are growing better and better and that they will someday be perfect; but our remark is about what they are, not about what they will be. Moreover, even perfect *prints* would still remain substantially different from *paintings*. Because their physical mode of existence is not the same, our aesthetic experience of them must needs be different.

The motives behind the industrialization of art are not here at stake. The fact alone counts, along with its consequences. The problem arises at the meeting point of three forces, two of which at least are not unrelated— namely, art itself, industrialism, and democracy. At any rate, their simultaneous appearance in modern history is a sure sign that mass production and production for the masses are two aspects of one and the same event. It would be vain to look at personal motives or at private interests for the main causes of events that no individual can either bring about or bring to a close. As long as these two collective forces prevail, the highest manifestations of the human mind, the highest aspirations of the human soul, the most rare, the most exquisite, and the loftiest products of human art will be sooner or later industrially processed, manufactured, and marketed so as to be put at the disposal of practically all men.

Any remark made on this point would be an imprudence, because it would seem to question one of the few myths really alive in our own times —namely, democracy. Fortunately, political philosophy is entirely irrelevant to this investigation. The problem at stake is not to know if it is *desirable* in itself to put all the great masterpieces of the art of painting at the disposal of all men; it is not even to know if all men are both desirous and capable of the loftiest aesthetic experiences; our only problem is to know if such an undertaking is *possible,* or if, on the contrary, it is not contradictory to the very nature of things.

Unfortunately, it is. The present imperfection of the techniques used in reproducing works of art is not what matters. It is possible to foresee a time when, owing to further technical progress, an extremely high degree of fidelity will be achieved in the rendering of colors. What seems to be unthinkable is that a time will ever come when a "reproduction," made up of materials completely different from those which enter the texture of a painting, will affect our eyes in the same way as a painting. Real paintings are made by the hand of painters on wood, canvas, or cardboard, with brushes or palette knives, by means of colored pigments they usually buy in tubes and whose physicochemical properties exercise such a determining influence on the finished product that its aspect is wholly different, depending on whether the painter has used oil, tempera, encaustic, or any other one of the many media at his disposal. It is no doubt possible to turn out still better reproductions than the best ones among those we know, but neither typographical inks nor any kind of sensitized surfaces will ever affect the retina in exactly the same way as touches or layers of colors whose substance is physically different. Printed plates are pictures; they are not paintings.[28]

Since, however, no proposition concerning the future is safe, let us content ourselves with saying that, such as they now are, the so-called reproductions of famous paintings can do little more than to familiarize their public with the subjects and the composition of these masterpieces, but when it comes to colors, which are the substance of paintings, they are likely to spread the misleading opinion that, provided their colors more or less resemble those of the original, a few differences in tones do not matter much. What, in the long run, will be the result of this effort to educate pictorial taste? Just about the same as that of a musical propaganda whose method it would be to ensure repeated performances of symphonies played on pianos out of tune. If the average optical sensibility of art lovers equaled that of their ears, most color plates would be unbearable to their eyes.

To conclude, without denying that the mechanical imitations of paintings may have their usefulness or, rather, while expressly affirming that they are indeed extremely useful in view of certain other ends, we must maintain, as a consequence of their individuation by their own matter, that paintings can be seen only where they are. Apart from all further considerations concerning form, and the part played by the hand of the artist in the execution of a painting, we can safely consider inconsistent with their very nature that paintings should be duplicated.

28. We beg leave to avail ourselves of the distinction there sometimes is, in common language, between the respective meanings of the words "picture" and "painting." A painting can be a picture; a picture is not necessarily a painting. The dominant notion in the word "painting" is that of paint. The dominant notion in the word "picture" is that of image. A picture, says the *Pocket Oxford Dictionary* (11th edn., New York, 1949, p. 617), is "a representation of something produced on a surface by painting or other means." Thus understood, pictures are essentially images. As such, they fall under the jurisdiction of a recently created science, namely, eiconics. See Kenneth Boulding, *The Image*, ch. 10, "Eiconics: a New Science."

CHAPTER THREE

DURATION

PAINTING is an art of space, but its products endure in time, and, to the extent that they do, problems arise concerning the various ways in which their being is affected by duration. Considered as an individual, any material object enters a specific relationship to itself from the sole fact that it enjoys a continuous mode of existence. Taken at any two moments of its duration, it can be recognized as being *the same* individual. This is what is called its identity.

The notion of identity is one more of the primitive concepts that point out fundamental properties of being qua being and that, because they cannot be explained by anterior ones, ultimately escape analysis. There is no difference, for any given thing, between being and being that which it is. To become something other than the kind of thing it is simply amounts, for that very thing, to ceasing to be. If these formulas sound somewhat abstract, let us ask ourselves this simple question: what would it mean to me to be turned into another man? It would mean at least this, that the two words "I" and "me" would completely lose their present meaning. *I* would have ceased to exist.

This fact has been forcibly stressed by Plato as well as by all the philosophers whose doctrines bear the imprint of Platonism: the notion of being cannot be separated from that of selfsameness in duration, that is, of immutability. In other words, the two notions of change and being are mutually exclusive, not, indeed, in the sense that beings do not change, but at least in the sense that, to the extent that they do change, they do not fully deserve the title of beings. To simplify the problem, let us suppose some material being enduring in time and, nevertheless, enjoying a practically perfect immutability. Its being would then be said to preserve, during the whole duration of its existence, a practically perfect selfsameness or identity. The following remarks will bear upon the extent to which the notion of identity, and its main consequences, are applicable to paintings.

1. Identity

IF WE consider it in the abstract, the notion of identity does not raise any particular difficulty. It is a notion immediately evident to the mind that, for a painting as well as for any other material object, to be is one and the same thing as to remain identical with itself, or, in other words, it is the same as to preserve its self-identity. Nevertheless, no character is more difficult to establish in the concrete than the identity of an object with itself. It sometimes happens that a famous painting is stolen from an art gallery; most of the time, although not always, stolen paintings are finally returned to their proper places, and the public is solemnly assured that the returned work of art is identically the same as the one that had been stolen. In such cases, however, the same question regularly arises in the mind of the public: is it really the same? Let us hasten to add that, owing to modern methods of identification, answers to such questions can generally be given with a high degree of probability and, in the case of world-famous paintings whose every detail is known, with absolute certainty. Yet this general remark suffices to show that the concrete problem of how to ascertain the identity of a painting is fraught with serious difficulties.

A second notion, distinct from the preceding one and yet closely related to it, is that of authenticity. It often happens that the identity of a certain painting can be traced to a very ancient date, or period, although we do not know who did it. Such is the case with Egyptian, Greek, Roman, or medieval murals whose continuous existence through many centuries is beyond doubt, but whose authors are unknown to us. To know the authenticity of a painting is to be able to trace it to the very artist who painted it.

The distinction between these two notions is clearly seen from the fact that many ancient paintings exhibited in art galleries bear the name of no painter. In some cases, the name of the painting becomes that of the painter. For instance, because we do not know by whom such works have been painted, we speak of the Master of the Moulins *Triptych* or of the Master of the Avignon *Pietà*. In other words, the only thing we know about the authors of these masterpieces is that, whatever their names, they did paint this *Pietà* or that *Triptych*. Often enough, we see paintings attributed to a certain artist, with this reservation, however, that the attribution is merely probable. A still more careful type of attribution simply relates the origin of a painting to the so-called "school" of a certain painter, that is, to any one of those among his successors who have undergone his influence.

An anecdote clearly illustrates the distinction between the problem of identity and the problem of authenticity. Incidentally, it also shows that these two problems are equally irrelevant to the artistic quality of the painting at stake. Maurice de Vlaminck happened to be in Vollard's shop when a man entered, carrying a picture under his arm, and asked Vollard to give him his opinion of it. "It is good," Vollard said, "I like it very much; it is very good." Whereupon the visitor asked Vollard if he thought that it was a true one. To which Vollard replied: "A true what? How can you ask me to affirm that this painting has been painted by such and such a man, and that it is not a replica or a copy of it done at about the same time? This thing was painted more than three centuries ago. I know absolutely nothing about it. Look here, why don't you go and ask my colleague across the street? It is written on his door: Expert."[1] And, indeed, a painting is artistically worth what it is worth in itself, and its value remains identically the same, as long as the picture lasts, irrespective of the name of its author.

And yet, distinct as they are, these two notions cannot be wholly separated. A sign that some relationship obtains between them is the obvious distaste of art galleries for anonymous works. The kinds of labels that have just been mentioned—"Attributed to X," "School of Y," and the like—

---

1. Vlaminck, *Portraits avant décès*, p. 88. Like so many other "good stories," this one may be, to some extent, a work of art.

bear witness to the fact that, in our imagination at least, our knowledge of a painting is not complete so long as we do not know its author.[2] The reason for this is probably the same that accounts for the common feeling that the identity of a man is not completely established until we know the place and the date of his birth as well as the names of his parents. If a man's description fits the person whose identity we investigate, there is probability that it is the same person, but if it can be established that this person is the same who was born at a certain date, at a certain place, and of identifiable parents, then indeed, unless there be fraud, all doubt is completely excluded.

A similar feeling prevails about paintings, especially where commercial interests are at stake. If he can help it, no art dealer will content himself with saying: this is a Delacroix, or this is a Manet. He will do his utmost to trace the painting that he is selling, from owner to owner, to the first person who bought it directly either from the painter himself or from the first art dealer who obtained it from the artist. Especially in the case of modern works of art, efforts are always being made to reconstruct the complete pedigree of each and every painting, but, in many cases, the thing can be done even with works dating from the early Renaissance. When we know for certain that a painting was done by Giorgione for a certain church, or that it was bought from Leonardo himself by King Francis I, no doubt is possible. This attitude seems to rest upon the conviction that, although the identity of a picture is independent from that of its cause, the knowledge of its cause is necessary for its complete identification.

2. In the fine arts, the word "school" signifies a group of artists whose works are similar in style owing to the common influence of the style of a certain master (school of Giotto) or local traditions (Umbrian school). The relation of this notion to those of identity and authenticity is obvious. A painting attributable to the school of Raphael is, up to a point and indirectly, a work bearing the imprint of Raphael's personality. When, without Raphael, it would not be what it is, a painting can be said to be, in a certain sense, his work. — On successes and failures in identifying such "pupils of," see the amusing anecdote concerning Amico di Sandro, one of the creatures of Bernard Berenson: S. N. Behrman, *Duveen*, pp. 156–58. After inventing him, B. B. finally redistributed his alleged works among Botticelli, Filippino Lippi, and Ghirlandaio. On the Botticelli that was not a Botticelli, p. 179. On the Giorgione that was a Titian, pp. 179–81 (but a "Giorgionesque" Titian, p. 183), which now hangs as a Giorgione in the National Gallery in Washington, pp. 184–85.

The only conceivable explanation for this paradox is that elements more or less foreign to the nature of paintings are included in common aesthetic experience. The most obvious one is our lack of faith in our own aesthetic judgment. The fame of the great painters of the past rests upon centuries of a practically unquestioned admiration for their works. Art historians and art critics are agreed that Botticelli, Titian, and Veronese are indeed great painters. Such glories now are beyond discussion, and any work attributed to such artists becomes admirable by definition. In fact, many visitors in art galleries look at the name of the painter before looking at the painting. First, they usually are more or less in a hurry; next, and above all, they do not trust themselves. Having been so often caught admiring the wrong thing or, on the contrary, not admiring, or not admiring enough, what they should have known to be a universally recognized masterpiece, they decide to save time. As John Constable so ably put it in a letter to John Fisher, we often go "by the *rule of name*."[3] If a painting has been done by Titian, then it should be good. And indeed, if one looks at it long enough, he will not fail to see how good it is. We are far from saying that the rule of name does not work. Rather, the trouble is that it always works, even when the name is wrong. Here is a mystery that deserves to be investigated.

Let us first eliminate the commercial point of view, not at all as unjustified in itself, but as irrelevant to art. Since there is a market for paintings, and a scale of rates for the works of the most famous among painters, it is normal that fakers should be prosecuted. The question is not: why should anyone care to make sure that the painting he likes was really painted by Manet? The point is that, since most people do care, any painter faking a Manet, or any art dealer who knowingly shares in such a deception, is guilty of fraudulent activities. If he knowingly sells a Trouillebert for the price of a Corot, an art dealer is simply being dishonest. This has nothing to do with art appreciation. It is a plain business proposition: right or wrong, the prices are not the same, and that is all.

This being said, the mystery remains whole. Our own contemporaries

---

3. "——— is annoyed by your designating his old masters trash. He goes by the *rule of name*." (Constable to Fisher, April 13, 1822; in Leslie, p. 90.)

have seen a Brittany landscape, exhibited as an early Gauguin, turned overnight into an Émile Bernard.[4] The next morning, although the painting at
stake had remained identically the same, it had lost nine tenths of its commercial value. This was not a fake; it simply was a false attribution. But
why should there be two so widely different prices for the same painting,
depending on whether it is supposed to be an Émile Bernard or a Gauguin?
From the point of view of aesthetic appreciation, the fact does not make
sense. Let us therefore disregard it as irrelevant, not indeed to art trade, but
most certainly to art.

The celebrated case of the pseudo Vermeer was a different one. This
time it was not a question of false attribution; the painting was a downright
fake. Here again, the problem is not interesting if asked at the level of commercial transactions, but it becomes fascinating if asked at the level of art
appreciation. For indeed, a hundred years ago, the commercial value of a
Vermeer of Delft was so low that it would not have been worth the trouble of
faking it. A Rembrandt then was the thing to fake, and it has often been
done. Yet the artistic qualities of the works of Vermeer and of Rembrandt
are today exactly what they were a century ago. Today, successfully faking
a Vermeer is a highly profitable venture, but when the fraud is detected,
what happens to the painting at stake? Strictly nothing. The only question
is to know why, if an artist[5] can paint as well as Vermeer of Delft in   [25a, b]

4. This incident, which we witnessed, took place in 1937. The real story was a much
more complex one. When he learned the true origin of the picture, its owner reproached
the art dealer with having sold him a pseudo Gauguin, to which the art dealer replied
that, given the price he had asked for it, a man had to be out of his senses to believe that
he was buying an authentic Gauguin. The combination (for there was a clever calculation
behind the incident) would have worked without the accidental presence of Émile
Bernard. After being exhibited several times under the name of a painter, a picture
acquires a pedigree; it progressively becomes authentic. — On the painter Bernard, see
Bernard Dorival, *Les Étapes de la peinture française contemporaine*, I, 99–102. We shall
quote from Bernard's irreplaceable *Souvenirs sur Paul Cézanne, et lettres*.

5. On the Vermeer incident, Malraux (*The Voices of Silence*, p. 369) shows the pseudo
Vermeer forged by van Meegeren. Another faked Vermeer is shown in *True or False?*,
p. 36 (see n. 14, below, p. 89). — The art of faking can boast of a very honorable ances-
try. The engraver Marcantonio (1480?–?1534) is said to have counterfeited, on copper,
the thirty-six woodcuts by Dürer on the Passion of Christ "with the A. D. with which
Albert signed his works"; "Marcantonio succeeded in making them so like that no one
could tell the difference who did not know, and they were sold and bought as Albert's
works" (Vasari, *Lives*, III, 71–72). Michelangelo himself "made copies of various old

December of a certain year, his work should become a practically worthless fake in January of the following year.

To this question, the ready answer naturally is that competent people suspected from the very beginning that it was a fake. And not only do we not deny this, but, rather, we do believe that it is partially true. Most of the time, when it has become scientifically established that a certain painting is indeed a fake, there first has been somebody to feel that it was a fake, when the fact could not yet have been proved. The painting itself is in no way altered by such a demonstration; yet, as soon as it has been proved to be a fake, even those who, until then, had entertained no suspicion as to its authenticity cease to see it with the same eyes. It then becomes "evident" to them that the painting is not authentic. The "rule of name" dominates the mind of experts almost as much as it influences the judgments of laymen. But there really is no reason it should be so. After all, the proper function of an art gallery is to exhibit works of art, not attributions; what was worth looking at when it was supposed to be the work of one of the great masters of past time should be just as worthy to be admired after experts have proved it to be thirty years old. The explanation of this mystery does not lie in the nature of art; on the contrary, it lies in the fact that paintings fulfill many functions besides that of being works of art.

[26, 27]

In this connection, it seems difficult not to quote a curious remark recently made by Malraux, the inventor of the "museum without walls." Fully aware of the deep significance of the problem at stake, this brilliant novelist observes that if, for argument's sake, the *Victory of Samothrace* were proved to be a fake, "it would be killed." In other words, it would at once cease to interest us. Obviously, such a remark means little from the point of view of art itself. Nobody will consider it at all likely that this perfectly authenticated masterpiece could ever be proved a fake; yet there

masters, making them look old with smoke and other things so that they could not be distinguished from the originals. He did this to obtain the originals in exchange for the copies, as he wanted the former and sought to surpass them, thereby acquiring a great name" (ibid., IV, 110–11). On the life-size sleeping Cupid done in marble by Michelangelo and sold as an antique by Baldassare del Milanese, see IV, 113–14. — These anecdotes may themselves be contrived; the point is that Vasari, who related them, does not seem to have felt indignant at these slight irregularities.

have been successful fakes boasting of a comparable antiquity,[6] and we should not forget that, by definition, the really successful fakes are like the perfect crimes: they never will be detected. But since the supposition has been conceived, let us imagine that, in a more or less remote future, the *Victory of Samothrace* may be proved to be a fake. We then would have to choose between two possible attitudes: either to continue to admire it as we now do, without worrying about its nonauthenticity, or else to forget it, as having ceased to be interesting from the very moment it has been proved a fake. But then we should also recognize the fact that our interest had always been less in art than in archaeology. For, indeed, it is true that a faked document is in no sense of the word a historical document, except in the history of fakes; but it is not true that the intrinsic value of a work of art, taken qua work of art, should be in any way affected by the answer given to the problem of its authenticity.[7]

To this conclusion, the ready objection is that to speak of experiencing a work of art exclusively qua work of art is to entertain an abstract view of an eminently concrete reality. Like artists themselves, art lovers are men,

6. Malraux, *Le Musée imaginaire de la sculpture mondiale*, p. 52. The opposite plate, p. 53, reproduces one of the Greek archaic fakes by Dossena. Malraux admits that these fakes are admirable; he also admits that the fact that they are fakes does not change the statues: "it only changes the feeling they cause in us"; finally, Malraux admits that this "is the most irritating of points in our relationship with art." The complete discussion of this attitude would entail an analysis of a new meaning given to the notion of "authenticity." It then means the reverse of imitation. Is "authentic" that which springs from the personality of the artist himself? In this sense, it can be said of Dossena that, had he exhibited his statues under his own name, "the multiplicity of the styles that he was imitating would have revealed the inauthenticity of his art" (Malraux, p. 52). This may be true, but it should not be taken for granted. Once more, it is a literary point of view on art: if it has no value as a historical document, a statue (or a painting) can have no value as a work of art. Nothing is less evident. Artists often take pleasure in creating in different styles; there is, at least, no contradiction in the notion of an artist's doing creative and "authentic" work in styles both different and dating from different historical periods. Critics have no patience with artists returning to one of their earlier styles, or to the style of an earlier historical period, but painters themselves love to do so. André Derain, Chirico, and, of course, Picasso have found no fault with the use of this perfect artistic freedom.

7. After saying that, if we learned that the *Victory of Samothrace* is a fake, that would kill it, Malraux adds with perfect candor: "But here is something that set us a-dreaming: were we to learn that it is a sixteenth-century fake, it would not be completely killed" (*Le Musée imaginaire*, p. 52). This remark implies that, in the complex of impressions caused in us by a work of art, a small number only are traceable to art.

and they cannot help apprehending works of art as objects loaded with many different qualities each of which is included in aesthetic experience. Rarity, antiquity, historical ties with famous artists or with brilliant periods in the past history of art—in short, the countless associations of ideas, judgments, and emotions infallibly evoked by such names as Athens, Florence, or Rome are undoubtedly at work in our global estimate of a work of art. From this point of view, we have fakes at a disadvantage. Once recognized as the work of van Meegeren, a painting has no right to our admiration beyond what it holds from its own merits. It stands before us in a sort of cold nakedness, having lost the halo of glory with which, as a work of Vermeer, it used to be surrounded. All this is true and nobody would deny it; but far from invalidating our previous conclusions, it sets off the essential fallibility of aesthetic experience. Of those who feel distressed at learning that a famous painting has never been, after all, anything else than a fake, how many ever looked at it as at a work of art?

For the same reason, the unpleasant misadventures of a few archaeologists deserve much less our blame than our sympathy. Their errors are unavoidable and founded in the nature of things. We all feel secretly ashamed at the possibility of such mistakes, not indeed for those who make them, nor for ourselves who are meekly following them in their errors, but, rather, for art itself. What is art worth if it can so easily be mistaken for something else? We would like to think that, like intellectual evidence, beauty shines forth with such unmistakable clarity that no error about it is possible. Obviously, it is not so, but the reason such errors are possible can help us to dispel the same recurring misunderstanding that separates us from the concrete reality of art.

However hard we may fight to overcome it, the illusion still obtains in our mind that painters communicate with us by means of signs, or symbols, which we have only to read to understand. In fact, paintings are the very art of the painters embodied in the matter of their works. Of what went on in the mind of an artist, a few years or many centuries ago, nothing is left for us to know outside this piece of wood or canvas now exhibited in some art gallery, where it is offered to the appreciation of the public. If there is any secret about it—for instance, its date or the probable name of its author—the key to it lies in the painting itself and, in the last analysis, nowhere else.

It is therefore no wonder that a human mind similar to that of the creative artist, and having at its disposal an art and a skill not wholly incomparable with those of its model, should succeed in turning out works of similar appearance. There would be no faked Corots if there were no authentic ones. What deceives us in a fake is the authentic presence of the model from which it derives its existence. It is likewise natural that the proof concerning the authenticity or nonauthenticity of such works should ultimately lie in the material elements of which it consists as well as in their disposition. This is nothing against the eminent dignity of art, since, on the contrary, it emphasizes the very reality in which, if painting is at stake, art itself consists. Why feel scandalized at the thought that the answers to the problems of authenticity lie in the physical structure of paintings? The products of this art are solid material substances; in a word, they are things.

These simple remarks may also help to solve another problem, no less puzzling than the preceding one, although, so far as we know, it has received very little attention. Why does public opinion react differently to pictorial fakes and to musical or poetic deceptions? For, indeed, this seems to be a fact. There have always been writers to attribute their own works to some famous author, or else to present them as the products of some form of popular art, as was the case, for instance, with Prosper Mérimée's *Théâtre de Clara Gazul.* Far from feeling indignant about it, we simply see there a practical joke or, at the utmost, an amusing deception practiced upon the simplicity of philologists. The history of music abounds in similar anecdotes. From Berlioz's oratorio, *L'Enfance du Christ,* to the pseudo-Pugnani or Vivaldi arrangements for violin carried for years and years through countless concerts by a certain contemporary virtuoso, many similar musical fakes could be quoted. Nobody minds it. On the contrary, everyone agrees that if a musician decides to write an *a cappella* Mass in the polyphonic style of Palestrina, his only chance to make people listen to it is to present it as a recently discovered masterpiece of sixteenth-century vocal music. Such things have recently been done, and when the deception was graciously acknowledged by its author, public opinion praised him for his cleverness. Yet, when all is said and done, what difference is there between selling a pseudo Vermeer to an art gallery and selling a pseudo Vivaldi to the concertgoing public?

In fact, there is at least one. Even apart from the difference in commercial value between the genuine work of an old master and the cleverest of recognized fakes, let us remember what has already been said concerning the unique relationship between a painting and the hand of the painter. Painters, Delacroix told us, are to themselves their own virtuosos. There is therefore a great difference between selling us the fleeting enjoyment of sounds caused by a performer, which nobody expects to take home at the end of a concert, and selling us the permanent ownership of a unique work immediately produced by the hand of a certain painter. If his hand has had no part in the making of a certain painting, to sell it under his name constitutes a tangible deception on the part of the faker. In this sense, the physical mode of existence proper to plastic works of art seems to account, at least in part, for the good-natured indulgence with which the public lends itself to a pleasant musical hoax and for the severity with which the law strives to discourage modern Rembrandts.

2. *Authenticity*

THERE is only one case in which the notion of authenticity is simple. It then means that a certain painting has been done by the hand of a certain painter whose name is known to us with absolute certainty. When, on the contrary, "authenticity" means a sort of spiritual quality owing to the fact that a work of art is born of the personal genius of an artist, not of any kind of imitation, the term means "genuine" rather than "authentic." Its meaning then becomes so vague that its analysis is hardly possible. But even taking it in its first and material acceptation, this term is far from signifying an absolutely simple notion.

Let us first mention an extreme case, which, infrequent as it is, cannot be considered impossible. In point of fact, we know that the thing did happen. Some painters have found themselves confronted with clever fakes done in their own manner. Most of the time, they simply refused to recognize such paintings as their own works, but there have also been cases in which, for various reasons, artists contented themselves with touching up the picture here and there and, finally, signing it.[8] Is such a painting authentic? No, since most of it has not been done by the painter himself. Yes, since, after being done in his own manner, this work of art has been completed by the painter himself and finally acknowledged by him as his own work.

Many famous works of art were born of such a collaboration, with the sole difference that, this time, it was a collaboration intended and organized by the artist himself. It is not believable that such painters as Rubens, Veronese, and Tintoretto were alone the authors of the great compositions that justly bear their names. They certainly needed, and received, material help in order to cover such wide surfaces with paint. In the case of Rubens,

8. In his catalogue for the Corot exhibition at the Lyon Art Gallery, 1936, Paul Jamot explained that Corot had probably carried charity to the point of touching up daubings done by some poor devils in order to turn them into something salable. Renoir is said to have pushed good nature still further than Corot, since he once touched up and *signed* a pseudo Renoir brought to him by a desolate amateur. Albert André had quoted this incident in his Preface to an album of reproductions of Renoir's pictures, but the art dealer Ambroise Vollard, who had read the galley proofs, was given assurance that Renoir would ask Albert André to suppress all allusion to possible fakes. And, indeed, it is bad business to let it be known that there are fakes. See Léon Werth, *La Peinture et la mode*, p. 114. — Cf. René Huyghe, "Simple Histoire de 2414 faux Corots," *L'Amour de l'art*, XI (Feb., 1936), 73–76. On the same problem concerning Manet, see Adolphe Tabarant, *Manet et ses œuvres*, pp. 96–98; on the many pseudo Manets, pp. 518–24. — Our modern scruples would have surprised such an artist as Rubens. He had different prices for the paintings entirely by his own hand and for those simply retouched by his own hand. But he had subtler distinctions. For instance: "1,200 florins. A Last Judgment, begun by one of my pupils, after one which I did in a much larger size for the Most Serene Prince of Neuburg, who paid me three thousand five hundred florins cash for it; but this, not being finished, would be entirely retouched by my own hand, and by this means will pass as original. 13 x 9 ft" (Jakob Burckhardt, *Recollections of Rubens*, Appendix, "Selected Letters of Rubens," p. 207). He does not want his customers to mistake for mere copies pictures so well retouched by his own hand "that it would be hard to distinguish them from originals" (p. 208). Yet, Rubens adds, these retouched pictures "are assigned a much lower price." Similar remarks, p. 209. In some cases, Rubens thinks that the pictures under discussion will become authentic: "I doubt not in the least that the 'Hunt' and the 'Suzanna' will appear amongst my originals" (p. 211).

for instance, we know that the master had fellow workers, some of whom were his pupils and were destined to become, in time, more or less famous masters. Art historians have spent a great deal of ingenuity in determining, in some compositions of Rubens, which parts are due to his own hand and which to the hands of assistants. In modern times, precise information is available concerning the origin of such composite works. The diary of Louis de Planet, who helped Delacroix with some of his murals, tells us which parts of these compositions were executed by Delacroix himself and which were done by his various collaborators. But the compositions are really the work of Delacroix, and, even in the order of execution, he had to teach each and every one of his assistants how to paint so as not to break the unity of his own style.[9] In such cases, the collaborators are simply hired hands.

Copies done by artists other than the author of the original cannot be considered authentic, but when such copies are done by good artists, familiar with the style proper to the author of the original, fully informed of his techniques, and using similar materials, it is not always easy to tell copies from originals. Vasari has related the imbroglio created by the exact copy, done by Andrea del Sarto, of Raphael's portrait of Pope Leo X. For some time, two distinct persons felt equally certain that they were owning the original, and even Giulio Romano, who had worked with Raphael, and under his direction, on the first portrait, was so thoroughly deceived that he pretended to recognize his own brushwork in the copy.[10] In our own times, we have seen two versions of *La Belle Ferronnière*, both considered authentic works of Leonardo da Vinci, the one in Kansas, the other in the Louvre. There was a long and severe dispute.[11] At present (December 1956), the painting exhibited in the Louvre is modestly "attributed to" Leonardo da Vinci. But it remains the same painting.

[28, 29]

9. See L. de Planet, *Souvenirs de travaux de peinture avec M. Delacroix.* Cf. *Journal de Eugène Delacroix*, I, 182, n. 4.

10. See Vasari, *Lives*, II, 317–18. — On the history of this comedy of errors: Jean Alazard, *Essai sur l'évolution du portrait peint à Florence de Botticelli à Bronzino*, especially pp. 121–22; bibliography of the incident, p. 122, n. 2. — Those who consider themselves practically infallible experts should remember that painters themselves are fallible. Constable called "a noble N. Poussin" what seems to be a copy done after one of Poussin's landscapes: "A man washing his feet at a fountain" (Leslie, *Memoirs of the Life of John Constable*, p. 84).

11. Harry Hahn, *The Rape of La Belle.*

After downright fakes and ancient copies come the false attributions, of which it can be said that public art galleries, as well as private collections, contain quite a few specimens. These false attributions are hardly less frequent in the case of modern paintings than in that of ancient ones. It often happens that a group of young artists, whose later works will reveal marked differences in style, exhibit a remarkable similarity. Among the Fauves, for example, an early Derain can recall a late van Gogh, while an early Dufy sometimes resembles early works by Braque or by Marquet.[12] Among the so-called Nabis and the Pont-Aven group, early Gauguins sometimes resemble early works by Émile Bernard, Sérusier, or even Bonnard. Since such problems of authenticity arise in connection with modern paintings, they are still more frequent in the case of works several centuries old. There is no end to this kind of controversy, not so much among artists as among the excitable tribe of connoisseurs and the learned company of art historians.

[30a, b]
[31–36]

This takes us back to the question asked by Vollard: how is it possible to establish the fact that a certain painting was done, several centuries or several years ago, by a certain artist rather than by another one? The two main methods followed by experts consist either in resorting to aesthetic intuition or in applying more or less scientific tests by means of which the personal style of an artist can be identified.

These two methods can be successfully applied, at least up to a point. Concerning the first one, it cannot be denied that, after devoting a long time to the study of certain schools, certain periods, or certain masters, some art historians, art critics, or even connoisseurs develop a sort of flair enabling them to recognize the hand of certain masters. It would be absurd to deny the fact, the more so as, in doubtful cases, any man responsible for a decision would ultimately take the judgment of such experts into consideration.

12. Speaking of some early pictures done by Derain: "I was going to write: these are Derain. But reflection convinces me that they are not yet true Derains. If they were mixed with pictures by Vlaminck, Dufy, and Braque dating from the same season, one would often hesitate on how to place the right signatures on all these canvases. Now that years have gone by, these *fauves* look terribly alike. Sagot, Vollard, and Bernheim [i.e., art dealers] may well have been able to identify them at first sight. Today, they leave us as puzzled as we are before certain cages in the zoo: jaguar or puma? One has to read the label to make sure." (Pascal Pia, "Derain au musée," *Arts*, XDXCIII [Dec. 8–14, 1954], 14.)

On the other hand, these experts are far from infallible in their decisions. On the contrary, no judge is less reliable than the famous "sixth sense" in virtue of which some experts feel qualified to give oracular decisions in matters of authenticity. Some of their errors are justly famous, but this is no reason they should be rashly judged. Experts simply attempt an impossible task. In our own lifetime, we remember having seen the *Concert champêtre* first attributed to Sebastiano del Piombo, then to Giorgione, then to Titian, then to Giorgione again. Now, both Louis Hourticq, who attributes the work to Titian, and Victor Basch, who maintains the authorship of Giorgione, honestly recognize that they cannot prove their respective conclusions. "Titian, such as I have seen and felt him," says Victor Basch, "cannot possibly be the author of this work." In short, it is all a matter of intuition. When two intuitions disagree, all hope of reaching any sort of agreement should be abandoned.

This is the less surprising as, contrary to what candid art lovers are likely to believe, painters themselves are not always infallible in identifying their own works. If caution were not indicated in these delicate matters, recent trials could be quoted during which famous painters have denounced as so many fakes works whose authenticity they themselves have later on been obliged to recognize. Nor are painters alone in this plight. The justly famous story of the sculptor Rodin suing an art dealer who had offered a perfectly authentic statue for sale should make us indulgent on this point.[13] No one is more dogmatic than some experts, but nothing is less safe than their conclusions. Nor should this fact disturb us in the least, for, indeed, the personal, historical, or commercial interests that poison such controversies are radically irrelevant to art.

The so-called "objective" methods of investigation aim to redress this

13. On errors committed by experts, see above, n. 5, and Hahn, ch. 9, pp. 99–106. — On the attribution of the *Concert champêtre* to Titian, see Louis Hourticq, *La Jeunesse de Titien*. On the rejection of this conclusion, see Victor Basch, *Titien*, p. 271. — On Rodin, see Vollard, pp. 281–82. After telling the story of a bronze by Rodin that was authentic and yet a fake, at one and the same time, Vollard relates that Rodin himself boasted that he was mistaken about the authenticity of one of his works only once in a lifetime. Even then he had an excuse. An art dealer was showing him a bronze called *Chaos*, whereas Rodin himself had listed it, in his own catalogue, under the title *L'Envolée*. Are we wrong in finding the excuse rather more distressing than the mistake?

a. JAN VERMEER. Diana and Her Nymphs

About 1654. Mauritshuis, The Hague

b. HANS VAN MEEGEREN. The Disciples at Emmaus

About 1936/37. (Vermeer forgery.)
Stichting Boymans Museum, Rotterdam

A faked Dufy
*International exhibition, "Le Faux dans l'art et dans l'histoire,"
organized by the French police, 1955*

A faked Utrillo

International exhibition, "Le Faux dans l'art et dans l'histoire,"
organized by the French police, 1955

The Hahn Belle Ferronnière

[*As titled by its owner: "The Hahn painting, Portrait of a Woman by Leonardo da Vinci, popularly known as La Belle Ferronnière—the only historically documented Da Vinci painting in the U. S. A."*]

The Louvre Belle Ferronnière

a. VINCENT VAN GOGH. The Olive Orchard
1889. Chester Dale Collection, National Gallery of Art, Washington

b. ANDRÉ DERAIN. Collioure, Mountains
1905. Mr. and Mrs. John Hay Whitney Collection, New York

30

a. GEORGES BRAQUE. The Harbor of La Ciotat
1907. Mr. and Mrs. John Hay Whitney Collection, New York

b. RAOUL DUFY. The Harbor of Le Havre
About 1905. The Art Gallery of Toronto

ALBERT MARQUET. Fourteenth of July in Le Havre
1905. Private collection

RAOUL DUFY. Fourteenth of July in Le Havre
1907. Mme Marcelle Bourdon Collection, Paris

ANDRÉ DERAIN. Three Trees, L'Estaque
1906. Mr. and Mrs. A. S. J. Zacks Collection, Toronto

34

Andé Derain. The Old Bridge
1910. Chester Dale Collection, National Gallery of Art,
Washington

ANDRÉ DERAIN. Amiens
1953. Pierre Lévy Collection, Troyes

uncertainty of subjective intuition. Generally speaking, their desire to eliminate purely subjective judgments makes experts resort to scientific and historical methods foreign to the order of aesthetics properly so called.

An attempt has recently been made to submit to certain rules the analysis of the personal style of any painter. This would lead to a sort of
"pictology" that, once fully constituted, would find itself with respect to
painting in about the same relation as graphology is to handwriting. Now,
precisely, graphology is one of those disciplines in which absolute accuracy
is hard to achieve and whose experts have been known to make mistakes. In
the case of pictology [14] the solidity of the conclusions rests upon that of one
of its presuppositions—namely, that the style of a painter exhibits constant
features recognizable from the beginning of his career to its end. This may
be true of certain artists, but there is no proof that it is true of all painters.
At first sight, it does not seem probable that, if he did not know beforehand
that they are the works of one and the same painter, a pictologist could
demonstratively establish that the author of the early works of Titian is the
same as the author of his last paintings. There is no great painter whose
style did not undergo some measure of transformation during the course of
his career. Nor is this all. For even while he finds himself right in the
middle of one of his successive manners, a painter may well yield to the
sudden urge of trying something different. To repeat, these remarks do not
mean that all attributions are equally uncertain; they simply mean that,
although they are not the rule, false attributions cannot be said to be rare
exceptions. [15]

14. M. M. van Dantzig, in *True or False?*, pp. 6–10. This book is based on an exhibition organized by the Stedelijk Museum in Amsterdam (Holland) and circulated in
the United States by the Corning Museum of Glass, Corning Glass Center, 1953–54 season. This pictological approach to the problem of authenticity is exemplified by an analysis of two Picassos (*Mother and Child*, 1905; *Composition*, 1924). The analysis aims
to establish by objective observation that these two works are by the same painter. However confident in the value of his method, the author first declares (p. 7) : "An absolutely
reliable method for the unmasking of forgeries does not exist—even the best experts can,
and do make mistakes."

15. See, in *True or False?*, p. 41, under the title "Principles of Pictology," a table
of the elements whose comparison enables us to tell original works from imitations. It
is enough to glance at this table to see that it compares creative artists with poor imitators.
When El Greco imitates Tintoretto, or, generally speaking, when an artist tests the manner of another one, the result is more difficult to appreciate. A continuous scale extends

If this conclusion seems unduly pessimistic, it will prove useful to observe that even if it implies a measure of historical skepticism, it also expresses a decided aesthetical optimism. There are such things as practically safe historical demonstrations. For instance, when a certain city has commissioned a sixteenth-century artist to paint an altarpiece, whose description is given in the deed, and which is still visible in the same city, above the same altar for which it was first painted, little hesitation is possible. The point we are enforcing is a different one. It is that this is *historical* evidence, and that while such evidence should be welcome wherever available, there is no *aesthetic* reason to worry in the countless cases where it is not available. From the point of view of art taken precisely qua art, there is nothing to lose in considering all paintings anonymous.

It is easy to foresee that these remarks will be construed as a glorification of ignorance and as a denial of the usefulness of art history in general. They are nothing of the sort. One should never hesitate to learn all that it is possible to know. The only question is: what is it to know art? More precisely: is the knowledge of art history, in any sense of the term, a knowledge *of* art? It certainly is a knowledge *about* art, but its object is not art, it only is its history. In the case of painting, as in that of poetry, it is entirely possible to know everything about their history without knowing much, if anything, about painting and poetry themselves. To limit ourselves to painting, it is not rare to see parents of good will undertake the artistic education of their children as early as possible, dragging them to art galleries, making them look at art books and at art postcards, forcibly stuffing their little heads with as many images of famous paintings and as many names of famous painters as possible (including even dates)—all this on the presupposition that it never is too soon to begin an artistic education. This is not the beginning of an artistic education; it is the beginning of a historical education. The fact that some children like it does not prove that they are gifted for aesthetic experience; neither does the fact that some

from downright fakes to original works influenced by the style and manner of another master. Since art historians sometimes hesitate between a mature Giorgione or a young Titian, intermediate categories should be introduced between authentic works and mere fakes.

children hate it prove that they are not gifted for the enjoyment of painting. Simply, it is a question of not confusing two distinct orders and of the perils that follow from their confusion. It is certainly better to like both art and its history, but it is quite possible to feel indifferent to art history while ardently loving art. The present tendency to confuse these two issues can do a great deal of harm. It can discourage artistic vocations without always encouraging historical ones. In short, this is one more example of the widely spread misunderstanding of the true relationship of intelligence and art.

What is wrong with this tendency is not that it attributes too much importance to the human intellect in the genesis of works of art. In all arts, and especially in painting, the intellect is at work everywhere, even in the painter's brush. The error that we wish to point out consists in letting cognitive activities foreign to its essence invade the art of painting and corrupt its notion in the minds of men.[16] It is natural for an art lover to take an interest in the lives of artists, in the history of painting, in the development of the various schools of painters, in the aesthetic problems connected with art in general and with painting in particular. All this is natural, but none of it is necessary. Above all, none of it should be allowed to take precedence over the very substance of the art. This is the ultimate reason why we suggested that, as regards art itself, the problems of authenticity are secondary in importance and should be relegated to their proper place. They are purely incidental to the substantial reality of painting.

3. *Life and Death of Paintings*

PAINTINGS are perishable, as are all material objects. There would be no point in reviewing all the accidents that can bring paintings to an untimely end. Earthquakes, floods, fires, wars, and vandalism are not causes of destruction proper to works of art and still less particularly to paintings.

---

16. "Art is not a thought; it is a fact. For the painter, the solution of his problem is in his color box just as it is in his ink bottle for the writer. Do not cultivate your personality; rather, draw closer to the rank and file. Originality is a monstrosity." (Raoul Dufy, in "Raoul Dufy," *L'Amour de l'art* (Paris), LXXVI–LXXVIII [1953], 48.)

On the other hand, even leaving aside the painter himself, whose relationship to his work is unique in kind, paintings have enemies of their own,
among whom, before any other one, we should list the customer.

The customer's behavior is a curious one. There is something mysterious in the gesture of the man who, rather than buying a car or a piece of
furniture, buys one of those unnecessary things which we call paintings.
On the other hand, it is only too true that, having paid for a picture, some
buyers feel that they own it and that they can do with it what they please.
Incidentally, no law in the world prevents the buyer of a masterpiece from
destroying it at once or even, which is worse, from repainting it. Without
going to such extremes, the owners of paintings sometimes do curious things
to them to improve their quality. The story of what Mr. John Allnutt did to
a landscape by Constable should not be held against him. For indeed, if he
himself had not told the story, we would not know it, but it deserves to be
preserved as a perfect illustration of our problem. From this point of view, it
is a classic.

Mr. John Allnutt had bought a Constable when very few people were
interested in his work. In point of fact, during the year 1814, when this
incident took place, John Constable sold only two paintings, and Mr. John
Allnutt bought one of them. He must therefore have been a man of taste.
Yet he wrote many years later to C. R. Leslie: "As I did not quite like
the effect of the sky, I was foolish enough to have that obliterated, and a
new one put in by another artist which, though extremely beautiful, did
not harmonise with the other parts of the picture. Some years after, I got
a friend of Mr. Constable to ask him if he would be kind enough to restore
the picture to its original state, to which he readily assented. Having a very
beautiful painting by Mr. (now Sir Augustus) Callcott, which was nearly
of the same size, but not quite so high, I sent it to Mr. Constable together
with his own, and expressed a wish that, if he could do it without injury
to the picture, he would reduce the size of it in height, by lowering the
sky, so as to make it nearer the size of Mr. Callcott's, to which I wished it
to hang as a companion." To make a long story short, let us say that this
refreshing candor on the part of the customer was fully rewarded by the

painter's angelic patience. When Constable told Allnutt that the work had been done and could be collected, Allnutt had two surprises in store. First, Constable refused to be paid; on the contrary, he declared himself under a great obligation to Allnutt, who had been the first stranger to buy one of his paintings when his own friends were still questioning his chances of success. Next, Constable, "wishing to make the picture as acceptable to me as possible . . . had, instead of reducing the height of the old picture, painted an entirely new one of the same subject."[17] Allnutt does not seem to have asked himself why Constable had preferred to do a new painting rather than to mutilate the old one. In this case, the painting was saved by the painter himself. In other cases, like Manet's portrait of Abbé Hurel, the mutilation was performed by the owner of the painting.[18] Nobody can say how many paintings have perished in this way.

Man, then, constitutes a serious threat to the survival of paintings, but even apart from natural accidents and from human intervention, paintings begin to change and to disintegrate almost as soon as they have left the painter's hand. Even stones get sick and ultimately perish; canvases, wood panels, and colors cannot be expected to endure indefinitely. During the first years of their lives, paintings do not always suffer from the effects of time. For a period of twenty years or more, especially if the media used by the painter have been well chosen and cleverly handled, oil slowly permeates the colored pigments, unifies the matter, and imparts to the work a mellowness that new paintings cannot possibly have.[19] Some painters strive to achieve this art-gallery effect by a series of artifices, but it is rather

17. Leslie, p. 47.

18. Tabarant, p. 27. — The portrait of Manet's friend Abbé Hurel was framed and given by Mme Manet to the model after the death of her husband. When it was given to Abbé Hurel, this portrait was 81½ x 72 centimeters; Abbé Hurel reduced to it 47 x 37 centimeters. On this point, artists are as dangerous as art lovers. See above, ch. 2, n. 1.

19. "A constant communion with pictures the tints of which are subdued by time no doubt tends to unfit the eye for the enjoyment of freshness; and Sir George [Beaumont] thought Constable too daring in the modes he adopted to obtain this quality; while Constable saw that Sir George often allowed himself to be deceived by the effects of time, of accident, and by the tricks that are, far oftener than is generally supposed, played by dealers, to give mellowness to pictures; and, in these matters, each was disposed to set the other right." Leslie, pp. 113–14. — Cf. Joseph Addison, *The Spectator*, no. 83 (June 5, 1711).

dangerous to do paintings that look already old in their youth. At any rate, young paintings are so different from old ones that it is not easy to exhibit works of the sixteenth century in the same room as twentieth-century paintings. Even to pass from a room to another one requires a few moments of adaptation when it makes us go from Jan van Eyck to Paul Cézanne, Matisse, and Renoir.

This common experience raises a rather disturbing question. What did the great masterpieces of the past look like when they had just been painted? What will the masterpieces of today look like three centuries from now? Above all, since philosophical problems are here at stake, what kind of being can we attribute to paintings if their so-called being is, in fact, a slow but irrevocable becoming? These speculative questions cannot be answered by philosophy, but, rather, by chemistry. Despite the rarefied atmosphere in which aesthetic discussions usually take place, the future of paintings is inseparable from that of the pigments used by painters. No masterpiece will ever survive the material elements that enter its structure. From this point of view, there is a sort of life and death of pictures. Each and every one of them unfolds its own history during a space of time whose duration is determined by that of its constituent elements.

This fact has given rise to new disciplines and techniques whose natural tendency is to subdivide and to multiply. There now exist a picture pathology, itself attended by an art of preventing picture ailments; a science of the way in which paintings are aging, either normally or abnormally; an art of restoring sick paintings; and other such disciplines or techniques that require laboratories, trained artisans, and, generally speaking, institutions and a specialized staff that are, with respect to paintings, in the same relationship as hospitals and physicians are to human beings.[20] The way specialists describe the qualities required of a good restorer of

---

20. On these problems, see M. C. Bradley, Jr., *The Treatment of Pictures*; Unesco, "The Care of Paintings," *Museum*, III (1950), 2, 3; IV (1951), 1. An excellent introduction is found in Caroline K. Keck, *How to Take Care of Your Pictures* (Bibliography, p. 54). On picture pathology, elementary information is found in A. P. de Mirimonde, *Pour mieux comprendre la peinture*, pp. 30–34.

paintings closely resembles the description of a qualified surgeon.[21] The only difference is that, while surgery is a regulated profession, there is no law to prevent anybody from doing anything he pleases to any painting. This situation may change with time, but there is too much uncertainty concerning methods and techniques to justify prescriptions and interdictions in such matters. We are still far from being able to implement the decisions made by certain international organizations to ensure the protection of painted works of art.

By and large, the main element responsible for the disintegration of paintings is color. The history of colormaking is long and complex, full of suppositions and clever guesses that are not always supported by facts. With respect to our own problem, it is often said that modern colors, mostly chemical in nature and factory-made, are far from equaling the old home-made colors, often vegetal in origin and less likely to fade than the chemical ones. Hence the kind of research work, already mentioned, that aims to recapture the secret formulas of the old technicians. And such efforts are certainly most useful, provided only that they do not make us believe in the existence of a golden age when color pigments were not reacting chemically and when paintings used to change but little after leaving the painter's easel.[22]

21. See, in Keck (pp. 36–40), the instructions concerning "first aid." Cf. p. 43: "Not every operation or medicine leaves a human being better off than he was before. Doctors and restorers both aim to preserve when they treat and not to destroy." — The destructive character of restoration work finds its explanation in the fact that the source of unity, without which a painting *is not*, lies in the mind of the artist by whom it has been conceived and by whom alone it can be executed. Speaking of the practice that consists in employing artists to finish pictures left incomplete by their predecessors, Leslie observes (p. 279): "The best painters know that a work of any value can only be carried through by the head and hand of him who planned it, and consequently, those only undertake to complete unfinished pictures who are the least capable of divining the intentions of their authors. Some of Constable's sketches have thus been *finished* into worthlessness, and what is a still greater injury to his reputation, entire forgeries have been made of his works. Multitudes of these I have seen, and with astonishment that their wretchedness should impose upon purchasers."

22. Jacques Maroger, *The Secret Formulas and Techniques of the Masters*. The object of the book is clearly defined in the introduction (p. 7). The author expresses a widely spread notion in saying that, for the last two centuries or more, "certain qualities of color and modelling and brilliance of surface which seem to have been the common possession of earlier schools of painting" are now inaccessible to modern artists "with the resources

As far back in the past as our records can take us, painters have always been less interested in making colors than in using them. The bills paid by the painters who decorated the walls of the Palace of the Popes, at Avignon, are still extant. We know exactly what colors they bought from the local dealer and what price they paid for them. It is likewise certain that those colors, as well as those used by other artists during the Middle Ages and in the Renaissance, have never ceased to change during the course of centuries. In some well-known cases, paintings done by such great artists as Leonardo da Vinci have totally disintegrated during their own lifetime. In other cases—for instance, that of Titian—the underpainting has so completely eaten up the colors that practically nothing of them is now visible.[23] When it is only a question of removing accumulated dust or successive layers of varnish, a carefully conducted cleaning can restore a painting to something more like its original condition. The operation carries its own risks, but it has often been successfully performed. When the color itself is the trouble, as it usually is, little or nothing can be done about it. Today, as in older times, and perhaps a little faster today but not noticeably so, some paintings become unrecognizable, as to color, during the lifetime of the artist. At any rate, what we now admire in the works of the old masters, and what their copyists are striving to imitate, is chiefly the damage caused to them by the passing of years and centuries. If he came back to life and revisited the Scuola di San Rocco, in Venice, Tintoretto would probably not recognize his own work.[24]

currently at their disposal." This may well be an illusion: who knows what certain modern paintings will look like two centuries from now? Moreover, when a modern painter succeeds in recapturing some of the qualities, not at all of the old masters, but of their works as they now are, he is accused of aping the style of museum pieces.

23. Titian's *Martyrdom of St. Lawrence,* in the church of the Gesuiti, Venice, has become wholly undecipherable because, in it, all the colors have been eaten up by the bitumens. Yet, in his *Titien* (pp. 241–42), Victor Basch has devoted two pages to the study of what, when we last visited it at least, exhibited to our eyes little more than the ruins of a painting.

24. A fragment of a frieze painted by Tintoretto in the Scuola di San Rocco, Venice, has accidentally retained its primitive freshness of colors. This enables us to measure the progressive darkening of the great murals done by Tintoretto for the same institution. This phenomenon has been noted and explained by Delacroix in his *Journal,* p. 238 (July 29, 1854): "When we copy a Titian or a Rembrandt we believe that we are keeping the same relationship between lights and shadows as the master's, but actually we are

In almost desperate cases, that is, when it becomes a question of life and death, restorers are called in to help. Owing to the discoveries of modern physics, sick canvases can be X-rayed, an operation that may lead to disturbing revelations. The painting we see sometimes covers the original work of the artist; additions, by unknown hands, have been made at unknown dates; ancient colors have been covered with entirely different ones. The reports on the work done on *The Mystic Lamb* of van Eyck eloquently tell us of the countless problems that restorers have to face. Far from blaming their efforts, which are often guided by a great love for art and for the works they are attempting to save from utter destruction, we should feel grateful to them for saving what can still be saved of so many masterpieces that, were it not for their skill, would soon cease to exist.

Yet, when all is said and done, the fact remains that the restoration of paintings is one of the surest methods scientifically to substitute new paintings for the old ones. The first harm can be done, not only during the lifetime of the artist, but even under his very eyes. An ill-advised application of varnish by another hand, a well-intentioned piece of repair work done to stop a hole—all degrees of intervention are possible until, because the color "is gone," another painter, resorting to pigments different from those in use in Raphael's day and trusting his own eye as if it were that of the old master, proceeds to cover the loggias of the Vatican with acid greens and canary yellows the like of which Raphael himself probably never used on any one of his own paintings.

To repeat, no blame is intended in these remarks: without such restora-

piously reproducing the work of time, or rather its ravages. The great artists would be most painfully surprised if they could see the smoke-blackened daubs that the pictures which they originally painted have become. The background of Rubens's *Descent from the Cross,* for example, must always have had a very dark sky, although one which the artist could imagine when he represented the scene, but it has now become so dark that one cannot distinguish a single detail." — See the similar remark (in Leslie, p. 114) made by John Constable to Sir George Beaumont, who was matching the colors of a small Gaspar Poussin so as to be "sure to be right": " 'But suppose, Sir George,' replied Constable, 'Gaspar could rise from his grave, do you think he would know his own picture in its present state? or if he did, should we not find it difficult to persuade him that somebody had not smeared tar or cart grease over its surface, and then wiped it imperfectly off?' "

tions, nothing of Raphael's murals would still be left for us to see. The only point at stake is that, from the moment a painting has been touched by another hand than that of the painter, it becomes another painting.[25] A world-famous picture such as Millet's *Angelus* has first been celebrated as an extraordinary masterpiece; the present tendency is to consider it an honorable piece of work that does not even compare with the best of what Millet has left us; in point of fact, what we now see may well be little more than the shadow of what it used to be in its pristine novelty.[26] Some restorations of works by Veronese and other great painters have been denounced by highly competent witnesses as amounting to pure and simple destructions.[27] Yet we have forgotten these restorations, and we now trust-

25. Contrariwise to what some seem to believe, the problem is not a new one: "A numerous class of men have risen up in this country [Great Britain], and indeed in all countries where the pictures by old masters are in demand, who, though unable to either draw or paint, assume a knowledge superior to the artists whose province it is to produce tints, and tones of colour of a corresponding quality. It is in vain to tell these men, that 'deep-toned brightness is produced only by repeated glazings, and that these glazings are composed of little more than varnish and transparent colour.' Many deny that such a thing as glazing existed, and consequently in removing what they consider 'dirt and varnish,' they remove every particle of richness of tint. What spirits will not reach, they follow into every crevice with the point of a lancer: until the picture becomes, not fresh and bright as it is termed, but raw and crude in the highest degree; as a judgment on Sir Joshua Reynolds, who had simply deplored the darkening of old paintings, no works have suffered more in this respect than his own, many of which have been cleaned down to the preparation for glazing, and when pointed out as examples of this destructive course, it is impudently asserted that his colours have fled." (Note of the painter John Burnet to Reynolds, *Discourses*, p. 24.)

26. The present opinion about Millet's *Angelus* is well enough expressed by Vlaminck, in his *Portraits avant décès*, where he says (p. 178) that, famous as it is for its subject, "the qualities of this painting are indifferent." But few people know that, in its present condition, this work of art differs from what it used to be before undergoing a severe restoration.

27. "Mme Villot returned in the evening. Perhaps rather imprudently, I said something about regretting the restorations to the pictures in the Louvre; but when I saw how warmly she defended her husband's skill I did not dwell too long on the subject of the large Veronese which that miserable Villot has destroyed by his attentions." (*The Journal of Eugène Delacroix*, p. 194 [Wednesday, October 12, 1853].) — See the entry, July 29, 1854 (pp. 238–39): "We are sometimes astonished that nothing remains of the painting of antiquity. We ought, rather, to be surprised at finding a few traces of it in the third-rate scrawls that still decorate walls at Herculaneum. . . . We should be even less surprised at their destruction if we reflected that most of the pictures produced since the Renaissance—that is to say, comparatively recently—are already unrecognizable. . . . Clumsy restorations only finish the work of destruction. Many people imagine that they do a great deal for paintings when they have them restored. . . . Each so-called restoration is an injury far more to be regretted than the ravages of time,

fully accept as authentic some paintings that their authors would not always recognize as their own works. There are two ways for a painting to perish: the one is for it to be restored; the other is for it not to be restored.[28] Opposite answers to the problem of what to do are always dialectically justifiable, but such discussions are of little help when it comes to practical decisions. Even if it were true that, in the future, paintings would be protected against inevitable death,[29] nothing could be done about past destructions. There are good reasons to hope that the average span of life promised to paintings will progressively lengthen. The difficulty that will never be

for the result is not a restored picture, but a different picture by the hand of the miserable dauber who substitutes himself for the author of the original who has disappeared under his retouching. Restorations to sculpture are less destructive."

28. On this point, perfectly balanced remarks are found in Keck, pp. 52–53: "Some curators feel that except in study rooms the public must not be asked to look at stripped down, time ravaged creations because they are mere ghosts of their original greatness. Others feel that even skillful restorations of a ruined masterpiece to make it whole again will destroy that faint but inspiring quality everpresent in the true original. At best, what a restorer impaints approximates the work of the original artist; it can never duplicate it. But both sides have good arguments. Which procedure is the wisest has not yet been settled, either between the public and curators or among individual owners." — See George Sand's answer (July 27, 1855) to Delacroix's letter of July 19, 1855: "The *loggie* are only seen with the eyes of faith; everything is in tatters; the *stanze* are so black that one can see there all that one pleases" (*Nouvelle nouvelle revue française*, I [1953], 573). See a recent article in favor of restoration work by Fernanda Wittgens, "Leonardo's *Last Supper* Resurrected," *Art News Annual*, XXIV (1955), 28–52, introduction by Bernard Berenson. One could not possibly disapprove of the heroic effort made to save what little was left of such a masterpiece; the question, however, remains to know what relation there is between the ruin that has been saved and the original work by Leonardo. Compare the copy of the original done c. 1500 by Marco d'Oggiono, pupil and companion of Leonardo, with the present mural. The differences are not only in details of architecture, but also in the relationship between the heads of Christ and St. John, on the one hand, and their background, on the other hand. Besides, in his *Lives* (II, 161), Vasari assures us that Leonardo had left the head of Christ unfinished (and also that of Judas), and he adds that, in his own time, the picture was becoming undecipherable. — Another simple experience is to compare the description of *Mona Lisa* given by Vasari (II, 164) with whatever of the original painting is now left in the Louvre. If the description of the colors given by Vasari was correct, what we now see is the portrait of a ghost, or the ghost of a portrait.

29. Delacroix felt sure that the causes of destruction, so manifold since the Renaissance, would still multiply in the future "thanks to the increase in sharp practice and knavery in every branch of the art, whether it be adulteration of the materials that go to make up the colours, oils and varnishes, or substitution by the manufacturers of cotton for hemp in canvases and of poor quality boards for the well-seasoned wood formerly used for panels" (*Journal*, p. 238 [July 29, 1854]). — Much more optimistic is the point of view of the restorers, at least at first sight, but if we read the conclusions of one of them as carefully as they were written, we shall entertain very few illusions: see Keck, pp. 52–53.

removed, so far as one can see, is to decide in good time which paintings deserve to be protected and which ones can be allowed to perish.

Here again, a summary comparison with music will no doubt help us to realize how deeply such problems are rooted in the physical nature of these two classes of works of art. A painter leaves behind him works completely defined in their structure. Painters are so truly the total causes of their works that these cannot be modified in any way without undergoing a change in their individuality and suffering a loss of authenticity. Every decision made in such matters is irrevocable: a restored picture will never again be quite the same picture it used to be before its restoration. It even will begin to change again, following another rhythm and in a new way. This is so true that, as has been said, certain restorations practically amount to downright destructions.

On the side of music, things are rather different. Since each and every musical composition requires a mediator to exist, the intervention of artists other than the author himself is not only not scandalous, or sacrilegious, it is even natural, beneficial, and necessary to the work. When Artur Schnabel was performing one of Beethoven's piano sonatas, he was not proceeding to a restoration of some original but, rather, to the original creation of one of its possible interpretations. Let us buy four recordings of this same sonata by four different artists; the result will be four different renderings of the same musical work, and nobody will ever be able to prove that one of them is *the* ideal and absolute self-subsisting sonata No. 32 in C minor, Opus 111. The poverty-stricken mode of subsistence that is proper to music ensures its indestructibility. A painter can say: this is my painting. A musician is seldom able to say: this is exactly my music. Interpreting a musical composition is not an absolutely free matter, but it allows a great deal of liberty for which there is no ground in painting.

For the same reason, musicians can take many liberties with written music that it would be criminal for painters to take with paintings. True enough, all musicians and all music lovers do not react in the same way on this point. Some of them vigorously object to any kind of change inflicted upon the work of a musician by other musicians, but it is impossible to maintain that the problem is the same in the case of music and in the case of painting. The reason for the difference is that, in these two cases, the consequences are entirely different. When a painter modifies the painting done by another artist, the original work of this artist is forever altered. The new picture may perhaps be better than the old one, but it will certainly be different. Hence the scruples that any painter should experience when asked to restore a mural by Giotto, Raphael, or Leonardo da Vinci. Not so in the case of music. First of all, musicians themselves have often re-written their own compositions, to say nothing of those written by others, in order to reduce orchestral scores for the piano, or to turn cello concertos into violin concertos, or to orchestrate compositions written for organ, for piano, or even for human voices. Since Wagner himself did this with certain scenes of *Tristan* and *Parsifal,* why should not similar "arrange-ments" be perpetrated by other musicians? The result is what counts. If the result is good, its author is justified.

However each of us may feel about the Passacaglia and the Preludes and Fugues of Bach orchestrated by famous maestros or, on the contrary, transcribed for the piano by well-known virtuosos, the fact remains that no harm has been done by the authors of these transcriptions. Bach himself subjected the works of many other musicians to similar alterations, but this has not destroyed them. In like manner, it will always be possible to perform *Boris Godunov* either in its original orchestration or in its highly popular version by Rimsky-Korsakov. Those who prefer Bach's pre-lude for harpsichord to its metamorphosis into Gounod's *Ave Maria* are perfectly justified in sticking to their own aesthetic judgment, the more so as, in this case too, to remove the *Ave Maria* is all there is to do to recover the original prelude. Even then, some will prefer to have it performed on the harpsichord rather than on the piano, but if there is no harpsichord and if the pianist is good, the piano will have to do, the more so as Bach is no longer here to tell us which way he himself would prefer to have it per-formed.

These considerations should not make us lose sight of the fundamental fact that painting is an art of space. As has already been said, a painting is entirely given to us at once, and our first apprehension of it is practically instantaneous. No doubt, this initial experience can be protracted, but even while it is enduring in time, it remains a global and simultaneous apprehension. The onlooker is not being shown first a certain part of a picture, then another one. He has not to keep the whole structure of the work in his mind by an effort of memory similar to that which one spontaneously makes while listening to music. The same remark can be worded differently: a certain amount of musical memory is required for the enjoyment of a musical composition, whereas little visual memory, if any, is necessary for the enjoyment of a picture. If the work is a small one, memory is not required at all.

A painting is experienced as a given whole at any one of the moments of its duration, but not necessarily as identically the same whole, unless we call it the same as we say that an old man is the same man as the child that he once was. Some artists are so fully aware of the fact that they enlist time as their best collaborator. Time, Ingres used to say, will finish my work. For all painters, however, time ultimately proves an interfering collaborator, and, here again, the materiality of painted works of art is inscribed in their aesthetic existence. Many Greek and medieval marbles, or carved stones, used to be covered with bright colors under which, should these coats of paint still exist, we would today refuse to recognize what we hold to be exceptional masterpieces of ancient art. What is true of painted sculptures is no less true of paintings.[30] If some frolicsome genii decided overnight to restore to their pristine condition all the paintings in the Louvre, it would probably become necessary to rewrite the whole history of art, and many of us would pray the same genii promptly to turn again these bright young things, pleasing to see but a bit loud for our soberer taste, into the respectable masterpieces we used to know and love. We all admire the best van Goyen landscapes and seascapes, but what did they look like when they were new? This is a question nobody can answer. To be

30. On what happened to Greek and medieval sculpture, see Bernard Berenson, *Aesthetics and History*, pp. 58–59 (refers to Johan Huizinga, *The Waning of the Middle Ages*, p. 235).

sure, we like them as they are; what we do not know is in what measure the paintings we now like are really those done by this master of the seas and the plains. There would perhaps be some truth in saying that the only paintings that can give us a fair notion of what the works of Tintoretto looked like in their primitive novelty are the most recent paintings done by those among our contemporaries who do not have the ambition to turn out modern museum pieces. Any youth resembles any other youth more than he resembles the old man he will someday have to be. If we want to enjoy the old masters as they once really were, let us first cherish contemporary painting.

CHAPTER FOUR

ONTOLOGY OF PAINTINGS

GIORGIO VASARI seems to have been one of the first artists to attempt a definition of painting. This definition itself presupposes another one, that of design. By the word "drawing" (*disegno*) Vasari means the art of outlining figures by means of appropriate curves. There is a certain amount of design in every painting, but to paint is something more than merely to make an outline. "A painting is a plane surface—be it a wood panel, a piece of canvas, or a wall—covered with spots of colors disposed around an outline which, because its curves have been well designed, circumscribes the figure." [1]

A similar definition occurs in Hippolyte Taine's classic *Philosophy of Art*,[2] and again, more recently, in a famous article by Maurice Denis. The

1. Vasari, painter and architect, born at Arezzo in 1511, died in Florence in 1574. His famous book, *The Lives of the Painters, Sculptors and Architects*, is found in an English translation by A. B. Hinds. This edition does not include the *Maniera* of Vasari, often prefixed to the *Lives* as introduction. It exists in a separate translation by Louisa Maclehose, *Vasari on Technique*, ed. G. B. Brown. — Since the definition of painting found in the *Maniera* has been generally overlooked, we beg to quote it in the Italian original: "Ora, avendo di cio [i.e., design] ragionato abbastanza, seguita che noi veggiamo che cosa sia la pittura. Ell' è dunque un piano coperto di campi di colori in superficie o di tavola o di muro o di tela, intorno a' lineamenti detti di sopra, i quali per virtù di un buon disegno di linee girate circondano la figura." "Introduzione alle tre arti," ch. XV, in *Le Opere di Giorgio Vasari*, vol. I, p. 38.

2. "By themselves and apart from their aptitude to imitate, colors as well as lines have a meaning. Our impression varies according to the way they are assembled. A painting is a colored surface on which the various tones and the various degrees of light are distributed with a certain choice; this is its intimate being; the fact that these tones and these degrees of light make up figures, draperies, or architectures is with them an ulterior property that does not prevent their primitive property from having all its importance and all its rights. The value proper to color is therefore enormous, and the de-

formula is well known, but it is so often misquoted or misunderstood that it will not be amiss to quote it once more: "Remember that before being a war horse, a nude woman, or telling any story whatever, a painting essentially consists of a plane surface covered with colors assembled in a certain order."[3] Maurice Denis did not know the passage of Taine at the time he himself had written his own definition,[4] but even if he had, the fact would be of little importance. There is no common measure between a casual statement made by a philosopher and the same statement, or a similar one, made by an artist fully aware of the exigencies of his own art.

Although it may seem too obvious to be worth quoting, this was, and it still remains, a highly controversial definition. We sometimes find it quoted under this abridged form: "A painting is a plane surface covered with colors assembled in a certain order." But the gist of Denis' definition was that, *before* being the representation of any subject whatever, a painting is made up of colors assembled on a plane surface according to a certain pattern. To say what a thing *essentially* is does not amount to giving an exhaustive description of it.[5] As to Taine, the fact that his definition ap-

cision made about it by painters determines the rest of their work" (II, 334–35). Taine wrote these words at the end of the second volume of his work, when it was too late for him to do anything with it. In fact, the whole trend of Taine's aesthetic is against it. One cannot help wondering if, when Taine was about to write the last sixteen pages of his *Philosophy of Art*, some charitable painter did not remind him that colors play an important part in painting.

3. Denis, "Définition du néo-traditionnisme," in *Théories*, p. 1. This same definition is restated, with an important addition, p. 27: "Before being a representation of any thing whatever, a painting is a plane surface covered with colors assembled in a certain order, *and for the pleasure of the eye*." This raises the problem of the final cause of the paintings. It will be considered separately in another section of this book.

4. Denis, *Charmes et leçons de l'Italie*, p. 177, n. 1.

5. Denis himself has sometimes abridged his formula: "The fruitful notion of the plane surface covered with colors assembled in a certain order . . ." ("The Influence of Paul Gauguin," *Théories*, pp. 166–71). But some historians have deliberately reduced it to this sole element: "Remember that a picture . . . is a plane surface covered with colors assembled in a certain order" (Bernard Dorival, *Les Étapes de la peinture française contemporaine*, I, 110). In this "axiom," the ellipsis stands for all that has been suppressed. Going further still, some critics reproach Denis with having eliminated from the notion of "painting" all that is not color: Charles Lalo, "Classification structurale des beaux-arts," in *Formes de l'art*, p. 20, n. 2. Lalo reduces Denis' definition to the following formula: "Visual perception of two-dimensional forms on a continuous surface." The notion of order has thus been replaced with that of forms. This substitution agrees with Lalo's description of painting as "a technical interpretation of the laws of theoretic optics" (p. 20); but men have painted masterpieces for millenniums without even

pears only at the end of his work suggests that it is of secondary importance in his aesthetics.[6] At any rate, it seems difficult to deny that the two notions of color (or of light values) [7] and of order sufficiently determine the nature of painting considered as distinct from pure drawing. Of these two notions, that of order is of especial importance for the ontology of painted works of art, but its definition presupposes a certain understanding of the notion of form, to which we now must turn our attention.

[37]

1. Form and Becoming

AT THIS moment of our inquiry, it may prove profitable to ascertain the technical meaning of some terms whose use is unavoidable in the present discussion. These terms are borrowed from the philosophy of Aristotle, and their practical necessity appears from the fact that no aesthetician wholly succeeds in doing away with them. Modern phenomenologists, and even existentialists, openly or tacitly return to Aristotle's terminology every time they attempt to describe the relationship between artists and the works created by their art. And no wonder, since the philosophy of Aristotle, in its very essence, is a reflection on the operations in consequence of which things come to be. Now, art is distinct from nature, but, like nature, it is a cause in consequence of which a certain class of beings come to be. It seems therefore advisable to consider a few general notions applicable to becom-

suspecting the existence of optics and its laws. Denis' definition simply aimed at recovering a clear awareness of the essence of painting conceived precisely as one of the fine arts.

6. "I am now coming to the last element, a capital one, namely, color" (*La Philosophie de l'art*, II, 355). Despite his theories about climate, race, and so on, Taine did not completely overlook the fact that, at the origin of painting, there is an aptitude to feel pleasure at the sight of certain colors.

7. Some painters have practiced a voluntary asceticism with respect to color (see Denis, "Le Renoncement de Carrière," *Théories*, pp. 213–14), but nothing forbids us to call "painting" a preparation in black and white, such as, for instance, those of Seurat. — Black and white can be held to be, in a certain sense, colors. See *Webster's:* "All colors are divisible into two classes: *chromatic colors*, as reds, greens, purples, browns and pinks; *achromatic colors*, including black, white, and the series of grays intermediate between black and white, which differ from each other only in the degree of resemblance to white or difference from black." The notion of achromatic (i.e., colorless) colors appears paradoxical, not to say self-contradictory. But these problems of terminology should not prevent us from acknowledging the fact that light values suffice to constitute a painting.

ing under all its forms—that is to say, in the order of nature as well as in the order of art.

Let us come back to the notions defined by Aristotle in connection with the problem of knowing how things come to be. His first remark about it is that, for any conceivable thing, to become is "to come to be from another thing" (*Physics*, I, 7, 189b, 33). The other thing from which it comes to be is called its matter. This notion can point out different objects. Matter can be something very modest in both being and commercial value, such as paper, plaster, or clay. It can also be something exceedingly precious and expensive, such as the gold a goldsmith uses as a matter in making a gold ring. Moreover, a matter can be a very complicated structure, itself the result of long natural preparation or of an elaborate industrial or artistic processing. In order to make things clearer, let us say that matter is both a certain way of being and a certain way of causing something else to be. Apart from absolute prime matter, which has no being of its own, any concrete substance can serve as a matter for the becoming of another being.

Because of the generality of its notion, Aristotle often calls matter a "substratum," that is, the underlying element "from which proceeds that which comes to be" (*Physics* I, 7, 190b, 1–4). Among the five examples quoted by him of the different ways in which things come to be from a certain matter, three are relevant to art: by change of shape, as a statue; by taking away, as the Hermes from the stone; by putting together, as a house. A fourth example of becoming—by addition—is borrowed by Aristotle from living things (things that grow), but he could as well have borrowed it from the art of the painter. In all these cases, a thing comes into existence, starting from something else (its matter) that becomes the thing in question. That from which becoming originates, in which it takes place, and which constitutes the very body of the being at stake is its matter. Such are marble, stone, or bronze in a statue; such also are the colored pigments in a painting.

One of the points stressed by Aristotle in connection with matter is that its notion is not merely negative. Matter is not a simple absence of being. On the contrary, in any process of becoming, that which becomes is often a highly complex entity, as are the germs and seeds in the generation of living beings. The matter from which becoming proceeds is sometimes called its *subject,* in order to stress the positive nature of its entity. At the same time, every generation, or becoming, presupposes the nonbeing of something—that is, the nonbeing of that which is going to be at the term of the process. This notion is really a very simple one: that which already is cannot possibly come to be; in other words, all becoming is the coming to be of something that, at the beginning of the process, is not.

This point led Aristotle to a curious notion, whose meaning appears in full when artistic production is at stake. It is the notion of privation.

Let us suppose a matter, or substratum, that will become the subject of some process of becoming. The very nature of this process will consist in turning the subject at stake into its very contrary. What Aristotle means thereby is this: if we want to obtain a colored surface, the starting point of this process should be a noncolored surface, or, in plain language, a white surface, just as, if we want to turn a man into a musician, he must first be innocent of musical skill at the beginning of the process. Privation then can be conceived as the absence, in a subject matter, of what it is going to possess at the end of the process of becoming. Thus, matter always is a certain thing that is becoming, and because it is always the matter-of-a-substance, it itself nearly is substance; on the contrary, as Aristotle himself expressly says it: "the privation in no sense is" (*Physics,* I, 9, 192a, 3–6).

This negative notion assumes a positive meaning as soon as we ask ourselves: of what is it the privation? For, indeed, this question immediately introduces the notion of a third principle of becoming, which is form. At the origin of any process of becoming, there is the privation—that is, the nonbeing—of a certain form that is coming to be. In other words, to be the cause of a certain becoming is to produce something, not indeed from absolute nothingness, but at least from the nothingness of the very form that is to be produced.

The aesthetic inspiration of Aristotle's philosophy of nature is clearly felt in his remarks on this curious notion of privation. Taken in itself, it first gives an impression of mere verbalism. What can be more commonplace than such a statement: it is contradictory to suppose that something already is that which it is about to become? But this Aristotelian notion is best understood in connection with the remark often made by the Philosopher, that negative as it is, the notion of privation points out the nonbeing of something that ought to be or, in other words, the absence of something that should be there. In this sense, the becoming of every work of art consists in substituting the presence of a certain form for the privation of that form in a certain matter.

The reason becoming takes place is precisely that, taken in itself, a given matter is neither pure nonbeing nor pure being. Placed, so to speak, betwixt and between, it always is both a substance determined in itself, such as a piece of canvas or masonite, and a possible subject for further determinations, such as the support of a possible painting. Expressed in terms of common experience, this means that in perceiving things, we often perceive, at least as much as what they are, what could be done with them or, in other words, what would become of them if they were used as so much material for the production of new beings.

The awareness of this fact is the probable source of Aristotle's remarkable doctrine concerning the origin of becoming in material substances. Having at his disposal three elements to account for this phenomenon—matter, form, and privation—Aristotle observes that he cannot find its explanation in form, because, being wholly defined in itself, form has nothing to desire; nor can he find its explanation in privation, for the simple reason that, having no entity of its own, privation cannot be the seat of any yearning; there then remains matter as the sole possible source of such desire, and this is what Aristotle finally affirms in a formula justly famous for a brutality verging upon crudity: "The truth is that what desires the form is matter, as the female desires the male and the ugly the beautiful" (*Physics*, I, 9, 192a, 20–25).

It is easy to misunderstand this doctrine and even to make it look ludicrous. There seems to be a naïve anthropomorphism in a position that attributes to matter desire and yearning as if matter were endowed with a soul capable of such emotions. But Aristotle's doctrine is not that simple.

It describes a complex experience in which the formal vocation of a certain matter is perceived by such a human mind as that of an artist. More deeply still, it describes a complex reality in which nature itself is unconsciously working after the manner of an artist and obscurely groping its way toward always higher ends. Is it really absurd to conceive of the universe of material things as animated from within by a sort of desire for perfection? Assuredly, this is not a scientific notion, but it has at least the merit of accounting for a fact that contemporary science leaves unexplained, namely, the progressive and quasi-creative character of evolution in general. At any rate, and without entering controversies we can avoid, let us say that, even if Aristotle had been mistaken in conceiving nature as a sort of unconscious human agent, his philosophy of nature would, for this very reason, provide a fitting interpretation of the genesis of works of art.

Reduced to its essentials, Aristotle's teaching on this point is that there is in matter a craving for any form that can turn its privation into some positive mode of being. Obviously, the fulfillment of this craving cannot be the work of privation, which is nothingness, or of matter, which is the seat of privation; it must therefore be the work of form, whose notion it remains for us to describe.

The word "form" now belongs to everyday language. In its common acceptation, it simply means the visual appearance of a thing or, in other terms, its figure and its shape. These meanings are correct, but they express less what Aristotle used to call form than its external manifestations. In the sense we shall give it, the word "form" designates the essential nature of a thing or, still more precisely, that nature itself considered as determining the thing in its species and, by the same token, in its figure and in its shape.

We know form much less in itself than by its effects. Every time certain effects are present, we can safely infer that a form is there, as their cause. Among these effects, let us first note a literally universal one: form is that through which each and every being has existence. For instance, wood is a thing of nature; it is a bed only potentially; to turn it into an actual bed, some artisan has to give it the shape of a bed, but as soon as it has been given this shape, the wood in question becomes a bedstead; in short, it *is* a bed. So the bed exists only through its form (*Physics*, II, 2193a, 30–35).

Aristotle expressed the same notion in different words when he said that, for any substance, or thing, that which "is only potentially a *this*" (for instance, a bed) "only potentially *is*" (*On Coming to Be and Passing Away*, I, 3, 317b, 26). Consequently, in giving actual form to a shapeless matter, we cause it to be actually *this*, we give it actual being.

Our next question then should be: how does form give actual being? It does so by isolating, within matter, a whole that, because it is endowed with determinate size, shape, and position in space, is capable of separate existence. We are here reaching a point where all the notions related to being are given at once as included in every one of them. Let it suffice to list the principal among these notions and to characterize their meaning in a summary way.

Form is that on account of which a certain thing is the very thing that it is. In this sense, as has already been said, form is, for each and every thing, the cause of its being.

By positing a thing as a definite being, form separates it from all that which it is not. This separative power of the form is easily observed, especially in the art of drawing, in which a few lines suffice to isolate a portion of space from the surrounding ones, and, thereby, to delineate a distinct being: angel, man, or beast. Under the hand of Albrecht Dürer, minor worlds, all complete in themselves, seem miraculously to separate themselves from nothingness and to acquire actual being. On a more abstract level, it can be said that, from the fact that something is that which it is, it becomes distinct from all the rest. [38, 39]

This separative power of the form manifests itself by delineation, if the operation takes place in space; or by definition, if the operation takes place in the order of abstract intellectual knowledge. The very word "definition" reveals the relationship between the two operations of defining and separating. To define is "to mark the limits or boundaries of." The definition of a notion therefore marks the limits, or boundaries, that separate it from other notions. This twofold operation, or, rather, this twofold effect of one and the same operation, is what classical philosophy used to express in saying that form is the *ratio*, or "reason," of the thing. Inasmuch as it is "reason," form is that in any reality which makes it intelligible (*Webster's*, p. 828). This "reason" (*ratio, logos*) can be experienced by sense, as when sight perceives the unity of an arabesque in space, or when hearing perceives the unity of a melodic line in time. In any case, the definition, reason, or intelligible formula of a thing results from its form, whose function it is to gather together a multiplicity of elements and to include them in the unity of a distinct being.

From this point of view, the Greek notion of form entails, as its highest characteristics, totality, wholeness, completion, and perfection. When the privation that was in matter has been replaced with a being fully determined by its form, the process of becoming is completed. For the same reason, this process is said to have reached its "end." Here again, language has its own logic. In the light of its Latin etymology, that is "perfect" which "has all the properties naturally belonging to it." In other words, it is that which has been "perfected." In the light of the Greek etymology of the word, that is perfect which has attained its end. In a remarkable passage of his *Physics* (III, 6, 207a, 12–14), in which he strives to establish that to be unfinished is also to be imperfect, Aristotle remarks: "*Whole* and *complete* are either quite identical or closely akin. Nothing is complete [*teleion*] which has no end [*telos*]; and the end is a limit."

It now remains for us to realize the fact that all this analysis is dominated by the notion of form. For, indeed, the sole function of matter is to be the receiver of some form, to be informed by it, and thus to pave the way for determinations of a still higher type. From the beginning of this process to its end, form is the active energy that, in its effort to fulfill the obscure yearning of matter, quickens it from within and gives rise to fully constituted beings.

To this analysis the ready objection is: what is it about? Is this a description of the generation of natural beings, or is it a description of the production of works of art? It is both. One of the most important lessons we can learn from Aristotle is that, distinct as they are, natural causality and artistic causality are far from being unrelated. Nature works as a determined and unconscious artist, while artists work as free and more or less clearly conscious natures. This philosophy of being is, at one and the same time, a philosophy of nature and a philosophy of art.

To be sure, the philosophers who undertake to deduce from their ontology or their phenomenology some systematic interpretation of the fine arts, or of the various classes of works of art, are usually led to conclusions widely different from those of Aristotle. On the contrary, it is worth noticing that when they undertake to draw a philosophical interpretation of art from the direct observation and analysis of art itself, modern aestheticians, even though they have little use for Aristotle, spontaneously rediscover the fundamental notions of Aristotelian philosophy. If Aristotelian forms were not endowed with a dynamic spontaneity closely similar to life, nothing would happen in the order of nature any more than in that of art. Every time we start talking about matters, forms, and the "life of forms," our mind is simply recapturing ancient intuitions that are as valid today as they ever were. At any rate, there is no reason for deciding a priori that these intuitions are not worth testing in an introduction to the ontology of painting.

2. Nothingness and Creation

T H E notion of form is familiar to painters, but it presupposes other notions whose presence in their mind is certain, even though it is not always perceived with complete clarity. The obscurity of these notions is due to their high degree of abstraction, itself inseparable from the mystery of being. Yet the most elementary aesthetic experience attests the reality of their objects.

Let us consider music. Its very existence presupposes that of silence. We recognize as nonmusically gifted the well-known class of persons whom music inspires at once with an irresistible urge to talk. The reason for this is that talking is making noise and that to make noise is to make music impossible. Hence, on a larger scale, the many precautions taken by the conductors of orchestras to ensure complete silence at the beginning of any concert or any operatic performance. The existence of musical sounds presupposes the absolute nothingness of all other sounds. In this sense, music can be said to be created *ex nihilo musicae,* just about as the world is said to have been created by God from a nothingness of world, or as being was first created from a nothingness of being. There is nothing paradoxical in such statements. On the contrary, they could rather be reproached with stating what is too obvious to stand in need of restatement—namely, that the nonmusic that is silence is a prerequisite for the creation of music.

Let us now consider the poet. Confronted as he is with his sheet of white paper, he sees it as the place of infinite poetic possibilities, any one of which can materialize precisely because none of them is already there. The same remark applies to the canvas, wood panel, or wall selected by the painter as the support of his future painting. Whatever its nature, the first care of the painter will be to prime it—that is, to lay on it a coating or preparation that will ensure its perfect uniformity and neutrality with respect to any possible pattern of lines and colors it may have later on to receive. This initial nothingness of figures corresponds to the nothingness of sounds that is the silence created by conductors at the beginning of a musical performance. Like music, painting can be said to be, in a certain sense, created from nothing.[8]

After priming his canvas, the first thing usually done by a painter is to sketch an outline of his future work. This, of course, is an extremely complex operation in which intelligence, imagination, and draftsmanship are equally involved, but we can arbitrarily simplify it to facilitate analysis. More precisely, we can consider in it the sole initial motion of the hand whereby a painter (or a child) delineates the first outline on a sheet of white paper. Even reduced to these simple terms, the question evokes at

8. It is remarkable that modern artists have sometimes spontaneously resorted to the language of Holy Scripture in expressing their own experience on this point. For instance, speaking of his glass pictures, which he began by drawing with a needle on a blackened piece of glass, Paul Klee found it natural to say: "I begin logically with chaos, that is only natural" (Grohmann, *Paul Klee,* p. 115). Speaking of Piet Mondrian: "To create emptiness is the principal act. And this is true creation, because this emptiness is positive; it contains the germ of the absolutely new." (Michel Seuphor, *L'Art abstrait,* p. 120.)

once such a variety of answers that it remains necessary to make a further choice or, at least, to adopt a certain order.

Expressed in the simplest possible terms, the result of this initial operation is to make "some thing" appear where, heretofore, there was "no thing." This is what is meant by the term "creation" when it is applied to works of art. In this, art is unique, and the fact is especially evident in the case of the plastic arts such as design, drawing, engraving, or painting.

In a loose sense, all the productions of the human mind can be called its creations. Science is something added to nature by the minds of scientists, but it is not another thing added by scientists to the world of already existing things. Science is not an artifact. It is not even a mental image of reality that we could conceive as duplicating and enriching it in the mind of the scientist. As a construction of the mind, science remains contained within the very reality it strives to describe. And what is true of science is also true of philosophy, particularly of metaphysics. The aim and scope of philosophy is to know the ultimate nature of reality. At a different level, and by methods different from those of science, metaphysics, too, is essentially speculative; its ultimate aim and purpose is not to produce a new being, or thing, but, rather, to know given reality exactly as it is. To the extent that it is art, painting is an activity specifically different from both scientific and metaphysical cognition.[9]

This does not mean that there is no art in science and that a philosopher cannot be, at the same time, an artist.[10] The unity of the human mind is such that, just as there is intellectual knowledge in all that man does, or makes, there seldom is complete absence of art in what man knows. Elegance is a quality highly prized in mathematical demonstrations. The same elegance is perceptible in the dialogues of Plato, so much so that some of them—

9. See E. Gilson, "Art et métaphysique," *Revue de métaphysique et de morale,* XXIII, No. 1 ᵇⁱˢ (Jan., 1916), 244–46.

10. Thomas Aquinas has noted that "even in speculative matters there is something by way of work"; we *make* speeches, reasonings, demonstrations, expositions, etc. The arts related to the operations of the mind, and in which the body does not share, are called, for this very reason, *liberal* arts: *Summa theologiae,* Ia, IIae, 57, 3, reply to obj. 3. — On the many different answers given to the question "What is art?" see the excellent ch. III, "The Meanings of Art," in Thomas Munro, *The Arts and Their Interrelations,* pp. 49–109.

for instance, his *Symposium*—constitute in themselves exceptionally perfect specimens of literary art. But this is not our question. Even if it is
truly aesthetic in nature, mathematical elegance is entirely at the service
of cognition: it aims to achieve an expression of truth highly satisfactory
to the mind. As to such works of art as Plato's *Symposium*, what of philosophy they contain could be stated in a much simpler, shorter, and less
artistic way without losing any of its truth value, although it would lose all
its beauty and much of its persuasive force. But this reduction of art to
any kind of cognitive process is particularly impossible in the case of
painting. The work of the painter is there, materially present in space, for
everyone to see. While a scientist is explaining his science, he himself and
his science occupy the same place in the lecture room; when a painter
presents his works to the public, he himself and his paintings do not occupy
the same space in the exhibition room. This is what we mean in saying that
the art of painting is not a particular species included in the genus "cognition."

This point is of decisive importance, and the answers to so many other
problems depend upon it that we should not let important difficulties pass
unnoticed. One of the best known follows from the popular definition of
art commonly attributed to the novelist Émile Zola: art is a fragment of
nature seen through a temperament. If this were true, nothing would be
more common than artistic creativity, for, indeed, each and every man
has a temperament through which he cannot help seeing nature, but very
few men are endowed by nature with the gifts that it takes to create works
of art worthy of the name. This elementary confusion lies at the origin of
many pseudo-artistic vocations. The most exquisite sensitiveness to natural
beauty requires neither science, nor philosophy, nor even any kind of intellectual culture in general; between the charm of nature and ourselves,
there is nothing, but between our sensibility and any painting that we may
attempt to do, there is art. In the case of painting, art is not nature seen
through a temperament; rather, it is the ability to create a new being that
nobody would ever see, either in nature or otherwise, unless the art of the
painter caused it to exist.

A similar formula, attributed to Francis Bacon, defines art as "man added to nature" (*homo additus naturae*), and it raises similar difficulties. Like so many other brilliant definitions, this one does not bear the acid test of critical examination. Since man is part and parcel of nature, he cannot be added to it. Rather than as man added to nature, art should be conceived as man adding to nature, or, better still, as nature enriching itself by all the additions that it receives at the hands of man. As has been said, the painter is neither a philosopher nor a scientist in whose mind nature mirrors itself; but he is not, at the same time, one of those engineers whose cleverness harnesses the forces of nature and puts them at our disposal; he is one of the creative forces of nature, in this sense at least, that he gives existence to certain beings that, in nature, nothing else than himself could possibly have produced. And not only nothing else, but no one else. It is not evident that, at the present stage of scientific progress, the premature death of a great scientist renders impossible the scientific discoveries that a longer life would have enabled him to make. On the contrary, the death of an artist certainly brings to a close the production of the kind of painting that bears the imprint of his hand. Many men can now know the paintings and enjoy them, but no other man than himself could cause them to exist. The lineage of these beings, which resemble one another as the children of the same father, is now extinct, and neither the admiration nor the zeal and cleverness of his most faithful pupils will ever increase it by a single unit. The creative artist is for us the only empirically observable example of a force analogous to the still more mysterious one in virtue of which the works of nature come into being. No painting, drawing, or etching done by anyone else will ever replace those which a still longer life would have enabled Matisse himself to create. The death of a great painter is an irretrievable loss of substance for the world.[11]

In the light of what precedes, it may well be asked if paintings should

11. See the epigraph (borrowed from Gabriele d'Annunzio's *Il Fuoco*) to our essay of 1915 on "Art et métaphysique": "Ah, Stelio, t'aspettavo! Riccardo Wagner è morto. — Il mondo parve diminuito di valore." ("Ah, Stelio, I was waiting for you! Richard Wagner is dead. — The world seemed to have lost some of its value.") — This page was written on the very day the Toronto radio announced the death of Henri Matisse (November 5, 1954).

simply be classified among the artifacts. And, indeed, they are artifacts, at least in the sense that they are products of human workmanship; but even granting that all paintings are artifacts, it cannot be granted that all artifacts are works of art. Considered as a genus, artifacts include, besides works of art properly so called, the densely populated class of the many and manifold tools, instruments, and machines due to the inventiveness and skill of *homo faber*. Now, whatever their differences, all these tools, instruments, and machines have this in common, that their final cause lies outside themselves. Not one of them is made for its own sake. One does not look at a timepiece (taken precisely qua timepiece) except to know what time it is. An ornamented shotgun may well be considered a work of art, but then it is no longer seen as a shotgun, whose intrinsic qualities, taken precisely qua shotgun, are foreign to the notions of ornamentation and decoration. Not so in the case of paintings. We call "tool" anything that serves as a means to an end, but, precisely, a painting cannot be used as a means to any end extrinsic to itself. A painting is not there to permit any kind of operation to be performed such as carrying goods or persons, talking from a distance, or shooting game. There is nothing that one can do *with* a painting. True enough, there is something that one can do *about* it, but, precisely, there is only one such thing, and it is to look at it. If he considers a painting as a means to any other end than its contemplation, a man does not see it as a work of art. He may look at it as an art dealer looks at the particular brand of merchandise he tries to sell, or as an investor looks at a more or less promising kind of stock. He may even consider it something to be talked about, if he is a lecturer; or something to be written about, if he is an art historian or an art critic.[12] In every one of these cases, the end of the work of art lies outside it, as in money, in a lecture to give, in an article or in a book to write; consequently, in every one of these cases, the work of art will be used as a means to another end; it will cease to act as a work of art.

12. Critics themselves do not like discussing the question of their own attitude toward works of art. It seems hardly possible to consider their position as identical with that of common art lovers. Critics are at their best when they deal with works of art with which they used to be familiar before they began to speak, or to write, as critics. At any rate, to look at a painting *in view of* writing about it must somewhat interfere with the aesthetic apprehension of the work in question.

We can now return to our question and give it an answer. The question was: in what sense is it true to say that the term "creation" fittingly designates the initial operation of artists, and quite especially of painters? The answer is: because the immediate and direct effect of such an operation is to cause something to be or, in simpler terms, because the effect of such an operation is the actual existence of a new "being." Here again a comparison with theology can help, not at all because we should attempt in any way to deduce aesthetics from theology, but rather, on the contrary, because in certain matters theology has based its inferences upon the experience of artists as well as upon the nature of art. Such is particularly the case with the notion of creation. In his *Timaeus*, under the form of a mythical narrative, Plato has presented the world as the work of a divine artist whom he called the Demiurge. We shall have later on to ask ourselves what light this dialogue throws on the nature of artistic production; for our present problem, it will prove more important to consider the notion of creation such as, on the strength of Biblical data, the Christian theologians have understood it.

If we leave aside the history of this religious notion and consider it merely as it became at the very time it reached its point of perfection, this notion points out the act by which a certain being causes other beings to be. Strictly speaking, only one being can thus be the cause of existence for other beings—namely, God, who, because he himself is the pure act of being, is eminently able to impart actual existence. Obviously, no artist can create his works, as God does, from an absolute nothingness of existence. Some material must be at his disposal before he begins his work; even the forms he creates are the forms of something, and he has seen them in nature, or in the art of his predecessors, before he himself began to create.[13] Moreover, the kind of existence an artist imparts to his works always presupposes his own existence, which, unlike that of God, is a received one. Incidentally,

13. This point is forcefully developed by Delacroix in his *Journal*, p. 386 (March 1, 1859), particularly: "But not only did these great men create nothing in the proper sense of the word, which means making *something* out of *nothing*, but in order to form their talent, or prevent it from getting rusty, they had to imitate their predecessors and, consciously or unconsciously, to imitate them almost unceasingly." Delacroix himself always had Rubens in mind; Manet could not forget Velázquez during his "Spanish period," and Picasso, perhaps the most inexhaustible source of new forms in our own times, cannot help remembering somebody or something else's style the very moment he is inventing a style of his own.

this is the reason why aesthetics need not carry its investigations beyond the philosophical level of ontology to the properly theological level of the divine act of existing. The actual existence of the matter to be informed by the art of the painter, as well as that of the painter himself, are two necessary prerequisites for the very possibility of art. The problems that belong to aesthetics presuppose the fact that there are works of art, and although aesthetics can investigate the mode of being proper to this specific class of artifacts, its inquiry stops at the level of substantial being specified and determined by its form. Actual existence is presupposed as already given, for all its ingredients, from the very beginning of the operation.

This does not mean that actual existence is not at stake in the making of a painting. The actual existence of the painting to be done is the final result that the artist intends to achieve. Since God alone is the pure act of being, no secondary cause, be it even the art of a creative artist, can conjure up a new being from total nonbeing. But the artist himself, his art, the matter and the forms he puts to use, all are enjoying an actual existence they have received from the Prime Cause. Artists can impart or communicate to their [40] works the actual existence that is their own. Some pen drawings by Corot are enough to give existence to charming landscapes that seem to be made from nothing, and almost with nothing. An etching done from a pen drawing by Pieter Brueghel succeeds in educing the most complex landscape from the blank surface of a plate. The mere interplay of the lines, ordered as they are by a supremely lucid imagination, even permits him to pretend that [41] the very Journey to Emmaus is included in this creation of his hand. In this sense, the production of plastic works of art truly extends to their very existence. Himself an existent, the painter is an efficient cause of actual existence for other existents.[14]

14. "To act is nothing else than to communicate that by which the acting being is in act" (Thomas Aquinas, *De potentia*, qu. 2, art. 1, answer). Thomas presently adds to this: "to the extent that it is possible." Now, God, who is the Prime Cause, is the pure act of Being. Consequently, "all the created causes communicate in one single effect, which is actual existence [*esse*], although each one of them has its own effects, by which they differ from one another. For instance, heat makes something to be hot, and an architect causes a house to be [*aedificator facit domum esse*]. Created causes thus agree in this, that they cause being [*conveniunt ergo in hoc quod causant esse*], but they differ in this, that while fire causes fires, an architect causes a house" (qu. 7, art. 2 answer).

GEORGES SEURAT. The Black Bow
About 1882. Black conté crayon. Private collection

MARTIN SCHONGAUER. Angel of the Annunciation
Engraving. Rosenwald Collection, National Gallery of Art, Washington

ALBRECHT DÜRER. St. Eustace
Before 1505. Engraving. Rosenwald Collection, National Gallery of Art, Washington

J.-B.-C. COROT. The Broken Bridge
About 1855. Pen, and ink. Louvre

EVNTES IN EMAVS

PIETER BRUEGHEL THE ELDER, The Journey to Emmaus
About 1555. Engraving. Rosenwald Collection, National Gallery of Art, Washington

PAUL KLEE. Uncomposed Components in Space
1929. Water color. Private collection, Bern

a. PAUL KLEE. Family Promenade: Tempo 2
1930. Pen and colored inks. Paul Klee Foundation, Bern

b. PAUL KLEE. Around the Fish
1926. Museum of Modern Art, New York

GEORGES BRÉTEGNIER. The Studio of Meissonier
1891. Engraving after the painting

EugÈne Delacroix. Corner of a Studio
About 1830. Louvre

45

MICHELANGELO. God Dividing the Light from the Darkness
1510. Fresco. Sistine Chapel, Vatican, Rome

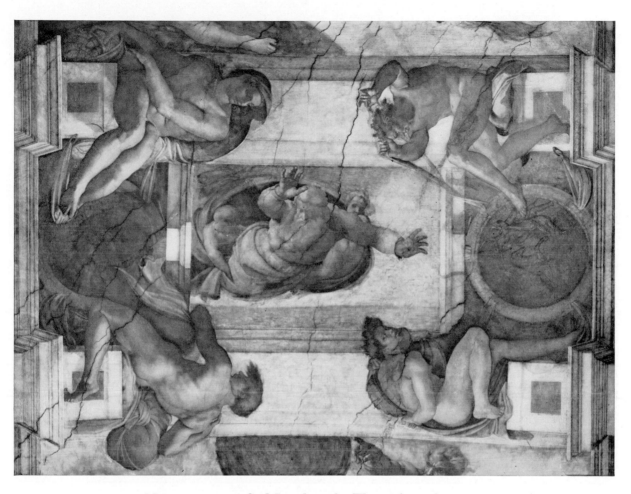

MICHELANGELO. God Dividing the Waters from the Earth
1510. Fresco. Sistine Chapel, Vatican, Rome

MICHELANGELO. The Creation of Woman
1509. Fresco. Sistine Chapel, Vatican, Rome

These notions will have to be reconsidered at a different level in discussing the proper kind of causality a painter exercises with respect to his works. For the present, let it suffice to observe that thus to relate art to metaphysics, and even to theology, is by no means to attempt a deduction of art from these lofty sciences. On the contrary, when theologians started from the visible world in order to conceive, as best they could, the invisible nature of God, they first borrowed from art the pattern of the most perfect kind of causality given in human experience, and then transcended it in order to make it attributable to God. In their effort to do so, the theologians have unveiled to us the very Idea of what an absolute artistic creation would be: an act in which, because the intellect, the power, the will, and the art of the artist are identically one with his own act of being, the total cause of the total effect is included. Artistic creation is not such an act, but it remains for us the least imperfect image there is of what the theologians call creation. And no wonder, since it is found at the origin of the notion that the theologians have formed of it. Supposing, therefore, that painters can communicate existence to their own works, we must now ascertain the sense in which it is true to say that, because they also produce forms, painters truly produce beings.

3. Form and Being

L E T us now consider the initial moment an artist's pencil, chalk, or brush begins to delineate a figure. This figure does not necessarily represent a thing. Whether it does so is irrelevant to the present problem. What matters is the fact that the figure itself *is* a thing. Even though it may consist of only one single straight line, it has a shape and a structure of its own. We distinguish at once a straight line from a circle, we give it a name, and we can always recognize it for the specified reality that it is—namely, a figure consisting of one single line lying evenly throughout its extent or, in other terms, having an invariable direction.

The characteristic property of such figures is that each of them *is* a particular way of occupying space. Our starting point is a nothingness of forms and figures. At the very beginning of our analysis, we find the painter face to face with the practically empty space represented by the uniform priming of his canvas.[15] As soon as he draws the first line or the first figure, which can be a single straight line or a single curve, the painter begins to fill up the initial vacuum at his disposal. In other words, he begins to substitute beings, or things, for nothingness. Since he is working on a plane surface—that is, in a two-dimensional space—the painter must content himself with drawing lines. In the beginning of his operations, even his figures are generally mere outlines—that is, lines suggesting the visible boundaries of the place that, were they real objects, their volumes would occupy in space. To denote it by its most general name, let us say that, whatever his pencil or his brush may design, the painter begins by creating a shape or form. We thus find ourselves confronted with one of the most baffling notions that philosophers have to handle. There would be no point in trying to avoid it under pretense that its complexity may defy analysis. For, indeed, it does, but while it is disturbingly complex, the metaphysical notion of form is constantly present in practical life and in everyday language. No man aware of what he does and says can refuse to consider it.

The reason for these difficulties is, once more, that the notion of being is

15. The notion of space should be understood as that of a painter's space. There are mathematical and physical notions of space; there even are biological ones. The pictorial notion of space is distinct from them all. It can be defined as a pure possibility of visual forms; or else, as that whose whole nature it is to be occupiable by visual forms. In occupying space, visual forms determine it, define it, enclose it, or cover it. — The notion of space must not be confused with that of "spatial element," which seems to be proper to the terminology of Paul Klee. In his "Creative Credo," Klee distinguishes four formal elements in painting: dot, line, plane, and space (Grohmann, p. 97); but space is here understood as something already determined by the painter; it is a painted space—that is, in Klee's own terms, "a cloud-like, hazy spot made with a loaded brush and including several shades." Yet these two notions fundamentally agree, for, indeed, the spatial element defined by Klee is essentially formless—that is, without definable formal determinations. In fact, some modern pictures are five tenths unpainted canvas, cardboard, masonite, or even wrongside-foremost plywood; there is no essential difference between pure paintable space and what Klee calls a spatial element. Despite the confusion of his terminology, Piet Mondrian does not seem to think differently: "At this point, I became conscious that reality is form *and* space. Nature reveals forms in space. *Actually all* is space, form as well as what we see as empty space. To create unity, art has to follow not nature's aspect, but what nature really is. Appearing in oppositions, nature is unity; form is limited space concrete only through its determination. Art has *to determine space as well as form* and to create *the equivalence of these two factors*." (Mondrian, "Toward the True Vision of Reality," in *Plastic Art and Pure Plastic Art,* p. 13. Cf. p. 19: "The predominance . . .")

involved in the discussion. Generally speaking, "Form is the aspect under which a thing appears, especially as distinguished from substance or color" (*Webster's*). For us to see a form, then, practically amounts to seeing a thing, or the figure of a thing. Consequently, it amounts to seeing a being, or the figure of a being. There is no doubt about the equivalence of these notions in common language. We recognize objects by their forms, and each typical form is signified by a distinct name. In human experience, the two notions of being and of form cannot possibly be separated.

The preceding analysis chiefly bears upon cases in which a drawn or painted form is the symbol of a natural object, such as a tree or an animal, or else of any artifact known to us and designated by a common name, such as a "table" or a "house." But the same conclusion applies even to simple lines or figures that signify nothing else besides themselves. Contemporary artists and critics are agreed in distinguishing between representational art, whose forms imitate the visual appearance of things, and abstract art (i.e., nonrepresentational art), whose forms represent nothing other than themselves. From the point of view of our problem, there is no difference whatever between these two cases. For, indeed, even considered in themselves and apart from any possible signification, straight lines, angles, diagonals, triangles, rectangles, curves, circles, spirals—in short, all possible geometrical figures—are in themselves forms and, consequently, are definite objects. [42]

Abstract painters and representational painters are likewise creating forms [43a, b] and, by the same token, beings.[16]

There is something mysterious in this divisive function exercised by

16. That abstraction is creation is the common root of many notions that have become fundamental in modern painting. Most of them are found, gathered together, in the contribution of Paul Klee to *Schöpferische Konfession* ("Creative Credo"). First, "Art does not render the visible; rather, it makes visible." Secondly, since to design is to define, to separate, or to set a part of space apart from the rest of space, "a tendency towards the abstract belongs to the essence of linear expression" (to abstract, from the Latin *abstrahere:* to separate by an operation of the mind). With deep insight, Klee has perceived at once the ultimate implication of this property of lines: "The purer the artist's work (i.e., the more he stresses the formal elements on which linear expression is based), the less well equipped he is for the realistic rendering of visible things" (Grohmann, p. 97). These remarks of Paul Klee, if meditated and understood, clearly show that far from representing a belated and decadent form of the art of painting, non-imitational art is the development of one of the most essential tendencies of design.

forms. One should perhaps rather say that to be a form essentially consists in occupying a certain portion of space by means of an outline that separates it from all the rest. Moving pictures and television have not been slow in exploiting the feeling of passionate interest we all experience in watching the tip of a painting brush or a pencil while it actually delineates objects, or men and women, that seem to spring from nothingness before our very eyes. And yet, the hand of the unseen artist does nothing more than to isolate, within the uniform indetermination of empty space, a certain number of zones circumscribed by their respective outlines or determined by their plastic properties. In this sense, to define a being, to set it apart, to abstract it, and to produce it are one and the same operation.

This truth can be verified by any onlooker watching a painter at work. Still more simply, it can be personally experienced by anybody attempting to perform the same operation. And it can be described at the various levels of theology, philosophy, or plain artistic experience.

In describing the creative activity of God, theologians usually distinguish two effects of the divine power. The first one is creation properly so called, whose effect it is to confer existence upon creatures. The second one consists in distinguishing among creatures, and it necessarily attends the act of creation since, without it, even God could not create a plurality of creatures. The only way to have two beings is to produce two separate beings. Hence, in his *Summa theologiae* (I, 47), the words used by Thomas Aquinas: "After considering the production of creatures, we must turn to the consideration of the *distinction* among them." This is in no way a deductive inference. Thomas Aquinas simply takes it for granted that to cause a plurality of beings is to distinguish each one of them from the rest. More remarkably still, to make sure that the distinction and plurification of things is included in the creative act of God, our theologian quotes a text borrowed from Holy Writ, which is, in this case, from Genesis. And, indeed, the sacred book uses the same expression twice in order to say that the multiplication of created beings was an effect of their mutual separation by God.[17] In the be-

17. Cf. Gen. 1:14: "Let there be lights . . . to divide the day and the night"; 1:18: "to divide the light and the darkness." These expressions are the source of the intimate

ginning "the earth was void and empty, and darkness was upon the face of
the deep"; then God made light, that is, he "divided" the light from the
darkness (Gen. 1 : 4). The rest of the text is known: God "divided" the waters that were under the firmament from those above the firmament (Gen.
1 : 6–7). Even the creation of Eve is an act of separation. But this divisive
action itself follows from a still more primitive one that we can attempt to
describe, this time with the help of philosophers.

[46, 47]

[48]

As has been said, things numerically differ from one another, because,
within a certain species, each of them has its own matter by which it is individuated; but before this individual distinction within a certain species,
there is a specific distinction between species and species within a certain
genus. Now, what is the cause of this specific distinction? Once more, it is
what philosophers call form. This time, it means "the essential nature of a
thing as distinguished from the matter in which it is embodied." Plato
calls it an Idea—that is, the ideal pattern of a material thing. In a more
Aristotelian way, form can be defined as "that in a thing which determines
it in its kind or species" (*Webster's*). In short, form is what makes a thing
the specified being it is and, by the same token, distinguishes it from all
individuals belonging in a different species. To make a thing what it is is
the same as to distinguish or separate it from all the rest.

In order not to interrupt this analysis, we beg to push it slightly further
than is strictly necessary for our present purpose. Among the many meanings
of form, there is one that, perfectly classical in Latin (*formosus,* beautiful),

relationship established by the Scholastics between the work of creation and that of
distinction. The same Scriptural texts have been quoted, in full awareness of their significance for aesthetics, by Jeanne Hersch, *L'Être et la forme,* pp. 103–10. For instance:
"In the beginning God created heaven, *and* earth." First separation: as soon as God
creates, he separates—but the earth was not yet separated within itself. "The earth was
formless. . . ." Ever since the first distinction, surfaces come to be: "and darkness was
upon the *face* of the deep. . . ." When God creates light, it looks as though he first ascer-
tained its goodness, but it is its *separation* from darkness that definitively gives it existence: "And God saw the light that it was good; and he *divided* the light from the darkness." "And God said: Let there be a firmament made *amidst* the waters; and let it
divide the waters from the waters. And God made a firmament, and *divided* the waters
that were under the firmament from those that were above the firmament, and it was so."
Thus the work of creation implies a work of distinction, before which there was nothing,
except the Creator. Only owing to separation can there be reunion, repartition, order,
form.

is now archaic in English and yet, unless we are mistaken, still remains understandable. In this ancient sense, it used to mean "pleasing external appearance; beauty" (*Webster's*). We shall have later on to ask why the cause of being is, at the same time, the cause of beauty. For the present, let it suffice to note that every one of these notions naturally leads to the others. Yet the central one is that of the relationship between the two notions of creation and distinction.

Among the properties of form, the most striking one is its aptitude to confer being upon the matter that receives it. In the structure of being, the primitive element is the act in virtue of which a certain thing is, or exists; but existence itself is that of some actually existing thing, and since a thing is what it is owing to its form, it is through its form that it receives existence. Hence the classical position according to which existence comes to things through form.[18] If this is true, we were right in saying that artists, and particularly painters, exercise an activity that closely resembles an act of creation, not only because they communicate actual existence, but also because they fashion and mold the very being they cause to exist. By imparting form to a given material, they turn it into a subject capable of actual existence —that is to say, into a substance. Ancient as it is, this doctrine is still valid in our own day; contemporary exponents of existentialism have reinterpreted it with penetration;[19] and even among painters themselves, some perfectly sober minds do not hesitate to speak of their works as of so many creations

18. Boethius, *De Trinitate*, 2: "Omne namque esse ex forma est"—i.e., "For every being is in virtue of form" (tr. H. F. Stewart and E. K. Rand, Loeb Classical Library, pp. 8–9). Among many other texts: Thomas Aquinas, *Summa theologiae*, I, 9, 2; I, 14, 4; *Contra gentiles*, I, 68, 3. The notion that existence comes to things through form is not hard to understand if one relates it to this almost identical one, that to be always is to be a certain kind of being determined or specified by a form. It is strictly impossible for us to conceive a being otherwise than as a specified being. See Thomas Aquinas, *Summa theologiae*, I, 17, 3. For a commentary, E. Gilson, *Being and Some Philosophers*, pp. 164–66.

19. This essentially creative nature of the art of painting is the central theme of the already quoted book of Jeanne Hersch, *L'Être et la forme*. For instance (p. 205): "He [the Poet] is, at the scale of man, the most integral creator; without creating from nothing, he makes something exist that did not exist. He creates by imparting form to something given—that is, by conferring upon it existential coherency."

ex nihilo.[20] And, indeed, *insofar as its artistic mode of existence alone is at stake,* nothing of it is given to the painter in natural reality.

The same problem can be discussed at the level of art itself and wholly apart from any theological or metaphysical implications. It then becomes a question of knowing if paintings are a particular form of language, whose function it is to impart knowledge, or if, on the contrary, it is of the essence of a painting to be a self-signifying substance and an addition to the sum total of already existing reality.

Delacroix is sometimes quoted as having said: "A picture is nothing but a bridge between the soul of the artist and that of the spectator."[21] Even if it were complete, this formula should not be mistaken for an attempt, on the part of Delacroix, to define paintings. Painters themselves know very well what paintings are. They are not likely to mistake them for bridges, especially not for the particularly unsubstantial bridges that span the chasms between souls. When he wrote these lines, the point that Delacroix was enforcing was that, in paintings, "cold accuracy is not art." He then was criticizing the so-called conscientiousness of "the great majority of painters," which, to him, was "nothing but perfection in the art of *boring*. If it were possible, these fellows would labour with equal care over the backs of their pictures." As Delacroix saw it, the reason for their error is simple.

20. We are simply copying Constable, who was neither an abstract painter nor a metaphysician: "It is the business of a painter not to contend with nature, and put such a scene, a valley filled with imagery fifty miles long, on a canvas of a few inches; but to make something out of nothing, in attempting which, he must almost of necessity become poetical" (Leslie, p. 124). And rightly so. In his *Treatise on Landscape Painting* (p. 11), André Lhote has this perfect definition: "The representational element, that is, the part that does not contribute to the structure of the picture." In other words, whatever is not representational in a painting presupposes a creative act of the painter. On the other hand, an element is not representational because it represents, but because, doing nothing else, it performs no plastic function in the painting.

21. Quoted by Thomas Bodkin, *The Approach to Painting*, p. 56. This author does not make the mistake of quoting this sentence as a definition of painting. His interpretation of it is that, once we recognize the purpose and the stability of a picture, "we ought to pass over it with all possible speed; and we can then look back at leisure to enjoy the grace of its proportions, the quality of its material and the skill that was spent upon its building." Who could affirm that Delacroix had nothing like this in mind? But it is at least certain that he also had in mind something else—namely, that a picture is not a word, a symbol, a sign, but a thing.

It is that most painters conceive pictures as means of conveying knowledge; so they never tire of explaining, whereas, on the contrary, the privilege of pictures is to enable mind to speak to mind, "and not knowledge to knowledge." In short, a picture is a bridge precisely because it does not teach; it does not explain; it does not talk; it just is one more thing among other things.[22]

The true meaning of this alleged definition of painting is therefore different from what it seems to be. The veritable intention of Delacroix was to contrast painting with literature, but, in so doing, he found himself led to observe that, while writers content themselves with explaining their thought by means of symbols, painters confront onlookers with concrete objects, real things, or beings, which they themselves have made and before which we all find ourselves in the same situation as before the things of nature. For, indeed, nature does not explain; nature does not impart knowledge; nature simply is there for us to see. In like manner, instead of giving us words to understand, painting places under our eyes realities on which to meditate. Whence, according to Delacroix, the superiority of painting (and, incidentally, of music) to literature. With deep insight, Delacroix observes that the words that a writer has to use always lose something of the thought that they strive to convey, whereas, when he meditates in the presence of a picture, the onlooker has the thing itself before him, including that in it which is not expressible by means of words.[23]

22. " 'In painting, and especially in portraiture,' says Mme Cavé in her treatise, 'mind speaks to mind, and not knowledge to knowledge.' This observation, which may be more profound than she knows herself, is an indictment of pedantry in execution. I have said to myself over and over again that painting, i.e. the material process which we call painting, is no more than the pretext, the bridge between the mind of the artist and that of the beholder." (*Journal*, p. 127 [July 18, 1850].) Cf. "To sum up, the painter says nothing, he keeps silent, and I still prefer it that way" (*Lettres de van Gogh à son frère Théo*, p. 469 [not dated, but later than September 17, 1888]).

23. "When I have painted a fine picture, I have not given expression to a thought! That is what they say. What fools people are! They would strip painting of all its advantages. A writer has to say almost everything in order to make himself understood, but in painting it is as if some mysterious bridge were set up between the spirit of the persons in the picture and the beholder. The beholder sees figures, the external appearance of nature, but inwardly he meditates; the true thinking that is common to all men. Some give substance to it in writing, but in so doing they lose the subtle essence. Hence, grosser minds are more easily moved by writers than by painters or musicians. The art

The consecution of ideas, here, is clear. Since the painter creates a form, by means of which he gives existence to a new being, all his obligations are to the very form that he creates and to the new being to which his art aims to impart existence, not to any external object, being, or landscape that he might try to imitate.[24] This fact, as Delacroix aptly remarks, compels even the most realistically minded painters to "use certain conventions of composition or of execution."[25] These conventions simply express the exigencies proper to the form that the painter aims to embody in a certain matter.

of the painter is all the nearer to man's heart because it seems to be more material. In painting, as in external nature, proper justice is done to what is finite and to what is infinite, in other words, to what the soul finds inwardly moving in objects that are known through the senses alone." (*Journal*, pp. 7–8 [October 8, 1822].) "In Mme de Staël I find exactly the same method that I use to develop my own ideas about painting. This art, like music, *is higher than thought*; hence it has the advantage over literature, through its vagueness." (*Journal*, p. 24 [January 26, 1824].) — On this notion: "*Vagueness*. In one of my little blue note-books there is a quotation from Obermann on vagueness. The church of Saint-Jacques at Dieppe in the evening. Painting is vaguer than poetry in spite of the definite appearance it presents to the eyes. One of its greatest charms." (*Journal*, p. 332 [January 13, 1857].) Cf. *Journal*, p. 201 (October 20, 1853). — An important passage of Delacroix, too long to be quoted here, will be found in the Appendix II, pp. 312–13.

24. Albert Gleizes and Jean Metzinger, *Du Cubisme*. For instance (p. 8): "Let the picture imitate nothing and let it present its *raison d'être* in its nudity." Yet (p. 17), the same authors grant that "the memory of natural forms cannot be absolutely banished, at least now." — Cf. Léonce Rosenberg, *Cubisme et tradition*. These sixteen pages are a reprint of the preface written by Rosenberg for the catalogue of an exhibition of French paintings at Geneva, February, 1920. A quotation of *Philebus*, 51, is found in pp. 6–8 of the reprint: "I do not mean by beauty of form such beauty as that of animals or pictures . . . but . . . understand me to mean straight lines and circles, and the plane or solid figures which are formed out of them . . . " etc. (*The Dialogues of Plato*, tr. B. Jowett, IV, 625).

25. The fundamental convention that all painters have to observe is the necessity arbitrarily to construct a self-contained whole endowed with a unity of its own. This, Delacroix says, is one of the essential differences between painting and photography. "In a photograph of a view you see no more than a portion cut from a panorama; the edges are as interesting as the centre of the picture and you have to guess at the scene of which you are shown merely a fragment, apparently chosen at random. In such a fragment, the details have as much importance as the principal object and, more often than not, obstruct the view because they occur in the foreground. . . . The most striking photographs are those in which certain gaps are left, owing to the failure of the process itself to give a complete rendering. Such gaps bring relief to the eyes which are thereby concentrated on only a limited number of objects. . . . And what shall we say of the disturbing effects produced by actual perspective, especially where human figures are concerned? . . . The confirmed realist corrects this inflexible perspective which, because of its very accuracy, falsifies our view of objects. Even when we look at nature, our imagination constructs the picture . . ." etc. (*Journal*, pp. 387–88 [September 1, 1859].)

Their common justification is to keep out of the art of painting a cause of corruption that Delacroix has consistently opposed under the name of "realism." By this word, Delacroix understood the attitude of those who see the ideal of the art of painting in a faithful rendering of things and beings as they are in external reality. If it is a question of duplicating reality, no sculpture done by an artist will ever equal a plaster cast done from nature. Nor will any painting ever equal the accuracy and completeness of a good photograph. But a true painter does not borrow his subject from reality; he does not even content himself with arranging the material provided by reality so as to make it acceptable to the eye. His starting point is fantasy, imagination, fiction, and all the elements of reality that do not agree with the creature imagined by the painter have to be ruthlessly eliminated. In [44] this sense, "Realism should be described as the antipodes of art." At the very least, it is one of the most dangerous temptations that beset the artist in his work. It is imperative that he should reject from his models, however real and even pleasant they may be in reality, all the elements that are not at least compatible with the plastic form of the work of art to be made. Hence the remark often made by Delacroix: "The first of all principles is the need to make sacrifices." [26] This principle is but another name for the primacy [45] of creation over imitation in works of art.

In adopting this attitude, Delacroix was announcing and even initiating a movement whose consequences are still felt in contemporary painting, but he also was positing a principle whose consequences were, or should have been, far reaching in the history of the philosophy of art, in art criticism,

26. *Journal*, pp. 396–97 (February 22, 1860). This passage is a criticism of the notion of "realism" in art, especially in sculpture and painting. By "realism" Delacroix means the servile imitation of reality. Against this attitude, Delacroix maintains: (1) that the starting point of art is imagination, invention; (2) that this invention, or imagination, or "personal feeling," is the only thing that can give unity to a work of art (nature itself has no such unity); (3) that in order to create this unity, the painter must eliminate from his work all that is irrelevant to it: "Personal feeling alone can give unity, and the one way of achieving this is to show only what deserves to be seen" (p. 397); (4) this systematic elimination of what, because it is irrelevant to the painting in question, does not deserve to be seen is what Delacroix calls "sacrifice"; in this sense, the need to make sacrifices exactly measures the distance between art and the reproduction of physical reality.

and, generally speaking, in all the disciplines that are in any way concerned with the interpretation of painting.

The first corollary of what Delacroix said is that the final cause of all the operations performed by the painter is to cause the existence of a self-subsisting and autonomous being—namely, the particular painting freely conceived by his imagination. From this first corollary, important consequences follow concerning what can be called the ultimate foundation for aesthetic judgments. This foundation must be sought in the very essence of the works of art under discussion, and in nothing else. This does not mean that works of art are not subject to other tribunals judging them on the strength of other rules, such as those of religion or of morality; but it does mean that, if it is a question of judging a painting precisely qua work of art, the principles to be followed in judging it should be borrowed from the notion of art understood as the creative activity that has just been defined. In the case of painting, these principles should be borrowed from the very essence of the class of beings that we call paintings.

Hence, what the painter is attempting, consciously or not, is to bring to completion the new being to which his art is imparting existence. For him to succeed is to create such a being, just as not to succeed is to fail to create it. There is no other criterion of success or failure in the art of painting than this golden rule: a painting is good when it actually exists as the fully constituted being that art can make it; inversely, a painting is bad when it fails to achieve actual existence as a fully constituted being. As has rightly been said, the true work of art is "the one which *is*." In other words, if it is a question of judging them as works of art, paintings are not to be justified, or condemned, by norms of morality, or by norms of any kind of knowledge, historic, scientific, philosophic, or otherwise, but "by ontological norms only." [27] One could not better express the fundamental truth that all

27. "This is where the power of *making to be*, at the human level, appears in the purest and most absolute manner. For it seems evident to me that, in art, the form is not to be justified by norms of moral goodness, nor by norms of true knowledge, but by ontological norms only. This simply signifies that the true work of art is the one that is—that is to say, the work of art whose form truly is a capture of being, under the formal conditions imposed by the human mode of existence. So also, in art, the misfit is not malice, nor is it ugliness understood in the sense of disobedience to a set of aesthetic

problems related to paintings must ultimately be answered in terms of being.

Art criticism is directly interested in the recognition of this truth. There is a positive art criticism. Whether what it praises in a painting is its composition, its coloring, or its execution, positive criticism always is about some actually existing reality, which can be perceived by the critic, pointed out by him, and then seen by all. On the contrary, there is nothing harder, nor perhaps more vain, than to indulge in negative criticism and to attempt to justify it.[28] If a bad painting is something that, as a work of art, has failed to achieve actual existence, negative criticism can do little more than either to overlook the presence of a reality that escapes the eye of the critic or else futilely to point out the empty place where something that ought to be there is not to be found. Now, there is no way to prove that something does not exist: between what one does not see and what is really not there, the distinction is not easy to make. If an artistic misfit is, on the whole, a non-entity, the best attitude toward it is silence. As the saying goes: "It does not exist."

These general rules are of little help when it comes to judging particular works of art from the point of view of their own structure. The starting point of this inquiry was the fact that paintings are physical beings—more precisely, solid bodies—endowed with an individuality of their own. It now

rules, nor is it ignorance or deficiency in knowledge, but, rather, it is inexistence, non-being, lack of a coherency whose ontological efficacy would be due to the force of one single law." (Hersch, pp. 17–18.) These lines so perfectly express what we are striving to establish that we would not hesitate to assume the responsibility for what they say. Only one line ("under the formal conditions imposed by the human mode of existence") recalls to us that, writing under the spell of idealism, the author has perhaps not yet found the true ontology of her phenomenology.

28. Even Baudelaire, who had a good command of words, sounds somewhat naïve in his negative criticisms. For instance, concerning Horace Vernet's *Prise de la Smalah d'Abd-el-Kader:* "It is truly painful to see an intelligent man floundering about in such a mess of horror. Good Heavens, has M. Horace Vernet never seen the works of Rubens, Veronese, Tintoretto, Jouvenet?" (*The Mirror of Art*, p. 9.) We all have seen them, and still we cannot paint as Veronese did. Again (p. 16): "Boulanger's *Sainte Famille* is detestable. His *Bergers de Virgile*, mediocre. His *Baigneuses*, a little better than Duval-Lecamuses or Maurins; but his *Portrait d'homme* is a good piece of painting." Again (p. 17): "Schnetz. Alas! what is to be done with these vast Italian pictures? We are in 1845, but we are very afraid that Schnetz will be giving us the same kind of thing ten years from now." The truth of these appreciations is not at stake; we only wish to suggest their utter vacuity. When negativism in judgments extends even to paintings that have not yet been done, it seems to overstep its own limits.

begins to appear that, still more than it is an individual, each painting that meets the requirements of a true work of art is a completely self-sufficient system of internal relations regulated by its own laws. In this sense, paintings are mutually irreducible beings, each of which needs to be understood and judged from the point of view of its own structure. Painters have often made this remark, and although art critics and art historians have seldom subscribed to it (for it seems to make art too easy for artists and criticism too hard for critics), it can be said that, in this case, the truth about art is again to be found on the side of the artists.

A remarkable expression of this truth is to be found in a saying attributed by Leslie to Constable. As the family physician, Dr. Gooch, had just said in Constable's presence that he found "every individual case of disease a new study," the painter "applied this to painting, and said 'In like manner every truly original picture is a separate study, and governed by laws of its own; so that what is right in one, would be often entirely wrong if transferred to another.' " [29] To the extent that it succeeds in achieving its own mode of artistic existence, a painting is justified in being exactly what it actually is.

These conclusions hang on the mysterious power that forms have to create organic ontological units, that is, beings. Like all the concepts that are inseparable from the primary notion of being, the concept of form cannot be reduced to any other one by which to elucidate its meaning. The only other way to approach it than through straight metaphysical speculation is to ask painters themselves what it means to them when they envisage it from the concrete point of view of their own art.

29. Leslie, p. 281. — Cf. the fragment of a letter of William Collins to Leslie (pp. 278–79): "I mentioned to you his [Constable's] admirable remark upon the composition of a picture, namely, that its parts were all so necessary to it as a whole, that it resembled a sum in arithmetic; take away or add the smallest item, and it must be wrong." "The world is wide; no two days are alike, nor even two hours; neither were there ever two leaves of a tree alike since the creation of the world; and the genuine productions of art, like those of nature, are all distinct from each other" (p. 273).

CHAPTER FIVE

THE CAUSALITY OF FORM

THE poetics of Aristotle is dominated by the notion of what he called "imitation." What he himself understood by that word is not always clear (for instance, in the case of music), but there is no doubt that, in his own mind, art was essentially imitative and that the diversity of the fine arts was due to the diverse media to which they resorted in order to imitate. In all arts, the means used by artists consist of a form and of something that is informed by it. We have called that something a "matter." Some artists use language as a medium to be informed by their art, and the result is poetry. Others, such as painters, use color and form as means to imitate diverse things, and the result is painting (*Poetics*, I).

The same notions to which Aristotle resorts in describing the structure of works of art apply in his doctrine to the structure of natural beings. For instance, in his *Metaphysics* (V, 2, 1013a, 24) Aristotle lists, as the first one among the four natural causes, "that from which, as immanent material, a thing comes into being, e.g. the bronze is the cause of the statue and the silver of the saucer."[1] As to the form, which is here described as the pattern (*paradeigma*), its notion is obviously derived from that of the models after which artists mold the matter of their work. The shape or figure of anything is inseparably tied up, in Aristotle's mind, with the notion of a typical scheme that, although individuated by accidents, remains one and the same

---

1. We are quoting Aristotle's *Poetics* from the translation by Ingram Bywater (included in *The Basic Works of Aristotle*, ed. Richard McKeon, pp. 1455–87). The *Metaphysics* is quoted from the translation by W.D. Ross (same volume, pp. 682–926). — Interesting considerations in F. Battaglia, "Forme naturalistiche e forme estetiche," *Convivium*, n.s. 5 (Sept.–Oct., 1954), pp. 513–33.

in each species. The visible forms, or shapes, of natural beings simply express their essential natures in ways that, because what is being thus informed is matter, are perceptible to sense. The two processes of nature and of art are therefore, although distinct, yet analogous and even parallel. Looking for an illustration of the relation of matter to form in nature, Aristotle does not hesitate to say: "For instance, both the art of sculpture and the bronze are causes of the statue not in respect of anything else but qua statue; not, however, in the same way, but the one as matter and the other as source of the movement" (*Metaphysics*, V, 2, 1013b, 2–9).

This last remark is worthy of note. For, indeed, the art of the sculptor, which plays in works of art the same part as form plays in the work of nature, is here described as the cause of movement. More precisely, it is the cause of the movement that turns bronze into a statue. Now, when it is a question of natural beings, what is the cause of the movement that makes them to be? It is form, of course, but, this time, instead of being a form introduced into matter from without by the art of an artist, it is form as an inner cause of the movement whose ultimate term is the actual being of the natural thing. In traditional Aristotelian metaphysics, the name of such a form considered as working from within until matter is turned into a wholly formed being is "nature."[2] And, indeed, Aristotelian nature is, before anything else, the very form considered as the cause of "the genesis of growing things" (*Metaphysics*, V, 4, 1014b, 16).

How is it that nature works consistently and coherently enough to account for the coming to be of beings answering a specific type? The answer is: because, just as it is an operating nature, form is the final cause of the genesis of the being whose form it is. In the same way as it is its principle, or beginning, the form of a natural being is what this being is striving to become and finally to be. In short, it is its end. Understood in the fullness of its meaning, the natural philosophy of Aristotle considers the good and

---

2. The Greek word for nature (*phusis*) is derived from the verb that signifies "to be born." The same remark applies to the Latin word *natura*, derived from the verbal root *nasci, natum:* to be born, born. Even the English "nature" still connotes the notion of "innate" qualities in persons or things. When a man does something as if it were in its nature to do it, we say of him that he is to the manner born.

the beautiful as the origin of the movements by which the noblest among things are brought forth. Nature chiefly works in view of goodness, art chiefly works in view of beauty, but goodness is beautiful and beauty is good. Such being the ultimate causes of all the generations that take place in Aristotle's universe, how could its Prime Mover be understood, if not as the prime and universal object of love that, directly or indirectly, all beings and all things desire? [3]

Thus understood, nature is a sort of immanent art. This traditional notion has lost much ground in the minds of our own contemporaries. Chiefly under the influence of idealism, there has been a growing tendency to sever art from nature and to set it up as a separate order whose interpretation requires other principles than those which apply to physical and biological reality. There was nothing wrong with stressing the specificity of art as distinct from nature. Especially under the form of phenomenology, which does not necessarily require the metaphysical presuppositions of idealism, recent research has accumulated useful information concerning the actual genesis of works of art. Yet, without denying the usefulness of such investigations, one may well wonder if the times are not ripe for a return to a more realistic attitude in such matters. It is not a question of identifying art with nature. As will be seen, these really are two distinct orders. But artists themselves are beings of nature, and it might prove profitable to consider their creativity as a particular instance of the general productivity of nature. At any rate, there is little to lose in attempting this approach to the function exercised by form in the genesis of paintings.

1. Form and Subject

AMONG the painters who have attempted to analyze their own activity, very few have failed to place at its origin, so to speak as its seed or germ, a

3. On this point, see Aristotle, *Metaphysics*, bk. XII, ch. 7, 1072b, 3. The theory is verified by constant aesthetic experience. In art galleries, the great masterpieces set visitors in motion; they move art lovers, without themselves being moved, simply because they are being loved. This, Aristotle says, is true of all the objects of desire. Now, being is object of desire, "but the beautiful, also, and that which is in itself desirable, are in the same column" (*Metaphysics*, XII, 6, 1072a, 34–36).

confused feeling of some painting to be done. They do not agree on its name, or always on its description, but this is not surprising, because what they have in mind is in itself something fluid, still indeterminate, and more akin to becoming than to true being.

On the contrary, most of them would agree that, in normal cases, this feeling is embodied in a more or less vague and changing image, which arises on contact with reality and, as often as not, on the occasion of some sensation. This phenomenon is dominated by the creative imagination of the artist much more than by the perceived data of reality. Everybody has experienced the suggestive power of rhythmical noises: the wheels of a railway carriage running over rails, or the singsong of drops of water heard in the silence of a sleepless night, invite the auditive imagination to inform this raw material with a melodic line, sometimes even with the unifying continuity of verse and song. Most painters are likewise used to respond to the perception of the vaguest patterns perceived on any colored surface by the invention of fully constituted images, each of which is a sort of ready-made sketch provided by nature.

It does not take a painter to verify this fact. The mere sight of colored spots or of lines casually distributed on a plane surface, or perceived in three-dimensional space, is enough to evoke in most minds figures and scenes fit to be painted. Vasari's remarks concerning the almost pathological aptitude of Piero di Cosimo in this respect should not make us overlook the significance of the anecdote that he relates with some crudity: "He [Piero di Cosimo] stopped to examine a wall where sick persons had used to spit, imagining that he saw there combats of horses and the most fantastic cities and extraordinary landscapes ever beheld."[4] To which Vasari presently

---

4. "Life of Piero di Cosimo," *Lives*, II, 177. Leonardo da Vinci has raised this personal habit of Piero di Cosimo to the dignity of a method. See: "A Way to Stimulate and Arouse the Mind to Various Inventions. I will not refrain from setting among these precepts a new device for consideration which, although it may appear trivial and almost ludicrous, is nevertheless of great utility in arousing the mind to various inventions. And this is that if you look at any walls spotted with various stains or with a mixture of different kinds of stones, if you are about to invent some scene you will be able to see in it a resemblance to various different landscapes adorned with mountains, rivers, rocks, trees, plains, wide valleys and various groups of hills. You will also be able to see divers combats and figures in quick movement, and strange expressions of faces, and outlandish

adds: "He cherished the same fancies of clouds." Hence, perhaps, the uncanny ability of Piero di Cosimo to create satyrs, fauns, and perfectly convincing monsters, conceived in beauty.

[49]

These remarks help us to understand that the origin of the creative process is not sensation itself, but, rather, the response of imagination to the
stimuli of sense perceptions. This point should be carefully kept in mind
because of its consequences concerning the ambiguous notion of "subject"
in painting; for, indeed, these answers to sense perception given by the mind
of the painter actually are, and will remain for us, the very subjects of his
paintings.[5] Here, however, let us first consider these answers in themselves,
such as painters seem to understand them.

Paul Cézanne made such abundant use of the word "motive" (Fr. *motif*)
that, after him, it became a technical term in writings devoted to the aesthetics of painting. In fact, it is not a badly chosen term. According to a usual
definition, motive is "that within the individual, rather than without, which
incites him to action" (*Webster's*). In the case of Cézanne, however, it
must be noted that he always refused to isolate the internal image from the
externally perceived object. To him, the "motive" was reality itself perceived as suggestive of a painting to be done; in other words, it was the
confused feeling and image of this painting experienced by the painter *in*
the very reality whose perception provoked it. We shall leave it to art critics
to discuss the consequences of this symbiosis with respect to Cézanne himself. Rooted as it is in actually perceived reality, his art feeds on images
endowed with the realness and intensity of sensations. Like the poet, the

costumes, and an infinite number of things which you can then reduce into separate and
well-conceived forms. With such walls and blends of different stones it comes about as it
does with the sound of bells, in whose clanging you may discover every name and word
that you can imagine." (*The Notebooks of Leonardo da Vinci*, II, 250–51.) This is what
some psychologists call the phenomenon of "creative perception." Incidentally, this suggestive power of dots and spots is included in the calculations of some nonrepresentational
painters, and it contributes to the pleasure caused by the sight of their works. The onlooker, too, is then called upon to exercise creative or constructive perception.

5. This attitude is the very reverse of that of scientists. Delacroix's comic hatred of men
of science ("I have a horror of the usual run of scientists," *Journal*, p. 155 [May 6, 1852])
proceeds from this opposition between the respective attitudes of science and of art toward nature. This is the only trace of narrow-mindedness we remember finding in the
Journal of this supremely intelligent man.

painter thus becomes a "visionary of reality." What is directly relevant to our own inquiry is the fact that, in the case of Cézanne, what other painters would call their subject finds itself reduced to the condition of motive—that is, not of a model to copy, but of an incentive to create a plastic substitute for reality. [6]

The same notion was implied in what Cézanne used to call his "little sensation" [7]—that is, his own personal way of experiencing a mental vision in, and as, a perceived reality. The same notion was involved in his oft-quoted announcement that, henceforth, the problem would be to do paintings according to a stylistic pattern, as Poussin had done, but to do them from nature.[8] This organic complex of perception and vision is what André Lhote felicitously calls Cézanne's "hallucinations from nature." A few lines further, the same painter describes this experience as beginning "by forgetting all that has been done before, all that has been seen, and by wholly surrendering oneself to sensation. For indeed every object, if for one moment one renounces the knowledge one has of its form, of its color and of its matter, becomes a source of unexpected images which, captured in ecstasy, provide the poetic imagination of the spectator with an unprecedented springboard." This is the true meaning of the word "inspiration"—namely, those "crucial moments in which the painting to be done reveals itself" and in which the "everyday world vanishes to be replaced with a world exclusively composed of appearances, of phantoms." [9]

6. A fine natural landscape was not necessarily for Cézanne a "motive"—that is to say, an invitation to paint: Cézanne to Émile Zola, May 24, 1883 (*Paul Cézanne, Correspondance*, ed. John Rewald, p. 194). To go hunting for motives ("aller au motif"), to work "on the motive," to discuss a picture "on the motive," etc., are common expressions in Cézanne. And no wonder, since, according to him, "Everything is, especially in art, theory developed and applied in contact with nature" (to A. Vollard, January 9, 1903, p. 252). Cf. letters to Charles Camoin, September 13, 1903, p. 255; and to Camille Pissarro, July 2, 1876, pp. 126–27. Cf. Bernard, *Souvenirs sur Paul Cézanne, et lettres*, pp. 19–20, 44, 55, 56, 82.

7. The fear of being robbed of what was peculiarly his technique seems to have been a source of anxiety to Cézanne (Bernard, p. 34). Among his most cherished possessions was what he used to call his "little sensation" (Lhote, *Treatise on Landscape Painting*, p. xii). By these words, he seems to have meant his own manner of transfiguring reality in the very act of perceiving it.

8. According to Bernard, Cézanne once said: "Imagine Poussin done all over again from nature—that is classicism as I understand it" (Bernard, p. 93, n. 1).

9. Lhote, *Traité du paysage*, p. 8; cf. English translation, p. xiii.

This description of the initial phase of artistic creation wholly agrees with what modern painters usually say about it. Not only Monet, the great master of impressionism, but also van Gogh and Cézanne used to begin with an actual perception of reality that put them directly in a state of "continuous ecstasy." [10] Not, of course, a mystical ecstasy, but a state in which actually given reality is completely transfigured by the response it elicits from the mind. From now on, this response is the real subject that the painter will continually keep present in his mind.

But is there any reason to contrast modern painters with their classical predecessors on this point? Some modern artists feel justified in so doing because, while they themselves start from actual perception, or, as they say, "feeling," traditional painters used to start from some "idea," that is, from a definable "subject."

Assuredly, ideas, stories, definable subjects of every description, played, in traditional art, a much more important part than they do in modern painting, but there might well be an illusion in the belief that those earlier painters found their starting point in the stories told by their paintings, or in the "ideas" that their works now suggest to our own minds. We ourselves might well be mistaken in thinking that what is for us the subject of a painting while we are looking at it also was the subject present in the mind of the painter while he was doing it. Our own tentative answer to the problem would rather be that the anecdotes or events represented by traditional painters were just so many springboards for their imagination, similar to those

10. Lhote, *Traité du paysage*, p. 8; English translation, p. xii. In this passage, Lhote contrasts the attitude of the modern painter, working in a state of continued ecstasy born of an initial sensation, with the classical self-control and the traditional way of working around an *idea*. It would perhaps be more nearly correct to describe the classical approach as concerned with an image rather than an idea. The power of fantasy seems to have been underrated ever since the time of Cézanne, in whom, let us remember, this power was rather weak. The "motive" was for him a constantly present necessity. See Bernard, p. 55: "Cézanne's imagination was poor, he had only a very keen feeling for arrangement; he did not know how to draw without a model, which is a serious obstacle to all valid creation." See (pp. 54–55) the incredible project of a *Homage to Delacroix*, which, fortunately, he never painted. Delacroix, dead, is carried to heaven by angels; one of them holds Delacroix's brushes, another one his palette; in a corner, a barking dog symbolizes art critics, etc. Now, precisely, Delacroix was the very type of painter who does his preparatory work from nature and his works from imagination.

which, nearer us—real landscapes, scenes, or objects—were for the creative imagination of Monet, Cézanne, and van Gogh. Many modern painters have lost contact with the historical and mythological worlds of classical antiquity as well as with the religious world of Scripture; they fail to realize the emotional power wielded by these venerable writings, and the force of their impact on the minds of such men as Giotto, Michelangelo, and Tintoretto.[11] Before contrasting the traditional manner of painting with modern art on this point, it will not be amiss to examine what painters seem to have really done, from the time of Giotto to the last decade of the nineteenth century.

Let us first set apart the, on the whole, rather exceptional cases, in which painters have been expressly commissioned by sovereigns or governments to perpetuate by their works the memory of some historical event. For instance, when David was requested to paint *The Coronation of Napoleon I*, at which he was bodily present, the painter was not provided with a mere "motive," but with a ready-made subject. In fact, his work can be considered a historical document.

But this was a rather rare occurrence. When painters decided to paint certain mythological scenes, or to represent certain religious events, their real starting point was the creative image evoked in their minds by the literary description of such scenes or by their faith in such religious events. When he painted his *Jupiter and Thetis*, from a passage in Homer's *Iliad*, Ingres had certainly no intention of representing the true face and figure of Jupiter or of Thetis. What he was trying to achieve was the plastic construction of two figures, now in the Museum of Aix-en-Provence and so remarkably analyzed by Louis Gillet.[12] In other words, for us onlookers, the subjects of such paintings are the mythological incidents they represent, but,

---

11. In our own day, the meaning of even Christian subjects is not always clear to all, and the countless pictures representing scenes borrowed from mythology or from the history of ancient Greece and Rome are unintelligible to most of the visitors to our art galleries. In so far as subjects are concerned, this humanistic art of painting has largely lost its public. *Pausias and Glycera, The Rape of the Daughters of Leucippus, Queen Tomyris Receiving the Head of Cyrus*, these and many other similar subjects treated by Rubens have become meaningless to most modern onlookers.

12. Homer, *Iliad*, I, 493–516. — Louis Gillet, "Visites au musés de Province: III. Aix-en-Provence," *Revue des deux mondes*, 8th per., XI (Sept. 15, 1932), 315–44.

to the painters themselves, the true subjects were the plastic forms these mythological anecdotes, or religious events, suggested to their imagination. For us, the thousands of paintings that represent the Nativity of Christ have one and the same subject; for the painter himself, his true subject always is his own personal way of representing the Nativity of Christ in the particular piece of work he is doing. The same historical subject can give rise to an infinite number of different pictorial subjects. The scenes depicted by Michelangelo on the ceiling of the Sistine Chapel are identically the same ones that have been depicted, before and after him, in so many different ways. Many more different renderings of the same scenes still remain possible. Such scenes are, for a creative artist, so many occasions to conceive pictorial subjects.

The same problem can be approached from the opposite direction. Just as one and the same anecdote can give rise to many different pictorial subjects, so also paintings that have practically the same pictorial subject can represent several different anecdotes. We have long lists of "subjects" culled by Delacroix himself from the literary works he used to read with the hope of finding incentives for his pictorial imagination. But who will believe that he ever felt interested in representing for their own sake such mythological subjects as *The Education of Achilles*, or such literary subjects as *Ovid in Exile with the Scythes*, or such historical incidents as *The Execution of Doge Marino Faliero*? Delacroix had never seen any of these events. To represent such incidents was not what he was interested in. Any anecdote acting as a motive and suggesting to his creative imagination the confused form of some possible painting was for him a good starting point. For instance, he would see richly dressed warriors on fiery horses surrounded with dejected figures scattered on the ground. This common visual scheme runs through *The Massacre at Scio, The Battle of Taillebourg, The Taking of Constantinople by the Crusaders, The Justice of Trajan,* and even *The Expulsion of Heliodorus from the Temple.* Another group of paintings by Delacroix exhibits a similar unity: *Dante and Virgil in the Infernal Regions, The Shipwreck of Don Juan, Christ on the Lake of Gennesaret* (done seven times). In all these paintings, despite the variety of the titles and of the scenes described by the painter, the visual scheme is about the same oblong form of a boat tossed upon a heavy sea and carrying a group of frightened people. Incidentally, the common ancestor of this family of plastic forms probably was the famous painting by Géricault, *The Raft of the Medusa* (Louvre), for which Delacroix always felt a warm admiration.[13]   [50–51] True enough, there is a human element common to all these situations— namely, the conflict between the weakness of man and the overpowering forces of nature. Delacroix certainly included it in the subject of these works, but, in the last analysis, what lies at the origin of the paintings constituting such a group is a dynamic pattern of lines, figures, and forms that Delacroix was particularly fond of painting.

The same truth can be expressed in still another way. One has spoken of Delacroix's "literary sources," and, indeed, it is enough to read his *Journal* to know their names, but one may well wonder in what sense it is correct to use the word "source" in connection with a painter's reading. When we ourselves read Homer, Virgil, Dante, Shakespeare, or Goethe, do we experience an irresistible urge to embody in a picture some of the events narrated by these writers? Unless we are painters, we do not. But painters do. Several different painters will go to different books for the source of their inspiration, or, if they open the same one, they will not necessarily find in the very same passages the subjects of their own works. His own pictorial imagination remains for every one of these artists the ultimate reason for his own choices. It is the painter who creates his own sources; he is their source, or, rather, in him their true source is his creative imagination.

There is a remarkable parallel between the long outdoor walks of Cézanne hunting for "motives" and the long readings of Delacroix hunting for "subjects." In both cases, all that the artist really needed was a sort of

---

13. On the "sublime Raft," see the *Journal*, p. 27 (April 1, 1824). Delacroix has several times compared *The Raft of the Medusa* with Rubens' *The Raising of the Cross*, in Antwerp: pp. 134–35 (August 10, 1850) and p. 199 (October 20, 1853). Cf. p. 153. Incidentally, let us note that Delacroix has deeply modified the pictorial theme of the *Raft* by reducing the proportion of the boats in comparison with the sea; the poetic meaning of the paintings became at once different.

springboard for his creative power. In both cases, what he conceived at the contact of the things he saw, or read and imagined, was that in them which could be incorporated with the substance of a painting. Ingres was far from enjoying the imaginative powers of a Delacroix. He was less interested in inventing subjects than in stylizing his models.[14] Yet, even in reality, he seems to have been haunted by a certain type of feminine beauty exemplified by the series of his celebrated nudes, *Bathing Woman* (1807, Bayonne), *Bathing Woman of Valpinçon* (1808, Louvre), and the *Grande Odalisque* (1814, Louvre). Each one of these paintings was just a nude, but when he chanced upon a letter of Lady Mary Wortley Montagu describing a Turkish bath, his plastic imagination caught fire. Ingres realized at once that many such nudes could be included within one and the same picture. Whence

[52a, b]   came the *Bather*, the *Small Bathing Woman, Interior of a Harem* (1828, Louvre), and, finally, the fantastic riot of Ingrian nudes that constitutes *The Turkish Bath* (1859, Louvre). If there ever was an instance of the "life of forms," this is one. We can follow it almost step by step from the chance reading of a letter by Ingres to its perfect and ultimate incarnation.[15]

These facts can hardly be denied, yet they leave the mind unsatisfied because what is here called a "subject" is not clearly defined. But, precisely,

---

14. Ingres defined his own notion of style when he said that a painter should not attempt to learn how to create beauty in character: "one must find it in one's own model" (*Ingres raconté par lui-même et par ses amis,* p. 59).

15. The successive stages following which a literary motive becomes a subject can be followed in the case of *The Turkish Bath,* a picture completed by Ingres in December, 1859. Ingres had read one of the letters of Lady Mary Wortley Montagu, April 1, 1717, describing her visit to the public hot baths of Adrianople (now Edirne). This description was copied twice by Ingres in his notebook (n. IX). His notes leave out most of the anecdotic elements of the motive, which, anyhow, could not be included in the subject— for instance, the friendly words addressed by some of these naked women to Lady Mary, herself in traveling dress; the remarks made by Lady Mary on the respective importance of the beauty of faces and of bodies; her reflections on what the painter Jervas would have learned, had it been possible for him to be invisibly present, etc. In his notes, Ingres retains almost exclusively the plastic elements of the descriptions and the general impression of the scene: about two hundred women, all of them naked but without trace of impudicity, standing, walking, or reclining in various postures, while young girls do the hair of these women in a thousand different ways (text of one of Ingres' notes in *Ingres raconté par lui-même,* pp. 238–39; text of Lady Mary's letter, ibid., pp. 239–40 n., the edition of these letters, indicated p. 239 n., is that of London, 1764). On the successive stages in the evolution of this work, which, once finally completed as an almost perfect square, Ingres himself truncated and turned into a circle (Pls. 53a and 53b), see Georges Wildenstein, *Ingres,* p. 230, n. 312.

it cannot be. We cannot say what the subject of a work of art is in itself. While he is doing his work, even the artist himself does not know it yet, at least not with complete clarity. And this seems to be true of other arts than painting. In Pascal's own words, the last thing that one knows in writing a book is its title. What is true of the titles of books also applies to their subjects. The only definition of his subject that a creative writer can give is: that which now is the finished book. In the case of paintings, the subject is the initial plastic form that we now find embodied in the new being produced by the painter. In some cases, this form will express itself only once; in other cases, it is so full of vitality that it can embody itself in a chain of kindred works without sinking into self-repetition and exhausting its power; in all cases, the plastic form acts as a living germ whose inner potentialities cannot be wholly foreseen, even by the artist himself, until they actualize themselves in a completed painting.

In explaining these things, one feels divided between two opposite fears, either to make them sound more subtle than they are or, on the contrary, to make them look clearer than it is in their nature to be. A concrete example will perhaps help us to realize the import of these conclusions.

The Boston Museum owns a well-known painting done by Gauguin   [54] in 1898 and about which we are fortunate in having commentaries by the artist himself. The art critic André Fontainas had written in the *Mercure de France* (January, 1899) an article on some paintings exhibited at the Vollard Gallery. Among these was the large Boston canvas, about which Fontainas observed that, although obviously symbolic, nothing in it would reveal the sense of the allegory if Gauguin himself had not given to his work this abstract title: *Whence Do We Come? What Are We? Whither Are We Going?* Here is, as it seems, a clear case of a painting whose subject can be explained by means of words.

In fact, it is not so. When, in March, 1899, Gauguin read Fontainas' article, he was in Tahiti, in extreme poverty, sick as usual and as systematically averse to answering criticisms as he had always been. Yet, this time, he felt a passionate urge to answer Fontainas, not indeed to justify himself, but because the meaning of his whole work was then at stake. A detailed commentary on this exceptional document would cover most of the

problems connected with the art of painting, but we shall restrict ourselves
to those of Gauguin's remarks which are relevant to our own problem.

Answering Fontainas, as much as he could by means of words, Gauguin
straightway returns to the initial setting in which he had first conceived his
work. There he is near his Tahiti hut, surrounded with deep silence, in-
toxicated with the fragrance of tropical nature, and experiencing a bitter-
sweet delight shot through with the sacred awe that the proximity of primitive things and beings always inspires. Under the stimulus of this emotion,
his mind begins to be haunted by confused images: violent harmonies of
colors; animal figures of statuesque rigidity, with something ancient, august, religious in the rhythm of their attitude, in their uncanny immobility.
In their dreamy eyes, the opaque surface of a baffling enigma. Night has
come, everything is at rest: "My eyes close in order *to see without understanding* the dream, in the infinite space, that flies ahead of me, and I perceive the mournful procession of my hopes." In these lines, let us note that
Gauguin himself has underscored the words: "to see without understanding." And, indeed, this is the whole point. As Gauguin presently adds: "My
dream cannot possibly be grasped, it contains no allegory." Whereupon,
availing himself of formulas applied by Mallarmé to poetry, our painter
specifies: "Because it is immaterial and superior, the essential in a work of
art precisely consists in that which is not expressed: it implicitly *follows*
from the lines, without colors or words, but it is not *materially constituted
by them*." [16] This is what inhabits the soul of the artist, "painting and
dreaming at one and the same time, without having any distinctly graspable
allegory at hand. This is perhaps due to some lack of literary education.
When, the work now being completed, I awake, *I say to myself, I say:*
Whence do we come? What are we? Whither are we going? A reflection that
no longer is part and parcel of the canvas, but which is placed, in written
words, wholly apart, on the surrounding wall that encompasses it, not as a
title, but as a signature." Here again, let us note that the words, *I say to
myself,* and *I say,* have been underscored by Gauguin himself. And not

16. Letter to André Fontainas, Tahiti, March, 1899 (*Lettres de Gauguin à sa femme
et à ses amis,* p. 288). Cf. letter to the same, Tahiti, August, 1899 (pp. 292 93).

without good reason, since their exact meaning is that spoken or written language only begins after the painting is completed. "Emotion first, comprehension next." Once more, the true subject of a painting is given to us by the artist as something to be seen, and no wonder, since it is that part of the painting which could not possibly be expressed by means of words.[17]

This letter to André Fontainas (March, 1899) is remarkable for its lucidity, but it raises a complementary problem that the painter himself could not completely avoid. So long as paintings remain representational, nothing can prevent the onlooker from approaching them from what, to the painter himself, is their most external side. True enough, the artist can do much to prevent this misunderstanding. For instance, he can avoid painting classical symbols, whose meaning is known to all, and which turn paintings into so many rebuses. Gauguin reproaches Puvis de Chavannes, whom he admired so much, with resorting to that sort of conventional language and thus to "write" rather than to paint: "Puvis explains his idea, yes, but he does not paint it. He is a Greek, whereas I am a savage, a collarless wolf in the woods. Puvis will entitle a picture *Purity,* and then, in order to explain it, paint a young virgin holding a lily in her hand.—This is a known symbol; consequently it is understood. Under the title *Purity*, I [Gauguin] shall paint a landscape with limpid waters, unpolluted by civilized man, maybe a figure."[18] All this is crystal-clear, but it does not wholly justify Gauguin's conclusion: "There is a whole world between Puvis and me." Is there a whole world between symbolizing purity by a pure girl and symbolizing it by pure waters? Probably the only reason onlookers would think of purity is that the word is written on the frame; otherwise, they would only see water, or

---

17. Same letter, p. 289. In order not to break the continuity of Gauguin's thought, let us quote here the end of this letter (p. 290) for the light it throws on the problem, which will be examined separately, of the relationship between art critics and art. The key to the problem is that, because they write, critics are bound to reduce painting to literature. "Serious, full of good intentions, and learned, the art criticism of today tends to impose upon us a method of thinking, of dreaming, and this would result in another kind of slavery. Engrossed in its own business, its special domain—namely, literature—criticism would lose sight of what concerns us—namely, painting. Were it to be so, I would haughtily repeat to you the words of Mallarmé: 'A critic! a gentleman who minds somebody else's business.'"

18. Letter to Charles Morice, Tahiti, July, 1901 (*Lettres de Gauguin à sa femme,* pp. 300–01).

a girl holding a lily, which are things very different from the abstract notion
of purity. Above all, as long as there is a symbol, there must be a meaning.
Thus, while it should have its own meaning in itself, a painted figure cannot become a symbol without pointing out something else—namely, the very
thing it symbolizes. From this point of view, the difference between these
two painters would reduce itself to this, that Gauguin cleverly keeps his
public guessing, whereas Puvis de Chavannes sees no harm in using the
most naïvely obvious symbols. But his reason for doing so probably is that,
precisely, the symbol itself is of no importance; what really counts is the
[55]   painting. While he was doing his *Summer,* now at the Cleveland Museum of
Art, Puvis de Chavannes did not intend to depict the simple pleasures of a
nudist colony in summertime. A representation of some harvesting scene, as
in the *Harvesters* of Brueghel the Elder, at the Metropolitan Museum; or
any one of the countless *Pleasures of Summer,* as in the panel by Boucher,
in the Frick Collection; in short, practically any kind of illustration not
incompatible with the title would have done just as well. Most of the time,
the plastic form causes the picture, and, in turn, the picture causes the title.
If, as happens in the case of a commission, the title comes first, it merely
circumscribes an area of wide possibilities in which the artist remains
wholly free to conceive a certain form and to embody it in the matter of a
completely determined individual.

The words in which this truth is formulated are of no importance. For
instance, one can say, as has been done, that every painting has a "double
subject": one is the form embodied in the painting; the other is the painting itself read as a picture because, borrowing its elements from reality, it
seems to represent it. Or else it can be said, with Maurice Denis, that every
painting is a "symbol," [19] because what it seems to represent merely points

---

19. The notion of "symbol" applies to creative painting in general and far beyond the
limits of the so-called symbolist school. Like all denominations, this one is likely to become
misleading. Its meaning can be inferred from several letters of Gauguin. Even in his own
works, one must be careful not to mistake the allegorical explanation of the picture with
its subject. In his letter to Daniel de Monfreid, February, 1898 (*Lettres de Paul Gauguin
à Georges-Daniel de Monfreid,* pp. 201–02), Gauguin gives an allegorical explanation of
the Boston picture. At the center of the picture, a standing figure is picking fruit from
the Tree of Science; on its right side, a crouching figure, intentionally painted too large

out the plastic form, present in the mind of the painter, that has molded its matter into an actually existing reality. Whatever language we may choose to use, what matters is the clear realization of the fact that, as soon as it is seen as a describable picture, justifiable in the light of a title, the work of the painter has lost its true subject.

2. Germinal Forms and the Possibles

S I N CE it is anterior to its own plastic incarnation, the form conceived by the painter cannot be described in itself; it is known by its effects only. Yet one could not speak about art without saying things about the initial form that is the origin of the whole creative process, and the way one speaks about it is not in itself a matter of indifference. Every time creative work is under discussion, it is important to remember that the starting point of the painter—that is, what he first has in mind—is a more or less fluid image, or, rather, a sort of moving scheme that is much less a model properly so called than the germ of the work to be. Unless he is a mere copyist of himself or of others, in which case no problem of creation arises, a painter cannot distinctly know what he is doing until his work has been completed. To "put the last touch to a painting" is much more than the

for the rest, raises its right arm: it is marveling at two dim figures, standing, which have the audacity of thinking about their destiny. On the left, an idol, with mysteriously and rhythmically raised arms, seems to signify the Beyond. A seated girl listens to the idol; an old woman, near death, expresses acceptance and resignation; "at her feet, a strange, stupid white bird, holding a lizard in its claws, represents the vanity of idle words." Then Gauguin asks the excellent question: "If one told the students of the Beaux-Arts, for the Rome competition: The picture that you have to do shall represent: 'Whence do we come? What are we? Whither are we going?'—what would they do? I have completed a philosophical work on this theme compared with the Gospel. I think it is good; if I have the strength to copy it, I shall send it to you." In short, we should distinguish among the legibility of the picture (reading what it represents), the allegorical meaning of what it represents (understanding ideas that could as well, or better, be expressed in a philosophical treatise), and the symbolic meaning of the picture (the plastic rendering of the painting to be done). The second meaning, so abundantly represented in the murals of Puvis de Chavannes (Grand Amphithéâtre, Sorbonne, Paris), corresponds to the order of what Gauguin calls his parables. See the letter to André Fontainas, Tahiti, August, 1899 (*Lettres de Gauguin à sa femme*, p. 293). This is the letter in which he says: "You are doing me pleasure, *a great pleasure*, in acknowledging that you had *wrongly* believed that my compositions, like those of Puvis de Chavannes, started from an a priori abstract idea that I was trying to quicken by means of a plastic representation."

description of an act; it expresses, in the painter's mind, the end of a period of uncertainty that is coextensive with the duration of his work.

This does not mean that artistic creation is an unconscious process, or
that the intellect is not necessarily required in order to conduct it. The only
point at stake is that the knowledge that an artist has of his future work
little resembles the determinate knowledge we have of already given objects.
Rather, knowledge accompanies the progression of the work of art, throw-
ing a feeble light on the path ahead of the painter and offering him possible
answers to many problems he has to solve. Even in the *Timaeus* of Plato,
when the Demiurge is working with his eyes fixed on the Ideas, there is at
least one Idea that he himself has to conceive—namely, the form of his own
work.[20]

This is so true that one may well wonder if, in the case of painters, the
best word to use in order to point out their starting point is "intuition."
Taken in its primitive meaning, "intuition" signifies the same thing as
"sight." True enough, philosophers have restricted it to mean "immediate
apprehension or cognition; the power of knowing or the knowledge obtained
without recourse to inference or reasoning; insight; familiarly, a quick or
ready apprehension" (*Webster's*). Now, precisely, even if the "little perception" of Cézanne, or the ecstatic perception of Lhote, can rightly be
called an intuition, it is still very far from representing the completed work

20. In Plato's philosophy, the Ideas were the self-subsisting principles of intelligibility,
unchangeable and eternal, which account for what of being there is in becoming. In
Plotinus' philosophy, the Ideas became the thoughts of the second highest principle (after
the One)—namely, the divine Intellect (*Nous*). In St. Augustine's theology, the Ideas became the patterns, eternally present in the second person of the Christian Trinity—namely,
the divine Word (*Verbum*)—according to which God created all the beings that constitute
this world. Thomas Aquinas took up Augustine's doctrine and developed it along the lines
of his own Christian philosophy. The Ideas are in God as "the likeness of a house pre-
exists in the mind of the builder. And this may be called the idea of the house, since the
builder intends to build his house like the form conceived in his mind." (*Summa theologiae*, I, 15, 1, answer [*Basic Writings of St. Thomas Aquinas*, I, 163].) The Ideas are one
with God, and since the Christian God is the living God, the divine Ideas are life. Such had
already been the teaching of St. John in his Gospel (1:3, 4): "Without him was made
nothing that was made. In him was life." Hence, in Thomas Aquinas' doctrine: "The likeness of these things, which do not have life in themselves, are life in the divine mind, as
having a divine being in that mind" (*Summa theologiae*, I, 18, 4, reply to 2nd obj. [*Basic
Writings*, I, 193]). In Christian philosophy, as in the experience of artists, the forms of the
works to be done are conceived, by analogy with the divine Ideas, as so many living and
creative realities.

as it is going to be. To the extent that an Idea is a pre-existing pattern of a certain thing to be made, painters have real ideas. The execution of their work is not preceded by its perfect precognition in their mind. This is an important difference between the art of God and the art of man.[21]

The reason some aestheticians place the starting point of a painter's activity in some sort of intuition is their tendency to reduce all problems to terms of knowledge and speculation. And, indeed, where there is no mind, there is no art, but because it is production, not speculation, art does not start from cognition alone, but also from action. Art itself does not necessarily require the actual exercising of a will. Idle artists are by no means a rarity. Sometimes because they need time to permit the ripening of an idea, sometimes for psychological or physiological reasons foreign to art, artists fully equipped with all the tools needed for the production of works of art simply do not feel like working. If no men had the will to paint, there would be no paintings.

This truth should not make us lose sight of another one, which is that, although it itself is not yet art, the desire to acquire it and to exercise it lies at its origin. Once more, this desire resides much less in the mind of the artist than in the man himself, and quite particularly in his hand. Many men feel an irresistible urge to use a pencil in order to draw figures: this does not mean that they have the brains required to be a painter; but unless he feels in his fingers the curious itching that must have put a piece of charcoal in the hands of the men who painted the bisons of the Altamira cave, nobody will ever acquire art, much less use it.

A man has no creative perceptions such as those of Cézanne unless, at the very same moment that he perceives certain external spectacles, he feels in his hand an obscure urge to translate them into colors and shapes. These

---

21. The notion of what an artisan will do pre-exists in him (Thomas Aquinas, *Summa theologiae*, I–II, 94, 1). It is likewise true that "no line must come from the hand of a painter unless it has previously been formed in his mind" (Maritain, *Creative Intuition*, p. 67). But during the whole conception and execution of a painting there is no single moment when its complete pattern, up to the final touch, has been totally present in the painter's imagination. "When a painting is in the making, we seem to recognize it little by little, but without ever knowing ahead of time what its true visage will exactly be" (Jean Bazaine, *Notes sur la peinture*, p. 27). This, Bazaine says, is a particular case of Pascal's: "Thou wouldst not search for Me if thou didst not possess Me."

two moments of aesthetic perception are inseparable, and both infallibly disappear if abstract analysis isolates one of them from the other one. Let us remember the meaning of the word "motive": the motivity of artistic perceptions or of artistic images is as essential to them as their cognoscibility.

Unless the impulse to do something with the hand is there from the very outset, nothing will ever happen. Under its elementary aspect, this impulse assumes the form, familiar to all, of doodling—that is, of covering white surfaces with aimless scrawls while one's attention is engaged elsewhere. There is in doodling the same initiative of the hand that, when creative perceptions, or images, are experienced, makes the same hand immediately translate these images, or perceptions, into sketches that are so many seeds of future pictures. But despite its efforts to be as slow as possible, our analysis still goes too fast, for, indeed, another mystery waits for us on this threshold of the art of painting.

Why is it that the hands of so many men cannot leave any sheet of white paper uncovered with their scrawlings? This is one of the many cases in which all we can do is to take stock of a primitive fact that, precisely because it is primitive, does not admit of explanation. Among the Aristotelian principles that modern science makes out to be obsolete, there is one that, from the point of view of mathematicized physics, sounds extremely comical indeed. It is that "Nature abhors emptiness." And one must grant that, unless Nature be conceived as a sort of living being, endowed with knowledge and able to experience feelings, one does not clearly see how it could either like emptiness or, on the contrary, dislike it. But, precisely, artists are living beings, and Paul Valéry was certainly remembering the much abused scholastic formula when he said: "The poet abhors emptiness."

Setting the poet aside, because his case is perhaps still more mysterious,[22] let us ask ourselves whether it is not literally true that painters,

---

22. Fromentin has spoken for both writers and painters in his novel *Dominique* (p. 169): "I told you once, not so long ago, that I had a hankering, not to be a somebody, which seems to me absurd, but to produce something, which is the only justification for our poor little lives. I said so then, and I still mean to try; not, I beg you to believe, in the interests of my dignity as a man, or my pleasure, or my vanity, or other people, or myself,

PIERO DI COSIMO. The Death of Procris
About 1490/1500. National Gallery, London

a. THÉODORE GÉRICAULT. The Raft of the Medusa
1818/19. Louvre

b. EUGÈNE DELACROIX. Dante and Virgil
1822. Louvre

a. EUGÈNE DELACROIX. The Shipwreck of Don Juan
1840. Louvre

c. EUGÈNE DELACROIX.
Christ on the Sea of Galilee
1854. Walters Art Gallery, Baltimore

b. EUGÈNE DELACROIX.
Christ on the Lake of Gennesaret
1853. Metropolitan Museum of Art,
New York

a. J.-A.-D. INGRES. Bather
1826. Phillips Collection, Washington

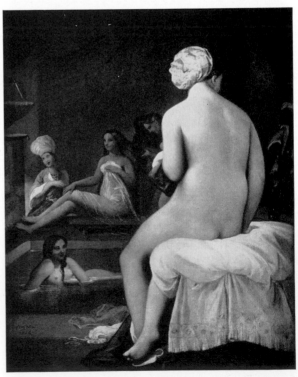

b. J.-A.-D. INGRES. The Small Bathing Woman
1828. Louvre

a. J.-A.-D. INGRES. The Turkish Bath
State in 1859. Louvre

b. J.-A.-D. INGRES. The Turkish Bath
Present state, 1862. Louvre

Paul Gauguin. Whence Do We Come? What Are We? Whither Are We Going?
1898. Museum of Fine Arts, Boston

PIERRE PUVIS DE CHAVANNES. Summer
1891. J. H. Wade Colection, Cleveland Museum of Art

JOHN CONSTABLE. Sketch for "Salisbury Cathedral from the Bishop's Grounds"
City of Birmingham Museum and Art Gallery, Birmingham, England

56

JOHN CONSTABLE. Salisbury Cathedral from the Bishop's Grounds
1825. Metropolitan Museum of Art, New York

J.-B.-C. Corot. The Narni Bridge (sketch)
1826. Louvre

a. Jacob van Ruisdael. A Landscape with a Footbridge
1652. Frick Collection, New York

b. J.-B.-C. Corot. The Narni Bridge
1826/27. National Gallery of Canada, Ottawa

a. Frans Hals. The Jolly Toper
About 1627/30. Rijksmuseum, Amsterdam

b. Édouard Manet. Le Bon Bock
*1873. Caroll S. Tyson Collection,
Philadelphia*

at least, experience this feeling. When the born painter finds himself confronted with an empty surface, he experiences an obscure desire to cover it with forms.[23] If the surface at hand is, for instance, a sheet of white paper, the hand of the painter will seldom resist this temptation, as though it were a shame to allow nothingness when it is possible to fill it with beings. Those who seem to believe that, in drawing, the artist merely lets his hand follow a model that his mind contemplates are deceptively simplifying a more complex operation. Without pretending to describe it in clear and distinct terms, this at least we can say, that in this continuous exchange between the hand and the eye of the painter, the hand is giving at least as much as the eye. Its proper contribution seems to consist in producing, for the eye to see, the very form that was but confusedly conceived by the imagination. What is true of drawing is equally true of painting. The creative artist, whose imagination is haunted by rudiments of indistinct forms, is a man whose hand will make them really be what they obscurely aspire to become. To enable him to see his own images, the hand of the painter must give them actual being.

Can an operation of this kind be considered one of the particular cases of knowledge? To be sure, knowledge accompanies artistic production from its very beginning to its end. It precedes it, it guides it, it judges it, and it

but simply and solely to get something off my mind that makes me uncomfortable." — Compare Charles Morgan, *Sparkenbroke* (p. 274) : "George, contrasting with Piers' impatience in all else the steadiness of his approach to his art, said, with a hand on the manuscript: 'Is this what you care for most in life? What do you want out of it—fame?'—'To do it,' Piers said.—'But why? It must go beyond that?'—'If it does, it goes beyond my reach.'"

23. "Plastic art cannot be the simple expression of space. Empty space has no other function than to make life possible. Plastically it does not represent life. It leaves us isolated with our thoughts and feelings. Reciprocal action between us and the environment is not possible and without this action, human development (culture) cannot exist. For our feelings empty space is unbearable. Think of the solitude one feels in the desert and on the ocean. It evokes all kinds of subjective sensations and fantastic images. Contact with the plastic expression of reality is lacking. Even limited spaces and forms of great size displease us. Churches, factories, etc. can depress us; objects and creatures can awe and frighten us when the space determination is incomplete. It must be noted that empty space can evoke universal conceptions, create mental and moral activity. But this activity is in the abstract domain and always requires the remembrance of the world of oppositions. The action of plastic art is not space-expression but complete space-determination." (Piet Mondrian, "A New Realism," *Plastic Art and Pure Plastic Art*, p. 18.)

corrects it until the work at stake has reached its completion. Yet, to the extent that it is creative, art is not reducible to any particular kind of knowledge, for the simple reason that what has not yet been "made to be" does not yet exist; consequently, it cannot possibly be an object of cognition. Artists sometimes speak of truth as of one of the ideals they hope to attain, or to approach, by means of their works; but if truth is understood, in its traditional meaning, as a perfect conformity between the mind and its object, there can be no truth in the knowledge that an artist has of his future work, because such knowledge has not yet found its object. The truth pursued by the poets is not the conformity of their knowledge with a poem that is not yet there. Nor is it the conformity of their work with a fully defined pattern already present in their minds. In speaking of artistic truth, a poet means to say that something that was but an indistinct and shadowy image in his mind has now become a concrete reality in his own work. A completed poem is a dream come true. In Keats' own words: "The Imagination may be compared to Adam's dream—he awoke and found it truth." [24] Eve is the truth of Adam's dream: Eve, that is; not the image of a reality, but the reality of an image.

The same notion of artistic truth has been expressed by Richard Wagner, with respect to both poetry and music. In one of his letters to Mathilde Wesendonk, written when he was completing *Tristan and Isolde*, the musician remarks that there is a great deal of truth in the doctrine of Kant according to which space, time, causality—in short, the whole structure of the world—are hanging on the thought of man. Is not human thought an anticipation of reality? Then, after quoting the remark of Schiller that what the poet knows is *true*, precisely because it has not yet *been*, Wagner asks himself if what is miraculous in artistic genius is not precisely the fact that what has not yet *been* finally *is*. And, indeed, because the form embodies itself in a work of art, what first was but an image in the mind of the artist

24. Letter to Benjamin Bailey, November 22, 1817 (*Letters*, ed. Maurice Buxton Forman, p. 67). On Adam's dream, see Milton, *Paradise Lost*, VIII, 460–90. Cf. the penetrating remarks of Lionel Trilling, *The Opposing Self* (pp. 40–41), where the ethical implications of the doctrine appear in full.—In the same sense, Klee, *Über die moderne Kunst*, p. 49.

ultimately reaches concrete existence under the form of a material and perceptible reality.[25] This kind of truth would be more correctly called a substantiation.

Painters, at least those among them who scrutinize the nature of their art, feel the same way. In his *Journal*, under the date June 6, 1851, Delacroix observes that, in his own mind, "*truth* is the rarest and most beautiful of all qualities," but, precisely, this is the long entry in which he criticizes "Poussin's method of arranging the effect of his pictures with the help of small models lit by studio lighting"; and Raphael's habit of "conscientiously drawing each figure in the nude before he draped it." Rembrandt, Delacroix says, "would never have achieved his power of representing character by a significant play of gestures, or those strong effects that make his scenes so truly representative of nature, if he had bound himself down to this studio method. Perhaps they will discover that Rembrandt is a far greater painter than Raphael." The truth of Rembrandt's works lies in their relationship, not to external models, but to themselves.[26] As Delacroix wrote about himself at another date: "Who would ever believe it? The things that are most real to me are the illusions which I create with my painting. Everything else is a quicksand." [27] Gauguin seems to have had in mind something like this when he wrote to Émile Schuffenecker: "A piece of advice: do not paint too much from nature. Art is abstraction. Extract this abstraction from nature while you are dreaming before it, and think rather of the creation that will result from it. This is the only means there is to ascend toward God, namely, to do as our Divine Master himself does: to create." [28]

The written testimonies of painters should not be understood literally as if they were the works of philosophers or of theologians. In fact, rather than to compare the painter with God, one should understand the primitive

25. E. Gilson, *L'École des muses*, p. 135.

26. "When Courbet painted the background of the woman bathing, he copied it faithfully from a study which I saw hanging near his easel. Nothing could be colder; it is like a piece of mosaic. I began to make something tolerable of my African journey only when I had forgotten the trivial details and remembered nothing but the striking and poetic side of the subject. Up to that time, I had been haunted by this passion for accuracy that most people mistake for truth." (*Journal*, p. 198 [October 17, 1853].)

27. *Journal*, p. 25 (February 27, 1824).

28. August 14, 1888 (*Lettres de Gauguin à sa femme*, p. 134).

form conceived by the painter as analogous to the natural forms by which Aristotle used to account for the coming to be of all beings. The most striking feature of the development of a natural form is that it seems to be directed toward a certain term.[29] The Aristotelian philosophy of nature, precisely because to a large extent it derived its inspiration from art, had vigorously opposed the mechanistic interpretation of the world that had obtained before the time of Aristotle and was to be revived after him. In the case of artistic creation, at least, it cannot be doubted that the forms are the living germs of the works of art to be. For this reason, they can justly claim the title, of Stoic origin, that used to point out this aspect of their nature: germinal forms. Transmitted by Plotinus to St. Augustine (*ratio seminalis*), this expression designated a living germ that, in the course of time, would develop according to a specific type of being. In the case of paintings, however, the germinal form is the origin of an organic process of development whose end is a fully constituted individual work of art. No one can predict the course of such developments. They never repeat themselves. In some cases, the hand is allowed to play for some time in a more or less idle way, as if the mind contented itself with letting it free; in other cases, the dialogue between the hand and the mind becomes so animated that it looks like a furious battle; and there are still other cases in which, after doing nothing to a painting for quite a long time, except perhaps thinking about it, an artist will finish it in half an hour, as if his hand no longer needed the guidance of the mind. In no case does the finished work follow from its germinal form in a necessary and predictable way, and still, unless it does follow from such a form, the painter is sure to fail in his undertaking.

The first critical moment arises when, at the beginning of his work, a painter proceeds to the kind of operation often called *"chercher l'esquisse."* The problem is not for him to know why he should start sketching. As had

---

29. The modern emphasis on the notion of "form," not only in psychology but also in zoology and botany, authorizes the hope that the two orders of science and art, dissociated since the rise of mathematical physics, will reopen an era of co-operation. See Adolf Portmann, *Animal Forms and Patterns*; Agnes Arber, *The Natural Philosophy of Plant Forms*; same author, *The Mind and the Eye.*

been said, unless he feels an urge to know what he has in mind, and to see it, a man is no painter.[30] This initial move should therefore be conceived neither as an operation of the hand nor as an operation of the mind, but as that of a man, and, more precisely, of one of those men whom we call painters because of the special symbiosis that obtains among their eyes, their mind, and their hand.

This initial operation can be described, in an allegorical way, as the moment a germinal form sets out in search of a body. The Greek philosophers often marveled at the fact that, instead of peacefully enjoying the contemplation of intelligible beauty, souls seem to be impelled by an irresistible urge to join bodies. What is the cause of such an impulse? Is it the passionate giddiness of a fall? Is it the generosity of a love that invites the form to communicate itself to matter? Whatever the answer, the fact is there, and similar ones can be observed in other domains. Language is a case in point. Why do the inner conceptions of the mind embody themselves in spoken words, sentences, reasonings, and discourses? But why is it written in the Gospel of St. John that "the Word was made flesh, and dwelt among us" (1 : 14)? We should remember that "word" stands for the Greek *logos*, itself closely associated with the notions of "idea" and "form." The only thing to add, when it is a question of painting, is that the form should not be conceived first in itself and next in its effort to give itself a body. In Focillon's own words, "the form is not only, so to speak, incarnate, it always is incarnation."[31]

Modern painters have given summary descriptions of their personal approaches to the problem, and despite inevitable differences from person to person, the process generally appears as a particular application of the method of trial and error. The first moment always is the sudden invasion

30. "What is certain, is that if I were to pick up my palette at this moment, and I am longing to do so, I should be obsessed by that lovely Velázquez. What I want to do, is to spread good, fat paint thickly on to a brown or red canvas, and therefore what I must do to find a subject is to open some book capable of giving me inspiration, and then allow myself to be guided by my mood." (*The Journal of Eugène Delacroix*, p. 30 [April 11, 1824].) Compare the deep remark made by Gauguin: "I have no pretension to invent something new. What I am coveting is a still unknown corner of myself." (*Lettres de Gauguin à sa femme*, p. 163.)

31. *Vie des formes*, p. 52.

of some matter by a germinal form, usually followed by a more systematic effort of appropriation that requires careful calculation. Several different incarnations of the form are always possible. That certain ones select themselves rather than other ones can be due to the size, shape, or color of the paper or of the canvas at hand.[32] But it sometimes happens that a painter's imagination is occupied, at one and the same time, by his desire to work in a certain format and by a contradictory desire to do a work unfit for that format. A compromise then has to be reached and a number of sketches have to be tried. But even in normal cases it may take a long time before a germinal form reaches the term of one of its possible incarnations.[33]

In a first sense, we call possible whatever is not intrinsically impossible —that is, any object whose notion is not self-contradictory. In a second sense, we call possible whatever, after being conceived by the mind, can be made to exist in reality. These two kinds of possibles have in common only one feature—namely, that they are not intrinsically impossible. For all the rest, they are entirely different. As long as we remain in the order of abstract possibility, whatever is not contradictory can be said to be, not only possible, but even compossible. As soon, on the contrary, as we enter the order of actual existence, incompossibilities begin to multiply. In other words, we can impart existence to any one of the possibles that we have in mind, but the sole fact that we cause one of them to be makes it impossible

32. "Nowadays, I rarely start a picture from hallucinations as I did in the twenties, or as later, about 1933, from forms suggested by collages. What is more interesting to me today is the materials I am working with. They very frequently supply the shock which suggests my forms much as the cracks in the wall suggested form to Leonardo. I start a canvas, without a thought of what it may eventually become. I put it aside after the first fire has abated. I may not look at it again for months. Then I take it out and work at it coldly like an artisan, guided strictly by rules of composition after the first shock of suggestion has cooled. Forms take reality for me as I work. In other words, rather than setting out to paint something, I begin painting and as I paint the picture begins to assert itself, or suggest itself under my brush. The form becomes a sign for a woman or a bird, as I work. Even a few casual wipes of my brush in cleaning it, a flaw in the canvas, a stain on the board may suggest the beginning of a picture. The second stage, however, is carefully calculated. The first stage is free, unconscious; but after that the picture is controlled throughout in keeping with that desire for disciplined work which I have felt from the beginning." (Joan Miró, in James Johnson Sweeney, "Miró," *Art News Annual*, XXIII [1954], 187.)

33. See the sequence of images (plates on pp. 77–78) that accompanies the same article by Sweeney. — In the same article (p. 70), see an excellent example of what a germinal form can be when it attempts to express itself in both lines and words.

for many other ones to exist. By far the largest number of the misunderstandings that separate painters from art critics, art historians, or simply art lovers arises from the fact that, because they have to *make* things, painters are always concerned with existential possibility, whereas, because they only *look* at things and *think* about them, possibility always remains for onlookers at the level of abstraction. "A thought," Odilon Redon says, "cannot become a work of art." [33a]

Considering paintings from the point of view of painters themselves, two kinds of impossibilities limit the creative liberty of the artist. To simplify the discussion of the problem, let us call these the objective limits or objective impossibilities, and the subjective limits or subjective impossibilities.

The most general of these objective limits arises from the very nature of the art of painting. Such as we found it defined by Vasari, painting was included among the arts of *disegno*, but, in turn, it included color. This duality of elements makes itself felt in almost everything that can be said about this art. It introduces in painting an inner tension hard to relieve, impossible to suppress. Drawing is an art complete in itself. It has its own masters, who may also happen to be great painters, but are not necessarily so. Ingres, who was a master in both arts, knew full well that one cannot concede everything to color if he wants to respect the rights of drawing. To him, expression was inseparable from a complete mastery of the art of drawing. Now, "Expression, an essential part of art, is intimately tied up with form. The perfection of coloring is so little required for it that the best painters of expression have not exhibited the same superiority as colorists. To blame them is not to know enough the nature of arts. One cannot require from the same man contradictory qualities. Besides, the rapidity in execution that color demands in order to preserve its prestige does not agree with the deep study that the extreme purity of forms demands." [34] Personal gifts account for the choice that each particular painter

33a. *À soi-même*, p. 90. To which Redon adds: "except in literature. Art borrows nothing from philosophy, either."

34. *Ingres raconté par lui-même et par ses amis*, p. 62. — Cf. Baudelaire, *The Mirror of Art*, pp. 51–52.

ultimately has to make. Anyone who has seen lead drawings by Ingres will know at once why, in his own case, the choice was not likely to be in favor of color. But the very existence of the choice, its inevitability, and the nature of its terms are independent of the personal gifts or dispositions of any particular artist.

Another option seems likewise unavoidable; not, this time, between drawing and color, but, rather, within color itself, between the local tones and the modeling of the volumes. The necessity to choose is less absolute in this case than in the preceding one. Compromises have often been reached between these two orders, and if, in some paintings like those of Rubens, El Greco, or Delacroix, there seems to be an excessive boldness in laying intense colors on strongly contrasted values, the reason for this may well be that value contrasts have a natural tendency to become exaggerated in the course of time. It must likewise be conceded that the distinction of these two plastic elements may have been overstressed in modern times. Yet, when all is said and done, there remains a great difference between the marvelous compromises by which the great paintings of the Renaissance reconcile local tones with volumes and the resolute use of flat local tones that becomes conspicuous in the works of Gauguin. His best works, as well as those of many recent painters, achieve, by means of flat local tones boldly laid and hardly broken by any perceptible modeling, effects that more strongly marked volumes would annihilate.[35]

35. On the antinomy "local color—volume," see Kahnweiler, *Juan Gris*, p. 153. If the painter wants to stress the modeling of the volumes, he must sacrifice local color or local tones. — This point had already been developed with great clarity by Lhote (*Parlons peinture*, pp. 306–07). A painter should avoid marriages between mutually hostile families. For instance, to join pure color with modeling is to sink into the most shameful vulgarity. Lhote then divides the painters, from the point of view of technique, into two families: the "valuists" and the "colorists." The "valuists" have an architectural vision of reality. These are the pure plasticians (Leonardo, Georges de La Tour, Corot, etc.). The colorists are, so to say, "the musicians of painting." They only gather from reality its most subtle and most directly perceptible elements (Fra Angelico, Fragonard, van Gogh, Bonnard, etc.). "Between these extreme families is that of the courageous equilibrists. After their sensibility has made its choice between value and color, these artists attempt to introduce into their works the permitted maximum of the contrary element. These are the heroes of painting: Tintoretto, Rembrandt, Rubens, El Greco, Cézanne. But even when they come to terms with these hostile elements, they do not superimpose them on the same part of the

To these general limitations, let us add accidental and particular ones. All the specifications attached to certain commissions should be counted among these. The dimensions of the work, the shape of the surface to be painted, its location with respect to light (opposite a window, between two windows, on a ceiling, in corners, in cupolas), its relation to the other parts of a decorative or architectural whole: all these conditions must be taken into account by the painter, and they constitute so many limitations to the existential possibilities at his disposal. The nature of the material at hand exercises a no less decisive influence. In short, the fact that all matters are not capable of receiving all forms should be counted among the causes that preclude many an abstract possibility from becoming an existential possibility. From this point of view, the choices made by painters are, if not determined, at least directed by necessities that are beyond the control of their wills.

Their wills themselves, however, impose a still larger number of limitations on the choices that are abstractly possible. The first decisions of the hand, the choice made of a fundamental color, considerably narrow the field of the remaining possibilities. Every further decision will restrict what is left of it with an increasing severity. This is the more important as the first decisions of his hand sometimes take the painter himself by surprise. Just as writers do not always write the books that they were planning to write, so painters feel sometimes nonplussed at the sight of what they are painting. Now, the true possible is not the one that, speculatively speaking, it is not impossible to actualize; it is the one that, because its productive causes are already at work, is already enjoying an inchoation of existential actuality.

The same distinction accounts for the constant recurrence of the feeling of disappointment experienced by every artist after the completion of one picture." Sometimes, carried away by their game, some of them "put a little too much polychromy in their modeling; despite their genius, they then stand on the very limit of the possible, on the borderline of vulgarity. Greco's *Pentecost*, certain Rubens, and certain Delacroix, in which intense blues and reds are laid on excessively contrasted values . . . cause an uneasy feeling that is not usually caused by their works, more noble because born of a more severe choice of means."

of his works. The painting had been so beautiful, so powerfully moving, so truly radiant, and so wonderfully alive as long as it still was a pure possible in the limbo of creative imagination! Now that the work was done, all that was left of such hopes was a poverty-stricken reality. Artists then have nothing else to do than to resign themselves to the fact:

> *Whither is fled the visionary gleam?*
> *Where is it now, the glory and the dream?*

In the case of painters, the answer is easy to find. At the origin of every painting, an indefinite number of abstract possibles are given together, and the visionary gleam of the artist, in which they all are present, includes incomparably more than what can be embodied in the actual realization of any one of them. Any single germinal form is pregnant with many different possibilities, but the greatest of painters will never be able to actualize more than one of them at a time. As he is looking at his finished work, the artist still has in mind the confused crowd of the other incarnations of the same form that he himself has had to eliminate in order to ensure the realization of this one. No actually existing painting can compete with an indefinite number of possible ones each of which, being imagined as real, includes in itself the substance of all the others. But there is a compensation. Many an artist has had the pleasant experience, when seeing his work again after a certain time, to find it much better than he remembered it. This is a sure sign that, the work having already ceased to live in his mind, the painter begins to see his painting as it is in itself, stripped of the glorious but deceptive halo of imaginary possibilities.

On the contrary, the critics and the public compare the finished painting, not with the germinal form that it first was in the mind of the artist, but, rather, with the abstract possibles that the sight of the picture at stake conjures up in their own imagination. No wonder, then, that they often feel disappointed. Had they had to handle such a subject, *they* would have seen it in an entirely different way. Which is quite possible, but even they themselves cannot know for sure that this is true. One should never forget the remark once made by Georges Braque: "I do not do as I will; I do as I can."[36] Between those who do what they can and those who imagine what they please, the misunderstanding is unavoidable and inscribed in the very nature of things.

3. Life and Death of the Forms

AFTER it has begun to take shape, the germinal form requires a certain time to develop and to reach its completion. This space of time can be so short that the whole work seems to develop within the limits of the initial experience. Most of the time, however, a more or less long duration is required for the form to find its body. There are even cases in which certain paintings that nothing would designate as the result of severe struggles have had to wait for years before being brought to completion. Ingres' *Source*, which now looks like a somewhat conventional composition in the classical style, long remained in the painter's studio in the condition of a nude that had not yet found its head.

The fact that it takes an artist more or less protracted efforts to achieve clear awareness of the kind of work that is asking to be done is wholly unrelated to the particular nature of his style. Everyone knows the anecdote about Cézanne's obliging his models to sit almost indefinitely for their portrait,[37] but if one imagines that this was due to the fundamental dissatisfaction that inhabited Cézanne's soul, he will change his mind after reading, in Amaury-Duval's memoirs of Ingres, the description of the scenes that took place while this worshiper of Raphael was painting the famous portrait of Émile Bertin. If those who now see this remarkable work in the Louvre had any objection to formulate, it would probably be that, for a painted portrait, it looks too much like a snapshot. Now, in a way, this is what it finally came to be, but it is not what the portrait was at the beginning. After trying time and again, with so little success that, on certain days, Ingres actually cried in despair, he decided to interrupt his efforts. It was only

36. *Le Jour et la nuit*, p. 10.

37. "After one hundred and fifteen sittings, Cézanne gave up my portrait in order to return to Aix. When he left, Cézanne told me: 'I am not too displeased with the shirt front.' He made me leave in his studio the suit of clothes with which I had sat for him. It was his intention, when he came back to Paris, to work again on certain parts of the portrait." (Vollard, *En écoutant Cézanne*, p. 64.)

later on, while he was no longer working at it, that he suddenly said to
Bertin: "Come and sit for me tomorrow, your portrait is done." And, indeed, this time, the work was successfully completed within a month.[38] Ingres
crying in despair before his model, who would have believed it? And yet,
Bertin himself assures us that it was so: "He was crying," Bertin says, "and
I was spending my time consoling him." Perhaps there is no such thing as
a painless birth.

Whatever its duration, this process is dominated by something that, if it
is not exactly a law, appears at least as a sort of necessity. Despite its essential plasticity, there is a point beyond which the germinal form cannot
be stretched without losing its nature. As soon as the artist's imagination
wanders away from it, his work is lost. Painters' studios are full of unfinished works, most of which will never be completed. These are the proj-
ects during whose execution the artist lost contact with the creative perception, or image, that had inspired him at the beginning of his effort. Most
of the time, if we knew the detailed history—so to speak, play by play—
of certain masterpieces that seem to have sprung from nothingness at the
first call of genius, we should hear a tale of hesitations, doubts, moves, and
countermoves that, seen from without, makes no sense. When they assist at
this excruciating process, onlookers remonstrate with the painter. They often
are desolate witnesses to what appears to them a wanton destruction of
paintings that, after seeing them one day in what they considered their
final state, they could not recognize the next day. Seen from within, struggles of this sort are meaningful to the painter. The reason for these cease-
less efforts of most painters to correct themselves and even to do their
works all over again is their inability to distinguish, among the countless
abstract possibilities of which their imagination is full, the only one to which
they are really trying to impart actual existence. The remedy, well known
to artists but not easy to apply, is to find out at what precise point of their

---

38. Amaury-Duval, *L'Atelier d'Ingres*, p. 97. The *St. Symphorian*, now in the Cathedral of Autun, was first commissioned in 1824. According to Baudelaire (*The Mirror of
Art*, p. 60), it "was entirely re-painted several times, and at the outset it contained far
fewer figures." The work was completed in 1834. See, in Wildenstein, *Ingres*, p. 206, pls.
131 and 132.

execution they went off the track. To ascertain this precise point, to start again from there as if what has been done this side of it had never existed —in short, to reintegrate the painting into the line of its germinal form— is the only way there is to salvage a work that, otherwise, is doomed never to reach its completion.[39]

An easy way to understand what precedes is to compare the experience of painters with that of writers. In creative prose and in poetry the problem often is for the writer to ascertain, by a careful scrutiny of his work, the precise point where, having unconsciously lost sight of the particular form whose incarnation was in process, inspiration has ceased to flow, leaving the gate open to the flood of irrelevant developments. There is no point in continuing to write without having first recovered the germinal form that is the living seed of the book; for, indeed, inspiration is but another name for it, and its own unity is the very unity that the work itself must have if it ever is to *be*.

Some writers have described this experience with vivid accuracy.[40] But it does not take a great artist to realize the meaning of such expressions as "to lose the thread of one's own discourse" and "to wander from one's own subject." The only difference is that, in the case of creative art, no logical calculus will ever suffice to ascertain the critical point where the execution

39. Speaking of the artist, Hersch (*L'Être et la forme*, p. 206) excellently remarks: "Sometimes he loses this unique road, he loses contact with being, he no longer feels the constraint exercised by the form, and, straightway, his freedom empties itself and confounds itself with nothingness. The artist no longer creates, he only alters given reality; he modifies fragile materials. He absolutely must find back that which is the only possible condition under which *this one* form can possibly be. It is the unity of this form that possesses him; this it is that he struggles with all his forces to preserve; this it is from which flows toward him the extraordinary choiceless liberty. Because this is *one*, he does it; and because it is one, it *is*." The import of this truth concerning the problems of art criticism is defined on p. 207.

40. Charles Morgan, *Sparkenbroke*, pp. 272–73. In this work of art about art (and a few other things), the poet attempts to determine the exact word that has jerked a reader back out of his poetic illusion. See the penetrating remarks that follow: this search must be conducted from the point of view of what should be said in the poet's world, not in everyday life: "Probably it twists further back. . . ." "It's more than one sentence, George. It's everything that leads up to it. What the girl says is right; the rest is wrong. I must go back." — "You say it like a peasant who has come ten yards down the wrong lane. It's two days' work. . . ." "I must go right back." See the conclusion of the episode, p. 350.

first went astray. The problem is the more complex as there is no way for an artist to determine with absolute certainty if he himself has lost contact with a form that can still be recaptured, or if the form itself has lost its efficacy. Some forms have not the vitality that it takes to bring the intended work of art to completion.[41] In such cases, the only choice is, for the painter, either to palliate this deficiency by resorting to artificial devices or else to turn his canvas to the wall. Countless paintings look completed, but are not. The holes have simply been filled in with forms in which it is obvious that the painter was not interested.

For purposes of clarification, let us consider the meanings of "to complete," "to finish," and "to sketch."

The verb "to complete" is not immediately clear. Like all words, it is susceptible of several different interpretations, all of which are legitimate. In its present context, "to complete" simply means to bring a certain painting to the point where there is nothing more that the artist can still do to it. At that moment, the germinal form has completely informed its matter; in so doing, it has exhausted all its productive energy. For this very reason, the completed work now stands apart from the artist, subsisting in itself as having received the fullness of the determinations required for its actual existence. The form that once lived in the mind of the painter is now living, according to a different mode of life, in the completed painting. Nobody exactly knows how many millenniums ago the Altamira bisons were first completed; we all can see that the germinal forms from which they then were born are still alive, attracting countless visitors, acting and operating as the fully constituted individual beings that they are. When the painting *is*, the work of the artist has come to an end.

In common language, "to finish" is frequently used in the same sense as "to complete." In the language of the painters, however, "to finish"

41. See the curious reflections of a shy artist about what he himself called "the seasoned painter" (*le peintre d'expérience*), who, instead of pouring all his inspiration into his sketch, saves it, so to speak, in view of the completed picture to be done: "He will know how to contain the flame always ready to flare up, so that the sketch, done in cold blood, does not engage the work that is to follow." Once the sketch has been well established and quite dry, let the painter frantically attack his canvas. (Jules Breton, *La vie d'un artiste*, 1890, pp. 284–85.)

sometimes conveys the notion of bringing a certain piece of work to its last degree of perfection by attending to all its details and, in certain cases, by polishing it to give it a glossy finish. The so-called "perfectionists" are likely to be unduly finicky. There is a certain notion of the art of painting that imperiously demands that pictures should be "finished" in this precise meaning of the term. Whether to finish is the same thing as to complete is a problem to be discussed, in each particular case, with reference to a certain particular painting.[42]

A study is a drawing, or a painting, done as a preliminary attempt to handle some part of the future work. Private collections and art museums conserve a great many studies by masters. Some of them are mere indications of lines, movements, and attitudes, but others are in themselves fully completed works of art. They are complete studies that, taken precisely as studies, have reached their point of completion. In many cases, such studies are not only complete, they are "finished." Such are, for instance, the quasi-miraculous studies for hand, arm, head, single figure, or drapery left us by Leonardo da Vinci and preserved in the Royal Library at Windsor Castle. These fragments of future works are in themselves completely finished pieces of work. In fact, some of them are so strikingly complete that they could not have been integrated with a painting as they are without ruining it. The painting would have been killed by the conspicuous self-sufficiency of fragments so complete in themselves that they could not enter the structure of another complete whole. A study may well be left unfinished by a master, but the reason it is unfinished is not that it is a study.[43]

42. Defending Corot against the reproach of not "finishing" his landscapes, Baudelaire has said: "Next [they are unaware] that there is a great difference between a work that is *complete* and a work that is *finished*; that in general what is *complete* is not *finished*, and that a thing that is highly *finished* need not be *complete* at all" (Baudelaire, *The Mirror of Art*, p. 29).

43. Another division is found in Malraux (*The Voices of Silence*, p. 109): (1) "the working sketch (or study)"; (2) "the sketch which records the artist's direct *raw* impression"; (3) "the expressive sketch," as exemplified by the lithographs of certain masters, such as Degas or Toulouse-Lautrec. Concerning these two latter classes, Malraux observes (p. 109): "The rough sketch is a memorandum; the expressive sketch an end in itself. And being an end in itself, it differs essentially from the completed picture." See (opposite pp. 110 and 111) the plates showing a detail of Delacroix's *Pietà* and the final version of the same work. — Malraux's interpretation of the reason such an artist as Constable

The notion of "sketch" calls for similar remarks. This notion itself can be understood in a twofold sense.

In a first sense, the sketch is the first outline, or rough draft, of the work. Such a sketch is part and parcel of the painting. It is therefore correct, in comparing it with the completed work, to say that such a sketch is an uncompleted painting.

In a second sense, a sketch is a sort of memorandum done by a painter, either from nature or from imagination, in view of some future work. Since, as has already been said, there is nothing absolute in matters of art, it cannot be said that such sketches cannot possibly be turned into completed paintings. The thing is being done by especially clever artists who, even while they are doing the sketch, already have in mind the future painting. In general, however, a sketch is destined to provide motive and inspiration for another painting, derived from the original sketch but distinct from it. It seems clear that, when the word is used in this second sense, the kind of painting that it signifies is not necessarily an unfinished piece of work. On the contrary, there is a point at which a good sketch has to be stopped if one does not wish it to degenerate from its condition of finished sketch into that of an unfinished painting.[44]

This is so true that one would sometimes hesitate to choose between the finished work of a painter and its sketch. This often happens with landscapes, especially in the case of painters whose notion of a "finished" painting invites the peril of academicism. By way of example, let us compare

added a realistic "finish" to his sketches (namely, to gratify the spectator by a more complete realism) is not a complete answer to the problem. The sketches of Leonardo da Vinci do not differ from his completed works by any lack of realistic "finish." A scrupulously "finished" picture may not even have begun to exist as a painting.

44. There is no difference between doing something and completing it. To the extent that a thing has not been completed, it has not been done. This is true of all kinds of arts: "Omnis ars infinita repudiat" (Thomas Aquinas, *Contra gentiles*, I, 63: "All art repudiates unfinished works"). In the present case, however, painters have to clear an obstacle that seems proper to their own art, at least under this form: "Everyone must have observed, on looking over the studies and drawings from nature of any celebrated painter for a great work, how much of their interest and beauty is lost, when they become transferred to the canvas: many of the delicacies of drawing and sentiment disappear by being embedded in the depths of shadow; or requiring to be stronger pronounced so as to give them distinctness from under the rich tones of color with which they necessarily become charged." (Note of John Burnet to Reynolds, *Discourses*, p. 29.)

the vigorous sketch done by Constable for *Salisbury Cathedral from the* [56, 57]
Bishop's Grounds with the "finished" version of it now in the Metropolitan
Museum of Art; or, again, the sketch done by Constable for *The Hay Wain*
in the Victoria and Albert Museum with the completed painting in the
National Gallery (London). If an art lover were offered a choice between
Corot's sketch from nature for *The Narni Bridge* now in the Louvre and the [58, 59a]
painting, which one would he choose? The sketch is pure Corot, but one
cannot help wondering if there is not the memory of a Ruisdael landscape [59b]
between Corot and his final version of the work. In the Ruisdael painting,
the road keeps the structure together, because it leads the eye both to the
left outside the frame and to the right across the bridge; one would like
to feel sure that, in the final version of the Corot, the road added to the
sketch does not endanger the unity of the work, and if its unity, then its
being.

If this be true, it can be said that the notion of completion applies to
all sorts of painted works, with the sole exception of those whose initial
destination is to be the starting point of a work still to be done. In this sense,
a work of art—study, sketch, or painting—should always be completed,
since to be completed and to be are for it the same thing. On the other hand,
a painting, or a study, or a sketch, is always complete when its execution
has been pushed to the point that is required for the fulfillment of the
germinal seed from which it proceeds. In Baudelaire's own words, a work
of art is always well executed when it is *sufficiently* so.[45]

According to the preceding definitions, there is no necessary relationship, for a painting, between being completed and being finished. Many
people feel convinced that, if it is not finished in all its details, a painting

45. Baudelaire, *The Mirror of Art*, p. 29. — Cf. "I'm satisfied with the sketch [of the
Entombment], but when I come to put in the details how am I going to preserve this impression of unity that results from very simple masses? Most painters, and I myself did so
in the past, begin with the details and deal with the effect last. But however distressing
it is to see the impression of simplicity in a good sketch vanish as one adds the details, there
still remains far more than could be obtained with the other method." (*The Journal of
Eugène Delacroix*, p. 68 [March 1, 1847].) See the whole note, pp. 68–69 (March 2, 1847).
Among the best reflections on this problem are those of a minor master whose writings denote a comprehension of aesthetic problems much superior to his own powers of execution:
Jules Breton, *Nos Peintres du siècle*, pp. 246–49.

is a failure. As will be seen later, one might perhaps object that they are mistaking the notion of image for that of painting; but even so, since every man is entitled to his own taste, there would be no point in arguing against such an opinion. The real trouble rather is that, in their zeal for the defense of true art, some painters have gone so far as to oppose the two notions of "finishing" and of "completing." The truth of the case is that there is between these two notions neither such a necessary tie nor such an opposition. If it is necessary for a painting to be finished in order to be complete, then the painting at stake must be finished, indeed. If, on the contrary, a painting cannot be finished without losing the individuating completion that it has already received at the hands of the painter, then to finish it would simply be to destroy it.

The common taste of art lovers seems to confirm this opinion. The vogue of modern paintings has not destroyed the taste for meticulously finished works. Who would dare to maintain that the miraculous landscape of the Rollin *Madonna,* by Jan van Eyck, does not find admirers among the lovers of modern art? The same remark would apply equally well to many works done by Memling, Gerard David, and others. In *A Small Country House,* by Pieter de Hooch, we can almost count the number of bricks in the wall and tiles on the roof. Given this style of painting, the work would not have been completed if it had not been so carefully finished. Here again, to complete a painting is to bring it to the point of completion required for its actual existence as a completely determined individual. Inversely, and for the very same reason, Frans Hals was well inspired not to consider an infinite accumulation of petty details necessary for the completion of his [60a] *Jolly Toper.* The apparently slapdash suddenness and liberty of his brush is the surest cause of his success in bringing to completion a painting to which any addition would bring a loss of substance. If anyone doubts this, let him compare the drinker of Manet with that of Hals. Two supremely [60b] skilled painters, indeed; but are we wrong in suggesting that, in *Le Bon Bock,* Manet was courting disaster? The work of Manet is dangerously near the level of plain illustration; the work of Hals is nothing if it is not straight painting.

When these confusions are cleared up, the problem still remains for the painter himself *to know* when a painting is really completed. Experience shows how difficult it is for artists themselves to be good judges in the matter. Most of them, however, have a proper feeling for the degree of precision required in the execution of each one of their works. A good example is the story of Constable's *Opening of Waterloo Bridge,* a painting whose first idea entered his mind in 1819, on which he worked, off and on, during twelve years without wholly satisfying himself about it. Finally, he exhibited it in 1832, but it failed to please the public, perhaps because it lacked the sentimental value of Constable's usual meadows, brooks, and mills, but more probably, Leslie says, "for its want of finish." [46] Yet twelve years was a long space of time to spend on a supposedly unfinished painting. The truth of the case was that, again in Leslie's own words, "the expanse of sky and water" that had tempted Constable to do the painting did not require any further finishing for the work to be completed.

That great painters usually know when to stop does not tell us how they know it. They themselves have acknowledged, first, that the initial

46. Leslie, p. 227. A more complete explanation is given by Leslie, pp. 207–08. It clears up the case so perfectly that we beg to quote it in full: "With Constable chiaroscuro was the one thing to be obtained at whatever cost. 'I was always determined,' he said, 'that my pictures should have chiaroscuro, if they had nothing else.' In the pursuit of this indispensable quality, and of that brightness in nature which baffles all the ordinary processes of painting, and which it is hardly possible to unite with smoothness of surface, he was led by degrees into a peculiar mode of execution, which too much offended those who were unable to see the look of nature it gave at the proper distance. In the 'Waterloo Bridge' he had indulged in the vagaries of the palette knife (which he used with great dexterity) to an excess. The subject challenged a comparison with Canaletti, the precision of whose execution is wonderful, and the comparison was made to Constable's great disadvantage; even his friend, Mr. Stothard, shook his head and said, 'Very unfinished, sir,' and the picture was generally pronounced a failure. It was a glorious failure; I have seen it often since it was exhibited, and I will venture to say that the noonday splendour of its color would make almost any work of Canaletti, if placed beside it, look like moonlight. But such pictures ought not to be compared, each has its own excellence, and nothing can be more true than Constable's remark that '*fine pictures neither want nor will bear comparison.*'" Since we are about this unfortunate picture, let us recall one more of its misfortunes. Speaking of this same *Waterloo Bridge,* Leslie wonders (pp. 227–28) what would Constable have felt, "could he foresee that, in little more than a year after his death, its silvery brightness was doomed to be clouded by a coat of *blacking,* laid on by the hand of a picture dealer! Yet that this was done, by way of giving *tone* to the picture, I know from the best authority, the lips of the operator, who gravely assured me that several noblemen considered it to be greatly improved by the process. The blacking was laid on with water, and secured by a coat of mastic varnish."

sketches often exhibit a bold simplicity of outline mainly due to the fact
that no unnecessary details have yet come to obscure it; next, that they
nevertheless experience an almost irrepressible tendency to complete their
paintings, be it at the necessary loss of some of the best qualities of their
sketches. There is in the germinal form an inner urge to externalize the
totality of its content. To allow a plastic form to remain in the condition
of a sketch is like trying to stop the development of a living organism in
the hope that, if it never reaches the maturity of adult age, it will preserve
the flower of its youth. But natural forms spontaneously cease to grow as
soon as they reach the term of their evolution. Born of the free will of the
artist, the painting has to be brought to its completion by a free decision
of the same will.

The main source of the difficulty seems to lie in the very skill of the
artist. The painter is looking at his sketch, wondering how to complete it.
If he is a master in his art, the temptation will be for him to add anything
anywhere. If he yields to this temptation, his work will be promptly finished,
it never will have been completed.[47] The details he has to find and to paint
are those which are required for the complete unfolding of the form, and
no other ones will do. The problem is for him to allow the "egg or embryo
of the idea"[48] to reach its complete development.

The painter knows that this end has been achieved in exactly the same
way in which we all know that an organism has ceased to live. It no longer
moves, it does not act, it does not operate. The germinal form is now dead
in the mind of the artist, nor is there any use in attempting to revive it or,
simply, to pretend that it is still alive. If the painter fails to see how to
correct, modify, or complete his work for the last time without completely
wrecking it,[49] or without having to do it all over again, it is a safe bet that

47. See Delacroix's remarks in his *Journal*, April 23, 1854. The passage is reproduced
in our Appendix II, pp. 316–17.

48. See Appendix, p. 316.

49. "I am simply trying to lay in colors that express my sensation. There is between
tones a necessary proportion that can make me modify the form of a figure or transform
my composition. So long as I have not achieved this proportion for all the parts, I continue to seek it and I pursue my work; then there happens a moment when all the parts
have found their definitive relation, and from that very moment it would become impossi-

the painting is really completed. In Georges Braque's own words: "A paint-ing is completed when it has wiped out the idea."[50] One more form has succeeded in saturating its matter. One more individual has been added to the substance of the world.

What happens to painters when they attempt to exploit a germinal form after its vitality is spent is so well known that there would be no point in describing it. Too many painters have to commit this error, in the full awareness of what they do, simply because they want to live. Art dealers know how difficult it is to get the public accustomed to a certain style; if they buy a Corot, customers want a Corot that really looks like a Corot; so the painter has to turn out a more or less uniform series of paintings—that is to say, he has to become the faker of his own art.

Philosophers, art critics, and historians, usually protected as they are against extreme poverty, would be ill advised to pass judgment on such abdications. The tragic side of the problem appears in full in the case of those unfortunate artists whom the awareness of their degradation finally leads to suicide. In this respect, no document that we know of surpasses in sadness Benjamin Robert Haydon's *Journals*. Painting and repainting, time and again, his famous *Napoleon Musing at St. Helena,* he himself became acutely conscious of the progressive degradation of his art: "Began and finished a Napoleon in two hours and a half; the quickest I ever did, and the twenty-fifth." It is no wonder that he himself added to this remark: "The art with me is becoming a beastly vulgarity." And again: "The soli-tary grandeur of historical painting is gone."[51] Such is the price to pay for sinning against the essential necessities of true art under the still

ble for me to modify ever so slightly my picture without doing it all over again. One must achieve a construction." (Matisse, quoted by Dorival, *Les Étapes de la peinture fran-çaise contemporaine*, II, 85.)

50. *Le Jour et la nuit*, p. 27.

51. *The Autobiography and Journals of Benjamin Robert Haydon*, ed. Malcolm Elwin, p. xi. Cf. "Painted a Napoleon musing (front), and sold it for twenty guineas, all in six hours" (p. 602). "Painted a little Napoleon in four hours." "Nearly finished another Na-poleon in four hours—nine to one." "Worked hard, and finished another Napoleon—'Haydon, patent for rapid manufacture of Napoleons Musing.' This is the eighth" (p. 618), and so on (pp. 620, 621); "I have painted nineteen Napoleons" (pp. 626, 627, 628, 633).

stronger pressure of the necessities of practical life. Yet Haydon was very far from being of a mediocre character. On the last day of the year 1841, he could justly write in his *Journals:* "I have loved my Art always better than myself." This is the very reason he finally died by his own hand, "hoping through the merits of Christ forgiveness." [52] Art would never end in tragedy, as it sometimes does, if its deepest problems were not directly related to the very life of man, himself at grips with the most primitive necessities of matter. In the poet's own words: "Art is an eminently earthly thing." [53]

52. Haydon, pp. 596 and 654. — See a similar story concerning the painter Marchal (in Jules Breton, *La Vie d'un artiste,* pp. 263–64). A diptych painted by Marchal, *Penelope and Phryne,* was a tremendous success. For two or three years, unable to sell anything else, Marchal exhausted his talent in replicas. Finally, he committed suicide "in evening dress, with all the correctness of a gentleman."

53. "L'art est une chose éminemment terrestre" (Pierre Reverdy, *Le Gant de crin,* p. 11).

CHAPTER SIX

THE WORLD OF PAINTINGS

IF WE consider paintings as man-made objects, the problem of the ultimate reason for their existence does not arise. *Homo faber* delights in making things, and, in this respect, painters are in no way different from other artisans who take so much pleasure in imparting existence to things that, without them, would not exist. It seems, however, that painters, and probably sculptors as well, experience a particularly intense feeling of domination over their work. Consequently, the pleasure they take in producing it is remarkably intense. Some of them speak of it as of an exaltation similar to that which would no doubt arise from the exercise of a truly creative activity. The works of the painter are his own creatures much more deeply and genuinely than if they were the products of a merely mechanical mode of production. The reason for it is not hard to find: born of his hand under the guidance of his mind, paintings are made in the image and in the likeness of the painter.[1]

Another question, much less easy to answer, is why certain men seem to attach so much importance to the production of painted works of art.

1. "A great painter concentrates the interest by suppressing details that are useless, offensive, or foolish; his mighty hand orders and prescribes, adding to or taking away from the objects in his pictures, and treating them as his own creatures; he ranges freely throughout his kingdom and gives you a feast of his own choosing, whereas, with a second-rate artist, you feel that he is master of nothing" (*The Journal of Eugène Delacroix,* p. 227 [April 28, 1854]). — Cf. Reynolds, *Discourses,* p. 42, and the personal experience related by Eric Gill, below, ch. 8, n. 37. — The following anecdote concerning Théodore Rousseau and the rustic is found in the memoirs of the painter Jules Breton (*La Vie d'un artiste,* p. 291).

And, indeed, the question is a puzzling one. Artisans make tools and objects of all sorts in view of their practical usefulness in everyday life. Although, occasionally, a man may take pleasure in making perfectly useless things, for the mere pleasure of making them, the practical advantages to be derived from fabricated objects is the normal justification for their production.

Not so in the case of paintings. There is some depth in the apparently naïve question of a peasant to the painter Théodore Rousseau: "Why are you painting that oak tree, since it is already there?" To duplicate real objects by a series of images without substance of their own is, to say the least, a pastime more suitable to youth than to persons who have reached intellectual maturity. The only explanation for this phenomenon is that paintings serve some purpose of their own that is not served, or that is less well served, by the things and beings constituting the world of nature. In other words, it is to be supposed that paintings constitute a universe of their own whose purposiveness, although different from that of nature, can probably be discovered.

This can be done, at least in the beginning of the inquiry, without bringing into play any other elements than the painter himself and his work. Reduced to its simplest terms, the activity of the artist can be described as an effort to cause the existence of an object that its creator desires to see but that he does not find, ready-made, in natural reality. At the same time, the progress of artistic creation is, to the painter himself, a progressive revelation of the new being he is producing. In this sense, the artist is to himself his first public, and if we ask what he is expecting from his own work, the answer is: the pleasure of seeing it. With the artist himself begins the first moment of the long chain of expressions of like and dislike that will attend, through years, centuries, and sometimes millenniums, the existence of the work of art. True enough, there already were countless other paintings, all of them capable of giving pleasure to the eyes, even to the eyes of the painters who made them, but there still was room in the world for one more of these strange givers of pleasure. The immediate purpose of the painter is to give existence to a certain artistic being that is irreplaceable in the sense that the sight of no other one can give to its author the particular kind of pleasure this one painting is able to give. Having reached this point, the analysis must go beyond empirically given facts in order to proceed to their interpretation.

1. Paintings and Beauty

TO ENTER a universe peopled with objects whose function is to give pleasure is also to establish contact with the order of pure beauty.

The words "beauty" and "beautiful" have become unfashionable, not indeed with artists, who use them quite freely even in our own day, but rather with the school of those aestheticians who intend to handle the realities of art with the same scientific methods that befit the realities of nature. The beautiful then is rejected as a "metaphysical" notion unworthy of our attention. But nothing is simpler, more concretely evident, than beauty, and its experience is familiar to all. In reading books, we usually content ourselves with understanding the meaning of the sentences, pages, and chapters. If we stumble upon some passage whose meaning escapes us, either on account of the obscurity of the style or because of the intrinsic difficulty of the subject, we read it again, but not for pleasure. We never desist from reading the passage in question until, owing to our renewed efforts of attention, its meaning becomes clear to our mind. Then, at last, we *know* what our text means. But precisely because we then are in the order of knowledge and of truth, we stop reading the sentences that have so long detained our attention. If we read a book to learn the truth it contains, the aim and purpose of our reading is to rid ourselves of the need of reading the same book again in the future. This is the kind of book of which one says: "I do not need to read it because I know what there is in it."

But there is an entirely different class of books. We have already read them, understood them, and some of them are so familiar to us that we could recite parts of them, as the saying goes, "by heart." Still we want to read them at least once more. We shall always desire to repeat our past experience, not in the least because we hope to learn from such books something they have not yet taught us, but simply because of the pleasure we are sure to find in reading them. This well-known experience usually attends our first contact with certain sequences of words and sounds that leave in us a sweet wound more desirable than many material satisfactions. At first, this is not a question of understanding; usually, the understandable element of the sentence is very simple, so much so that, as often as not, there is nothing to understand at all. It can be just a singsong, or one of those playful lyrics which sound so much like a lovely nursery rhyme:

> Lawn as white as driven snow;
> Cyprus black as e'er was crow;
> Gloves as sweet as damask roses;
> Masks for faces and for noses;
> Bugle bracelet, necklace amber,
> Perfume for a lady's chamber . . .

Any time we feel an irresistible urge to stop, to linger upon such an experience, to repeat it for the mere pleasure of experiencing again, we can feel sure that beauty is there.

When joy is experienced by sense, and in sense, its true name is pleasure. Words always betray such experiences. In the present case, it should be made clear from the outset that, because to see is to know, the pleasure of aesthetic experience is that of cognition. The desire to repeat it is the desire of repeating an act of cognition. Moreover, since the cause of pleasure lies in the very apprehension of a certain object, the desire to repeat it expresses itself in a series of intellectual efforts whose aim and purpose it is to deepen, to clarify, and, in a word, to perfect our knowledge of its cause. This is one of those cases in which a continuous exchange takes place among pleasure, love, and knowledge, the desire to know springing from the pleasure that the sight of a certain object can give and, in turn, the pleasure itself feeding on an always more intimate knowledge of its source. The pleasure that is here at stake is exactly of the same sort as that of contemplation. And, indeed, aesthetic experience is, first and foremost, a sensible contemplation that blossoms in an intellectual inquiry into its cause. Therefore, in saying that aesthetic experience is that of a pleasure, we shall always point out the kind of emotion a man experiences in contact with an object whose apprehension is desirable for its own sake. The beautiful is that which, in the object itself, is the cause of such emotions, or of such pleasures, of such acts of cognition.

Read in the light of these simple facts, many ancient doctrines recover the fullness of a truth that has been obscured by too many misunderstandings. The Scholastics used to define the beautiful (*pulchrum*): that which pleases when seen.[2] A similar position was upheld in the seventeenth century by Nicolas Poussin, when he defined painting: "An imitation of anything visible that is under the sun, done on a surface by means of lines and colors. Its end is delectation."[3] To be sure, the word "delectation" conveys the notion of an emotion more complex than what is commonly called pleasure, but, precisely, whatever the mind contributes to the pleasure of the eyes is there in view of turning this pleasure into a protracted delectation. In the very last lines of his *Journal*, Delacroix has noted in pencil this ultimate reflection: "the first quality in a picture is to be a delight for the

2. "Beautiful and good in a thing are identical fundamentally, for they are based upon the same thing, namely, the form; and this is why good is praised as beautiful. But they differ in the mind. For good properly relates to appetite (since good is that which all desire), and therefore it has the nature of an end (since desire is a sort of movement towards a thing). On the other hand, beautiful relates to a cognitive power. For those things are said to be beautiful which please when seen. Hence beautiful consists in due proportion, for sense delights in things duly proportioned, as in what is like itself, because the sense too is a sort of proportion [other texts: reason], as is every cognitive power. Now since knowledge is by assimilation, and likeness relates to form, beautiful properly relates to the notion of formal cause." (Thomas Aquinas, *Summa theologiae*, I, 5, 4, ad 1.) — Cf. Ia, IIae, 27, 1, ad 3. In this latter text, note the important remark that, just as desire finds its rest in good, so also does apprehension, be it that of sense or that of intellectual knowledge, find its rest in beautiful: "Sed ad rationem pulchri pertinet quod in ejus aspectu seu cognitione quietetur apprehensio." This nature of aesthetic apprehension, conceived as the intrinsic perfection of cognitive apprehension as such, will remain for us, as will be seen later, the last word on the question. — A different approach to the problem is to be found in Harold Osborne, *Theory of Beauty*, especially ch. 3, pp. 32–60 ("Metaphysical Aesthetic Theories"), and ch. 4, pp. 61–90 ("Subjective and Objective Theories of Beauty"). Elements of bibliography (pp. 205–15) give a faint notion of the multitude of studies devoted to the question. Cf. Thomas Munro, "The Concept of Beauty in the Philosophy of Naturalism," *Revue internationale de philosophie*, XXXI (1955), 33–77.

3. As quoted in *Artists on Art*, ed. Goldwater and Treves, p. 151. — The French original is found in a letter of Poussin to M. de Chambray, Rome, March 1, 1665 (reprinted in Lhote, *De la Palette à l'écritoire*, p. 57).

eyes."[4] It would be a pity to lose sight of a position that has obtained the support of Aristotle, Poussin, and Delacroix. But the best way to ensure its survival is perhaps to examine its ultimate implications.

As has been seen in its place,[5] an object is said to be a work of art for the elementary reason that it owes its very existence to the art of an artist. But it owes to the same art to be such as it is, and if it has been of such nature that its sight gives pleasure to those who experience it, the cause that makes it an object pleasing to human eyes remains inherent in it, or consubstantial with it, as long as it remains in existence. This is to say that the beautiful hangs on our actual experience of it as far as its aesthetic mode of existence is concerned, but its physical existence is as independent of the fact that it is being experienced or not as the physical existence of the work of art itself is. And no wonder, since for a work of art to be and to be fully actualized as an actually existing work of art are one and the same thing. Here, as in all similar cases, there is nothing to prevent a philosopher from adopting an idealistic attitude. We can *pretend* to believe that the intrinsic physical characteristics that make some Egyptian paintings such an unexpected joy to the eye simply ceased to exist during the millenniums they spent in complete darkness, invisible to human eyes. The least that can be said about such a supposition is that it is a wholly gratuitous one. Successfully achieved works of art are not beautiful because they please our eyes; they please our eyes because they are beautiful. Their beauty is coextensive with their duration as it is consubstantial with their being as works of art.

On the other hand, it is true that the beautiful reveals itself and reaches one of its ends in the human act of cognition by which it is being actually apprehended. In this respect even the classical formulas in which the Scholastics used to speak of the beautiful are apt to be misleading. In saying that the beautiful is that which pleases when seen ("id quod visum placet"), one seems to say that the beautiful consists in the pleasure that it gives to

---

4. The note (*Journal*, p. 414) ends as follows: "This does not mean that there need be no sense in it; it is like poetry which, if it offend the ear, all the sense in the world will not save from being bad. They speak of *having an ear* for music: not every eye is fit to taste the subtle joys of painting. The eyes of many people are dull or false; they see objects literally, of the exquisite they see nothing."

5. See above, p. 12.

those who perceive it. But their complete view of the problem was more complex than one might surmise from this abbreviated formula. First of all, since the beautiful is apprehended by an act whose repetition is desirable, it is an object of love. But that which is an object of love is apprehended as a certain good. For this reason, the beautiful is a particular case of the good. It is the kind of good found in the very apprehension, by sense, of any kind of being so made that there is pleasure in the very act of apprehending it. This is not an exclusive property of works of art. Every sense perception whose act is enjoyable for its own sake is an intimation of the objective presence of beauty in its object. Things of nature, such as landscapes, seascapes, animals, human figures and faces, even the works of man's industry, such as cities, utensils, and the most modest of man-made objects—in short, everything that in any sense of the verb can be said "to be" is susceptible, under favorable circumstances, of becoming an object of pleasurable experience. One then realizes that the thing *is* beautiful. The nature of this experience is the same with the works of nature as it is with the works of art. The beautiful is the same in both cases. Not, indeed, our own apprehension of it, but that, in reality, whose nature is such that there is for us pleasure in the very act by which it is being apprehended: "id cujus ipsa apprehensio placet." [6]

There is, however, a real distinction between the naturally beautiful and the artistically beautiful. Their difference lies in their respective origins and, by the same token, in our awareness of the difference. Natural

---

6. Thomas Aquinas, *Summa theologiae*, Ia, IIae, 27, 1, ad 3 (ed. André Blot, vol. II, p. 298). The text says: "We do not speak of beauty in connection with the sensible qualities perceived by other senses [i.e., other than sight and hearing]; for we do not say that tastes or odors are beautiful. And thus it appears that beautiful adds to good a certain relationship to cognitive power. So, something is called good simply because it gives satisfaction to desire, whereas something is called beautiful because its very apprehension pleases [*id cujus ipsa apprehensio placet*]." — Cf. "Beautiful things are those which please when seen—and, of course, I mean mentally seen, and therefore pleasing to the mind. . . . Anything is beautiful if it be made in such a way as to give pleasure to the mind which perceives it, and the question as to what should or should not give pleasure to the mind is no more and no less difficult than the question as to what should or should not give annoyance." (*Letters of Eric Gill*, p. 259: letter to *The Architect's Journal*, March 4, 1931.) — On the "indestructible relationship of . . . aesthetic beauty, to the kingdom of intelligence," see the excellent passage in Maritain, pp. 165–66.

beauty belongs to things considered as so many works of nature. Artistic beauty belongs to objects considered as works of art. This is so truly perceived by artists themselves that one can find in this elementary fact one of the deepest reasons for their creative activity. To the question asked by the rustic, Rousseau could have answered: "I am painting an oak tree because the one we are seeing is not quite the one I would like to see." At the origin of the art of painting there is a vague feeling that, admirable and even unequaled in its works as it is, nature does not provide man with all the objects of apprehension he would like to perceive. The primary function of art is to provide man with such objects as nature itself does not provide, because their only aim and purpose is to be beautiful. This implies no dissatisfaction with nature qua nature; it only implies the feeling that there is a whole order of beings whose production is the responsibility of man himself, or, at least, of man as an artist.

Artists could almost be defined as the special class of persons who do not find in nature a certain class of objects that ought to be there—namely, objects whose existence, essence, and structure are exclusively justifiable by the pleasure found in apprehending them. Paintings are not simply objects that are pleasant to see; they are objects that have been produced by artists in such a way that their sight pleases the eyes. This is the cause of their existence. Because they do not find in nature objects whose exclusive *raison d'être* is the aesthetic pleasure derived from their perception, artists set out to produce such objects. There are no such things in the physical world; so let us make them.

This also is one of the causes of the creative nature of the aesthetic perception, or imagination, in which we have found the germinal forms of pictures to be done. Owing to their creative imagination, painters live in a universe of their own, a sort of earthly paradise in which, because they have been made to serve this precise purpose, all objects, beings, and scenes are as they should be in order to please the perceiving powers by which they are apprehended.[7] Last, not least, this is the cause of the very struc-

---

7. "To a lady who, looking at an engraving of a house, called it an ugly thing, he [Constable] said, 'No, madam, there is nothing ugly; *I never saw an ugly thing in my*

ture of the particular class of works of art called paintings. Each of them
is such that all the elements that enter its structure, and their very order,
contribute to make it an object whose apprehension delights the eye.[8]

At this point, the question inevitably arises: What is there, in some forms,
that makes them pleasant to see? However this question is answered, and
even though we failed to agree on a satisfactory explanation of the fact, the
fact itself at least is there, and its reality cannot be denied. As to the theory
by which it can be accounted for, although all seem to agree on its principle
ever since the time of Aristotle, its scientific formulation has made little
progress.

The problem of the aesthetic pleasure experienced in seeing paintings
is usually conceived by analogy with the clearer case of music. The musical
sounds are perceived vibrations of air, and the combination of two or more
musical sounds either pleases the ear or displeases it, according to the
numerical relations that obtain between their respective vibrations. At the
time of Aristotle, Greek ears seem to have lagged far behind Greek eyes
in their aptitude to perceive such relations. In his treatise *On Sense and
the Sensed*, Aristotle explains that colors are like sounds, in this at least,
that the cause of the pleasure they give is the same. Harmonies are most
pleasing to ears when they obey numerical proportions, such as, for instance, unison, which is the perfect identity in pitch; such is also diapason,
which sounds the consonance of the octave and in which, therefore, the proportion is that of two to one. Aristotle still mentions the proportions of
three to two (*diapente*), and of three to four, and so on. In short, all combinations of sounds that can be expressed in terms of numerical proportions
are pleasant to hear; the others are not. The same remarks apply to colors.
In his commentary on this text, Thomas Aquinas observes that, just as, in
consonances, or harmonies, the most pleasing to hear are those which consist in numbers, so also, in the case of colors, "those which consist in nu-

---

life: for let the form of an object be what it may,—light, shade, and perspective will always make it beautiful. It is perspective which improves the form of this'" (Leslie, p.
280).

8. "But in referring to nature we in vain look for those combinations which, in the
works of Titian and other great colourists, produce such wonderful effects" (Burnet's note
to Reynolds, *Discourses,* pp. 24–25, n. 2).

merical proportion are the most proportionate, and the same seen also to be the most delectable, such as yellow [*croceus*] and purple [*purpureus*], that is, red. And just as few harmonies are pleasing to hear, so also few colors are pleasing to see. As to the other colors, which· are not pleasant to see, they do not consist of numerical proportions."[9]

As can be seen from these words, the problem was still in its infancy at the time of St. Thomas Aquinas. The fact that he does not even speak of the consonance of several colors, but only of the numerical proportion that constitutes a single color, does not modify the essence of the problem. On the contrary, it exactly localizes the difficulty, for, indeed, he whose eye does not perceive the presence of the numerical proportions whose apprehension would be for him a cause of pleasure is exactly blind to painting and excluded from the pleasures that the sight of its works can give. The pleasure itself is not the aesthetic experience; it accompanies it whenever it takes place. At its origin is found the perfect adaptation that there is between a certain eye and a certain visible object whose structure makes it a perfect object of apprehension. Sense perception is a biological function whose exercise is normally attended by pleasure. In the case of aesthetic experience, the structure of the objects to be experienced has been selected by the artist, from among many possible ones, precisely in view of its aptitude to cause pleasurable acts of apprehension.

To such a conception of aesthetic experience and of art, the ready objection is that it is one of the many branches of hedonism—that is, of the doctrine according to which pleasure is the supreme good. It suffices for our purpose to say that, without itself being the supreme good, pleasure is intimately related to it. The dignity of pleasure is proportionate to that of its cause. Do not theologians consider the beatific vision the ultimate end of man? In the more modest case of aesthetic experience, the pleasure at stake finds its source in the very intelligibility of being.

Assuredly, aesthetic pleasure is found in sense experience, but our sensibility is that of a man. In listening to the performance of one of Bee-

9. Aristotle, *On Sense and the Sensed*, ch. 3 (in Thomas Aquinas' commentary, ed. R. Spiazzi, p. 32, n. 101).

thoven's quartets, our ear perceives sonorous relations that would escape the apprehension of a nonrational animal. The formal structure of a fugue, of the first movement of a piano sonata, or of the finale of the second act of *The Marriage of Figaro* is as directly perceptible to a human ear as are the numerical relations that define the chords, the bars, and the musical phrases that constitute such music. What this interpretation of musical experience entails is that the pleasure it implies flows from the aptitude of human sense powers to perceive intelligible relations under the form of sensible qualities. In using the word "perceive," we mean to say that this experience is essentially distinct from intellectual knowledge,[10] but we also maintain its essentially cognitive nature as well as the essentially intelligible nature of its object.[11] This identity of object is unavoidable since, under all its forms, the nature of reality remains identically the same. It is the nature of being.

Similar remarks apply to painting. It is worth noticing that some of the most daring reformers in the history of this art, despite their personal divergences, have agreed on the notion that intelligible laws are at work in aesthetic experience, and this not only in music, as is evident, but also in painting. The intention attributed to Paul Cézanne of reducing material objects to geometric structures similar to those which constitute the universe

10. There is a curious reluctance on the part of some philosophers to accept the classic definition of the beautiful and of its aesthetic experience. It seems to them that it does not do justice to the part played in it by the mind. Hence, for instance, its modification by Eric Gill: "The aesthetic is that which is pleasing to the mind by means of the sense" (*Work and Property*, p. 49). One feels tempted to invert the formula and to say: "The aesthetic is that which is pleasing to the senses by means of the mind." — Besides, Gill himself adds (pp. 128–29) that the aesthetic pleasure is only mental pleasure "in exactly the same way as toothache is mental pain" and, in the last analysis, that "aesthetic pleasure is grounded in the physical rather than the spiritual."

11. Cf. Lhote (*La Peinture*, p. 26): "In order to sum up the method of Cézanne, one must distinguish two moments. First, at the contact of a spectacle, the painter experiences an *essentially plastic* emotion. Under the appearances, he discerns the existence of a hidden order that calls forth in his consciousness an adequate geometrical construction. Sensation here replaces inspiration in its classical sense, and it remains endowed with the same powers. The first work, direct, spontaneous, consists in enriching the fleeting structure of sensation with colored materials that contain the essential of the object at stake. The second part of the work, which takes place after reflection, consists in submitting to a mechanical rhythm—a reflection of universal rhythm—the elements born of the foregoing analysis." Cf. ch. 5, n. 32.

in the *Timaeus* of Plato,[12] the quasi-esoteric speculations carried by the so-called Nabis,[13] are so many signs that this conviction has never deserted the minds of painters. Above all, it should be noted that just as it is capable of giving perfect satisfactions to the mind, mathematics is capable of offering to sense perfectly satisfactory objects of perception. Who has not stood speechless before the perfect plastic beauty of certain plaster casts stored on the shelves of the department of mathematics in some faculty of sciences? Yet these objects are nothing else than straight geometric models, unless they represent the concrete development, in space, of some algebraic formula whose intelligibility thus becomes perceptible to sense. No wonder, then, that we can now see them, or very similar ones, no longer as mathematical models, but as works of art, in the *Developable Column* of Pevsner, in the *Spiral Theme* of Naum Gabo (Museum of Modern Art, New York), or even integrated by some modern painters with their own compositions.[14]

The significance of this fact is considerable. It helps us to realize the true nature of the forms handled by the painter. Behind every geometrical curve, or volume, even behind a simple line and its inflections, there is present an element of mathematical intelligibility. Leibniz was fond of repeating that there is no number of dots, thrown at random on a plane surface, that it is not possible to connect by means of a single line express-

12. For an interpretation of Cézanne's geometrical constructions and their relationship to sense perception, see Lhote, *La Peinture*, pp. 23–24. Note, however, that Lhote's personal views are involved in this interpretation. According to him, what Cézanne was painting at the time of his maturity was plastic equivalents of the relationship that obtains between the objects of sense perception and some transcendental figures (sphere, cylinder, cone) or some more complex figure resulting from their combinations. Thus conceived, paintings can be defined as "mental architectures born of the painter's sensation" (p. 29).

13. Paul Sérusier, *A B C de la peinture*, pp. 15–21. — Cf. Osborne, *Theory of Beauty*, pp. 174–87.

14. See the various polygons designed by Leonardo da Vinci for the book *De divina proportione*, by Fra Luca di Pacioli (in Matila C. Ghyka, *Le Nombre d'or*, I, pls. VII–IX; the extraordinarily beautiful samples of shells, pls. XV and XVI). — André Sainte-Laguë, *Le Monde des formes*, "golden number," pp. 110–16: representation (after the Swedish mathematician G. Gyllström) of the "integral curves of two complex differential equations"; geometrical surfaces made up of threads stretched out on brass frames, p. 200. Compare especially the figure on p. 201, which seems to have haunted the imagination of Pevsner and Gabo. — Incidentally, compare the trace left by the motion of a particle of matter in the Brownian movement (p. 179) with some drawings by Paul Klee.

ing a single law. The germinal form in the mind of the painter is not such a law, but it operates in accordance with a secret feeling for intelligibility. A sort of instinct rather than a knowledge, the germinal form gropes its way toward its final embodiment in a certain matter according to an inner tendency similar to that which orientates the form toward its end in the production of a natural being. The result of the operation, to borrow the words of Baudelaire,[15] is to bring about *"another* nature." Only, in the case of painting, the germinal form becomes incarnate in a matter exclusively structured to offer the eye a perfect object of apprehension and, so to speak, of sensible contemplation.

Thus understood, the germinal form is only perceptible to us under its first concrete expression, which is the painting; but it is the apprehension of that form in and through its body which constitutes the very core of aesthetic experience, the cause of the joy it implies, and, in short, its true object. It cannot be found in nature, or even in a revised and corrected version of nature destined to reduce it to average normality. The causes of visible forms are not themselves visible. Art is there to give them visible appearance and to reveal them to us through the medium of sense perception.

2. Being and Beauty

It is a commonly received theological truth that the universe bears witness to the existence and power of its Creator; a work of art likewise betrays at first sight the mastery of its author. It is to be regretted that the best words grow so hackneyed that the strength of their primitive meaning ultimately evaporates. In the present case, it is with good reason that painters have been called "masters," for, indeed, even apart from the fact that the germinal form is born of his own genius, an artist always remains the master of his work. A "master" is a person having control, and a painter is no master if, having conceived his work, he does not control its execution, as far as possible, in its smallest details.

Art lovers feel differently about this problem. They usually express their

15. *The Mirror of Art,* p. 61.

admiration for the boldness of conception that characterizes the great creators of art. And, true enough, inspiration (which is but another name for the germinal form) is necessary, but it is something about which artists themselves can do very little. Even when it is present, it is like unto the molten metal without which one cannot cast a statue; but the molten metal itself will never become a statue unless the sculptor forces it into a previously calculated mold. Art is essentially a know-how. It is much less inspiration itself than the wise management of inspiration. All the characters signified by the term "masterly" originate in this domination exercised by the painter over his work.

The main consequence of this fact is immediately perceptible to the eye. Dunoyer de Segonzac has expressed it in saying that one of the most essential elements in a work of art is *la tenue*. A man has *de la tenue* (*tenir:* to hold) when there is nothing slipshod about him or, in other words, when he holds himself well in hand, keeping a firm control over his own way of dressing, behaving, and speaking. A work of art, especially a picture, has *de la tenue* when it is at once experienced as the result of an attentively controlled effort.[16]

Artists of various schools and living in different times have resorted to different devices to ensure this domination over their works. Generally speaking, they have inserted between inspiration and execution a method, a doctrine, or theory, whose proper function it was to help them solve at least the general problems of composition and execution that arise in connection with all paintings.

Perhaps the oldest of these devices is related to the problem of dividing a surface into unequal parts, according to a universal rule and in such a way that it pleases the eye. It is called the method of the "golden number," or "golden section."[17] Its origin seems to be the teaching of Pythagoras, or of his school, but it has been revived in recent years by enthusiastic

16. Dunoyer de Segonzac, in P. Jamot, *Dunoyer de Segonzac*, quoted in Lhote, *De la Palette à l'écritoire*, p. 408. The same passage attributes to this *tenue* "rhythm, harmony, and the complete satisfaction given by certain works of art."

17. The most complete discussion of the problem is found in Ghyka, *Le Nombre d'or*. A large number of excellently selected and commented illustrations will convince any reader of the reality of the problem and of its relevancy to art.

disciples. Paul Sérusier, one of its exponents, has been blamed for having philosophized at the expense of his creative power as an artist,[18] but there is some illusion in the common belief that too much speculation must necessarily harm painting. It all depends on the painters. At any rate, in the case of Paul Sérusier, it can be said that, concerning the division of surfaces and the combination of colors, he simply codified general rules that had been brought into play by countless artists before his time.[19] The still more geometrical speculations followed by Juan Gris certainly did not impair his creative power or his originality.[20]

Another attempt to establish general forms, or canons, as guides for the painter is represented by the obscure doctrine of the pictorial "modes" imagined by Nicolas Poussin in imitation of the musical modes of the Greeks. What renders the doctrine obscure is its ambition to establish an exact correspondence between painting and music. Otherwise, the general intention is rather clear. A musician does not indifferently write in any key; he recognizes the existence of affinities between certain tonalities and the moods of the soul that he intends to express or to suggest. A universally perceptible instance is the difference between A and A flat or between any two major and minor modes. The Greek musical modes, Doric, Phrygian, Lydian, etc., were considered adapted to the expression of definite moods of the soul, and although there are no such clear-cut distinctions

18. Dorival, *Les Étapes de la peinture française*, I, 116. Ingres, Delacroix, Cézanne, Juan Gris, and many others have constantly speculated about their art; it never did them any harm. It is all a problem of mastery in execution. In some cases, it is a plain problem of nerves.

19. Those who deride Sérusier for having considered his own theories as one of the origins of cubism seem to have misunderstood the meaning of his statement. They mentally compare his own paintings with those of Picasso, Gris, or Braque, and they are quite right in failing to notice the resemblance. But Sérusier had in mind his Platonist conviction that beauty is essentially intellectual, as well as his speculations on the geometrical proportions observed by ancient painters (*A B C de la peinture*, pp. 15–20). This intellectualism was entirely shared at least by Juan Gris: "Artists have believed that they will achieve their poetic end by means of beautiful models or of beautiful motifs. We rather trust we shall reach it by means of beautiful *elements*, for indeed the most beautiful of elements are certainly those of the mind." (Kahnweiler, *Juan Gris*, p. 276.)

20. See Juan Gris' remarks: "Cézanne makes a cylinder out of a bottle, whereas I start from a cylinder in order to create an individual with a special type; out of a cylinder, I make a bottle, a certain bottle" (Kahnweiler, *Juan Gris*, p. 277). Cf. below, Appendix III, pp. 318–19.

between the general tonalities of pictures, Poussin conceived the idea of distinguishing them according to the musical modes of the Greeks. His letter of November 24, 1647, to Chantelou seems to have unduly puzzled his historians. In Poussin's own mind, a "mode" is one of those laws, or methods, which artists establish in order to help them in executing the work. In a way, such sets of rules entail certain obligations; so they impose restrictions upon the freedom of the painter, but, on the other hand, they facilitate his task by defining a general course of action whose observance is sure to lead to certain results.

How closely related to the notion of mastery this notion of modes is clearly appears from its definition by Poussin: "The good old Greeks, inventors of all beautiful things, discovered several modes by means of which they produced marvelous effects. This word *mode* properly signifies the reason or the measure and form we have to resort to in order to do something. It prevents us from overstepping it; it obliges us to proceed in everything with a certain restraint and moderation. Consequently, this restraint and moderation is nothing else than a certain manner, or order, both firm and determinate, found in the process by which the thing keeps itself in existence." [21] A method in execution keeps the artist within bounds and, by the same token, keeps his work within the limits that define its entity. This notion of "mode" represented, in Poussin's mind, the self-imposed disciplines without which painters find it hardly possible to achieve their works. When, two centuries later, Cézanne declared his intention to do Poussin all over again but, this time, "from nature," he clearly proved that to dominate the execution of his work by means of a set-up method was, for every artist, an objective necessity.

The first sign that betrays the hand of a true master is what philosophers, theologians, and even some artists have agreed to call the "integrity" of the painting.[22] The word itself can be given many meanings. In its application to paintings, however, it means that the painting at stake is a

21. This letter of Poussin to Chantelou is partly printed in Lhote, *De la Palette à l'écritoire*, pp. 49–51; English translation in *Artists on Art*, ed. Goldwater and Treves, pp. 151–53.
22. Thomas Aquinas, *Summa theologiae*, pt. I, qu. 39, art. 7, answer to the question. — The complete passage runs as follows: "Three things are required for beauty. First, integrity, or perfection [*integritas, sive perfectio*]; for indeed things are ugly to the

complete whole, lacking nothing of what should enter its structure as a perfectly completed being. Thus understood, the integrity of a painting is proportional to its being. If none of the elements that are essential to its structure is missing, then it enjoys wholeness and, consequently, the plenitude of being.[23]

Integrity should not be confused with the privilege, enjoyed by certain paintings, of causing a powerful impression of stability, of solidity, so much so that at times they seem to impart to what they represent a sort of independent reality.[24] It has rightly been said that "tactile values" are of great importance in paintings,[25] but the fact that some of them succeed in imparting to visible images the apparent solidity of real objects is not exactly the same thing as the integrity of the work. Some authentic master-

extent that they are incomplete [*diminutae*]. Then due proportion, or harmony [*consonantia*]. And again brightness [*claritas*], from whence it comes that things which have bright colors are called beautiful." Parallel texts are found in the *Summa*, IIa, IIae, 145, 2, answer, and 180, 2, ad 3m. — St. Thomas Aquinas' doctrine is a realism; according to him, beauty is being itself considered under one of its transcendental aspects. Modern idealism begins by turning the transcendentals into "values," after which it declares unsound the position it has thus deformed (Osborne, p. 69). A new definition then becomes necessary in order to eliminate its realistic implications from the notion of "work of art." It runs as follows: "A work of art is not a material thing but an enduring possibility, often embodied or recorded in a material medium, of a specific set of sensory impressions, which is characterized by what we call beauty" (Osborne, p. 202; cf. pp. 93–94). Cf. ch. 1, n. 10.

23. The notion of "integrity" takes us back to the previously studied notions of being, individuality, and even the personality of paintings: "In affirming the autonomy of the work of art, Cubists—unbeknowst to themselves, of course—were ambitioning for it that *integritas* which, according to St. Thomas Aquinas, is required before anything else *ad pulchritudinem*. The pictures which they created had to be 'individuals,' this term being taken in the precise sense of: an organized being that cannot be divided without ceasing to be the same person, each one of these 'persons' having its own unique 'personality' and occupying its own place in history." (Kahnweiler, *Juan Gris*, p. 142.)

24. James Joyce renders *integritas* "wholeness," which is a perfectly legitimate rendering, and he means by this word the property inherent in all being to constitute a self-sufficient whole, distinct from other beings. "In order to see that basket, said Stephen, your mind first of all separates the basket from the rest of the visible universe which is not the basket. The first phase of apprehension is a bounding line drawn about the object to be apprehended. An esthetic image is presented to us either in space or in time. What is audible is presented in time, what is visible is presented in space. But temporal or spatial, the esthetic image is first luminously apprehended as selfbounded and selfcontained upon the immeasurable background of space or time which is not it. You apprehended it as *one* thing. You see it as one whole. You apprehend its wholeness. That is *integritas*." (James Joyce, *A Portrait of the Artist as a Young Man*, ch. V.) This has been described (above, pp. 121–25) as the separative power of the form.

25. Bernard Berenson, *Aesthetics and History*, pp. 69–73. It should be superfluous to say that Berenson's tactile values are wholly unrelated to any kind of visual deception and *trompe-l'œil*.

pieces have very little tactile value; still, they have integrity if, for instance, intending to convey a dreamlike impression, they intentionally refrain from indulging in realistic accents. Odilon Redon, or even Turner, does not rely on tactile values to achieve his prupose. Integrity is there when the artist has succeeded in imparting existence to a fully constituted being.

There is one more reason why this first attribute of the beautiful should be situated in the relationship of the work of art to itself rather than to the density of the imaginary reality it represents. Two of the three panels by Botticelli preserved in the Prado tell a part of the rather long story of Nastagio degli Onesti. But the story itself is of little importance as compared with the immediately perceptible perfection of these two compositions. Since the colors cannot possibly be shown, the absolute integrity of these two works cannot be demonstrated. But it would be no less vain to attempt an analysis of these faultless paintings, because to understand them as works of art precisely consists in perceiving and enjoying, prior to any analysis, the total effect produced by the calculations of the painter. The [61] first of the two panels is perhaps still more remarkable than the other one in that, although the eye does not grasp it at once in its totality, each of the parts that it grasps is apprehended as a totality. Here, as in the case of Pisanello's *Portrait of a Woman* in the National Gallery or in practically any one of the panels that make up *The Legend of St. Ursula*, by Carpaccio, the painter has integrally realized the form that his art intended to actualize. The onlooker sees at once that this is true, and, like all evidences, this one is no object of demonstration.

Where there is integrity, there also is harmony, for, indeed, the mutual adaptation of the parts of the work of art and their over-all agreement with the whole are conditions necessarily required for its unity.[26] The presence of harmony is revealed by the feeling that any attempt to modify

26. "Harmony is an arrangement of sensations that we do not wish to be different. It satisfies, at one and the same time, our senses, whose functioning it facilitates, and our mind, which finds in it obedience to the laws by which it itself is ruled." (Sérusier, p. 10.) — Cf. Matisse's remarks as related by R. Escholier in Lhote, *De la Palette à l'écritoire*, p. 378.

SANDRO BOTTICELLI. Scene from the "Legend of Nastagio degli Onesti"
1487. Prado, Madrid

SANDRO BOTTICELLI. Scene from the "Legend of Nastagio degli Onesti"
1487. Prado, Madrid

SANDRO BOTTICELLI. Scene from the "Legend of Nastagio degli Onesti"
1487. Prado, Madrid

a. DOMENICO VENEZIANO. St. John in the Desert

About 1450. Samuel H. Kress Collection, National Gallery of Art, Washington

b. PAOLO UCCELLO. St. George and the Dragon

About 1455/60. Musée Jacquemart-André, Paris

the relationship that obtains among the colors, the masses, and the lines of a painting would result in the destruction of the whole. In the second of [62] the Prado panels, the need to represent at the center of the composition a double scene, corresponding to two distinct moments of one and the same story, has necessitated a flattening and a deepening of the perspective, compensated for by a narrowing of the central space delimited by the two front trees. The second panel is a sort of triptych whose three parts so felicitously communicate that a perfect harmony obtains between the unity of the whole and that of each of the parts. No calculation is required from the mind of the onlooker; it is not even certain that the painter himself did literally calculate his work, but the numbers are in it, and they are *seen* by the eye.

This is so certain that even a painter of genius is not always equally happy in his choices. The scene in which the hunted woman finally reaches [63] the scene of a banquet offers the eyes an unconvincing superposition of horizontals, from the tops of the tree stumps in the foreground to the two lines of the table, then to those formed by the heads of the figures, by the lake shore, and by the dark foliage of the trees. The vertical division of the painted space, faultless in the first two panels, is sadly lacking here. It is the same painter, the same colors, and the same style, but the charm does not operate. After a perfunctory glance at the third panel, the eye lovingly returns to the two other ones as to inexhaustible sources of joy. Once more, if integrity and harmony cannot easily be defined, they can easily and delightfully be seen.

The third and last element of the beautiful is also the downfall of the metaphysicians. For once, having to speak of a quality of matter whose apprehension is an emotion, they find themselves short of words. The Latins used to call it *claritas,* which means neither clearness nor lucidity, but, rather, the kind of property of a beautiful thing that one often expresses in saying that it "radiates" a light of its own. A "radiant beauty" should be considered a tautology. All beauty radiates.[27] A sort of diffused light

27. For a different interpretation, see Joyce, ch. V. This artist first tries to interpret *claritas,* in Thomas Aquinas, as meaning the artistic unveiling of the reality of which the work of art is the symbol. But he seems to reject this as "literary talk." He then suggests

seems to emanate from painted masterpieces and to enfold them in a transparent veil of which, perhaps, our own emotion is a part. This radiance is not that of color, or of form, or of any particular combination of lines; it is an effluence of the whole painting that owes its existence to the art of the painter and by which we feel softly invaded. Its veritable cause lies in the fact that we then find ourselves confronted by an object whose material elements are thoroughly spiritualized. Instead of being the colors, the shapes, the attitudes, and the motions of natural mountains, trees, animals, and men, all the sensible qualities that constitute such paintings are entirely subservient to the sole end pursued by the painter's art. And this end is a spiritual one—namely, to provide our powers of apprehension with an object integrally constructed in view of their own act. The radiance of a painting is that of a matter in a sort of state of glory, elevated by the art of man to the condition of a pure object of cognition. There are no such objects in the world of nature, but it is enough to look at the small

[64a, b]   *St. John in the Desert*, by Domenico Veneziano, or at the *St. George and the Dragon*, by Paolo Uccello, in order to realize that such is the very essence of authentic works of art. The painter has entirely disengaged himself from the physical reality of nature, and his reward is to have thereby given existence to a sensible reality of a specifically different kind in which the qualities of matter develop an intelligibility perceptible to sense. To be such a sensible being is truly to be a thing of beauty and a work of art.

This transfiguration of matter by art does not follow from a laborious process of composition going from the parts to the whole. A well-known engraving by Hogarth is entitled *The Analysis of Beauty*. If the point stood in need of demonstration, this plate would suffice to prove that the elements of beauty have very little beauty of their own. Apart from a few geometrical lines, two or three elementary solids, and some natural forms,

that the radiance of which Thomas Aquinas speaks is the Scholastic quiddity, the *whatness* of a thing, "felt by the artist when the esthetic image is first conceived in his imagination." One could object that this interpretation is "literary talk," too, if Joyce himself did not here issue a timely reminder that what he is saying refers to beauty "in the sense which the word has in the literary tradition." In the field of painting, the revelation of the *whatness* of things would give whole satisfaction to the aesthetics of academicism. See below, n. 32.

the rest consists of stays and of heads evolving from the normal to the ludicrous. Even taking into account the dry humor proper to Hogarth, one cannot help wondering how beauty could possibly arise out of such ingredients.

In point of fact, it does not. What comes first is the form of the whole painting, and so long as he works within its salutary limits there is no reason why the artist should care for anything else. Then is the time for him to say, with Eric Gill, that "beauty takes care of itself."

But where art comes to an end, philosophy begins. If they are irrelevant to art, these notions are directly relevant to the finished work of art whose apprehension is for the philosopher a fitting object of reflection. Even so, they should not be conceived as pointing out three distinct elements that enter the structure of the beautiful as our understanding conceives it. The beautiful comes first, and, as soon as it is there, the possible plurality of our points of view concerning it appears together with it. A sign that it is so can be found in the fact that every attempt to define one of these notions taken in itself unavoidably conjures up the other ones. Like the beautiful itself, they all share in the transcendental unity of being.

3. *The Quest of Beauty*

ACCORDING to what precedes, the very essence of painting is its power to actualize forms and, by the same token, to produce new beings whose perception is for us a cause of delectation. This creative power of forms has been acknowledged by modern aesthetics as the essence of plastic arts,[28] but this is no reason to ignore the fact that, for centuries, another

---

28. Focillon has stated his ultimate conclusion from the very beginning of his *Vie des formes*. The world of forms is not an image of the physical world; it is "a metaphor of the universe" (p. 2). Even when art borrows forms from nature, these forms acquire a new value and beget completely new systems from the very moment they are included in the world of art (p. 3). Only, because they still retain the mark of their natural origin, we find it hard to consider them as truly foreign to nature. We shall always remain tempted to consider artistic forms as meaning something else besides themselves. In other words, we are tempted to "confuse the notion of form with that of image, which implies the representation of an object"; we are particularly tempted to confuse the notion of form with that of sign. Now, "sign signifies, whereas form signifies itself" (p. 4). Focillon has firmly maintained this absolute position ("the fundamental content of form is a *formal*

notion of painting has generally prevailed. Living as we do in an age when painters take pride in their almost complete liberty, there is a real peril for a philosopher in neglecting the testimony of so many generations of artists whose works and words seem to tell an entirely different story. We have accumulated texts in which painters have stressed the creative side of their activity, but a no less traditional set of definitions could be quoted in which the notions of imitation and representation assume a great importance. And, indeed, these notions are almost inevitable. Even granting that the proper function of art is to create in beauty, one still has to concede that beauty is not exclusively produced by art. There is beauty in nature. In fact, there is so much of it, and of such a superlative sort, that great artists themselves sometimes wonder if there is any point in adding to natural beauty the more modest beauty of art. Hence the traditional effort carried on by generation after generation of artists to discover beauty in nature, or, rather, to find in natural beauty the very pattern of the beauty to be imitated by their art.

The fecundity of this notion is attested by the countless masterpieces accumulated in art galleries by the masters of traditional art. By and large, it can be identified with the doctrine according to which art in general, but quite especially the plastic arts, have their source in imitation. In this view, the beautiful in art has to be borrowed from the beautiful in nature and, so to speak, to be embodied in the matter of the works of art. There would be no point in attempting a dialectical discussion of a notion whose object is concerned with a definite type of action, but it will not be amiss to consult the very representatives of the schools of art whose task it has been to submit their own doctrine, along with its practice, to the acid test of artistic creation. As will be seen later, the modern conceptions of paint- ing are not free from ambiguities, but it would be a serious error to imagine

content," p. 5), but, at the same time, he has clearly seen that, as soon as it appears, form can be read in several different ways. To read it as signifying itself is to read it as an artist, but it can be read as representing a natural being (a man, a horse, a tree, etc.) or as *signifying* a meaning (a crucifix). The problem raised by these other ways of reading the forms is to know if they are relevant to painting taken precisely qua painting. — Cf. Luigi Pareyson, "Contemplation du beau et production des formes," *Revue internationale de philosophie*, XXXI (1955), 16–32 (particularly pp. 19–21).

that the traditional interpretation of the plastic arts did not experience difficulties of its own.

If he sets out to look for beauty in reality in order to reproduce it or to interpret it in his art, a painter must have a certain notion of both reality and beauty. Now, painters are not philosophers in the usually received sense of the term. When one of them interrogates himself about reality, the meaning of his question simply is: what is paintable reality? In other words, such an artist is simply wondering what there is, in visible reality, that he could, and should, try to represent or to imitate. But since reality is one and the same for all men, it is difficult for painters not to remember, or not to rediscover by themselves, one of the few possible answers given by philosophers to the same question.

This is eminently true in the case of Plato and Aristotle, of whose doctrines Bergson used to say that they were the kind of philosophy that comes naturally to the human mind. The easiest way for a painter to define the place of the beauty he strives to achieve is to resort to the philosophy of Plato or to some simplified version of it. But there is a price to pay for a mind that finds its rest in the truth of Platonism, and since no one can define it better than Plato himself did in book X of *The Republic*, the only thing to do is to let him speak for himself.

The dialogue is between Socrates and Glaucon. It presupposes the recognition of a truth established at great length in other parts of the same work—namely, that true reality does not consist in the changeable becoming of the individual objects perceived by sense, but, rather, in the self-subsisting and unchangeable Ideas of which each concrete being is but a particular expression. The feeling often experienced by artists that they are engaged in a quest whose object will always elude their best efforts finds a sort of bitter satisfaction in this answer to the problem. Their perennial sense of frustration is justified by their knowledge that, even if they were endowed with the most powerful creative genius, their works would still fall short of the ideal goal of their art. Apart from this negative consolation, the notion of an ideal beauty does very little to help artists in their work. In point of fact, as Plato himself has admirably established, it reduces the work of the artist to an imitation, not of the ideal beauty itself, but, rather, of any one of its particular embodiments in natural beings.

Starting from the hypothesis that there is an eternal Idea of the bed, and that the ambition of the painter is to imitate it, Socrates first recalls that the real beds made by joiners already are so many imitations of this Idea or Form. This leaves us confronted with three kinds of beds: the ideal and unique form of the bed, created by God, the many beds made by joiners after the model of this form, and all the beds made by painters, in doing their paintings, after the model of one of these beds. This, as Socrates makes Glaucon see it, leaves the painter far behind God, and even behind the joiner in the order of creativeness:

"Then," Socrates said, "painter, joiner, God; these three are set above three kinds of bed."

"Yes, three."

"Now whether it was that God did not elect to make more beds than one, or that some species of necessity lay on him to prevent his making more than one in nature, at all events he has produced but one, unique, which is the veritable Bed. Two beds like that, or more than two, have not been formed by God in nature, nor will they ever be."

"How so?" said he.

"Because," said I, "if God were to make but two, then yet again a single bed would be revealed whose form the other two would share, and this would be the real bed, not they."

"Correct," said he.

"God knew that, I believe; he wished to be the real maker of a real bed, and not a certain artisan of a certain bed, and so created this unique authentic bed in nature."

"So it seems."

"Then you wish to call him the Creator of this form, or to use some similar term?"

"Yes, that is only just," he said, "since by creation he has made this thing along with all the rest."

"What about the joiner? Are we not to call him the artificer of a bed?"

"Yes."

"And the painter, too? Shall we call him the artificer and maker of the like?"

"Never!"

"What name then, do you say, has his relation to the bed?"

"The name," said he, "in my opinion, that best applies to him, is that of imitator of the object which the other makes."

"Good," I said. "So you denominate the author of something at the third remove from its creation 'imitator'?"

"Precisely so," said he.[29]

In thus reducing painting to the imitation of an imitation of a unique model, Plato was not only turning it into a strictly noncreative activity, he also condemned it to work in utter ignorance of what it is said to imitate. As a model to be imitated by painters, the ideal Form of which Plato makes so much has this irremediable defect, that it is invisible. To be sure, it helps artists to think that their confused but intense aspiration toward an inaccessible beauty is not without an object, but the very notion of imitating what they cannot see does not make sense. So their next move is to exchange the doctrine of Plato for the revised version of it provided by Aristotle, a thing that painters have often done in the past, even though they had no clear notion of what they were doing.

According to Aristotle, each individual is a concrete incarnation of its own species. The species itself, for instance, man, has no existence of its own; it only subsists as particularized in individual human beings, but the human intellect, starting from the sense perception of individuals, is able to form within itself the abstract notion of the species. In short, we see men only, but we can conceive the general notion of man.

Following this Aristotelian lead, some painters have imagined individuals as so many specimens of ideal types that it was their own task to

---

29. Plato, *Republic*, bk. X, tr. Lane Cooper, pp. 344–45. — See the perplexities of the Platonist painter in Jules Breton: "The truth of art is the essence of visible truth, and this essence is the beautiful" (*La Vie d'un artiste*, p. 292). The moments of his dialectic are as follows: (1) the goal of art is to achieve an expression of the beautiful; (2) but "this beautiful, what is it? Where is it?" (pp. 278–79) ; reason is powerless to answer this question, but the best solution of the problem is Plato's, the beautiful is the splendor of the true; it also is its "intensity"; and it still could be defined "the essence of life" (p. 279).

represent by their art. But the project was fraught with a fundamental difficulty. Although the point has been disputed, a philosopher can maintain that he actually succeeds in forming abstract concepts—that is to say, a common notion of man applicable to all particular men; but an artist would have a hard time proving that he can form such a monster as an abstract image. Like all visible objects, an image is an individual, and no individual reality can possibly imitate the totality of the other individual realities that belong in the same species. Artists know this even much better than philosophers themselves; they must therefore have something else in mind when they speak of types and of their beauty as of the object of their art.

The only other notion that can be present in their minds, however, is as little intelligible as the preceding ones. In the philosophy of Aristotle, the species itself does not exist apart from its individuals; otherwise it would be a Platonic Idea. On the contrary, if he turns it into an individual, such as its painted representation, the painter is attempting this impossible feat—namely, to impart artistic existence to a model of beauty that has no physical existence in reality.

To this problem, painters nevertheless have an answer. They consider themselves dedicated to the task of extracting from reality, by correcting, compensating for, or eliminating individual differences, the average type to which nature seems to be tending without ever succeeding in realizing it. In this sense, art would reveal to nature the true type that nature is eternally trying to achieve without ever completely succeeding.

If this is what the art of painting is really trying to do, then painters should first give up describing it as an art of imitation. By definition, the ideal type of the species is not to be found ready-made in reality. In order to represent it in the fullness of its perfection and of its beauty, painters have first to create it with the power of their imagination. But this requires an effort of which not all painters are capable, and to facilitate their task, many of those who are in quest of an ideal type of human beauty simply decide that the discovery of this type has already been made by the Greeks. To find it actualized in matter, it is enough to look at the classical Greek art of the Phidian period.[30] And the thing has abundantly been done; but here, too, there have been difficulties.

The first result of such an attempt has been to turn what had been intended to be an imitation of reality into the imitation of a particular interpretation of reality. From the very moment this type of art is turned into an ideal model, a conventionalism begins to obtain, in which art feeds on art instead of feeding on reality. When it attempts to contact physical beauty in nature, the result of the painter's decision to limit himself to average types is that impersonal figures and faces everywhere prevail, as if the goal of art were to produce plastic equivalents of abstract notions. Because artists then go to classical antiquity for their models, such an art is rightly labeled classicism, and because it necessarily proceeds by teachable rules borrowed from the study of classical models, the same art finds itself at home in schools, or academies, and is aptly called academic. The proper effort of academicism is to seek beauty in the imitation of classical art instead of seeking it in the imitation of reality.

There is no better example of this attitude than Sir Joshua Reynolds' *Discourses on Painting*. According to this excellent painter of portraits, that is, of individuals, the end of painting was to achieve a sort of typology. If we believe him, only the common run of painters can take an interest in the differences that distinguish individuals within the same species; whereas the true artist, "like the philosopher, will consider Nature in the

30. On this point, the best witness is Ingres. To him, the eternally beautiful and the naturally beautiful are one and the same thing. It has been found a long time ago. "Everything has been done, everything has been found. Our own task is not to invent, but to continue." (*Ingres raconté par lui-même*, p. 42.) "All the great study of art consists in learning to imitate these [earthly] objects" (p. 44). We must needs start from nature in order to form all our ideas, including that of the gods. "Phidias reached the sublime by correcting nature with the help of nature itself" (p. 44). The formula "ideal beauty," or the "ideally beautiful," is misleading. It must be conceived as pointing out the association of the most beautiful elements scattered in nature but gathered together by the artist (pp. 44–45). On the use of the model in which the beautiful is to be found, p. 47. The beautiful is found in the submission to nature (pp. 48–49). To sum up (p. 47), the beautiful, nature, and the ancients are one and the same thing: "Look at the model; it is like the ancients and the ancients are like that. . . . If you sincerely translate that which is there, you will be proceeding like the ancients, and, like them, you will arrive at the beautiful."

abstract, and represent in everyone of his figures the character of the species." [31] Yet, at the same time he was propounding this abstract notion of paintable reality, the same Reynolds corrected it by means of two felicitous inconsistencies. First, he observed that even if an artist turns to the Greeks for information about some species, or type, he will soon realize that there never was such a thing in their art. This is evident if we compare Greek art with itself at the successive epochs of its history, but the fact is no less certain if we consider Greek art at any given moment of its evolution. There has never been any fixed human type recognized as the model of human beauty by all the artists of ancient Greece. Secondly, Reynolds clearly realized that to paint average types—that is, cross sections of actually existing beings or things—also was to paint something that, precisely because it is abstract, cannot possibly exist. [32] When it is thus understood, the object of painting no longer is to represent reality, but, paradoxically enough, unreality.

This is exactly what academicism has always done, at all times and in all countries. The insipidity of its conventionalism is the penalty it must pay for its initial decision to break away from actually existing individual

---

31. Discourse III, pp. 47–48.

32. Reynolds has successively upheld all the possible positions, which does credit to his feeling for the realities of his own art. "The idea of the perfect state of nature, which the artist calls the Ideal beauty, is the great leading principle by which works of genius are conducted" (*Discourses*, p. 41). "By this Phidias acquired his fame" (ibid.). "Thus it is from a reiterated experience, and a close comparison of the objects in nature, that an artist becomes possessed of the idea of that central form, if I may so express it, from which every deviation is deformity" (p. 42). The investigation of this form is painful, but there is "one method of shortening the road"—namely, the study of the ancients (ibid.). To this principle, "that the idea of beauty in each species of beings is an invariable one," it may be objected that, in every species, there are various types; in "the human figure, for instance, the beauty of Hercules is one, of the Gladiator another, of Apollo another; which makes so many different ideas of beauty." Yes, but "perfect beauty in any species must combine all the characters which are beautiful in that species. It cannot consist in any one to the exclusion of the rest; no one, therefore, must be predominant, that no one may be deficient" (p. 44). — John Burnet, Reynolds' commentator, has his doubts. In his commentary (p. 41, n. 7), he observes that "this ideal beauty is different according to the different perceptions of the several artists." Although "the Ancients seldom varied the proportion of their figures from eight heads in height, yet . . . Raffaelle's are sometimes only six and a half, and Parmegiano frequently reduces the head to one tenth." This, of course, marks the end of the line in so far as the quest of artistic beauty in nature is concerned.

things. The deplorable products of Ingres' imagination when he had no model under his very eyes are a sufficient confirmation of this truth.

If reality is neither a Platonic Idea nor an Aristotelian species, only one way still remains open for the painter as well as for the philosopher. In the schools of the Middle Ages, those who did not believe in the reality of self-subsisting ideas, or in the reality of the species, had no other choice than to identify reality with concrete individuals. This is the very reason the reaction against the conventionalism of the schools and academies regularly assumes the form of a return to realism.[33] The fidelity of the painter to reality as given in actually existing objects or beings is a good cure for the anemia endemic in the abstract types favored by academic painting. Within the limits of imitational art, no other kind of reaction seems to be conceivable. Beauty has to be found where it is, and if concrete individuals are the only true realities, then the painter has to find beauty in them, taken as they are, or he will never find it. The solid realism of Courbet, not always pure of vulgarity, well exemplifies the normal reaction of a born artist against the mannerism of the schools.

Another illustration of the same problem is provided by the question endlessly disputed among painters: what use should one make of the model? If beauty has to be looked for in given reality, all the preceding problems arise again. If he simply uses the model as an invitation to conceive the very Idea of which the concrete reality is but a shadow, his work is likely to lack substance. If the painter reduces his model to some abstract type, he can do as well without looking at it. If he follows his model with close attention and almost slavish fidelity, the artist can hardly avoid the pitfall of vulgarity. At any rate, his only merit will be to offer to nature, in the mirror of art, an image of its own beauty, not an expression of the beauty of art.

33. This truth has been well expressed by Delacroix in a remarkable passage of his *Journal* (p. 397 [February 22, 1860]) : "Realism is the grand expedient which innovators use to revive the interest of an indifferent public, at periods when schools that are listless and inclined to mannerism do nothing but repeat the round of the same inventions. Suddenly a return to nature is proclaimed by a man who claims to be inspired. . . ." On this problem, see below, pp. 249–50.

It is hardly possible to read the writings of any traditional painter without finding him at grips with one or more of these difficulties.[34] An attentive examination of their works often reveals traces of this problem whose reality is beyond doubt. What makes it insoluble is the false belief that artistic beauty is found, not made. As soon as this illusion goes, all these difficulties go together with it.

Beauty certainly is found in nature, but it is the beauty of nature, not that of art. The power of illusion of painting must be very great indeed to make good minds hesitate on its very essence. A painter does not produce real beings, or moving and operating robots such as those which engineers produce. A painter does not even turn out solid bodies like the statues carved or modeled by sculptors. The flimsy films of colors produced by the painter have no substance beyond that of the surface they determine. Behind this envelope of imaginary beings, there is nothing but stone, plaster, wood, or canvas. But this lack of all other responsibility than that of pleasing the eye is precisely for painting the source of its aesthetic liberty. There is not a single real being that has not something else to do than to please. There is not a single work of art that, taken precisely qua work of art, has anything else to do than to cause in us the contemplative pleasure of enjoying its sight. Nature produces no works of art; nature produces artists who, in turn, produce works of art.

Nor should we imagine a painter as imitating in his limited way the activity of some higher artist whose example he is following. Aesthetic speculation is not qualified to determine the final cause of creation. This is the business of theology. So far no theologian has yet imagined that the end of creation was the production, by the Creator, of beings whose essential and unique function it is to be pleasing when seen. Yet, taken precisely as an artist, the painter does nothing else and his work serves no other immediate purpose. Art galleries represent the modest contribution of one of God's creatures to the embellishment of his own creation. In their own way, and judged at the level of man, they are a priceless contribution,

34. See Delacroix's remarks *On the use of the model* (*Journal*, p. 195 [October 12, 1853]).

but they are nothing else. God does not seem interested in creating paintings, nor does nature produce any such beings. Men, women, animals, trees, even stones, and the colossal masses of the mountains or seas, lakes, and streams that cover the planet are beings entirely different from works of art, and none of them is primarily intended to serve some artistic purpose. The remark has often been made that artists and their works teach us to see nature as a collection of works of art, and not only nature, but cities, suburbs, and discarded junk—down to the pathetic pair of old shoes in which, if he has the talent to do so, a painter can make us perceive the presence of some beauty. Man is too small and too weak a creature to create other objects of nature, but he is just engaged enough in matter to be able to mold parts of it in view of a spiritual end with which nature itself does not seem to be concerned. This is the portion of man; a modest one, indeed; it just so happens that he is the only being to which that share has been allotted:

> *Dein Wissen teilest du mit vorgezognen Geistern,*
> *Die* Kunst, *O Mensch, hast du allein.*[35]

These conclusions are not supposed to bring any controversy to a close. There is no obligatory point of view from which art should be considered, not even the point of view of art. Ever since the time of Plato, it has been customary to describe, to define, and to appreciate art from the point of view of truth rather than of beauty. The consequences are well known. The city needs carpenters because the city needs beds, but the city does not need people whose only job is to paint images of real carpenters or images of real beds that only real carpenters can make. Along with poets, painters should be politely invited to leave the territory of a philosophically ordered state. Under a less brutal form, a very large number of men, perhaps even the majority of those who stop to consider the nature of art, feel likewise inclined to conceive it as the expression of a second- or third-rate knowledge. The very last place they would think of in their quest of the source from which flows the beauty of art is themselves.

35. Friedrich von Schiller, *Die Künstler,* ll. 32–33: "Knowledge you share with other favored minds, / But art, Mankind, is yours alone." (Tr. B. Q. Morgan.)

But this takes us to the threshold of another problem. Why do we all have to resist a similar tendency? How is it that it takes us a special effort of reflection to reconcile ourselves to the notion that there is at least one human activity whose effects should not be judged with reference to an already given reality? The answer to this question cannot be found in the consideration of the art of painting alone. We now have to consider it in its relationship to a world foreign to its essence, the world of language. In the last analysis, the quest of beauty always ends in conversations.

CHAPTER SEVEN

PAINTING AND LANGUAGE

ABUNDANT as it is, the literature published about paintings concerns but a small proportion of painted works. By far the largest number of paintings have no history. They silently disappear without leaving any trace. Many of them are amateur work, fully justified by the pleasure they have given their authors but of little interest to the rest of the world. Other pictures are commercial stuff, produced either for industrial purposes or else for various classes of customers whose needs, although different, agree at least in this, that they are but indirectly related to art: family portraits of adopted ancestors for buyers of colonial houses, pictures of famous landscapes or views of foreign cities—in short, all the freshly painted canvases that crowd the Christmas market with mountain lakes, log cabins on the slopes of snow-capped peaks, sailboats tossed about on angry seas, hunting scenes, drinking bouts, and countless other images whose only function is to preserve memories of the past or to provide the kind of dream we all need to embellish the present.

This kind of production has always existed, and since it serves legitimate purposes, there is nothing to say against it. Why should not everyone take his pleasure where he can honestly find it? But masterpieces have another destiny. As soon as they leave the studios of creative artists, their works become so many signs of contradiction. Articles, books, and lectures pile up around them; specialized libraries collect writings about art; professors, teachers, and commentators of every denomination accumulate explanations, interpretations, condemnations, or justifications of masterpieces with an abundance that recalls the commentaries of the Middle Ages on Aristotle or those of modern times on Kant and Hegel.

And yet, one might well wonder why it should be so, because there is a difference in kind between using words to write commentaries about paintings and using words to write commentaries about other words.

1. Language and Aesthetic Experience

THE misunderstandings that arise between painters and their public are as manifold as their causes, but one of these causes is included in all the others. Painters are men who have made their choice of a silent medium; they express themselves by means of images, whereas practically all men express themselves by means of words. Some artists have had to make an early choice between becoming writers or becoming painters. This is always a momentous decision for such men. The novelist Ramuz, for instance, whose first education had been among painters, always regretted having at his disposal only the abstract words of the writer while his mind was full of vivid images and of the colors and lines by which painters can so perfectly express the visions of their mind.[1] On the contrary, when artists to whom such a choice was possible decided in favor of painting, they renounced the resources put at their disposal by spoken and written language. Naturally, to be a painter does not make it impossible for an artist to be also a writer, but he cannot be both at one and the same time. True painters know full well that, while they are painting, they are neither writing nor talking.

This proposition is easy to understand, but it is harder to realize the fullness of its implications, and to conform one's conduct to what these consequences prescribe is harder still.

The first and more general one is the heterogeneity of the art of language and the art of painting. Taken literally, this proposition means that, because paintings and words themselves are heterogeneous in nature, it is

1. Charles-Ferdinand Ramuz, *Questions*, pp. 7–12.

as impossible to paint by means of words as it is to speak by means of paintings. To this, of course, the ready objection is that, in point of fact, paintings do explain things, so much so that, in many cases, a good picture is considered, and is, infinitely easier to understand than many words. This is true, with this reservation only, that, when it acts as a substitute for language, a picture is not a painting. This is to say that, in Maurice de Vlaminck's own words, "When a picture can be explained, when it can be made to be understood, or felt, by means of words, it has nothing to do with painting." [2]

A corollary of this conclusion is that, when there is a great deal to be said about a painting, one has reason to fear that the work at stake belongs less to painting than to literature. It is a bad sign for a painting when it inspires people with an urge to translate it into words. In articles published in the *Revue indépendante*, November 10 and 25, 1847, the art critic Louis de Ronchaud had devoted a study to French murals and, on this occasion, had praised the work done by Delacroix for the Senate as well as for the Chambre des Députés in Paris. Naturally, Delacroix felt pleased by this homage, but it also caused him misgivings. He wrote at once to George Sand: "If it were not about myself that all this has been said (forgive the modesty), I would tell you that it is just too bad for the kind of painting that makes people see so many things. The beauty of this art mainly consists in things that the language is not able to explain." [3]

This truth can be verified by the art lover as easily as by the painter himself. There is no greater pleasure than to share the privilege of aesthetic experience with others. Thus admired in common, the beautiful simply is fulfilling its vocation, which is, since it partakes of the nature of good, to diffuse itself and to communicate itself in virtue of some innate generosity. Let us suppose that, once more, the miracle has been performed. Beauty certainly is there, and we see it. As the saying goes, we are "struck speechless" with admiration. How could one say it better? We all know the peculiar kind of silence created by the presence of recognized beauty; but man is a

2. *Portraits avant décès*, p. 177.
3. *Correspondance générale*, II, 332.

talking animal, and it is certain that, sooner or later, someone will break the silence by expressing his admiration. This is a most natural thing to do, and it even is a harmless one so long as the admirer does not attempt to justify his feeling by means of words. If, on the contrary, he starts telling us why the painting that all admire is indeed an admirable one, his remarks are sure to break the spell. Even when men agree on beauty, they seldom agree on its causes or, at least, on the words to define such causes and thus to render them perceptible to others. Usually, if a painter is there, he is most likely to disagree with all the rest of the group. At any rate, his own approach to the painting will be an entirely different one. The unanimity so often observable on the objects of our common admiration very seldom extends to the motives by which this feeling can be justified.

Older men usually know how to keep their peace in the middle of such discussions and, better still, how to keep away from these controversies. Yet it is most natural that such disagreements should arise; their cause lies in the very essence of the beautiful. If, as has been said, the beautiful is being itself as an object of a pleasing apprehension, then it must share in the intrinsic characters of being, which, because it is the first principle in reality as well as in knowledge, escapes description and definition. If we say of a being that it is *this* rather than *that,* we simply define it by itself. In short, we can absolutely not think otherwise than in terms of being, which is the very reason we cannot place it in front of us as an object to be seen. The same is true of the beautiful. If and when it is there, it confronts us with the wonder of a man-made being whose apperception alone is enough to fill us with pleasure. Whatever one can say about it will really be about something else. This is a primary ontological experience; as such, it is ultimate in its own order.

The aesthetic judgments that express these primitive experiences are, on account of their very immediacy, almost impossible to compare. They usually exhibit two strikingly opposed characters: on the one hand, they are passionately dogmatic assertions; on the other hand, they are as fickle and inconsistent as they are dogmatic. For the same reason, they are practically incommunicable. To be sure, the formulas in which they express themselves are easily communicated, but it is extremely difficult to communicate their justifications. It is of the essence of teaching that the teacher can cause the truth present in his mind also to become present in the mind of his pupil. If he can follow the order of the demonstration, the pupil is bound to assent to the conclusion that is propounded to him as true. Not so in the case of aesthetic judgments. Because these ultimately rest on sense experience, one cannot make somebody admire a certain work of art on the strength of any demonstration. Suggestion is always possible, and it sometimes works. Between kindred spirits of comparable culture and sensibility, such exchanges are possible, but even then "contagion" would be a better word than "communication" to describe them. Since aesthetic experience takes place in a universe other than that of language, how can it communicate itself by means of words?

Still, aesthetic judgments are in no way arbitrary, objectless, or without foundation in reality. On the contrary, they gather certitude to the extent that, instead of seeking for their justification in combinations of concepts essentially foreign to the nature of their object, they rather seek for it in the unique relationship that the matter of every painting entertains with its form. Metaphysics, mathematics, physics, biology, social sciences, and many other disciplines offer themselves to the choice of the human intellect avid of concepts, reasonings, and conclusive demonstrations. Each one of these sciences has its own method, its own object, and its own approach to communicable truth. Plastic beauty, with which we are here concerned, is of an altogether different kind, and although there is little hope ever to discourage men from arguing about it, true art lovers should not be allowed to consider themselves as wasting their love on mere trifles for the sole reason that aesthetic experience cannot be communicated by words. They can follow with good conscience artists of all times, all countries, and all the styles in their constant quest for the still unknown forms of creatable beauty. Nor should they feel ashamed of not having demonstrations to proffer in support of their aesthetic judgments. In deepening our understanding of the paintings of which it can truly be said that they *are*, and these can only be understood in pleasurable contemplation, we are practicing the only kind of art criticism that is not wholly foreign to the nature of its object. For, indeed, when paintings are at stake, judgments of existence and judgments of beauty are one and the same thing.[4]

But why speak of judgments? Aesthetic experience includes no other judgment than the delight of the spectator in the object of his apprehension. True enough, this experienced pleasure is partly determined by the sensorial and intellectual gifts of the spectator; all his past is involved in every one of these new adventures, and all that which, because he has had to become it, he now is. Yet, in the last analysis, the experiencing of beauty in a painting first consists in letting oneself go, or, rather, in offering oneself to the domination of art wherever art is to be found. It is not enough for art lovers to consent to their pleasurable defeat when it comes; they go out of their way to provoke it and to expose themselves to it. When the aesthetic experience takes place, their quest has once more reached one of its possible ends, and yet it must go on and on, as long as life lasts, because, good in itself as it is, every beautiful painting is but one among many other goods, each of which is desirable in itself and none of which is absolute beauty or absolute being.

2. Painters and the Talking World

By "TALKING WORLD," or world of language, we understand the world of nonpainters, including painters themselves while they are talking instead of painting. And they certainly do talk. "Painters," André Lhote says, "are great chatterboxes."[5] And he should know, being one of them. Even when they do not write, which many of them love to do, and do very well indeed, they cannot always help talking about their art. When they do, their remarks usually deserve to be carefully weighed, especially when they spring from the personal experience of the artist and attempt to formulate it. Yet, even in the most favorable of cases, a writing painter is a writer, not a painter.[6] The most unfavorable cases are those in which, instead of analyzing

4. See above, pp. 131–32.
5. *De la Palette à l'écritoire*, first sentence of the Preface.
6. Nevertheless, an amusing study could be devoted to the personal experience of Delacroix in this respect. Deceived by the facility with which he was writing his own

his personal experience, the painter sets out to philosophize. He then becomes little more than a weak echo of trite philosophical ideas, as we saw Reynolds become in his doctrine of nature and type. As to the never-ending flow of discourse about painting that springs from nonpainters, perfectly legitimate in itself as it certainly is, the main question it raises is to know to what extent it truly is about painting.

The most general of all approaches to painting, outside that of painters themselves, is that of philosophers. On this point, painters agree to a man that they do not understand what philosophers are talking about; at any rate, they cannot believe that what philosophers are talking about is what they themselves call painting.

Among the many experiences that can be quoted in support of this contention, a particularly remarkable one is that of Delacroix invited to attend a lecture by the philosopher Ravaisson, going there, and availing himself of the first break to run away from it. What lends a particular interest to this anecdote is the fact that Ravaisson was not only the author of an excellent study on the metaphysics of Aristotle, but also a great art lover, an educationist deeply interested in the teaching of drawing in French schools, and therefore a man highly qualified to speak intelligently about art. Yet, in so far as Delacroix was concerned, the experiment was a failure. "After the first part of the lecture," Delacroix says, ". . . I slipped away, perhaps rather disgracefully, but I was encouraged by seeing one or two other people who, like myself, felt that they had been sufficiently edified on the subject of the Beautiful." [7] Such was the effect produced on a painter by what Delacroix himself rather irreverently calls in his *Journal:* "a lecture on art, or on the progress of art, by a certain M. Ravaisson."

The same lack of enthusiasm makes itself felt in his remarks about an article on Rubens published in the *Journal des débats* "by a certain M. Taine." Besides, Delacroix had not waited that long to form an opinion

Journal (the easiest of all literary genres), he began to wonder why writing was so much easier for him than painting. This lured him into writing an article on Poussin. Problems of literary composition then entered the picture and nearly drove him to despair. See the *Journal*, p. 182 (May 10, 1853).

7. *Journal*, pp. 179–80 (May 4, 1853).

about the author of *The Philosophy of Art*. "I had already decided," Delacroix says, "from other things he has written, that he was a thorough-going pedant and full of the faults of which I have just been speaking. He, too, says everything, and then he says it all over again."[8] Who would blame Delacroix for his harshness? Or, for that matter, any one of the painters who have expressed similar opinions about philosophers and their aesthetics? What philosophers can say about art is too abstract to fit the subject.[9] In point of fact, philosophers may well avail themselves of art as an occasion to philosophize, but what they say is not art, it is philosophy. No wonder that artists do not recognize themselves in it!

Painters should have more luck with writers who, though using different media, are themselves busy producing works of art, but such does not seem to be the case. What has just been established concerning the incommunicability of aesthetic experience applies to this new problem. Precisely because their own medium is language, writers have no other choice than to limit themselves to those of the problems related to art which can be handled by means of words. In this respect, their ingenuity has no limits. Leaving aside art criticism, whose problems require a separate treatment, writers can, if they are novelists, undertake to depict painters in their novels, which provides them with an opportunity to express their own opinions about the art of painting; but the painters thus described by novelists are little else than writers who pretend to be engaged in the task of doing pictures, and the opinions about painting they are supposed to hold are those of men unacquainted with specifically pictorial problems.

Van Gogh's judgments on the achievements of Zola in this matter do not permit any illusions.[10] If he has not the creative imagination of the novelist,

---

8. *Journal*, p. 382 (July 27, 1858).

9. See Renoir's outburst about a newspaper article that contained something on Art (capital *A*!); the article was signed "Henri Bergson" (Vollard, *En écoutant Cézanne, Degas, Renoir*, p. 277). Under this form the anecdote is slightly suspect; Bergson was not given to writing in newspapers. — Compare the vicious attack against a philosophy of painting based upon the doctrine of L. Brunschvicg (Vlaminck, pp. 169–70). — Cf. also Paul Klee's remarks on the hairsplitting that he regrets in Lessing's *Laokoon* (Grohmann, *Paul Klee*, p. 98).

10. Van Gogh read Zola's essays, *Mes Haines*. It taught him to know "the weak sides" of Zola, whom he found full of prejudices and ill informed about painting. Speaking of

a writer can at least write biographies of masters, studies on their spiritual evolution, psychological portraits, etc. The genre has never been as flourishing as it now is, but painters themselves have their doubts as to the relevancy to art of most of the facts related or invented by such biographers. The wildest speculations about heredity, the influence of the environment, the sentimental life of the artist, the climate, the historical moment, the so-called spirit of the time—in short, about countless circumstances either real or imaginary but always unrelated to the art of the painter—are brought into play in these studies. As Paul Klee aptly said: "Captivating though it may be to tackle problems of personality such as van Gogh or Ensor, far too much biography gets muddled with art. This is the fault of the critics, who are, after all, literary men."[11]

The same complaint applies to the countless studies devoted by writers to the critical history of the art of painting. The impossibility of translating forms and colors into words has surprising consequences, the most common one of which is that art historians sooner or later have to eliminate their hero and to substitute their own work for his. Such is particularly the case with the endless descriptions of "subjects" in which these writers willingly indulge because it is for them an interesting exercise of virtuosity in artistic transposition; but the result is the literary description of a scene, not the description of a painting.

André Fontainas has given an excellent written description of Delacroix's *Noce juive au Maroc:* "The glaring light of a southern sky grows more subdued as it overflows the tops of bright walls. Men are standing or sitting in

Zola's articles on the Salon (*Lettres de van Gogh à van Rappard*, p. 177): "I find them very poor and entirely wrong, except, in part, his appreciation of Manet. I, too, find Manet first class, but it is interesting to hear Zola talking about art. It is as interesting as, for instance, a landscape done by a portrait painter." "Zola has this in common with Balzac, that he does not understand much about painting. I only find two types of painters in the works of Zola. Claude Lantier, in *Le Ventre de Paris,* and the other one, in *Thérèse Raquin,* are comical shadows of Manet, impressionists of a sort. Well . . . In Balzac, the painters are ponderous and boring personages." (P. 178.) "I wish to add, however, how pleased I am to see him [Zola] let fly an arrow against Taine. Serves Taine right, for indeed Taine is sometimes annoying with his mathematical analyses." (P. 178.)

11. Grohmann, p. 10. This sentence is borrowed from Paul Klee's *Journal,* 1909. Critics are sometimes also biographers, but the two varieties should be, if not isolated, at least distinguished.

that light. On the left . . . better sheltered women watch the supple and flexuous movements of a dancing girl," and so on up to a complete verbal description of the picture. Let us now listen to what a painter has to say about it. In the *Souvenirs* of his collaboration with Delacroix, Louis de Planet has left us an entirely different set of notes about the same picture: first, what brushes to use; how to lay in the gray underpainting; then how to do the whole painting, including buildings, objects, and figures, in the same gray upon gray tones, always proportioning the sizes of the brushes to that of the painted objects; when he comes to colors, Planet not only quotes each of them by name, but also says in what order Delacroix wants them to be placed on the palette, and for what reason madder lacquer and Robert lacquer No. 7 or 8 should be placed well apart, on the left, isolated from the rest, so that they are always at hand, to be used either pure, or broken, or again for glazing. Four full pages of these sorts of cooking recipes fill up the *Souvenirs* of Louis de Planet, and, indeed, for a painter this is exactly what this painting actually is.

The difference is clear: while Fontainas has not said a word about colors, Louis de Planet is speaking about nothing else; he says nothing about the subject. And, indeed, why should a writer worry about brushes, palettes, colors, and all those material tools whose use is unknown to him? Were we to believe the excellent Fontainas, the whole art of a painter could be explained in terms of exceptionally acute and remarkably well-balanced intellectual qualities: "The gifts of invention that dominate Delacroix are never disorderly in him; one could not exhibit more sensibility or more precision than does Delacroix in composing a picture; only, before establishing his composition, he has allowed his poetic spirit to warm up; the movements that express it have grown passionate, ardent, epic; in fine, when these movements have reached the highest point of expressive perfection of which they are capable, after they are fixed in the memory of the painter, now sure of his vision, his skillful and exacting sagacity transfers their image to his canvas." [12]

12. André Fontainas, *Histoire de la peinture française au vingtième siècle*, pp. 128–29 and p. 113. Louis de Planet, *Souvenirs*, pp. 23–27.

How simple, indeed, all this is! If nature has imparted to one such a wonderful gift of invention, all he has to do is *to transfer its images to the canvas!* The most vivid imagination, the most skillful and exacting sagacity, in a painter has finally to incarnate itself in some matter by means of his hand. The dramas of the painter's technique do not seem to be known to men whose problems are wholly contained in their mind.[13] This is the reason the literary effusions of writers about pictures are generally considered unrelated to the art of painting by painters.

The masters of words, are they more successful when they apply language to art criticism? There is at least one case to which most of the preceding reservations should not apply: it is the case in which a painter himself assumes the responsibilities of the art critic. Even though he may be writing about it, a painter cannot mistake his own art for another form of literature. Yet, as is too well known, nothing is more monotonous than the list of the active dislikes and sometimes of the downright hostilities that have opposed some famous painters. On this point, however, it is necessary to introduce a distinction between the art criticism of painters and the art criticism of the public.

In a sense, the painters, too, are part of the public. There is, however, a fundamental difference between the aesthetic judgments of painters and those of mere art lovers—namely, that the judgments of painters are part and parcel of their creative effort. Here again, the personal temper of the artist has to be taken into account, but creators with a marked personality usually have little patience with the art of other artists. Having to make a choice between their own form of creative work and that of other artists, they do not hesitate a moment. If there ever was a clear case of struggle for life, this is one. Creative artists are very far from feeling always pleased with their own ego, but they certainly have no use for anything that is entirely foreign to it. In this battle between sameness and otherness, otherness has simply no right to exist.

No systematic survey of the artistic tastes of artists has ever been con-

13. See the remarks made by Vlaminck, *Portraits avant décès*, p. 37.

ducted. On the basis of limited and personal inquiry, however, it appears that the tastes of each creative artist form an organic whole endowed with a coherency similar to that of a living organism.[14] In simpler terms, this means that, in agreement with the old Greek saying that everything likes its own like, we generally find great painters liking the artists whose works seem to justify their own, while, on the contrary, they utterly dislike painters whose works imply an opposite conception of art.

The obvious implication is that the possibility of his own work is at stake in each and every one of an artist's aesthetic judgments. This inference is the more likely to be correct if one restricts it to the field in which this artist does creative work. Like all personal tastes, those of artists are wholly

14. Such a consistent system of reactions is observable in Vlaminck, *Portraits avant décès.* A self-taught artist, Vlaminck regularly refuses to study with his friend Derain at the Académie Julian; this appears to him a sort of betrayal of their personal efforts and technical discoveries (pp. 71–72); the problem for him is to preserve his own personality intact (p. 116; cf. p. 71, a personal "order," "a way of being," a "character"); this applies to his subjects as well as to his technique; Vlaminck goes to Provence on Derain's invitation, but he brings back practically nothing from a country where everything, "landscape, people, and sky," was foreign to him (p. 102); although he considers himself a born "revolutionist," even an "anarchist" (the best symbol for the Fauves is the anarchist Ravachol), Vlaminck detests cubism as born of Negro art (pp. 107–15); he is against traveling, at least for artistic purposes (p. 116); born in simplicity, the work of art "must continue to live in the same climate, in the same atmosphere" (p. 117). To travel or to visit art galleries in order to renew oneself is, for a painter, to admit that he has nothing more to say (p. 118); the new fad is "invention," the changing of themes and of technique, or "manner," so much so that, to our contemporaries, such "homogeneous" monuments as the works of Beethoven, Wagner, Mozart, Corot, or Renoir seem to be lacking in "modern qualities" (p. 119). Hence Vlaminck's criticism of Gauguin's "mad craving for invention" (p. 140; see the extraordinary pp. 140–41: Gauguin's work is that of a man who has deserted wife and children); he does not like Degas (see below, n. 18); "the painting of Cézanne is the art of a repentant" (p. 146); on the contrary, as compared with Manet, who is a dandy, and with Cézanne, who is always hinting at "possibilities," Courbet is a fighter, a man without afterthoughts and always expressing himself by acts, never by reasonings (pp. 147–51).

These reactions are of a piece with Vlaminck's early refusal to study with Derain at any kind of school; they also agree with the remarkable stability of his manner and technique (as opposed to the subtle evolution of Matisse and Derain: in the case of Matisse, even Fauvism was already an evolution); in short, Vlaminck's reactions are those of a painter who places nothing above his uncompromising faithfulness to his own artistic personality. To the extent that he embodies this grim independence, he is well founded in considering himself an "anarchist." His vicious attacks against the "about-faces" of Picasso (p. 186), and still more against the facilities offered by cubism to those who want to paint without knowing how to do it (pp. 187–90), spring from the same conviction that, in an artist, change is incompatible with sincerity.

unpredictable outside their own art.[15] Still more precisely, even if we knew what kind of music a painter liked to hear, this would still tell us nothing about the kind of music he would aspire to write if he were a creative musician. There is nothing surprising in the fact that such a classical painter as Ingres, who literally worshiped Raphael in the order of painting, should have preferred Mozart to all the other musicians; but when Ingres describes the kind of music he would have liked to write for the Sistine Chapel, even Hector Berlioz looks tame in comparison.[16]

The summary way in which some painters dispose of their fellow painters should therefore not distress us too much nor induce us to believe that, since such great artists utterly disagree in some of their aesthetic judgments, we ourselves should consider all opinions about art a matter of indifference. The antagonism that always existed between Ingres and Delacroix, for instance, can be accounted for by the direct opposition between their respective

15. Laurent, the librarian of the Chambre des Députés, once said to Delacroix that he was "the Victor Hugo of painting"; Delacroix answered, "Sir, I am a pure *classique*." See Joubin's introduction to the *Journal de Eugène Delacroix*, I, xxi. A *classique*—that is, in French, the opposite to a *romantique*. In this respect, the musical tastes of Delacroix are interesting to observe. He prefers Mozart to Beethoven (*Journal*, p. 109). "Beethoven seems to us more moving because he is a man of our own time. He is romantic in the highest degree" (p. 70). He detests "this monstrous work, *Le Prophète*," by Meyerbeer, but he also dislikes "men like Berlioz and Hugo and other would-be reformers" (p. 90). Among these is Richard Wagner (p. 299): "This fellow Wagner wishes to revolutionize music and he is convinced that he is right. He suppresses many of the musical conventions believing that they are not based on any law of necessity." Delacroix sincerely admired Chopin. — On the musical tastes of Chopin himself, see the admirable passage by Franz Liszt, *F. Chopin* (Leipzig: Breitkopf & Härtel, 4th edn., 1890), pp. 194–97. In the works of the masters, Chopin looked for that which corresponded to his own nature only; see his reservations on some brutalities in Beethoven, on harsh moments in Schubert, and even on some commonplace passages in Mozart's *Don Giovanni:* "His cult for Mozart was not diminished thereby, but it was, so to speak, saddened" (p. 197).

16. See Ingres' note, Florence, 1821 (*Ingres raconté par lui-même*, pp. 113–14). Just after hearing Mozart's *Requiem*, Ingres notes that, if he could write the music of a Mass for the dead, he would add to it certain devices to create unusual effects of terror or of pity, as in the *Eumenides* of Aeschylus: "I would make voices of dead men come from underground, howlings, orchestral effects as in Gluck . . . the laughter of the devils and the tortures of the damned. . . . One would not see the musicians, so that nothing would divert the mind from the effects of the music itself in this so terrible and so solemn subject. The Church, obscure; tombs here and there," etc. So this classical painter, who considered Haydn the "daily bread of whoever studies music" (p. 115), imagined before Wagner to conceal his dream orchestra and went much further than Berlioz ever did in the romantic stage setting of his imaginary music.

styles.[17] Since we ourselves are not painters, we should have no objection to
the fact that Ingres favors drawing rather than color, or, inversely, that
Delacroix stresses the importance of color rather than that of drawing. But if
we were Ingres, being convinced as he was that the whole art of painting was
at stake, we would be just as intolerant as he was. Rather, since much more
than a matter of speculative opinions is here at stake, instead of speaking of
intolerance, let us rather say that the uncompromising exclusiveness of his
judgments expresses a quasi-biological necessity. If the art of painting was
what Ingres thought it was, then such a man as Delacroix should not have
been permitted to paint. Other artists than these two great men have exhibited the same spirit of absolutism,[18] and nothing is more common among

17. Ingres' god was Raphael: "Raphael was not only the greatest of painters; he was
beautiful, he was good, he was everything" (*Ingres raconté par lui-même*, p. 97). He
would have had Géricault's *Raft of the Medusa* removed from the Louvre (p. 111).
To his pupils going to the Louvre, Ingres recommended (pp. 182–83) going straight to
the Raphaels and, if they had to go through the Rubens rooms, to do so without looking
at his pictures. Some anecdotes on his attitude toward Delacroix are not perfectly safe
(Amaury-Duval, *L'Atelier d'Ingres*, p. 93)—for instance, the scene in which, after stumbling upon Delacroix in the room of the Louvre whose ceiling he had just painted
(*Homer's Apotheosis*), Ingres is supposed to have said, "Open all the windows; it smells
of sulphur." One thing at least is sure: Ingres voted eight times against Delacroix for
the Académie des Beaux-Arts. Delacroix was more understanding. He occasionally admired Ingres' technique (Amaury-Duval, ibid.) and even his results ("a delightful Ingres,"
Journal, p. 29 [April 11, 1824]). What he really detested was the neo-Gothic style of
some of Ingres' compositions (*Journal*, p. 131) and his constant glorification of the past.
"People like Ingres never get them [i.e., the authorities] out of their system" (*Journal*,
p. 194 [October 10, 1853]). "Ingres was lamentable; he has a completely warped mind;
he can see only one point of view. It's the same in his painting: no logic whatsoever, and
no imagination: 'Stratonice,' 'Angélique,' the 'Vow of Louis XIII,' his recent ceiling with
'France' and 'The Monster'" (*Journal*, p. 220 [March 24, 1854]). "The proportions of his
[Ingres'] ceiling are really shocking [i.e., *The Apotheosis of Napoleon I*, in the Hôtel
de Ville, Paris, which Delacroix has just called "The Monster"]. . . . Pretentiousness,
clumsiness, and a certain suavity in the details, which are charming in spite of (or perhaps because of) their affectation—this, I think, is about all that will remain for our
descendants." (*Journal*, pp. 228–29 [May 10, 1854].) "Saw the Ingres exhibition: highly
ridiculous, the complete expression of an incomplete mind!" (*Journal*, p. 276 [May 15,
1855].) ". . . the mixture of the Antique and bastard Raphaëlism of Ingres" (*Journal*,
p. 407 [November 25, 1860]). — Paul Cézanne was for Delacroix and against Ingres,
whom he considered "a very small painter" (letter to Émile Bernard, July 25, 1904, in
Correspondance de Paul Cézanne, p. 265). — On the contrary, Renoir used to prefer
Delacroix, but he refused to be blind to Ingres' merits, especially in the *Portrait of
Mme de Senonnes*, at Nantes, and even in *La Source*, in the Louvre (Vollard, pp.
274–76).

18. Thomas Couture on Delacroix: "Although he is no creator, he wants to play the
part of one. . . . There is in him something of a Titan and something of a monkey."
(*Méthodes et entretiens d'atelier*, pp. 198–99, as quoted by Tabarant, *Manet et ses*

painters than complete disagreement about the value of paintings.[19] In all such cases, we should remember that the aesthetic judgments of a painter are part and parcel of his own art.

The part of the public that consists of the art critics raises such thorny problems that one hardly dares to touch them. All painters admit that, from time to time, there appears an art critic more comprehensive than the common run, but they hasten to add that, as a rule, art criticism is irrelevant to the reality of art. Naturally, such feelings have been expressed with particular energy by those among the painters who have been exceptionally unfortunate with their critics. Delacroix could hardly mention critics without betraying a secret irritation, and the fact that, as often as not, critics exercise their arbitrary power through the no less despotic authority of newspapers did nothing to reconcile him with what he always considered an unnecessary evil.[20] But however long, varied, and picturesque it may be, a list of

œuvres, p. 11.) — "I despise all living painters, except Monet and Renoir" (*Correspondance de Paul Cézanne,* p. 250). "You will soon be turning your back on the Gauguins and the van Goghs" (p. 260). — "I do not like Degas" (Vlaminck, p. 142). "A painter? Lautrec is not a painter any more than Degas is" (p. 144).

19. During the short time they spent together, van Gogh and Gauguin used to disagree about many things, but especially about painting. In Gauguin's own words: "He [van Gogh] admires Daumier, Daubigny, Ziem, and the great Théodore Rousseau, all people that I cannot stand. On the contrary, he detests Ingres, Raphael, Degas, all people whom I admire." (*Lettres de Gauguin à sa femme,* p. 154.) Accordingly, being both in Arles and looking around, van Gogh would see things *à la* Daumier to paint, while Gauguin himself was rather seeing something like a Puvis de Chavannes, only with more color and a touch of Japan in it (p. 151). — On the three nineteenth-century painters whom "one cannot excel"—i.e., Millet, Delacroix, Meissonier—see *Lettres de van Gogh à son frère Théo,* p. 313.

20. Against critics: "L——, like most men living on the outskirts of the art, and like followers and attendants on armies, etc., is a great talker of what *should be,* and this is not always without malignity. Such persons stroll about the foot of Parnassus, only to pull down by the legs those who are laboriously climbing its sides" (Constable, in Leslie, p. 107). Cf. pp. 125–26. — "Impotence and insolence . . ." etc. (Delacroix, *Correspondance,* III, 121). This letter to George Sand is extremely violent: "Those people simply believe that they are making you, that you are their work, that their charitable advice, holding you in leading strings, has progressively opened to you the doors of the temple that they themselves will never enter . . ." etc. Cf. letter to George Sand, December 17, 1859 (*Correspondance,* IV, 139); letter to Charles Baudelaire, October 8, 1861 (IV, 276–77). — On the errors of even Baudelaire in matters of modern art, Tabarant, p. 49. — Collection of silly judgments on Ingres, in *Ingres reconté par lui-même,* pp. 263–65; Kératry thinks that, in the *Grande Odalisque,* the drawing is weak! — Similar collection concerning Corot, in *Corot raconté par lui-même,* pp. 195–99; J. K. Huysmans, the novelist and self-appointed art critic, distinguishes himself in this group by annihilating Corot's landscapes: "It was a disaster; his light pipe smoke had flown away . . ."

anecdotes has never proved anything. It should be more rewarding for us to consider the reasons, according to painters, such a fundamental disagreement exists between them and their critics.

The first and most important of these reasons has been summed up in a terse sentence by Delacroix: "Criticism follows the works of the mind as the shadow follows the body." [21] If art criticism itself were aware of the fact, little harm would be done; unfortunately, it so happens that, in virtue of its own essence, art criticism considers itself the qualified judge of art. The root of most misunderstandings on this point is an illusion of perspective that induces the shadow to imagine itself preceding the body it follows.

This illusion is practically inevitable. The painter is concerned with the problem of bringing a certain germinal form to the full awareness of itself. As has been said in its place, he himself is not quite sure what his own work will be. He is not even sure, after its completion, that this is the very work it should have been. All the other problems a painter has to solve—choice of a technique and skill in execution—are asked and answered by him in relation to this living germ of the work to be done. On the contrary, since he has had no share in this creative work, the critic is bound to judge the new painting on the strength of rules he has had to borrow from his knowledge of works already done by other painters. Now, these other works were so many answers to problems different from the particular one the painter himself had to solve, so that the point of view of the critic and that of the painter are very different. To be sure, there are general rules eternally valid for all paintings at all times, but, precisely, the painter differs from the critic in this, that he has to rediscover anew how these universal rules should apply in a particular case. The critic judges the answer given by the artist to a problem whose data are unknown to him, so to speak, by definition. [22]

etc. (p. 198). — The same phenomenon is observable in music; see Nicolas Slonimsky, *Lexicon of Musical Invective*. We do not know of any such collection of foolish judgments in the matter of painting in general, but abundant material is waiting to be collected. It is multiplying at such a rate that it will become more and more difficult to catch up with it.

21. *Journal*, p. 332 (January 13, 1857). Cf. Delacroix, *Œuvres littéraires*, vol. I, pp. 1–7.

22. "The French critics have begun with me, and that in the usual way, by comparison with *what has been done*. They are angry with the artists for admiring these

This initial difference entails others. If there were no art, the men who now are art critics could exist, but they would have to exercise another profession. Such as they are, however, they consider themselves, if not on the same plane as the artists, at least engaged in an activity exactly as artistic.

The reason for this illusion has already been given when a distinction was introduced between two kinds of possibles. The proper ground on which the painter stands is that of the existential possibles; the ground occupied by the critic is that of the abstract possibles. The paintings the critic has in mind are dreams of his imagination; yet he does not hesitate to pit them against the concrete realities that originate in the art of the painter. The critic finds a justification for his attitude in the power inherent in him, since he is a writer, to turn everything into words.

Art historians, art critics, aestheticians, all have in common two main features: a great love for art and the lack of the natural gifts that enable a man to become an artist. Their writings about art are for them a sort of compensation for the works of art they cannot produce. Such is the normal way of turning plastic works of art into literature. It has been aptly defined as an easy means of dreaming what one cannot do and, by dreaming it, of achieving greatness in the plastic arts: "This means is literature. One only has to *write* the painted work; one only has to *write* the statue. . . . Through the substitute of literary imagination, all the arts are ours." [23]

The will to judge reached its culmination when it became institutionalized. Official criticism carried by established academies has been tried at least once, in France, with the Académie des Beaux-Arts established by Colbert. Nothing is more tedious than the reading of its proceedings, except, perhaps, in the rare cases when, as happened with Le Brun's speech on Poussin's *Rapture of St. Paul*, the thing reaches the apex of the comic. [24] The most remarkable thing about this incident is that Le Brun himself was a competent painter full of admiration for the painting that was the subject matter of his speech. What officially recognized painters have not been able to do for

pictures, which they 'shall now proceed to examine,' etc. . . . All this comes of being regular critics." (Constable, in Leslie, p. 128.)

23. Gaston Bachelard, *La Terre et les rêves*, p. 95.

24. Text reprinted in Lhote, *De la Palette à l'écritoire*, pp. 87–91.

their colleagues does not seem to have been more successfully done by the many self-appointed judges who, simply because they could express their impressions about art, considered them worth expressing. One looks in vain for the name of a man whose opinions about the art of his time altered in any appreciable measure the course of its development.

Whether such a result can be achieved in poetry and other literary genres is an entirely different question. Literary critics create literature about literature; they write about writings. But art critics do not write music about music, nor do they paint about painting; they express themselves in words about an art that is not an art of words.

Each of us has firsthand information about the attitude of the general public with respect to paintings. By and large, its dogmatism is ten times more self-satisfied and prompter to approve or to condemn than the most cocksure of art critics.[25] How many times has everyone heard the classical formula: "I know nothing about painting, but . . ."? Artists themselves are only too familiar with it—so familiar, indeed, that most of them cease to listen when men begin to judge. The Reverend John Fisher, one of Constable's oldest and most faithful friends, wrote to him, on September 26, 1821, to tell him that a "grand critical party" was sitting in judgment on Constable's painting, *Stratford Mill*.[26] Short as it is, the anecdote is inexhaustible. First, after vainly arguing whether there was not too much sky in the picture, Fisher brought out of his portfolio two prints by Wouvermans and a van der Neer, "where the whole stress was laid on the sky, and that silenced them." A remarkable example, indeed, of the way onlookers have to rely on precedents. For, indeed, if too much stress on the sky was wrong in Constable's case, why not apply the same rule to all four paintings? The good Fisher must have thought something like this, for his next reflection is a rather melancholy one: "While in every other profession the initiated only

25. "The painter himself is totally unpopular, and ever will be on this side the grave; the subjects *nothing but the art,* and the buyers wholly ignorant of that" (Leslie, p. 190).

26. Incidentally, see the description of this painting by Leslie, himself a painter (p. 77). It is a graphic description: "On the extreme left of the spectator, the wheel and part of a water-mill are seen. In the foreground are some children fishing. . . . To the right . . . a barge lies . . ." etc. Not a word is said about what makes this piece, not a snapshot, but a painting.

are judges, in painting, all men, except the blind, think themselves qualified to give an opinion. The comfort is, that the truth comes out when these self-made connoisseurs begin to buy and collect for themselves." [27]

This latter class of onlookers would deserve a special study as being distinct from the common public, from the professional art critics, and even from the art collectors, although, in point of fact, the connoisseur often collects, sometimes carries on a small business in paintings, and always exercises his personal judgment in matters of art. Painters have a certain respect for the connoisseur to the extent that he also is a potential customer, but they know too well his propensity to give unsolicited advice not to be somewhat afraid of him. Let us symbolize this elite by the name of Sir George Beaumont, whom we meet at every one of the crucial moments in Constable's career. Leslie calls him "the amiable and accomplished Sir George Beaumont, at that time the leader of taste in the fashionable world. Few men better discriminated, than did Sir George, the various excellencies of the old masters; but he never considered how many beauties might remain in nature untouched by their pencils, and consequently he was averse to any deviation from their manner. It is curious that throughout the whole of his intercourse with Constable, Sir George assumed the character of a teacher." [28]

Isolated facts or judgments do not constitute proof. Accumulated facts would still prove nothing, but this at least can be said, that it seems rather

---

27. Leslie, p. 84. Cf. Silvestre, *Les Artistes français*, I, 1–8.

28. Leslie, p. 98. Cf. p. 126, the intervention of Sir George to make Constable try "the Venetian secret of colouring" recently discovered by a lady. On Mr. Ottley, introduced by Sir George: "He is more of a connoisseur than an artist, and therefore full of objections. A good undoer, but little of a doer, and with no originality of mind" (p. 127). Cf. p. 146. Sir George probably is the man whom Constable had in mind when he wrote the following deep remark: "Connoisseurs think the art is already done" (p. 273). Another character related to the connoisseur is the arbiter of taste in matters of painting; see the visit paid to Constable by Mr. Seguier (p. 216): "Did you do this? Really! Who made that drawing, you? really! very good indeed." After the visit of Mr. Wells, of Redleaf (p. 218): ". . . my pictures do not come into his rules or whims of the art, and he said I had 'lost my way.' I told him that I had, 'perhaps, other notions of art than picture admirers have in general. I looked on pictures as *things to be avoided*, connoisseurs looked on them as *things to be imitated;* and that too with such deference and humbleness of submission, amounting to a total prostration of mind and original feeling, as must serve only to fill the world with abortions.'. . . What a sad thing is it that this lovely art is so wrested to its own destruction!" — For similar cases on the French side, Vollard, pp. 257–65.

difficult to find evidence of any pre-established harmony between artists and the public. Nor is there any reason such a harmony should exist. Since they are its victims, it is only too natural that artists should take a gloomy view of the situation. Some of them at least seem to have entertained no illusions as to the aptitude of the common public to be open to the enjoyment of high art. "Taste is the best of judges," Cézanne once wrote to Émile Bernard; "it is rare. Art addresses itself to an excessively restricted number of individuals."[29] Yet, when the same Cézanne expressed his ambition to see his works exhibited in public art galleries, was he not implying that even his own art addressed itself to all? What is true is that, at the time of its creation and for a period of years afterward, art finds but an exceedingly restricted number of individuals whose taste is open enough to communicate with new plastic structures.

This is not surprising, for, indeed, the first friends of his works whom a painter meets, even when they themselves are not creative artists, must at least partake of a sensitiveness to forms and colors akin to that of the opener of new ways in the realm of art. Some of them may be art critics, others may be plain art lovers; in both cases, their number is bound to be very small, indeed. But they are the forerunners of the crowds that, in the years to come, will visit art galleries to enjoy those very same works, then become so many universally recognized masterpieces. The public taste is naturally limited on the creative side, but its powers of adaptation are unlimited. The traditional drama of the misunderstood artist, ignored by his contemporaries and worshiped by posterity, is probably destined to be re-enacted to the end of time; it is a necessary consequence of the normal relationship that exists between artists and their public.

3. *Paintings and Their Enjoyment*

RELIGIONS have churches; books have libraries; sciences and letters have universities; music has conservatories and concert rooms; paintings have art galleries or museums of fine arts. The origin of these institutions

29. Letter to Bernard, May 12, 1904 (*Correspondance*, p. 261).

seems to have been twofold. First was the desire to put under the eyes of the public all sorts of objects, curious, rare, or even very common, but apt to contribute to the information and education of the public. Secondarily, a museum was conceived as a possible aid to research,[30] but most museums were chiefly concerned with geology, natural history, or even national history rather than with paintings.

The second origin of modern art galleries was the private collections of pictures gathered by kings, princes, prelates, or wealthy men of taste in various countries. The psychological motives that impelled such men to collect works of art may have been diverse, and there is little doubt that they were not all of equal quality. What we are concerned with, in this study, is the general effect of these various motives—namely, the gathering together of collections of paintings and the increasing ambition of these collections to fulfill a public service.

This obvious fact confronts us at once with the main problem inherent in the very nature of public galleries of art. The natural tendency of public services is to justify their existence and the money they cost by rendering the public as many different kinds of services as possible. To limit ourselves to our own times, let us sum up the situation in the well-known formula: taxpayers should get something for their money.

To protest would be worse than useless; it would be foolish—the more so since, apart from any influence exercised by the growing pressure of the

---

30. Alma S. Wittlin, *The Museum, Its History and Its Tasks in Education* (especially pp. 109–12). — We are not including in the notion of "museum" the "imaginary museum" or "museum without walls" advocated by Malraux in *The Voices of Silence.* Delacroix had called painting a "silent art"; to him, this meant that painting has no voice, but Malraux has insisted that silent arts should talk. Accordingly, he has decided that, since "the plastic arts have invented their own printing press" (p. 16), it was becoming possible to have "museums without walls"—namely, illustrated books in which all the plastic works of art can be reduced to a certain uniformity of substance, size, and shape, and thus rendered comparable from the point of view of "style." Two remarks should suffice. First, the metaphor of the "printing press" is misleading, for, indeed, a printed word is still a word, but a printed painting is not a painting. Next, to turn all the plastic works of art—"miniatures, frescoes, stained glass, tapestries, Scythian plaques, pictures, Greek painted vases, details of paintings, and even statuary"—into so many plates is simply to annihilate them, qua plastic works of art, by eliminating the matter without which they do not exist. In Claude-Edmonde Magny's perfect words, this is "a Buchenwald of the plastic arts" ("Malraux le fascinateur," *Esprit,* CXLIX [Oct., 1948], 525).

democratic spirit in public institutions, these institutions themselves are essentially distinct from the causes they are called upon to serve. Scientists are
about the business of science, but universities are about the specifically
different business of teaching science by organizing and keeping together
more or less large bodies of teachers who, even when what they teach is
science, are not necessarily themselves scientists. The same remark applies
to philosophy: not a single one of the great seventeenth-century philosophers
ever taught philosophy. And the same remark also applies to painting. The
job of a painter is to paint his own works; the function of an art gallery is
to collect, preserve, and exhibit paintings done in all possible styles, at all
times, and in all countries, by artists upholding sometimes opposite notions
of their art. When an art gallery opens its doors, it opens them to all the possible forms of art.

Renoir once asked the statesman Gambetta for a job as curator of some
provincial art gallery at a salary of two hundred francs a month or so.
Gambetta answered: "My dear Renoir, ask me for a job as professor of
Chinese or as inspector of historic monuments, in short, for any job that is
not related to your craft, and I shall help you; as to appointing a painter
curator of an art gallery, everybody would laugh at us if I did." [31] And let
us add: rightly so. In a gallery of modern art directed by Delacroix,
there would not have been two Ingres; in a gallery directed by Ingres,
there would not have been a single Delacroix. Hard as the proposition may
sound, it is literally true to say that galleries of art are about works of art,
not about art.

This remark, which will perhaps be construed as a criticism of art galleries, should on the contrary justify them against many irrelevant objections. Some of these objections come from artists who protest against the
sterilizing influence exercised upon painters by the constant exhibition of the
masterpieces of the past. But even if the very same painters were not known
to spend weeks and months copying some of these masterpieces in order to
train themselves in self-expression, the central fact would remain that there
is no law compelling anybody ever to enter an art gallery. Painters are wel-

31. Vollard, p. 197.

come to avail themselves of this precious liberty. Nor would it be just on their part to prevent nonpainters from enjoying the works of the great artists of the past: simple art lovers have everything to gain and nothing to lose in exposing themselves to such influences. There would certainly be no harm done if all creative artists decided to keep away from art galleries and to abandon them to the rank and file of the visitors who, unable to increase the world's treasure of works of art, contented themselves with enjoying them.

On the strength of the same principle, museums and art galleries should feel free to organize themselves in view of serving the various needs of the community that sponsors their collections and provides for their keep.[32] The greatest service art galleries can render is to collect, preserve, and exhibit paintings that no private persons could possibly own in such large quantities and for whose preservation nobody would like to feel responsible to the world. Museums provide homes for aged masterpieces. It is most natural that modern communities, while generously discharging these self-imposed duties, should assure to their members all the benefits that can be derived from such institutions.[33]

32. This complexity of motives in public institutions is well exemplified in the history of the Louvre (as told by Wittlin, pp. 118–20). The nucleus of the collection was the private collection of King Francis I. It was first decisively enlarged because Colbert, Louis XIV's minister, bought a large number of pictures and drawings: "Colbert . . . wished to contribute to the training of contemporary artists by providing them with an opportunity of studying good pictures, and thus to further the interests of the country. True to the spirit of mercantilism, Monsieur Colbert regarded a country's independence from foreign import as the most favourable economic solution, and it appears that as a staunch rationalist he ranked works of art among other goods." Later on, "the collections began to form the background of intellectual and artistic activities" (p. 119), particularly the Académie de Peinture et Sculpture (1692), which initiated a consistent propaganda in favor of "academic" painting, and the Salon. French "academicism" was the price paid for this turning of an art gallery into a teaching institution. The problem is not a specifically French one. The usually mild John Constable could write like Marinetti and other futurists when he thought of the harm done by such institutions: "I could not help feeling as I did when I last wrote to you of what I saw at the British Institution. Should there be a National Gallery (which is talked of) there will be an end of the art in poor old England, and she will become, in all that relates to painting, as much a nonentity as every other country that has one. The reason is plain; the manufacturers of pictures are then made the criterions of perfection, instead of nature." (Leslie, p. 97.)

33. These fundamental functions properly belong to what Wittlin aptly calls the storehouse museums and the display museums. This excellent author, however, upholds the view that these two functions are better performed by two distinct types of institutions (p. 191). The functions proper to the "storehouse museum" are the storing of specimens

Among these benefits, by far the most important one, in the sight of modern communities, is education.[34] Few authors have suggested the possibility, much less the advisability, of an education entirely based upon the practice and knowledge of one or several arts. The thing could undoubtedly be done, be it only for the reason that the thorough mastery of any discipline requires a general culture whose area is practically unlimited; yet, feasible as it is, such an education could be only an exception. It would meet the needs of future artists exclusively. What modern communities are expecting from their museums is a major contribution to each and every one of the many other types of educations represented in any social group of some importance. One cannot imagine a modern man going through the full curriculum of modern schools, colleges, and universities, and leaving them without a minimum of information about such major arts as architecture, sculpture, painting, and music. In so far as sculpture and painting are concerned, civic or national museums and art galleries are obviously the centers around which these parts of complete education should be organized.

This is what is now being done on an always larger scale, but even the most generous of human undertakings have their own difficulties. In some cases, a visitor in contemplation before a masterpiece he is seeing for the first and last time in his life is firmly invited to move on so as to make room

and the longest possible preservation of these specimens, all done with maximum economy of cost. To these two functions, the same author adds a third that, as far as we can see, goes way beyond the aim and scope of a storehouse—namely, "to prepare for loan with the aid of experts in various fields, exhibitions on a variety of facts and ideas, in keeping with the progress of contemporary knowledge and standards of general education as recommended by educationalists untrammelled by party politics, commercial interest, or any other sectional bias" (pp. 191–92). The language alone suggests that the problem at stake is no longer exclusively related to art.

34. This is no place to discuss the notion of education in general. Still, I beg to suggest that the desire to get an education is one of the main obstacles on the road that leads to it. The idea that education is an end in itself represents the point of view of the educators. Since it is their task to provide it, they consider all the spiritual realities subservient to the end of their educational activity. This is the reason there is so much education in the schools and so little in their pupils.

Education is not an end to be pursued for its own sake; it is the by-product of the disinterested quest for all that deserves to be sought and loved for its own sake. If a man seeks beauty in view of acquiring an education, he will miss both education and beauty, but if he seeks the enjoyment of beauty for its own sake, he will have both beauty and education. Seek first truth and beauty, and education will be added unto you.

for twelve little girls, each of them carrying her own folding stool and all of them ready for a lecture on the masterpiece. Much less charming are the conducted tours that now prevail in all the great art galleries of the world. No stools this time, but a lecturer surrounded with any number of adults anxious to complete their education and erecting the solid wall of their backs in front of the painting.

All this is of minor importance. In every great art gallery there are days and hours when one can see paintings without being threatened with receiving an education. The days of Louis XIV, who got the whole Louvre collections transferred to Versailles for his personal pleasure, are irrevocably past. To be sure, most of us would prefer a little more solitude around certain masterpieces, but all citizens should be able to enjoy art treasures that belong to all, and all social groups should be entirely free to make their own art galleries serve their educational needs in whichever way they prefer. It is often said that since the public museum is a civic institution, its existence is justified to the extent that it serves the needs of the people. And nothing can be truer; but this is precisely the reason that, in the case of paintings, the more they are concerned with education, the less museums are concerned with art.

The dangerous pedagogical inflation that has taken place in modern times is one more instance of the growing aggressiveness of the disciplines of language. It should be the more fearlessly denounced since, on account of it, education itself is in danger of defeating its own purpose. Let us first make it clear that we are here speaking about art, and that any inference from what is being said here to anything other than art, and, within art, to any other art than painting, should be considered irrelevant. There is no such thing as useless knowledge; there is no knowledge related to the subject matter of any experience, be it even the contemplation of a painting, that cannot feed it and enrich it, provided it becomes really one with it. The only point we are enforcing is that, since aesthetic experience itself cannot be taught, whatever is teachable is only indirectly related to aesthetic experience. The great peril that threatens the future of the art of painting in modern democracies is the growing belief that there is no "distinction in princi-ple between enjoyment and learning."[35]

Only the pedagogical imperialism of some modern educators can account for the possibility of such a statement. To be sure, there is no opposition be-tween enjoyment and learning, but if there were between them no essential distinction, the feeling for the beauty of every art would reach its peak in the conscience of its archaeologists, which, to say the least, is not always the case. Inversely, we could enjoy nothing in a museum without having first absorbed as much information as possible concerning the objects of our en-joyment. Clearly enough, this never is the case. What we know about a work of art is what we had better forget at the very moment of enjoying it. For-tunately for us, we have very little to forget while admiring most of the masterpieces exhibited in one of the world's great galleries of art. Unless we are professors of archaeology, art history, or, at least, general history, what acquired knowledge can we combine with our apprehension of Egyptian paintings, Greek painted vases, engraved Etruscan mirrors, Byzantine mo-saics and paintings? Let us discount the treasures of Chinese, Japanese, and Hindu art, whose beauty so often overpowers our senses, despite our com-plete ignorance of the origin, date, and historical significance of these works. There is a great danger in letting people imagine that they do not "under-stand" art because they "know" little or nothing about it. If the mere sight of certain painted Greek vases does not fill a man with ineffable joy, he will vainly read the colossal literature accumulated on the subject in the hope of acquiring the aesthetic experience which, if he has an eye for beauty, the most unlearned of men will enjoy at once and without effort.

35. Here is the complete statement of the position at stake (Wittlin, pp. 190–91): "No justification seems to exist for a distinction between 'education' and 'enjoyment' as two separate functions of a museum, especially in connection with objects of esthetic qualities which are sources of general education contributing to intellectual and emo-tional sensitivization. It should indeed be one of the tasks of the museum of the future to convince people of the fallacy of a distinction in principle between enjoyment and learning, and of the ample possibilities of combining both in one and the same experi-ence." — There is much to be said in favor of the remark made by J. A. Gaertner: "The best education for art is simply education, which, if rightly performed, obviates all special art education" ("Art as the Function of an Audience," *Daedalus*, LXXXVI [1955], 84).

The fact that should dominate the discussion is the anteriority of aesthetic experience with respect to any form of discursive knowledge. Reflection comes second, and even when it contributes its share to the perfection of aesthetic intuition, a still incomplete aesthetic intuition has initiated the movement of discursive knowledge and reflection. We all are familiar enough with this experience, and there is no need to confirm it by the testimony of any artist. The art lover is competent to deal with the nature of his love, and the fact is that our love extends far beyond the reach of our knowledge. Nature has set no scholarly conditions to the enjoyment of beauty.

It is said that Kojiro Matsukata, a shipbuilder who also was a great art lover, having erected a museum near Tokyo, gave it the name of Kyoraku Bijutsu Kwan, which means, in Japanese, the Pavilion of the Pure Pleasure of Art. It is hardly possible to say with more precision and in fewer words what an art gallery will always remain to art lovers, quite irrespective of the many other legitimate and noble uses to which it can be put by civic communities. If people want to learn, by all means let them do so, but not there, because schools and universities, not art galleries, are the proper centers of learning. If museums of paintings should be compared with something else, it would be much wiser to liken them to places of enjoyment than to places of learning. Rather than give so many men and women a bad conscience on account of their ignorance in such matters, let us tell them that all they are invited to do is to enjoy themselves. Above all, let us avoid making them believe that all the mass of information put at their disposal is something they must learn to love if they wish to love painting. All men ultimately desire to know what they love, and find great joy in this kind of knowledge, but in aesthetic experience love comes first.

It is therefore up to us to put museums to good use and to avail ourselves of the multiplied possibilities of aesthetic experience that they place at our disposal. Even so, there are more stumbling blocks on the path to the enjoyment of art than most visitors to art galleries realize. To a great extent, walking through the exhibition rooms of the most modern of museums is like visiting the ruins of a past that cannot be brought back to life. Each and every picture we see in museums has first been meant to serve a purpose and to play its part in an ensemble that has now ceased to exist. It would be silly to deplore the fact, since what little is now left of such masterpieces often owes its survival to the fact that they have been torn away from their natural environment. The Elgin marbles should not now be in London, but if they had not been transferred to the British Museum, would they still exist? These are complex problems, often tied up with the political history of nations and about which philosophers have nothing to say.

The result, however, is there. As a consequence of wars, countless paintings have been forcibly removed from their mother countries; as a consequence of revolutions, many more masterpieces have been torn away from the places for which they had first been painted, removed from royal palaces or from churches and transferred to those repositories for homeless paintings which we now call art galleries. Like aged people, they are exceedingly well cared for, but they too now seem to have reached the age when it is time for them to retire and stop work.

This does not apply only to paintings removed from public buildings. Anonymous family portraits, pictures representing historical scenes whose memory we have lost, wall decorations for dining rooms or drawing rooms that have long ceased to exist, rows upon rows of still lifes or genre paintings, a single one of which used to be enough to confer beauty upon a whole house, all these and many other similar cases belong in exactly the same class as *Last Suppers, Crucifixions,* and *Virgins and Child* that lost their architectural frame and have ceased to exercise their normal functions.

Is it necessary to repeat that neither protest nor blame is here intended? Much worse might have happened to some triptychs than to be distributed among three cities, or even countries, one third for each. Their timely removal from their primitive homes has often saved masterpieces from being buried under the ruins of ancient buildings. But the fact that nobody is to blame for a given situation does not make that situation an ideal one. If it is not, to know how things stand is better for all concerned. Reduced to its essentials, the problem is that, although they themselves continue to live, paintings in art galleries have found a haven of safety at the loss of their normal connection with life. This deeply modifies the conditions in which it still remains possible to enjoy them; aesthetic experience is not the same in a private home and in a museum of fine arts.

The relationship between onlooker and painting is different in these two cases. The man who has seen a painting, has loved it, has coveted it, and has finally consented to a sometimes heavy sacrifice because he wanted it to grace his home is not in the same relationship to it as he is to the thousands of masterpieces that a nominal fee permits him to see in a museum. If he is not one of those art collectors who turn their homes into private art galleries, he can see every one of the few paintings that he owns in normal surroundings. He can see them only one at a time, and engage with each of them in a leisurely dialogue that can be interrupted and resumed at will.

Not so in art galleries. Modern museums have done wonders to avoid the peril of overcrowded exhibition rooms. Space has been generously provided, and it is now possible, in modern art galleries, to see one picture without having to see, at the same time, the sides, tops, or bottoms of at least four other ones. The grouping of paintings according to schools, periods, and styles likewise eliminates most of the shocking discrepancies that once permitted paintings freely to nullify one another in the eyes of onlookers. The problem does not rest with the art galleries so much as with their visitors, and visitors themselves are not always to blame. The roots of the problem ultimately lie in the nature of man and in the nature of things.

The more clearly to discern its nature, let us sum it up in the simple question of how to spend fifteen days in Venice. There are art galleries in Venice, among which the Academy would suffice for the happiness of a lifetime. But one of the admirable things about this glorious city is that, by and large, most of its masterpieces are still to be seen in public buildings, in churches, in *scuole* of various denominations, even in private homes or palaces, since Venice is the sort of city in which a man can rent murals by Tiepolo along with a house. The average art pilgrim knows from bitter experience that a fortnight in Venice happens every other twenty-five years or so. At such a rate his present visit may well happen to be the last one.

What is he going to sacrifice? The Palazzo Dogale? San Giorgio Maggiore? The Tintorettos of the Scuola San Marco, the Carpaccios of San Giorgio dei Greci, one Titian here, two or three Tiepolos there? What should one give up in order to derive the maximum enjoyment from such an art pilgrimage without losing one's sanity? The visitor to an art gallery is at grips with a similar problem. Our aptitude for artistic enjoyment is limited. It does not increase with the repetition of aesthetic experience. Museum giddiness is the price to pay for getting "painting-drunk."

Nobody is obliged to get drunk, even on paintings. The point is that, in virtue of their very nature, art galleries provide permanent possibilities for intoxication. A comparatively wise and sober man would not dream of looking at more than two or three masterpieces a day, no more than he would dream of sampling hundreds of symphonies and concertos during the two hours of a single concert. When he begins to feel that his head is swimming, the wise man gives up the fight. One single painting per room becomes a maximum until, utterly defeated, he suddenly decides to run away under the eyes of still more and more pictures whose mere presence sets the seal on his undoing.[36]

We wish we could make it clear that no such problems arise in connection with any other use that can be made of an art gallery. If it is a question of learning, any human being with a good visual memory can absorb names, facts, and figures about a large number of pictures without putting anything precious in jeopardy. On the contrary, if we consider the problem from the point of view of general culture, historical information,

36. See Paul Valéry's essay "Le problème des musées," *Pièces sur l'art,* pp. 93–99. Valéry first confesses that he does not like museums too much. First impression of constraint and regulations (no walking sticks, no smoking). A chaos of gesticulating creatures, "each of which demands, without obtaining it, the nonexistence of all the other ones." Entering the rooms dedicated to paintings, he finds himself in a strange place "partaking of the temple and of the drawing room, of the cemetery and of the school. . . . Did I come here to learn, or in search of my delight, or else to fulfill a duty and for decency's sake?" All this is inhuman. Nothing of this is pure. There is a paradox in thus placing side by side artistic marvels, each of them self-sufficient and yet mutually adverse, and the more so when they happen to be more alike (p. 95). The ear would not bear hearing ten orchestras at one and the same time. These paintings are "rare objects, which their authors would have wanted to be unique. As they sometimes say: This painting KILLS all the others around it" (p. 96). Still, they act all at once on our mind and our sensibility. What can we do? *"We become superficial"* (p. 98; italics Valéry's).

sociological studies, or nationalistic propaganda, there never will be too many conducted tours, too many specialized exhibitions, too many glorifications of this and that country's "national" art. Man can absorb practically unlimited doses of propaganda, information, and even learning,[37] but not of pleasure, not even when it is a question of the noblest ones.

It is therefore up to us to learn how to make good use of the museums at our disposal. The most modest ones usually suffice for the happiness of a lifetime, and from the point of view that is now our own, no statistics, no comparative sociological studies, will ever be able to say what has been the real significance of any one of them for the spiritual growth of some of its visitors. The attendance in conducted tours, the number of specialized shows and visitors, can be expressed in terms of numbers, but the comptometer that says how many people have passed a certain turnstile during the course of a year does not yet say how many of them entered the lofty building as a simple pavilion of the pure pleasure of art, and found it there. Yet, whatever else we may be looking for in an art gallery could be found as well, if not better, in any one of the universities or institutes for art history or for archaeology that have long ceased to be scarce. But the pleasure of art itself can be found only where art itself is—that is, neither in books nor in speech, but in paintings.

37. There is an incidental problem, which few would dare openly discuss, but which it would not be quite honest to conceal. Where are we going to find the qualified teachers or lecturers to introduce the public to the truth of paintings themselves rather than to any kind of truth about paintings? Is there no peril in letting teachers or lecturers spread among people the false belief that an artistic education consists in acquiring elementary information about facts incidental to art? In suggesting a syllabus for a "course in curatorship," Wittlin (pp. 252–53) observes that it would be beyond the capacities of a single man "to possess thorough knowledge of all aspects of work in a museum." Such a man would have to be a chemist; "a student of an almost encyclopedic range of interest"; an efficient buyer; a good educationalist; "a psychologist conversant with problems of human perception, memory, etc."; an organizer. Taste does not seem to be required, which, since taste cannot be taught, is most natural. One absolutely must read (pp. 253–54) the syllabus of the *one-year* course that will turn candidates (preferably, but not necessarily, graduates of a university or those holding a teacher's diploma) into so many acceptable curators. The first two subjects are "(1) The History of Civilization, illustrated by specimens of material culture and presented in relation to the facts of geology, geography and science; (2) General Outlines of the History of Arts and Crafts." Any commentary could but weaken such remarkable statements. Among the readings prescribed for future curators, a place should be made for Flaubert's *Bouvard et Pécuchet*.

The presence of the word "democracy" among the supporters of the contrary position is in itself a sure sign that the discussion is no longer being carried on the sole ground of art. It is difficult enough to form a clear notion of the art of painting without adding to the task the practically desperate undertaking of defining democracy. This, however, should be said: whatever its correct definition may be, there is no place for the notion of democracy in the definition of art in general or of painting in particular. Art does not include democracy, nor does it exclude it. Painting has been very brilliant in societies that cannot be better described than as aristocracies, and one could easily find, in our own day, self-styled democracies that have reduced art to a state of servitude incompatible with its prosperity. In point of fact, there are two opposite ways to misuse the word "democracy" in such matters, and we should strive to shun them both.

The first one consists in saying that, since it is democratic to place the very best at the disposal of all, democracies should not take an interest in that part of the very best which cannot be enjoyed by all. Democracy is a social and a political ideal; it is not a fact of nature. On the contrary, to the extent that it identifies itself with equality, democracy manifestly is an effort to counteract the effects of natural inequalities. Nature is not democratic; the survival of the fittest, which is exactly what happens when nature is left to itself, is an aristocratic law. No democracy pretends to replace natural inequality with a politically achieved physical, intellectual, and artistic equality. There is nothing antidemocratic in being an Olympic champion or in being a Michelangelo, a Shakespeare, an Einstein, or simply a man endowed by nature with the gifts, much more modest but no less necessary, that are required for the comprehension of Shakespeare or Einstein as well as for the enjoyment of Michelangelo. Even if the number of those who enjoy true art were much smaller than it actually is, this still would be no reason for the democratic state to change the primitive vocation of the public galleries of art, which consists, first and last, in being places where all can go, if they so choose, to find what the austere Poussin himself considered the true end of art: delectation.

The second error consists in inferring from the spreading of democracy in modern times that, since not all men are capable of aesthetic enjoyment, or not all to the same degree, democratic states will necessarily be the end of art. "Art," André Gide once wrote, "is doomed to disappear from the earth; progressively; completely. It used to be reserved for an elite; something closed to the common run. For these, the vulgar joys. But today the elite themselves are putting their own privileges in jeopardy; they do not admit that anything should be *reserved* for them. With a silly magnanimity, the best people today want *the best for all*." [38]

If it is democratic to want the best put at the disposal of all, then we all should hail this new era with unrestricted enthusiasm. The survival of such an antiquated specimen of the dog in the artistic manger as Gide seems to have been is enough to mark the reality of the progress achieved by democracy, as well as its importance. What is silly is not to want the best for all, but, rather, to think that the pure pleasure of art is in inverse ratio to the number of those who experience it. It is in the true interest of all that the best should be put at the disposal of all, despite the fact that not all are capable of enjoying the best. Extremely brilliant minds and gifted artists in certain domains are absolute Philistines in other domains.[39] This is an old commonplace: *non omnia possumus omnes.* The greatness and generosity of the democratic ideal consists precisely in this, that it aspires to make it possible for each and every citizen to develop his personal capacities, whatever they are, as fully as possible. This may mean the end of the aesthetic privileges of the happy few; it certainly does not mean the end of art.

What would portend the end of art—and, indeed, of all that is ex-

---

38. *Journal*, II, 227 (April 19, 1943).

39. G. K. Chesterton could hardly pass for a man deprived of artistic gifts, be it only in the field of literary art; yet, see his article "Our Note Book," *Illustrated London News*, March 10, 1923, and the passionate reply of Eric Gill (in *Letters*, pp. 177–80): "Mr. Chesterton has been a champion of mediaeval civilization. Yet he is so far a child of the Renaissance that he is ready to join company with a merely dextrous portrait-painter in spurning a great creative period and to suggest that Christian art only began with Giotto! Giotto, alas! was the end, not the beginning. But he is hailed as the beginning because he was the first great illustrator, and illustration, portraiture, criticism are the only functions of art honoured in an age in which men are no longer 'partners with God in the *making* of beauteous works,' in which artists are a class apart, spoiled & petted so long as they are able to purvey the lovable to their employers."

cellent—is the tendency, only too perceptible in certain minds, to think that because it goes by the rule of majority in the political order, democracy is bound to extend the same rule to all the orders of human activity. But there is no necessary reason this fatal error should be committed. Every political regime has its own main temptation to overcome; the blind hatred against personal superiorities, in short, plain envy mistaking itself for the love of justice, is undoubtedly the pet sin of democracies. At any rate, it certainly is the disease of which they die. They often confuse political aristocracies, which are self-perpetuating social classes, with an elite, which simply comprises all the superiorities, manual or intellectual or both, by which every social group lives and progresses at every moment of its history. Democracies rightly strive to rid themselves of their aristocracies, but they themselves cannot survive without their own elite. Nor is it enough for a democracy to tolerate the presence of such an elite. Because, unlike aristocracies, an elite is not a self-perpetuating social class, democracies have no other choice than to ensure its constant recruiting from all social classes, if there are classes, and without any distinction in the economic status of its citizens.

If the end of art is a certain kind of spiritual delectation caused by the perception of plastic structures and the contemplation of their secret intelligibility, then the true democrats are those who will not let the people believe that painting is a particular variety of the art of imagery. Their thirst for justice will not tolerate that an esoteric and true notion of what painting is should be considered the exclusive property of the happy few. On the contrary, because they want the best for all, such democrats will see to it that the best be permanently maintained at the free disposition of all. The best is the perfection of the good; if there is a democratic conception of the good that excludes the best, we do not want to have any quarrel with it; we shall simply decline to visit its art galleries. The only democratic galleries of art are those whose collections are good enough for the people because they would be good enough for a king.

CHAPTER EIGHT

IMITATION AND CREATION

THERE has always been a great deal of disagreement in matters of art appreciation. What seems to be proper to our own times is a much deeper kind of disagreement, no longer about certain works of art, but about the nature, object, and functions of art itself.

This is particularly manifest in the case of painting. While the vanguard of modern painters seems haunted by the ambition to create a new world of forms unrelated to the physical universe in which we live, many others keep faith with the traditional notion of painting conceived as an art of imitation. The public naturally feels bewildered by such a sight, the more so as, driven ahead by their creative instinct, some of the boldest among these artists seem to take a diabolical pleasure in baffling their public by unexpectedly returning to the most traditional forms of painting after trying the most daring experiments.

It is not the philosopher's business to arbitrate such conflicts, but they provide him with fruitful subjects for reflection. What is particularly remarkable, in the present divorce between these two main schools of painting, is that the supporters of the traditional conception of this art seem unable to understand for what reasons modern artists suddenly decided to do away with long-established and, on the whole, rather profitable traditions. Why, indeed, substitute incomprehensible daubings for the lovely landscapes, still lifes, and portraits bequeathed to us by the masters of past time? Most of those among our contemporaries who ask themselves this question would feel less surprised if they had examined the historical data of the problem. Nonrepresentational art certainly can be puzzling at times, but we seem to have forgotten how often the earlier painters themselves have been puzzled by the apparently simple notion of representational art.

1. The Labyrinth of Painting

THE ideal of an essentially imitational and representational art of painting has come to us, largely through Leonardo, from the early Italian Renaissance. One cannot read the Vasari's *Lives of the Painters* without being constantly reminded of the fact. In Vasari's historical perspective, the starting point of the evolution that culminated in the art of the Renaissance was the clumsy and conventional rigidity of the Byzantine painters, and the progress achieved by the Italian masters consisted in rediscovering, equaling, and finally excelling what he himself calls "the good manner of ancient Greece."

What was the nature of this progress? As Vasari conceives it, the contribution of Cimabue was to make the draperies, garments, and other painted things somewhat more lifelike, natural, and softer than the style of his predecessors. But Giotto went much further than Cimabue on the same way, and the very description Vasari gives of his work clearly shows what the great art of the Renaissance finally came to mean to the witnesses of its decadence. Already in Giotto's mosaic known as the *Navicella*, Vasari says, "the apostles are admirably represented, toiling in different ways in the midst of the tempest, while the winds fill the sail, which bellies out exactly like a real one." And even the feelings and emotions of men, or at least their visible expressions, are expressed with admirable faithfulness: "There is a fisherman who is standing on a rock and fishing with a line, whose attitude is expressive of the extreme patience proper to that art, while his face betrays his hope and desire to catch something." To which Vasari simply remarks: "All artists unite in praise of this work."[1]

The nature of the problem raised by this passage is clear. Let us grant that Giotto deserves to be praised for this remarkable mosaic, and still more

1. *Lives*, I, 74. Cf. I, 77.

for the paintings in which he describes all the emotions undergone by the characters engaged in his painted dramas. The question nevertheless remains: is this the job of a painter? Is this what makes a painting a painting? If allowed to proceed along the same line, the next improvement will consist for the painter in showing a scroll with written words issuing from the mouth of one or several of these painted men or women and saying in plain language what they want us to know. For instance, the crucifix saying to Thomas Aquinas in prayer, "Bene scripsisti de me, Thoma," [2] plus, as Vasari says, "A companion who stands amazed at hearing the crucifix speak." And, indeed, the companion has good ground to stand amazed, but so have we to see words written on a painting, except that comic strips have so generalized this ancient practice that most people now consider it a normal one.

It does not help to say that a line should be drawn somewhere and that this line runs between the painted representation of human expressions and the painting of actual words borrowed from spoken language. For, indeed, there is such a line. It is the line that divides a painting from a book, but the painting of written words is not necessary in order to turn a painting into a sort of book. A painting begins to become a book at the very moment it uses lines and colors to relate a story, or to describe human emotions, human passions, human thoughts—in short, whatever could be as well expressed by means of words.

This literary conception of the art of painting is well illustrated by Vasari's description of the frescoes in which Giotto has painted the life of the Blessed Michelina. Vasari praises Giotto for having "expressed with great realism a man afflicted with sores, as all the women who are about him, disgusted by the stench, turn away with various contortions in the most graceful manners imaginable." Is not this to praise Giotto for having used lines and colors to the very same end to which writers are using written

2. "Thou hast well written about me, Thomas." See the life of Filippo Lippi in Vasari, *Lives*, II, 111. The same device has been abundantly used in Annunciations. For instance: Simone Martini's *Annunciation with Two Saints*, in the Uffizi; Ambrogio Lorenzetti's *Annunciation*, in the Siena Gallery; van Eyck's *Annunciation* on the Ghent-Altarpiece; the Angel says, "Ave Maria," and Mary answers, "Ecce ancilla Domini," but the letters of the answer are inverted, precisely because this is an answer.

language? If this is true, our first conclusion should be that, ever since the early Italian Renaissance, men have been living under the spell of the doctrine according to which painting is an essentially representational art.

We are by no means criticizing or belittling the art of the Renaissance. It would be somewhat naïve to condemn a conception of the art of painting to which we are indebted for countless masterpieces contained in the most famous art galleries. We simply are suggesting that, to a large extent, the art of the Renaissance conceived painting as a sort of language. All the religious pictures, all the mythological pictures, all the allegorical pictures, all the historical pictures done by the masters of Venice, Florence, and Rome, as well as by their modern successors, are so many pictorial illustrations of printable stories. They say, by means of images, what a writer could say by means of words. The fact that such paintings were telling stories did not prevent them from being great masterpieces, indeed; but it was not what made them paintings. The text of the first chapter of Genesis, the printed images that illustrate this text in the picture books used for [46–48] teaching religion to children, the frescoes of the Sistine Chapel, all tell identically the same story, but not all of them are paintings. In short, even if it were true to say that painting and representation are always given together, it would likewise remain true to say that representationality is not of the essence of painting.

Let us consider the same problem from a slightly different point of view. Here again Vasari can be of service as a witness to the meaning of events whose origin is now buried in so old a past that we mistake their consequences for permanent necessities. In describing the rise of modern art Vasari lays great stress on the discovery of the laws of perspective. He attaches so much importance to this progress that we see him tracing it to its earliest manifestations. For instance, once more with reference to Giotto, Vasari praises this great artist for having represented beggars so cleverly deformed that his work should be considered the origin from which foreshortening is derived.[3] And, indeed, perspective, which is an application of

---

3. *Lives*, I, 77. The fact that the works thus praised by Vasari do not seem attributable to Giotto is irrelevant to the point under consideration. — Generalizing the problem,

certain optical laws, acquired a growing importance in the art of the Renaissance, so much so that, in relating the life of Paolo Uccello, Vasari himself could not help wondering if there was not something wrong with this passionate enthusiasm for the new technique. Paolo, Vasari says, "was always attracted by the most difficult things in art, and brought to perfection the methods of representing buildings, to the tops of their cornices and roofs, in perspective from their plans and elevations. This was done by intersecting lines, diminishing at the centre; the point of view, whether high or low, being first decided. He laboured so hard over these difficulties that he invented a method and rules for planting figures firmly on their feet and for their gradual foreshortening and diminution in proportion as they recede, a matter that was previously left to chance."[4] When engaged upon those matters, Vasari goes on to say, "Paolo would remain alone, like a hermit, with hardly any intercourse, for weeks and months, not allowing himself to be seen." Now, here again, we are not questioning Paolo Uccello's right to study the laws of perspective and to apply them in his own paintings; nor are we denying that the use of perspective is compatible with the art of painting at its very best; our only problem is to know whether, even in imitational art, perspective as such is of the essence of painting. There were painters and paintings for thousands of years before perspective

[65–67]

Lhote (*La Peinture*, pp. 16–17) interprets the same facts as a conversion from the primacy of sense (painting things such as they appear to sight). Yet the perspective of the Italians was very simplified, mainly concerned with horizontal perspective and careful not to lose contact with what we *know* about things. Nothing is more easily "readable," or intelligible, than Renaissance Italian painting: "The Italian prospective can be defined: a convention based upon visual sensations, but whose aim and scope it still is to generalize" (p. 17).

4. *Lives*, I, 232. Inversely, Vasari reproaches Paolo Uccello with having sometimes sinned against the laws of perspective in a manner incomprehensible in the case of such a learned painter (I, 236). His objections become quite amusing when he says that Paolo should not have "represented a horse as moving his legs on one side only, a thing horses cannot do without falling." Of which fact he presently offers this explanation: "The error probably was due to the fact that he could not ride, and had no practical knowledge of horses as of other animals" (pp. 236–37). — The problem is more general in scope. If it is true to say that to suggest depth by means of two-dimensional pictures is the eternal preoccupation of painters and their forbidden fruit (Lhote, *Treatise on Landscape Painting*, p. 6), then the eternal preoccupation of painters is to create an optical illusion. Cf.: "What is perspective? It is the art of substituting a *sensory illusion* for a moral certitude." (Lhote, *La Peinture*, p. 210.) Unless it totally renounces all representational elements, painting *is* indeed make-believe; it essentially is deception: *trompe-l'œil*.

was popularized by the men of the Renaissance. Since what has once been possible should always remain an open possibility, the correct answer to our own question probably is: geometrical perspective is not of the essence of the art of painting.

[68]

[69]

The same question can be asked in still different terms: is deception (*trompe-l'œil*) of the essence of the art of painting? By deception (*trompe-l'œil*) we mean the art of deceiving sight to the point of making painted figures look like solid material objects existing in reality.[5] To this question, practically all art critics and artists will answer that deception is an artifice unworthy of a true painter. Thus to create optical illusions may be legitimate, or even necessary, in the painting of panoramas, dioramas, or stage settings; it also can be resorted to, occasionally, just for the fun of it; but it cannot be considered an essential part of the art of painting.[6] And this answer is undoubtedly correct. But if we reject deception as foreign to the essence of the art of painting, then perspective should be eliminated along with it.[7] For what is perspective if not an optical deception practiced upon us by painters? But if perspective must go, then modeling should go too, and, by the same token, whatever, in both design and color, contributes to achieving a plausible appearance of reality. Nor can anybody say where

5. We shall often use "deception" as an English equivalent for the French *trompe-l'œil*. Our authority for this use of the term is Sir Joshua Reynolds, *A Journey to Flanders and Holland* (in *Works*, II, 355): "A Freize over one of the doors in chiaro oscuro, by De Witt, is not only one of the best deceptions I have seen, but the boys are well drawn."

6. Even academicism (because it advocates the *gusto grande*, or the *beau idéal*, or the *grand style*) is against *trompe-l'œil*, which is considered the wrong kind of imitaion of nature (wrong because mechanical): Reynolds, *Discourses*, pp. 36–38. Cf. p. 48: "If deceiving the eye were the only business of the Art, there is no doubt indeed, but the minute painter would be more apt to succeed; but it is not the eye, it is the mind which the painter of genius desires to address."

7. Fabrizio Clerici, "The Grand Illusion: Some Considerations of Perspective, Illusionism and Trompe-l'œil," *Art News Annual*, XXIII (1954), 98–178. The author of this remarkable article does not deny that *trompe-l'œil* shares in the nature of *"divertissement*, artfulness, elegance," but his conclusion is that those who see in it "simply a concession to virtuosity, and nothing more" should remember the names of the great painters who have indulged in that "game" (p. 121). — This is quite right—with this reservation, however, that, from the point of view of art, the question is not to know what *trompe-l'œil* is, but, rather, what use a certain painter has made of it in a certain work.

artists should draw a line, because painting is visual deception to the very extent that it is imitation.[8]

We thus find ourselves at grips with a sort of antinomy. On the one hand, traditional painting has always been imitational, so much so that some masters did not hesitate to push imitation to a point where it became downright deception. Countless Italian villas, palaces, and churches, some of them decorated by Veronese or Tiepolo, pretend to make us see columns, cornices, doors, and even real men and women where there are only two-dimensional surfaces covered with a thin coat of paint.[9] On the other hand, all painters feel insulted if they are told that deception is the end of their art. Yet, if its end is imitation, why should it not be deception, which, after all, is the perfection of imitation? At any rate, since there is no clearly defined boundary between imitation and deception, one should recognize at least the possibility of an art of painting that, in order completely to eliminate deception, would completely eliminate imitation.[10]

8. Paul Gauguin was consistent with himself when he said that he wanted to suppress shadows because a shadow is the *trompe-l'œil* of the sun.

9. Clerici, p. 121. See, in the same article (p. 120), the description of the achievements of the Fleming Domenick Remps in the field of pictorial illusionism (quoted from Father Orlandi, *Abecedario Pittorico* [A B C of Painting], 1719). — For *The Horse Room* (c. 1532), by Benedetto Pagni and Rinaldo Mantovano, in the Palazzo del Té, Mantua, art. cit., p. 136. For the little girl of the Barbaro family, by Paolo Veronese (1566/68), in the Villa Barbaro, Maser, p. 135. — Since virtuosity has practically no limits, the seventeenth century pushed illusionism much further than the preceding period; compare, in the same article, the plate representing Andrea Mantegna's ceiling in the Ducal Palace, Mantua (1461–74), p. 133, with the plate, p. 132, *Apotheosis of Alexander the Great*, by Angelo Michele Colonna and Agostino Mitelli (1638), in the Pitti Palace, Florence; and with the plate, pp. 130–31, *Apotheosis of St. Ignatius*, by Fra Andrea Pozzo, church of St. Ignatius, Rome (1676/78). This article on "the grand illusion"—that is, on illusionism in art, or on art as counterfeiting reality (p. 125)—is abundantly illustrated with well-chosen plates (pp. 123–78).

10. The techniques of *trompe-l'œil* were unexpectedly revived, at least for a time, by the cubists (c. 1912–14). False wood, false marble, concert programs, imitations of newspapers, and finally real newspapers, bits of glass, of leather, etc., were either painted or pasted by cubist painters on their abstract constructions. See above, p. 55. Various interpretations of this technique have been suggested. Kahnweiler thinks that the cubists wanted to demonstrate the solidity of a colored structure capable of assimilating real objects (*Juan Gris*, p. 172). Gertrude Stein thinks that, in using real objects in their pictures, or in painting these objects (a newspaper, a pipe) with intense realism, they hoped that the rest of the picture would "oppose itself to them" (*Picasso*, p. 23). In fact, as has been said above (p. 59), once integrated with a painting, these various objects cease to be *natural* things.

It is beyond doubt that for centuries such has been the doctrine of the most famous masters. In his praise of Leonardo's portrait of *Mona Lisa*, Vasari gives a description of the celebrated masterpiece that would befit a perfectly successful color snapshot. To Vasari, what makes this portrait seem rather divine that human is that it looks like a real being. Everything in it appears just as it is "seen in life"; it does not look like paint, but like living flesh; the pulse seems to be beating. And, finally, her smile, her divine smile, what is there in it that makes it truly divine? Simply this, that it is "an exact copy of nature." [11] One fails to see why such a conception of the art of painting should exclude the notion of visual deception. [12]

It will probably be objected that this is Vasari, not Leonardo himself. After all, the masterpiece is there, and we all see at once how different from a color plate it is. Yes, but the problem precisely is to know how, given his own theories, Leonardo was ever able to paint his *Mona Lisa*. According to him, "The painter contends with and rivals nature." Again, "The mind of the painter should be like a mirror which always takes the color of the thing that it reflects and which is filled by as many images as there are things placed before it." The classical text on this point is the recipe given by Leonardo "to represent a scene correctly." You first take a piece of glass and place it between you and the object you intend to portray. You must then "fasten your head by means of an instrument in such a way as to prevent any movement of it whatsoever." Then you close one eye and exactly delineate on the glass what you see beyond it. When this is done, you simply copy it from the glass on a thin sheet of paper, then on paper of better quality, and, Leonardo triumphantly concludes, you "paint it if you so

11. Vasari, *Lives*, II, 164.

12. From this point of view, the surrealism of Hieronymus Bosch and his modern successors is essentially different from *trompe-l'œil*. Surrealism does not intend to make painted things look like real ones, but, rather, to make imaginary beings represented in improbable settings please the eyes of the spectator. To the extent that it is "a process of liberation from conceptual, logical, discursive reason," and even "from reason, absolutely speaking" (Maritain, p. 80), surrealism is more interested in unsettling our perceptional habits than in giving them deceptive satisfaction. To transcend reality, even by visual means, is very different from resorting to visual means in order to achieve a fusion of the world of dreams with the world of realities. Lhote has humorously called surrealism a *trompe-l'esprit*. Cf. Maurice Nadeau, Histoire du surréalisme, p. 211: surrealist painting is "the handmade photography, in full color, of concrete irrationality."

desire, paying careful attention to the aerial perspective." After all, when Leonardo says that "the mirror ought to be taken as a guide, the flat mirror,"[13] one cannot help wondering how it is that we all are not as great a painter as he himself was. There must be something wrong with the theory. But what is it?

First, there is something wrong with the work of art itself. Among the instructions left by Leonardo to his successors, there is a particularly remarkable one—namely, that in painting their copy of nature, they should carefully observe aerial perspective. Naturally, Leonardo clearly saw that the art of modeling, in order to show relief, is but a particular case of the art of perspective, itself indistinguishable from *trompe-l'œil*, or deception. Generally speaking, since there is no intrinsic reason to stop short of deception in representational art, the conclusion follows that if, for any reason whatever, it is not desirable that painting should be integrally representational, then there is no necessity that it should be representational at all.[14]

Next, there is something wrong with the very notion of imitation in art. When asked if their object is to copy nature exactly as it is, painters unanimously protest that it is not so. On this point, there is such an abundant and even tedious literature that one hardly dares quote from it. The notion appeared, from the sixteenth century to the eighteenth, during the course of the endless discussions devoted by painters to the problem: is painting mere handwork? Or is it a liberal art?

A constant feature of these discussions is that the very same men who identify painting with the imitation of reality forcibly refuse to let it be called a "mechanical art." Leonardo is often quoted as having said that painting is "a business of the mind" (*cosa mentale*).[15] At any rate, he cer-

13. *Notebooks*, II, 235, 254, 281, 286.

14. Cézanne once told Émile Bernard: "There must be a measure of imitation and even a little bit of *trompe-l'œil*; it does no harm, if art is there" (Bernard, *Souvenirs*, p. 92). Kahnweiler (*Juan Gris*, p. 148) says that the main object of the cubist experiment was to represent three-dimensional objects on a two-dimensional surface. Is not this optical deception again?

15. "La peinture est chose mentale"; this formula is attributed to Leonardo da Vinci by Ravaisson, in Henri Bergson, *La Pensée et le mouvant*, p. 265.

tainly upheld the view that painters are serving a loftier art than that of the poets, since they can create fictions, as the poets do, and their fictions are more enduring than those of poetry. Painters are "grandsons unto God." [16] More modest than Leonardo, Reynolds nevertheless maintained that, in its own way, painting is "poetry," and it is so precisely because the true object of the painter is not to achieve a servile copy of nature, but, so to speak, to create it anew in a state of higher perfection. [17] The same conviction has been expressed anew in our own times by painters convinced that, if painting is mere imitation, then, by definition, it is not art. [18]

Hence an antinomy within the very notion of imitational art. If it is an art, painting must add something to its imitation of reality. In other words, it must create. Now, creation is the very reverse of imitation, and since art cannot be both, at one and the same time, painting is bound to follow this new road to its very end, once it enters it for any reason whatever. Just as *trompe-l'œil* is the logical term for representational art, so abstraction, or nonrepresentation, is the logical term for the notion of the art of painting that identifies it with poetry.

The problem must have been confusedly present in the minds of all creative painters. To the best of our knowledge, however, the clear awareness of its nature was first achieved about the middle of the nineteenth century. Significantly enough, Delacroix's attention was caught by an article of the musical critic Scudo in the *Revue des deux mondes*, December 15, 1857. Scudo had developed the idea that from Scarlatti to Gluck, then to Mozart and to Rossini, operatic music had constantly tended to assert the properties of its own language, and more and more "to cover the modest libretto that is its theme with a poetry independent of both dramatic interest and ex-

---

16. *Notebooks,* II, 227–28.

17. The object of Reynolds' "Third Discourse" precisely is to convince students that, because deceiving the eye is not the only business of painting, the painter's ambition should be to address the mind and to speak to the heart. This is "the great idea which gives to painting its true dignity, which entitles it to the name of a Liberal Art, and ranks it as a sister to poetry" (*Discourses,* p. 48). And, indeed, since the painter must express "the exact form which every part of Nature *ought to have,*" he himself has to invent what he does not find ready-made in reality.

18. "Every painter who is not in some way a poet is a bad painter" (Denis, "L'Ascétisme de Carrière," *Théories,* p. 209).

pression." Delacroix at once copied the whole passage in his *Journal* without omitting the conclusion of the critic: "Does not a painting by Titian, or Rubens, or any other great master give to those who love painting a pleasure quite independent of the subject that it happens to represent? Does such a language as the one in which *Polyeucte, Athalie,* or *Le Misanthrope* are written need the theatrical illusion that connoisseurs may perceive its beauty?"

Let us dismiss the questions raised by music and poetry as not directly relevant to our own problem. In so far as painting itself is concerned, the significance of Scudo's statement could not be exaggerated. Taken literally, it entailed consequences that would have frightened Scudo if he had been bold enough to deduce them from his own remark. The whole evolution of European painting between 1857 and 1957 was virtually included in it. For, indeed, if it is true to say that the pleasure caused by the paintings of any great master is *tout à fait indépendant* of the subjects they represent, one fails to see why a painting should represent any subject at all.

A similar idea had already occurred to Delacroix. In his *Journal*, he had casually remarked that "it is not always necessary that a painting should have a subject," but the most interesting expression of his personal reflections on this point is a page now included in his *Œuvres littéraires*, which, significantly enough, Gauguin himself later transcribed for his own use.

"The pleasure caused by a painting," Delacroix says, "is quite other than the pleasure caused by a literary work. There is a genre of emotion that is entirely peculiar to painting; nothing else gives an idea of it. There is an impression resulting from such arrangement of colors, of lights, of shadows, etc. This is what one might call the music of the painting. Even before knowing what the painting represents, you enter a cathedral, and you find yourself placed at too great a distance to know what the painting represents; still you often are seized by this magical accord." What Delacroix is here describing is for all art lovers a most familiar experience. In visiting an exhibition of paintings or an art gallery, who has not often been instantaneously attracted from afar by paintings whose authors, dates, and subjects were entirely unknown to him? This love at first sight is aesthetic experience itself in its state of natural purity. If it is so, however, important consequences are bound to follow. Most assuredly, Delacroix himself far from realized all the implications of his own discovery. On the one hand, he felt convinced that, in painting, the first and greatest commandment is the necessity of making sacrifices; on the other hand, he had discovered that the aesthetic impression caused by paintings has little or nothing to do with their subjects. What really counts in a painting is, to use a word Delacroix finds misleading on account of its literary connotations, *poetry;* unless, of course, we prefer to call it its *music,* while, in point of fact, its true name is *painting.*[18a]

As soon as they became aware of the true nature of the problem, modern painters discovered the principle that commanded its solution—namely, to eliminate from paintings all the merely representational elements and exclusively to preserve the poetic elements. This rule, more or less clearly conceived by a succession of great artists, became the driving force behind the evolution of modern painting.

There was a great deal to be said in its favor. Even in imitational art, the poetic element had consisted in discovering, selecting, stressing, and integrating with a structured whole the elements of reality that effectively please the eye. In doing so, painters had to take along with plastic elements a large number of merely representational elements without any aesthetic significance. Obviously, the intensity of the effect produced by a painting should increase in proportion to the plastic purity of its structure. Why not, then, eliminate all that, being merely representational, has no plastic value, and constitute a new type of painting containing nothing else than pure plastic elements?

18a. Scudo's article excerpted by Delacroix in his *Journal* (French text only), III, 51–53. Incidentally, there must be something wrong with the date of this entry (Jan. 25, 1857). The publication date of Scudo's article is given as Dec. 15, 1857; the same date concludes this development on *Execution* (III, 54); this is probably the correct date of the entry. — The following development is to be found in *Œuvres littéraires,* I, 63. — Cf. the Kantian idealism of Delacroix in matters of art, ibid., I, 65–67. In this passage, note (p. 66) the striking formula: "The impression caused by the fine arts has no relation whatever with the pleasure that is caused by any kind of imitation" (*L'impression qu'on reçoit par les beaux-arts n'a pas le moindre rapport avec le plaisir que fait éprouver une imitation quelconque*).

On the side of color, the problem was tackled by Gauguin and, after him, brought to its logical conclusion by the Fauves. If color is there because it pleases the eye, then it should be handled in such a way that its sight gives our eyes the maximum satisfaction. For instance, there are few pure and saturated colors in nature, but there is no reason painters should not substitute them, in their paintings, for the weaker colors of reality. On the strength of the same principle, there is no reason painters should not attribute to the objects they represent, not the colors that they have, but those they ought to have to please our eyes. There may be in nature no such thing as a really pink horse or a really red tree, but why should we paint a tree in its real color if its real color is dull, unpleasant, or merely indifferent? Let us rather paint everything in the colors it ought to have to please the eye. Hence a first kind of abstraction, which can be designated an effort to abstract colors from their objects and to distribute them according to the plastic exigencies of the painting rather than after the model of external reality.

But even before the Fauves, a deeper reformation had been undertaken by Cézanne. What is true of colors is also true of forms. Many elements of reality are not only nonplastic, but even antiplastic. Ingres already complained that heads and necks never dovetailed. Hence, in his own paintings, the remarkable proportion of necks afflicted with goiters or, on the contrary, heads reduced to the condition of extended necks. In one of his plates for *Lysistrata*, Picasso found another answer to the problem—namely, to behead the woman and put the head where, plastically speaking, it ought to be, on the left side of neck. Thus understood, the art of painting is dominated by the unique rule of the plasticity of the painted forms. It rests upon the presupposition that every form is plastic by itself and has a plastic "meaning" of its own. In the perfect words of one of our own contemporaries: "Every form has its specific mode of expression (the language of plastic), independent of its purely ideological significance (language of the sign)." [19]

The consequences of this principle, applied a long time before it found

19. Amédée Ozenfant, *Foundations of Modern Art*, p. 249. Cf. the penetrating remarks on the different uses made of geometry in Euclid and in modern painting (pp. 245–48).

its final formula, cannot be calculated. The long evolution that leads from Ingres and Cézanne to the completely purified art of Piet Mondrian has consisted in an always stricter application of the fundamental rule that has just been defined. In geometry, a set of straight lines and curves means a geometrical object. In imitational art, the lines that constitute a figure mean the real object they represent. In painting conceived as a truly plastic art, the lines that constitute a figure "mean" the aesthetic experience they cause, and nothing else.

One should understand in this sense the famous pages in which such painters as Cézanne and Juan Gris have defined the relationship between geometrical figures and their own paintings. They were not turning painting into geometry, but, rather, they were putting geometry to a painterly use. An attentive reading of their words would be enough to prove it. Pythagoreanism is inborn in the human mind. The notebook of Villard de Honnecourt shows that the game that consists in inscribing objects within geometrical figures was never forgotten during the Middle Ages. The so-called "egg" method for a time interested Delacroix,[20] and it still is put to good use by some professors of painting. At any rate, Cézanne certainly rediscovered an old ideal when he announced his intention "to interpret nature by the cylinder, the sphere, the cone, setting the whole in perspective so that each side of an object, of a plane, be directed toward a central point." [21] This was to submit nature to a Pythagorean treatment similar to that employed by the Demiurge of *Timaeus;* only, this time, the undertaking was a particularly risky one, and Cézanne knew this much too well for his happiness. His ambition to construct a geometry of visual appearances without destroying them, or, rather, to obtain this geometry from the visual appearances themselves, became a constant source of anguish for him.[22]

20. On what Delacroix used to call the "egg system"—that is, the use of ovoid forms in determining the structure of a painted object—see Planet, *Souvenirs,* pp. 33–34.

21. Letter to Émile Bernard, April 15, 1904 (*Correspondance,* p. 259).

22. "The writer expresses himself by means of abstractions, whereas the painter concretes his sensations, his perceptions, by means of design and color" (letter to Bernard, May 26, 1904 [*Correspondance,* p. 262]). This is why we heard him say that he preferred to discuss paintings "while on the spot [*sur le motif*] rather than talk about purely speculative theories" (*Correspondance,* p. 245; see above, ch. 8, n. 6). He wants to paint from nature in order to avoid academicism (pp. 261, 262, 265, etc.). On the other hand, he did

Some of his successors, among the very few who attempted to promote not his style but his problem, perceived with clear insight that it was difficult to stop on such a road. One had either to retrace his steps or else to proceed toward a still more nearly perfect purification of painting as a plastic art. The greatest names after Cézanne are Pablo Picasso and Juan [70, 71, 88a] Gris. Because Cézanne had found it hard to reduce nature to its geometrical elements, Juan Gris attempted to deduce nature from such elements. Instead of starting from landscapes and men in order to join geometrical figures, he decided to start from cylinders, triangles, and from there to join the structured composition of a painting. In his own words: "It is not picture 'X' which manages to correspond with my subject, but subject 'X' which manages to correspond with my picture." [23]

There would be no point in discussing the terms of a method that has given existence to so many glorious masterpieces, or, at least, has facilitated their creation. But Juan Gris himself had not reached the end of the road. Fortunately for him, as well as for us, he does not seem to have asked himself why a painter should worry about reaching, by any kind of method, either inductive or deductive, any kind of representational subject. This last step was taken, with admirable courage, by Piet Mondrian.

The thing had to be done, provided only there was someone bold enough to do it. Since, in any case, what matters in a painting is its plastic element, which we know to be geometrical in nature, why not present this plastic element in its perfect nudity? [24] To this decision we are indebted for the

not want nature to provide him with ready-made compositions (pp. 225–26). His ambition therefore was to develop and to apply theories "in contact with nature" (p. 253). More exactly, he wanted to achieve "la réalisation sur nature" (p. 258)—that is, to paint "constructions from nature" (p. 297) or "to realize from nature" (ibid.). But, precisely, this sounds a little like the squaring of the circle by means of ruler and compass.

23. See Appendix III, p. 318.

24. The plastic impurity of natural forms is due to the fact that their proper functions are not to confer plastic existence, but life, growth, and operation to the beings they determine. In this sense, natural forms necessarily limit, or restrict, what would be the liberty of a pure plastic rhythm or of a pure plastic form. Hence Mondrian's formula: plastic expression "is the clear realization of liberated and universal rhythm distorted and hidden in the individual rhythm of the limiting form" ("Pure Plastic Art," *Plastic Art and Pure Plastic Art*, p. 31). The fact that natural forms are functional by nature entails the consequence that they signify the beings they determine. The visual form of man says at once all that man is, or, at least, what we know about it. This is what Mondrian

series of paintings without any other titles than *Painting 1, Painting 2,* and so on, in which the only plastic element still permitted is the straight line, along with the figure whose plastic intensity is supreme—namely, the right angle, formed by two lines perpendicular to each other.[25]

No one having seen any of these paintings in the complete purity of their essence will ever forget them. That there have been faked Mondrians is one of the most extraordinary incidents in the history of painting. But Mondrian himself was not surprised. He did not consider his works abstract. On the contrary, he forcefully maintained that, since they themselves were concrete objects whose whole meaning was in themselves, and not in any aptitude to signify anything foreign to their own nature, his paintings were entirely concrete realities.

But the life of forms never stops, and since Mondrian had followed the road to its term, he was bound to verify the time-honored law that the end of a journey also is the beginning of the return trip. The last, unfinished [72, 73] production of Mondrian—namely, his *Victory Boogie Woogie*—adds to the static works that had preceded it a feeling for rhythm, almost for movement, that invites us to think that he himself felt that he had reached the term of an experiment. At any rate, and however we may feel about the results, it is beyond doubt that there is a positive meaning behind the enigma of modern painting. Far from resulting from an unexplainable aberration of the human mind, nonrepresentational art offers itself to our study as rooted in the very nature of representational art.

Seen in the light of its latest developments, the art of painting does not seem to have wandered aimlessly through its own labyrinth. When Delacroix laid down, as the first of all principles, the necessity for the painter to make sacrifices, painting was entering the way leading to pure plastic

expresses when he says (p. 31): "Limiting form [that is, the form that determines what a certain being is] always tells us something: it is *descriptive*." The painters who remarked that their art did not "talk" were entering the road to abstract art.

25. Mondrian, pp. 31, 50–53. — An incidental but visible consequence of the cure of abstractionism that painting has had to undergo ever since the beginning of the movement has been its liberation from sexuality. In Ozenfant's perfect words: "Cézanne gave us pears and apples that owed nothing to Eve: it was a brutal interruption to a flesh diet" ("Art Minus Erotics," *Foundations of Modern Art,* p. 82).

art. Where should one stop in making sacrifices? The answer is now known. Piet Mondrian seems to have gone the whole way, in this sense, that, if everything must be sacrificed to pure plastic form, the sacrifice at least has now been made. By the same token, since to sacrifice the rest to preserve a certain element in its purity is to abstract this element from the rest, the art of Mondrian marks the *terminus ad quem* of the long pilgrimage of painting on the road to total abstraction.

This is also the reason, after Mondrian, the situation becomes different from what it used to be. First, another kind of abstraction then becomes possible. Instead of sacrificing everything to the intelligibility of geometrical forms, especially the right angle, why not totally sacrifice this intelligibility to the ideal of absolute formlessness? The thing is now being done in the countless paintings that look like so many plastic symbolizations of what the philosophers used to call "prime matter": something that is ceaselessly striving to be but never quite makes the grade; a "near nothingness," or, in Augustine's own words, an "It is and it isn't." The only objection to prime matter is that it is rather monotonous. To distinguish one piece of it from another, a painter has no other choice than to resort to a minimum of form. By doing so, the artist renounces the pure abstract condition of total formlessness; he is making the first step on the way back to the pre-Mondrian situation in art.

A second consequence of Mondrian's heroic experiment is that, after him, painters can no longer engage in an always open competition as to who is to go one better in the way of abstraction. As a consequence, modern painting finds itself in the well-known situation of the revolutionist who, after struggling for years to conquer his complete freedom from certain oppressions, finds himself suddenly confronted, by his very victory, with the much harder problem of knowing what to do with it. If there is a drama of contemporary painting, it is this. The victory of abstractionism has been so complete that it now takes much more courage and independence for a painter to be more or less representational than to follow the crowd of those who find it more profitable to exploit, at their own profit, the facilities of shapelessness. There is no denying the fact: painting now is free. There no longer remains any career to be made by fighting for its complete liberation.

To the question, What use should painters make of their liberty? the painters themselves must find an answer. A philosopher can contribute nothing to the debate beyond the clarification of notions whose obscurity adds to the natural difficulty of the problem.

All true painters have always agreed on the necessity of making sacrifices, but they seem also to have been in the dark as to the precise nature of what they had to sacrifice. Their first notion of it, as is visible in Delacroix, was that a painter should sacrifice all the elements of reality that do not contribute to the plastic structure of his work. And, indeed, if they do not contribute to it, they harm it. Expressed in our own technical language (which should be read not for what it is, but for what it means), this signifies that "abstraction" essentially consists in the elimination of whatever is not required for the actual realization, under the form of a painting, of the germinal form present in the mind of the painter.

Taken in itself, this problem is much more general than that of representational versus nonrepresentational art. The degree and nature of abstraction cannot be determined a priori, on the strength of any universal principles; it is up to the painter to say what these principles should be from the problem he is trying to solve. This problem, of course, is the very painting he is now doing. A painting is not good because it is representational, but not to be representational does not suffice to make it good. If it is beautiful, an "abstract" painting is so for the very same reason that the most totally representational of the paintings left to us by Botticelli and Carpaccio are beautiful. Representational or not, a painting is a true work of art to the extent that it "abstracts" from all the elements that are not compatible with, or required for, the embodiment in matter of the germinal form conceived by the painter. In a word, because it is identical with the germinal form itself, abstraction is creation.

This more comprehensive notion of abstraction, which has recently been defined in different terms by the painter Jean Bazaine, essentially rests upon the decision to dissociate, once and for all, the two notions of "abstract" and "nonrepresentational." He himself should be allowed to express his own view in his own words.[26] What matters is the light it throws on the whole problem, and one could not have expressed it better than by calling Jan van Eyck, as Jean Bazaine does, the most abstract of all painters. This bold statement assumes its full meaning if one remembers his portrait of himself and his wife Margaret, now commonly called the "Arnolfini portrait." Dominated as it is by the round convex mirror around which everything seems to revolve, there is not a single line or shape in this painting, including the gloriously absurd headgear of the man, that is not, at one and the same time, both integrally plastic and integrally representational. It is the perfect reduction of the representational elements to the plastic requirements of the form. If the "representational" is not that which represents, but, rather, that which fulfills no other function in a picture than to represent, then the masterpiece of van Eyck is a perfect example of a painting that totally abstracts from the representational elements of reality.

It would be an illusion to imagine that, since it is so, there is nothing to prevent painters from once more indulging in the easy pleasures of imitational or representational art. In the new situation created by the art of Piet Mondrian, no particular type of art enjoys any privilege. If, as we think, what Jean Bazaine says is true, the correct conclusion to infer is that creative painting has never been representational. Even while it was representing, creative painting was doing something else than to represent. There is therefore at least one impossibility following from what precedes; it is, for any painter, to return to something that has never existed. And what

26. "If we wish to clear up the difficulty, it seems therefore necessary that we should once and for all dissociate the 'abstract' from the 'nonfigurative.' The power of interiority, and of getting beyond the visible, which creation implies, does not depend upon the greater or smaller degree of resemblance between the work and external reality, but, rather, upon its degree of resemblance with an internal world that entirely envelops the external one and that expands itself up to the *pure rythmical motives of being.* Zola is less resembling (less abstract) than Mallarmé. Cormon is less resembling (less abstract) than Klee, but Klee is less resembling (less abstract) than the Douanier Rousseau. And Kandinsky is much less abstract than Brueghel, Vermeer, or van Eyck. Van Eyck might well represent the most extreme point ever reached by abstraction in the whole history of painting." (*Notes sur la peinture,* pp. 56–57.) This entirely confirms the conviction that, in the last analysis, beauty is one and the same for both imitational and nonimitational art. Of course, here, the meaning of "abstraction" is: the resemblance of the painting to the internal reality present in the mind of the painter.

would this be? It would be to return to a style of representational painting that is painting qua representational. This simply would be a contradiction in terms. If this is not the end of the road, it certainly is the end of one of the roads. There is now no future for the "stories without words" that hope to be mistaken for so many paintings.

2. Pictures and Paintings

IN VIRTUE of its own nature, painting is inextricably enmeshed in another art for which there is no name, and for which it is hard to find a name because, so far, it has called itself "painting." Let us tentatively call this second art the art of "picturing"—that is, the art of doing pictures.[27] Why, and how, should it be distinguished from the art of painting?

If there is such an art, its very essence is to represent, or imitate, and whatever can make imitation more nearly perfect can be considered as serving the very end and purpose of this art. Deception is not necessarily its most perfect expression, but there is no ground on which it could be rejected as foreign to the essence of picturing.

Moreover, picturing is an art because it includes all the techniques that are conducive to its own end—namely, to turn out images that represent their models as faithfully as possible. The relationship, in the commonly received interpretation of Plato, between natural beings and their Ideas correctly applies to this conception of picturing as an art.

Picturing even is a "fine art," because it is beyond doubt that skillfully done images are extremely pleasant to see. Children delight in looking at picture books, and grown-up people remain pretty much like children in

27. If the principle of this distinction is accepted, usage will find the proper words to express it. To *illustrate*, or *illustrating*, mainly applies to the kinds of images that accompany, as visual aids, the text of certain books. *Image making* had for a while detained our attention, but Lionel Trilling, whose advice we sought on this question, dissuaded us from using it, for the same reason that one would avoid *imagery*; these two words "too much suggest the poetic process, the process of metaphor." Another noun, *imaging* (from the verb "to image"), also had to be eliminated because it "carries some overtones of the discussion of poetry." As far as we can see, *picturing* then remains the only possible candidate. A picture is a graphic representation of something. Trilling: "*Picturing* has to me the great advantage of a certain childish connotation: 'Picturebook,' 'See the pretty picture.' And *picturing* is exactly what a child does."

this respect. But pictures are at least as pleasant to do as they are to see. There is a specific pleasure in hitting the likeness of any given object, especially of human faces, as well as in seeing it. Contrariwise to what is true of the art of painting, comparatively young people, some of them hardly out of childhood, have an innate gift of drawing strikingly successful caricatures, usually profiles, of people around them. They do this not by chance, or in a haphazard way, but deliberately, intelligently, and consistently. Portrait painters without pretensions to genius, landscape painters, still-life painters, and even such recognized geniuses as Giotto, Botticelli, and Veronese—in short, all the masters of classical art—have left us a vast number of painted works, most of which are, at one and the same time, both pictures and paintings. And there is an invidious question that it probably is wiser not to ask. Among the countless visitors to art galleries, how many enjoy the works of Raphael as pictures, how many enjoy them as paintings? Is there any contradiction in imagining a visitor constantly delighted with the lovely images of men, women, landscapes, and still lifes that he sees in an art gallery, and returning home in a state of complete satisfaction, without even suspecting that he has been enjoying paintings as pictures much more than as paintings?

We do not intend to minimize the importance of pictures, or images. On the contrary, if one succeeded in introducing a distinction between pictures and paintings that looks so well founded, pictures would benefit by it as much as paintings. We need a history and an aesthetics of the art of picturing conceived in a spirit of sympathetic objectivity suitable to the importance of the subject.

Images are among the oldest products of the fabricative activity of man. They are inseparable from the magic rituals and from most of the religious cults: image makers have always helped men in imagining deities in which they believed but which they could not see.[28] Images are inseparable

28. Religious art is imagery to the extent that iconography has something to say about it. Thus understood, art, like nature, is the Bible (i.e., the Book) in which believers see, or read, the object of their religious beliefs. This is important to some religions; for instance, not to Judaism or to Islamism, but very much to Christianity. As subservient to religious instruction, painting has produced unsurpassed masterpieces (the ceiling of the Sistine Chapel); it has also produced countless charming pictures, including all the

from the political life of nations: image makers have always helped human groups in maintaining in their midst the memory of national heroes and their deeds.[29] Images are inseparable from domestic life: image makers have been doing portraits for centuries, and photographers are simply helping painters keep the common memories of family life alive for the members of this primitive social cell. Images are inseparable from sexual life: quite a few of the greatest painters have relied upon the attraction exercised by natural beauty to give at least this pleasure to those who derive little or none at all from the art of painting. But sex appeal naturally leads to advertisement, which, although it makes use of everything that can elicit a response from imagination, feelings, and desires, seldom neglects to enlist the services of this fundamental instinct.

The list could be extended endlessly, the more so as one and the same image can serve, at one and the same time, several different purposes. The most resolutely imitational form of art considers it its duty to embellish reality, and this is so true that the sacred images of national heroes or

Madonnas that are more rightly accounted lovely rather than beautiful, because they portray "that kind of woman who is lovable to those who love that kind of woman and in the attitude which is charming to those who are charmed by it" (Eric Gill, *Art-Nonsense*, p. 74) ; in fine, it has produced, and is still producing, a colossal number of artistically insignificant images, plus quite a few downright ugly ones, whose only justification, if there is one, is to serve the ends of religious instruction. On the contrary, if we forget about iconography, all true works of art are essentially religious, whereas all the works that present themselves as works of art but are not can be said to be (whatever they may represent) areligious. Eric Gill goes further still (pp. 72–73) : "The most irreligious modern work is to be found in churches and, on the other hand, the most religious is that of the men of the so-called post-impressionist schools; for these men have dared to proclaim in their work that worship is properly given to that which is beautiful in itself and not to those things which please merely by entertaining us." As an example of "godly" art, Gill quotes that of Matisse (p. 173)—a statement that, made in 1929, was an astounding prophecy.

29. So-called "history painting," in all countries without exception, is largely dedicated to the exploitation of nationalistic passions. As it is now developing in Russia or in Mexico, art is frankly at the service of a class propaganda that in no way differs from the czarist, monarchist, or patriotic propagandas of the recent past. See the pronouncement attributed to Orozco: "A painting is a poem, and nothing else. A poem is made of relationships between forms as other kinds of poems are made of the relationships between words, sounds or ideas." ("Orozco 'Explains,' " *Bulletin of the Museum of Modern Art* 4, VII (Aug., 1940), and *Masters of Modern Art*, p. 156.) Those who look at his *Zapatistas*, or, for that matter, at the paintings of Diego Rivera, will not find their "poems" very different, in inspiration, from those dedicated by Louis David first to the French Revolution, then to Napoleon I.

saints have not always drawn their models from the purest sources. The simplicity of those whom such images help in their piety is so perfect, and certainly so pure, that one probably would do more harm than good by quoting facts in support of these remarks.[30]

This is no place to attempt an aesthetics of imitation, or mimicry, which is one of the most fundamental among the natural instincts of man. Our only point is that, were it to be attempted at all, such a study should be carefully kept apart from that of the art of painting. Their confusion, which is everywhere apparent, never fails to provoke hopeless misunderstandings.

When Captain Cocq commissioned Rembrandt to commemorate his company of guards by means of a large canvas, he could have meant either one of two entirely different things. If what he wanted was a real painting to perpetuate the memory of his company, he should have left Rembrandt free to paint what he well pleased. This is what, in fact, Rembrandt did, but Captain Cocq did not like it. What he really had in mind, when he commissioned Rembrandt, was a group of portraits of himself surrounded with his men, more or less like the groups of portraits painted by Frans Hals for the companies of civic guards or for the boards of hospital trustees that wanted to perpetuate the memory of their faces. Captain Cocq could not guess that his name would survive the course of centuries precisely because *The Night Watch* did not seriously attempt to portray him or his guards. Yet this is exactly what did happen, and there would be fewer controversies about public monuments if, before commissioning artists, civic

---

30. A few indications should suffice for those who are not familiar with the facts in question. Since so-called religious art is still largely derived from the Italian Renaissance, see, in Vasari, how Fra Filippo Lippi selected his model for a picture of Our Lady (*Lives*, II, 4). This model became the unwed mother of Filippino Lippi. Even if the anecdote happened not to be true, Vasari's remark would still be worth meditating: "He was so highly esteemed for his abilities that many blameworthy things in his life were covered over by his excellencies" (II, 6; cf. p. 7). There is something humorous in the simplicity with which religious books or magazines (we beg to be excused from quoting titles, years, and pages) hope to feed the piety of religious souls with "reproductions" of the Blessed Virgin by . . . Sodoma. They would certainly not dare to print the name of this painter, as they do, if the purity of their intentions did not keep them miles away from realizing its meaning. See Vasari, III, 289, 292; especially III, 141: "Giovannantonio was a brutal, licentious man whose vices had won him the name of Sodoma, of which he was rather proud."

authorities made up their minds on the subject. Let us add that artists, too, should be quite explicit as to the spirit in which they accept a commission.

If an *image* is at stake, then imitation and likeness in representing are of the essence of the work to be done. This imposes such limitations upon the freedom of creative artists, and it grants such facilities to the others, that practically all commemorative monuments and pictures are bound to be, at best, indifferent works of art. But there is nothing to complain about in this fact. If we want a picture accurately to *represent* Joan of Arc liberating Orléans, George Washington crossing the Delaware, or, simply, one of the unknown soldiers of World War No. X, then we can demand a good picture, but we should not expect too good a painting. The reason is that too many details that must be included or excluded in order to obtain a good picture have to be excluded or included in order to do a good painting.

The alternative is to invite the painter to do as beautiful a painting as he possibly can, and to dedicate his work, after the manner of a commemorative stone, to the memory of a great man, a national hero, or some historical event. This time, imitation or representation should be, if not necessarily excluded, at least subordinated to the artistic end the painter aims to achieve. This is what Aristide Maillol rightly did when, as a monument to a great musician, he simply made one more of his beautiful statues and inscribed on the pedestal the simple words "To Claude Debussy." It was that, or else a statue representing Debussy himself, all complete from beard to shoelaces. There may be reasons in favor of either choice, but that a choice has to be made seems to be beyond discussion.

Two additional remarks can be made in favor of this distinction. The first one is that it disposes of the vexing problem recently created by the development of art photography. There is a great deal of truth in the famous saying of Jean Cocteau that "photography has liberated painting." It has liberated painting from the duty it had so long assumed, to imitate the visible appearance of things. But at the same time it was becoming itself, painting has liberated photography from its unsound ambition to be an inferior kind of painting.

To the often-asked question, Is photography an art? the answer to give

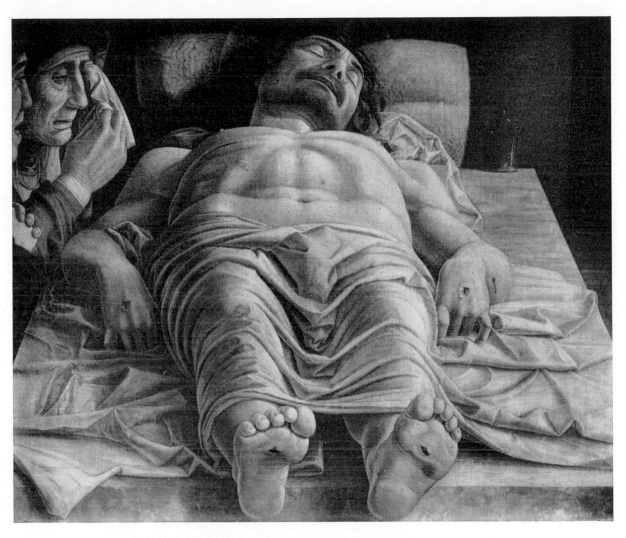

ANDREA MANTEGNA. The Dead Christ
A late work (after 1490). Brera, Milan

VITTORE CARPACCIO. St. Stephen Disputing with the Doctors
1514. Brera, Milan

JACOPO TINTORETTO. Finding the Body of St. Mark
About 1562. Brera, Milan

Antonello da Messina. St. Jerome in His Study
About 1460. National Gallery, London

ANDREA POZZO. The Apotheosis of St. Ignatius
About 1685. Sant'Ignazio, Rome

PABLO PICASSO. Still Life
1908. Solomon R. Guggenheim Museum, New York

PABLO PICASSO. Mandolin and Guitar
1924. Oil with sand on canvas. Solomon R. Guggenheim Museum, New York

PIET MONDRIAN. Composition in White, Black, and Red
1936. Museum of Modern Art, New York

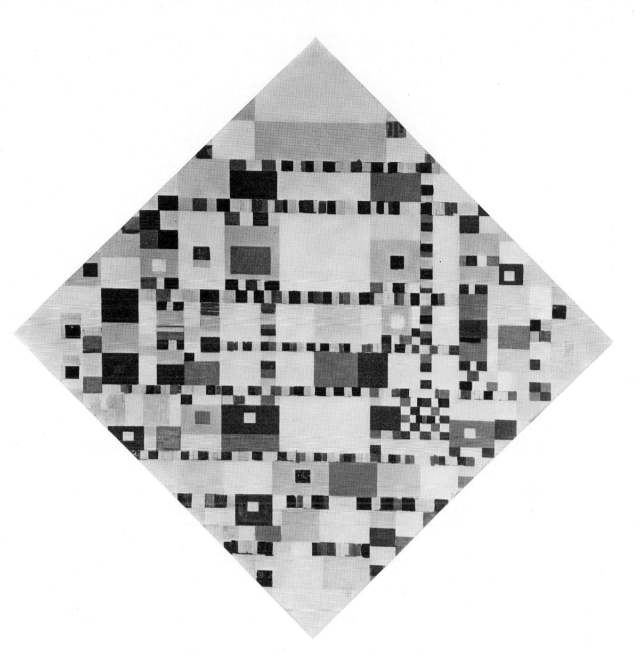

PIET MONDRIAN. Victory Boogie Woogie
1944. Paint and paper. Unfinished.
Miller Company Collection, Meriden, Connecticut

JAN VAN EYCK. The Marriage of Giovanni Arnolfini and Giovanna Cenami
1434. National Gallery, London

a. ERNEST MEISSONIER. The Flutist
1858. Louvre

b. ÉDOUARD MANET. The Fifer
1866. Louvre

ÉMILE RENOUF. The Helping Hand
1881. Corcoran Gallery of Art, Washington

MARY CASSATT. The Boating Party
1893/94. Chester Dale Collection, National Gallery of Art, Washington

a. NORMAN ROCKWELL. Thanksgiving, 1951
*The Saturday Evening Post Collection,
Philadelphia*

b. J.-B.-S. CHARDIN. Grace
1740. Louvre

ALFRED MANESSIER. Crown of Thorns
1954. Carnegie Institute, Pittsburgh

a. Jacqueline Gilson. Sketch for a "Pietà"

b. Jacqueline Gilson. Pietà
1952. In the possession of the artist

is, Yes, it can be an art, but because it is an art whose end is to imitate, photography is not a variety of the art of painting. Photography should rather be considered a mechanical variety of the art of picturing. Its immense popularity and the veritable passion sometimes put at the service of its pursuit bear witness to the natural love of man for the making of images. Photography is the draftsmanship of those whom nature has not blessed with the gift of picturing.[31]

The second remark is that, because they are specifically distinct, it is just as wrong to judge paintings from the point of view of pictures as it is to judge pictures from the point of view of painting.

A painting has its own rule, its own justification within itself. A picture has its criterion outside itself, in the external reality it imitates. Several critics have recently made the remark that nonrepresentational art has this major defect, that, being unrelated to any external reality, it has no criterion by which it can be judged. The argument would be valid if the art of painting were the art of picturing. As it is, all judgments and appreciations of paintings founded upon their relation to an external model are irrelevant to painting.[32]

[75a, b]

A painting is the embodiment of a form in a matter; the whole being of a picture is determined by the relationship that obtains between the image itself and some external reality. And since their aim and purpose is to represent things as they are, images have a right to be appreciated from the point of view of their success, or failure, in achieving their own end. As

31. Baudelaire, "The Modern Public and Photography," *The Mirror of Art*, pp. 225 31.

32. See Charles-Pierre Bru, *Esthétique de l'abstraction*, pp. 217–18. — Cf., on this problem, the remarks made by Lionel Trilling (*The Opposing Self*, pp. 97–98). The nature of the difficulty appears in full view in the essay of Raoul Ergmann, "The Chances of a Dialogue; Berenson and Malraux," *Diogenes*, VII (1954), 73–74. Incidentally, the chances of such a dialogue are nil: Berenson would have a great deal of listening to do. Still, the question itself is good (p. 73) : "If art may not be subjected to the discipline of representation, what measure of its value can be proposed?" And again (pp. 73–74) : In the compositions of Klee and Miró, even if pleasure is felt by the eye, we cannot judge of the "conformity [of the work] to a law which is as strict as it is secret." It is a hopeless undertaking to make a critic—who is a writer—understand that what he has to judge is the relationship between his own sensible pleasure and the painting, not the relationship between the painting and some externally given reality. To be sure, there is a secret there, but it is the critic's own secret as much as it is the painter's.

compared with a painting, whose ultimate end is to achieve a fitting object of contemplation, images are characterized by their ambition to represent all the objects they include, and to represent these objects with all the details that are compatible with their pictorial representation.

[76, 77] This remark applies not only to the number of the objects represented, but also to their visual appearance from the two points of view of shape and color. In short, a good image represents whatever is supposed to be visible in its object and represents it as exactly as possible as it would be seen if it were an externally given reality. In this sense, art critics are fully justified in judging images by the degree of their success in conveying an impression of reality. It is likewise understandable that, in judging paintings as if these were images, some art critics should condemn in them all deformation of what we take to be the real shape of external objects, all modifications of what we take to be their natural colors. What is justifiable in a painting, taken precisely qua painting, cannot be condoned in an image, whose proper function is to imitate reality.

[78a, b] These superficial differences are the signs of a deeper one. Since its proper end is to represent things, beings, scenes of human life, and, in short, the whole of visible reality, the art of imaging is a particular case of the general function of language. It is a branch of literature. In Odilon Redon's words, "There is a literary idea every time there is no plastic invention." [32a] Images always have a meaning, and they are rightly judged by the degree of their success, or failure, in conveying it. Consequently, the choice of the subjects to be represented by an image is of primary importance. Particularly the natural beauty, or charm, or power of suggestion proper to the objects, beings, or scenes represented by an image is lawfully taken into account in appreciating its artistic value precisely qua image. Images so obviously participate in the nature of their objects that to religious images, for instance, is often attributed a sort of inherent sacredness that really belongs to that which they represent, that is, to their meaning.

Innumerable consequences follow from this simple fact. To sum them up generally, let us say that, whereas images are likely to become more or

32a. *À soi-même,* p. 78.

less faithful historical documents, paintings very seldom serve the same purpose, and, when they do, the result is purely incidental to their nature. Good image makers have rightly been praised for having bequeathed to posterity a faithful picture of their country, its way of life, its people, and even the history of their own generation.[33] All the loves of a nation, all its hatreds, all its ambitions, all the successive images under which it depicts itself to itself can be represented by means of pictures, and when the image maker happens to be, at the same time, an authentic painter, as was the case of Honoré Daumier, it is often difficult to sort out, from among their immense daily production, what belongs to the art of picturing, what belongs to the art of painting, and what, as often happens, belongs to both. With a painter who is nothing but a painter, no such problems arise. From the whole production of Paul Cézanne, what can we infer concerning the history of his country? Derain, Matisse, and many other painters have left us countless paintings among which it would not be easy to find anything of historical significance. Their apples, their landscapes, and their odalisques are just as indifferent to the tragic events that shook their country, in 1870, 1914, and 1939, as the allegories of Botticelli are unconcerned with the local history of Florence during the second half of the fifteenth century. This is but the external symptom of the radical difference between a painting, whose meaning is in itself, and a picture, whose function is to point out something else, as do the words of spoken language and all the systems of written signs used by various nations ever since the beginning of civilization.

The distinction is particularly visible in the case of religious painting.

33. This social function performed by the maker of images, so foreign to the activity of the painter, is well expressed in the "Letters to the Editors" in *The Saturday Evening Post* for April 16, 1955. For instance: "Re Norman Rockwell Album (March 12), I doubt if history has or will again portray a complete cycle of a generation of Americans with equal nostalgic emotional power." Again: "The Rockwell covers on your magazine seem as typically American as apple pie and the Dodgers." Again: "Surely no artist of any period has ever bettered Mr. Rockwell in delineating a given subject." However great they are, these merits are entirely foreign to the art of painting. — On the need of an aesthetics of picturing, see the penetrating views of Baudelaire, "On the Essence of Laughter, and, in General, on the Comic in Plastic Arts," *The Mirror of Art*, pp. 133–34. In 1855, Baudelaire was writing: "The task still remains to be done." The sentence remains largely true in 1956.

As artists, Christians find themselves confronted with the same problems as other painters. The present situation itself is common to all. Like those of their contemporaries who have understood what this situation means for their art, the creative Christian painters are attempting to achieve plastic purification. In the case of religious painting, however, the additional difficulty arises that, inasmuch as it may be called upon to teach, or to recall religious realities to the mind and to the heart, representational elements are necessarily included in a large number of its works.

Two answers have been found to the problem. The first one is to substitute for the subject to be represented certain plastic equivalents of its meaning. The difficulty then is for the painter to remain readable without becoming imitational. The usual way to meet this difficulty is to insert, in the plastic form, at least some fragments of representational elements that direct the mind of the onlooker toward the intelligible meaning of the plastic forms at stake. A still more satisfactory compromise is simply to resort to the genre of painting in which art is less hampered by the nonplastic elements of the reality it has to express—namely, still life. Léger has left [24] us, in his stained glasses of the Audincourt church, a remarkable collection [79] of what can be called "religious still lifes." *Crown of Thorns*, by Alfred Manessier, is another religious still life. The formula is excellent, especially from the point of view of the painter.

For, indeed, this does not solve the whole problem. There are cases in which the direct representation of scenes including human figures may be required from the painter. Are we to say that no religious picture can possibly be conceived as a painting? There is no general answer to the problem, but the painting itself, in each particular case, is the answer. If he is asked [80a, b] to do a *Pietà*, it is up to the painter to invent some plastic form in which such a scene can be inscribed. His sketch of it will remain his constant guide during the whole execution. Still, what he has been asked to paint is not a plastic form; it has to be a *Pietà*. His problem then is to work *in the plastic form* so that, even while imitating a recognizable reality, everything in the work, from its fundamental color scheme to the natural forms it includes, be constantly supported, ordered, and bound together by the unity of the germinal form from which it originates. There is no general recipe for solving such problems. If there is such a recipe, painters, not philosophers, should be consulted about it.

3. A Qualitative Universe

NO PERFECTLY fitting name can be found to signify the essential tendency that, at various degrees and under various forms, seems to be common to modern painters. All of them are in rebellion against something, but sometimes also against themselves, so much so that one of their groups, at least—namely, Dada—could almost be defined as the very embodiment of the spirit of rebellion. There is another tendency, however, so general that several different names have been suggested to designate both itself and its opposition to older styles of painting. Here are some of these designations: objective–nonobjective; imitational or representational–nonimitational or nonrepresentational; figurative art–abstract art, etc.

It is easy to criticize any one of these names,[34] but it would be difficult to suggest a unanimously approved one. The main point is for us to understand that all these appellations point out one and the same tendency: to simplify the complexity of visual images, to reduce them to a small number of constitutive elements, and to substitute for the stylized representation of natural objects, or beings, certain structured wholes, made up of plastic equivalents, whose signification lies in themselves rather than in their relation to things. Let us call this tendency by its commonly given name, "ab-

---

34. "It is comprehensible that some abstract artists have objected to the name Abstract Art. Abstract Art is concrete and, by its determined means of expression, even more concrete than naturalistic art. In spite of the fact that the denomination 'Abstract Art' is right (abstraction means reducing particularities to their essential aspect), both names are equivocal; naturalistic art is also concrete. 'Non-figurative Art'—another denomination—is equivocal because abstract forms are figures as well as naturalistic forms. The intention of indicating the destruction of the particularity of forms, which this name expresses clearly, may not be understood. It is the same with the name 'Non-objective Art' which indicates that objects are not the means of expression, while Abstract Art strives for objective, that is, universal expression. 'Constructivism' might also be misunderstood, since Abstract Art requires destruction of particular form. Evidently every denomination is relative. However, it can be stated that all art is more or less realism. Men are conscious of life by the manifestation of reality. Reality here is understood to be the plastic manifestation of forms and not of the events of life." (Mondrian, "A New Realism," *Plastic Art and Pure Plastic Art,* p. 17).

stract art" or "abstractionism." Names are a matter of usage, and there is
no peril in keeping these, provided we give them a sufficiently definite
meaning.

From a certain point of view, this tendency is an invasion of the field
of art, particularly painting, by the Pythagorean spirit introduced in the
field of science in the fifth century before Christ. According to the testimony of Aristotle, Pythagoras and his disciples believed that the first principles of numbers were the first principles of all things (*Metaphysics,* I, 5,
985b, 23–986b, 8). This extremely surprised Aristotle, who found it strange
that one could resort to principles not taken from the sphere of sense to
account for things belonging to the sphere of sense (*Metaphysics,* I, 8, 989b,
29–990a, 32). Naturally, the fundamental numbers found themselves associated with the corresponding geometric figures, of which some still bear
the names, such as square, cube, etc. An ancient doxograph, Aëtius, in his
De placitis philosophorum (II, 6), summarizes as follows the cosmology
of Pythagoras: "The universe is made from five solid figures, which are
called also mathematical; of these he says that earth has arisen from the
cube, fire from the pyramid, air from the octahedron, and water from the
icosahedron, and the sphere of the all from the dodecahedron." [35] It goes
without saying that modern painters did not deduce from Pythagoras their
own notion of what a painting should be. Pythagoreanism is inborn in the
human mind. No wonder, then, that some of Cézanne's successors progressively liberated themselves from enslavement to visual appearances. Cubism,
under its various forms, then the different attempts either to eliminate all
traces of objective resemblance or, at least, to make it entirely subservient
to the plastic intentions of the painter, have achieved a sort of plastic purification of painting.

35. Milton C. Nahm, *Selections from Early Greek Philosophy*, p. 81. See pp. 74–77,
Aristotle's texts concerning Pythagoras. Plato's cosmogony, in *Timaeus*, clearly bears the
mark of the Pythagorean movement. — Concerning the remarks that follow in our own
text, note that Ozenfant has called painting "a geometry of sensation" (*Foundations of
Modern Art*, p. 260, n. 1). Cf. p. 256: "a mathematics of sensation." What Ozenfant intends to express is the notion that paintings are apprehended as "sensed structures"—
that is to say, mathematical relations, not understood by the intellect, but perceived by
sense.

The attempt was too paradoxical not to provoke resistance, and yet it did not result in a failure. This fact is one of the most fruitful subjects of reflection among all those which contemporary history offers to our observation. In the case of painting, the problem was successfully to overcome the visual appearances that are the very stuff pictures are made of. It certainly took modern scientists great courage to free themselves from imagination in order to conquer intelligibility, but scientists can speak the language of numbers, whereas, however he may conceive his own works, a painter has ultimately nothing else at his disposal but surfaces, lines, dots, and colors—that is to say, objects of sense perception to be apprehended as such rather than to be intellectually understood. The scientist may well decide to transcend sensible appearances to reach an intelligible Beyond, but how could a painter transcend sensible appearances? Even if he could do so, what could he hope to reach, by means of the senses, beyond the order of sensibility?

It is a commonly received view, in the history of ideas, that modern science first achieved full awareness of its nature about the first half of the seventeenth century, when physicists decided to account for all phenomena by submitting them to mathematical formulation. At the center of this scientific revolution, and as its philosophical spokesman, was René Descartes, whose physics, biology, and projected medicine entirely rested upon the two notions of extension in space and movement in time. The old qualitative physics of Aristotle was thereby eliminated, and not without good reason. To account for physical or biological phenomena by means of the four elementary *qualities* (cold, hot, dry, and moist) was tantamount to explaining natural events by means of human sensations. On this point, Descartes and his contemporaries carried the day. All the major steps of progress achieved by the sciences of nature from the seventeenth century to our own day have been made possible by a consistent substitution of quantity for quality and, therefore, by a systematic application of the language of mathematics to the interpretation of physical phenomena.

Still, there was a price to pay for this success. Thus eliminated from science, quality was not thereby eliminated from nature, for, indeed, man is in nature and he certainly does perceive qualities. What Descartes exploded once and for all is the illusion, common to so many people, that colors, for instance, such as red or yellow, are found in material objects under the form of unperceived perceptions. Aristotle never made this mistake. According to him, sense perception was the common act of the perceiving subject and of the perceived object. Both subject and object are necessary for a perception. Even so, however, there still are qualities in nature. There are sensible qualities as long as there are sense perceptions. Moreover, although science no longer accounts for anything by means of qualities, the language of the scientists remains as full of qualities as it ever was. As long as they continue to talk about light, sounds, weight, etc., scientists are still living in a qualitative world. This fact has been keenly felt by excellent minds, and even by at least one great artist— namely, Goethe—who never reconciled himself to the quantitative theory of colors proposed by Newton. Other attempts have been made to reintroduce quality into the very texture of science, but none of them has ever met with any success.

The upshot of this situation is that a vast area of reality is being left outside the order of scientific explanation and, consequently, is being abandoned to the arbitrariness of private judgments and opinions. There is no accounting for tastes, yet tastes are often necessary to life, and there seem to be very different kinds of tastes, some of which are better, while others are not supposed to be quite so good. Above all, these qualities about which personal tastes exert themselves constitute an important part of nature. An exceedingly small proportion of men could present a coherent physical explanation of the theory of colors, but practically all of them can tell red from blue and yellow from green. This is precisely the point at which painters have something to say. The qualitative world of perceived colors belongs to the art of the painter, as the world of light waves belongs to optics. Art is always about quality, even in the many cases when it is about the quality of quantity.

The notion of quality has been oversimplified by common sense no less than by science. Once more, certitudes that had been acquired by philosophers many centuries ago have been progressively forgotten. It may simplify things to speak of a world of qualities as distinct from a world of quantities, but such words should not be understood as meaning that, distinct as they are, quantity and quality are separate. There never is quantity without quality or quality without quantity. More generally speaking, there never is being without quality.

Taken in itself, quality simply is the particular kind of difference between any two beings in consequence of the primitive fact that every being is what it is. Whence the universal applicability of this notion. It applies to essences: to be a man is to exhibit the quality of that which exists after the manner of a man. It also applies to numbers: to be 6 is to be the number that enjoys the properties of number 6. It applies to the modifications of physical substances, including their changes in colors: whiteness, blackness, redness, and similar differences are rightly said to "qualify" beings and things. This is so true that in describing any object we are looking for, its color is likely to be the first indication we shall give as to its identity. Aristotle knew all these things.[36] His only error, and it was a serious one, was not to see that if the quality that is in numbers is a part of the quality (or difference) that is in essences, then the qualities that we call colors are likewise differences in essence, and the reason for this is that they

36. Technically speaking, "quality" is one of the ten primitive notions called "categories" by Aristotle's disciples. Like other primitive notions, quality can be described, but it cannot be defined. Generally speaking, quality is that which makes a thing to be such and such. It is the cause of "suchness." On the many classes of qualities, see Aristotle, *Categories*, ch. 8 (*The Basic Works of Aristotle*, pp. 23–20). For a study of the problems raised by this category, see *The Material Logic of John of St. Thomas*, tr. Y. R. Simon, J. J. Glanville, and G. D. Hollenhorst, pp. 367–87. The few remarks made by Aristotle about colors are irrelevant to our own purpose. What he says about the "fourth sort of quality"—namely, figure and shape—is more to the point. His remark that some qualities admit of variations of degree (a white thing can become whiter), while some others do not (all triangles are equally triangular, all circles are equally circular), gives an idea of the state of confusion in which his doctrine of quality remains. All forms of "suchness" are included in it, but no effort is made to carry the description of any particular class of quality beyond the level of elementary empirical observation. The remarks made in *Metaphysics* (bk. V, ch. 14) are shorter but more elaborate. Aristotle distinguishes two meanings of "quality": (1) that which differentiates an essence (including qualities in number and qualities in figures); (2) all the modifications in virtue of which, "when they change, bodies are said to alter" (including colors, virtues and vices, etc.). All these problems arise in Aristotle's mind in connection with science rather than with art.

themselves are qualities of numbers and, generally speaking, of quantity.

"Quantity" is defined, in a loose way, as "any amount capable of increase or decrease in kind" (*Webster's*). When applied to quantities either of space or in space, this notion leads to numerical expressions that point out the amount, or the ratio of certain increases or decreases, but all such calculations presuppose the notion of the line conceived as a unit and a whole. This notion itself reveals properties of the line not accountable for by the nature of any one of its points or even by the fact that such points are distributed in space so as to make up such a line. This means that, even in the order of pure quantity, wholes have properties transcending the nature of their parts. Any such property is a quality.

Let us consider a line drawn on a sheet of paper by the hand of an artist. It would be easy to show that it exhibits qualities due to the hand by which it has been drawn. There is a deep truth hidden in the old Greek anecdote about the painter who, not finding another one at home, left him, as a visiting card, a simple hand-drawn straight line. No painter has anything more personal than the touch of his hand.

But this is not the point. The kinds of qualities we now have in mind belong to quantitative wholes as such, and they are being actually perceived when such wholes are being actually apprehended by sight. Nature is abundantly provided with such wholes. What child has not found himself unconsciously fascinated by the perfect geometrical beauty of certain pebbles, sea shells, crystals, tree leaves, etc.? Why are most people so fond of flowers, not always for their colors, but often enough for the amazing perfection of their forms? The only reason for their admiration is that they are apprehending by sight the presence of a certain order among parts within a whole. Certain sea shells are so perfectly regular that their shape could be expressed by the algebraic formulas applicable to similar curves, but even such formulas do not make us see the curve; they only let us know why each one of the points of a curve, or of the lines of a surface, has to be found where it is. And just as the law of a geometrical curve is intelligible only to a mind, so also the order of its parts within their whole is perceptible only to such a sense as human sight. The order proper to each quantitative whole apprehended by sense perception is its quality.

Modern painters have been the explorers of this universe of visible qualities, just as modern musicians have been, and still are, the explorers of the universe of audible qualities. True enough, painters and musicians have always been engaged in the same pioneering work. In the beginning, both arts contented themselves with ascertaining the simplest and most elementary patterns of order in their respective fields. They now are far beyond these early experiments. Modern music, for instance, is as far ahead of that of the Greeks as our science is ahead of their science. Modern painting, too, is a striking advance in the field of sensible qualities falling under its jurisdiction. Modern painters have taught us to perceive by the organ of sight—that is, immediately to apprehend or *see*—a practically infinite number of intelligible relations in space, either colors, or forms, or structures, which our own intellect could *know* if it applied itself to a quantitative analysis of them.

This kind of exploration had to be a creation. After exploring the forms whose beauty is given to man in nature, or, rather, while continuing their exploration, modern painters have asked us to follow them in their effort to create quantitative structures exclusively made qualitatively to please human eyes. In this new undertaking, all the lovable beauties of nature, which so many painters cunningly offer for our enjoyment instead of their art, have to be dismissed by the artist. He cannot cheat any longer. There is then nothing left except the painter, the creature of his mind and his hand, and ourselves. For him, the quest of beauty has come to an end; for us, it is just beginning. Is there going to be any public to follow such guides in their creative exploration of the new qualitative universe? All the probabilities are against it, but man is constantly working against the general trend of natural probabilities.

The main condition required for the success of such an adventure is an absolute freedom of creative initiative on the part of artists and a no less absolute freedom of art appreciation on the part of the public. Both conditions have been happily fulfilled in the Western civilizations of our own times. No one would venture to pretend that the spirit of commercial speculation, greed, or gambling has played no part in the success of modern art, but there is nothing sordid in the substance of the story. When all is said and done, the fact remains that something almost unbelievable happens when some unknown man, as often as not of very moderate means, signs his first check to buy the work of some hitherto unknown painter simply because he likes it. All the sociological theories in the world will not make this simple gesture less mysterious than it really is. Caillebotte, de Bellio, Chocquet—let these three names stand for hundreds of others—can be said to have shared in the revolution that took place in the art of painting about sixty years ago no less actively than Cézanne and Manet themselves ever did.

Behind such forerunners, and sometimes close on their heels, came the first art critics to cast their lot with the pioneers of modern painting, then the growing crowd of the anonymous supporters of the new art, so much so that the very same works that were ridiculed fifty years ago are now hanging in art galleries especially created to keep these masterpieces under the eyes of the public.

The idea that this is all a big hoax or, at most, a comical misunderstanding simply does not meet the data of the problem. It particularly does not account for the experience, so common among art lovers of good will, that anyone with an open mind and an open taste has progressively graduated to the understanding and enjoyment of works of art that first were so many closed books to him. It still less meets the fact that, already in our own day, the most hermetic styles of painting are being aped by commercial artists, spread through a wide public by posters and advertisements, and put to the most practical uses by businessmen of all description. Fifty years ago, Seurat, Juan Gris, Gleizes, and Soutine would not have been able to sell one of their works at the price that people now are willing to pay for an illustrated volume devoted to their art. This conquest of the public by even the boldest among the creators of modern painting can hardly be without significance.

Why have so many art lovers agreed to follow modern artists in their ascetic effort toward an art stripped of the allurements on which it had traditionally relied to win the favor of the public? If he asks himself the question in the light of his own experience, every one of us will probably be conscious of having yielded to the confused urge of sharing in a bold adventure whose ultimate meaning was not clear to him or, perhaps, to his guides. On the whole, however, the very fact that we have thus been taken further and further away from visual appearances, and introduced to a new world of qualitative realities, has forcibly suggested the modest but real way in which man partakes of the creative energy in virtue of which the world of nature both is and operates. Here again the perspicacity of Delacroix has discerned the obscure aspiration latent in the hearts of all creative painters. There is no point in adding to reality images of natural beings, which, precisely because they are but its images, add nothing to reality. What really matters is to turn out, not an image, but a thing; not to add an image to reality, but a reality to reality. An obscure but inspiring note, to be found in the supplement to the original text of Delacroix's *Journals*, suggests that he himself had already experienced this ambition. We beg leave to render it, as it is found in the French original, under the form of an unfinished development: ". . . At the moment when his painting was still lacking that last breath which animates it; that breath whose effect is that a painting ceases to be a painting in order to become a being, an *object*, nay, an object that occupies its own place in the Creation, nevermore to perish; that breath which has got a name; which is called the transfiguration, etc. . . ." No wonder that Delacroix stopped short before finishing his sentence. There was something frightening in his Promethean thought, the more so as, when he formulated it, Delacroix was thinking nearly one hundred years ahead of his own art.

In our own lifetime the man-made artifacts inspired by the creative imagination of artists have progressively assumed more and more unfamiliar appearances, and still, on more protracted and closer acquaintance, they have finally succeeded in revealing their meaning to us. Since their apprehension was becoming a source of pleasure for us, their authors had certainly discovered the structure of possible objects, unknown to nature, but whose ultimate justification was to provide man with perfect objects of apprehension. No wonder that so many modern painters feel tempted to use anything rather than oils in their compositions. Oils are a perfect medium for a maker of images, but if the artist is ambitious to produce a real being, then his best chance is to attempt what A. Reth aptly calls a *Harmonie de matières*—that is, not an image made of colors, but a thing made of things.

Thus, at the very same time that man's scientific imagination was giving up being imitational in order to reach the deepest layers of physical reality, man's art was achieving an obscure but vivid awareness of the creative power whose fecundity has provided his knowledge with something to know. There certainly were perils in this experience. Some artists, especially among poets, misled by the spiritual nature of the concepts and images of which their own works are made, have aspired to exercise the creative power of God. What a temptation! Starting from nothing else but one's own creative power and the nonbeing of the work to be done, to confer upon it, at one fell sweep, existence, intelligibility, and beauty![37] Because they cannot forget the presence of matter and its exigencies, painters usually are more careful. They do not imagine themselves creating their works from nothing; still, they feel somehow associated with the work of creation and initiated into its mysteries.

Very modest artists have been aware of the nature of the problem, including its spiritual implications. "Art, then," says Jules Breton, "has not for its end the simple imitation of nature. But in what measure should one imitate? Up to what point must the artist create? How must he create? Is there no pride in believing that one can create?"[38] One could hardly

37. Description of the feelings of an artist toward the work he has made (Gill, *Autobiography*, p. 159) : "Lord, how exciting!—and not merely touching and seeing but actually making her [a carved young woman]. I was responsible for her very existence and her every form came straight out of my heart. A new world opened before me." The myth of Pygmalion has not ceased to be true. This proud joy of the creator is perfectly normal as long as he does not mistake himself for the Creator. On this point, see the famous letter of Mallarmé to Henri Cazalis, May 14, 1867 (in Maritain, p. 178, n. 29).

38. *La Vie d'un artiste*, p. 281. Remarkably enough, the same feeling of humility has led other artists to the contrary conclusion. They have refused to imitate, and therefore they have created nonimitational objects in order not to enter in competition with the Creator. This curious development is perceptible in Hans Arp, *On My Way*. For instance (p. 36) : "Man became a childish creator. In his megalomania, he wanted to create God and the world a second time. . . . Every painter, every sculptor wanted to be the most astonishing of creators. Anonymity and humility were replaced by fame and artifice." At the same time, this leads Arp to consider art as "of natural origin" and, consequently,

wish for a more candid confession of the misplaced modesty that probably accounts for the failure of Breton to reach the highest level of creative art. He felt a strange *moral duty* to imitate, and any resolute attempt to create appeared to him as something little short of impiety.

Not so with Paul Cézanne, who, having broken loose—not, indeed, from nature, but from its servile imitation—could write to Vollard: "I am working doggedly. I am in sight of the Promised Land. Will it be with me as with the great chief of the Hebrews, or shall I be able to enter it? . . . I have made some progress. Why so late and so painfully? Were it perhaps because Art is, indeed, a priestly function, requiring men both pure and wholly dedicated to it?" [39]

At any rate, this is what art was more and more tending to become as years were going by. In our own day, Paul Klee achieved full awareness of the true nature of the man-made things we call paintings as well as of the source from which they spring. No other modern artist has been so clear as Klee on the essential transcendency of the true work of art over nature: "In earlier times, artists liked to show what was actually visible, either the

destined to produce things, or beings, which are in themselves and by themselves: "in my opinion a picture or a sculpture without any object for model is just as concrete and sensual as a leaf or a stone" (p. 50). Against Mondrian, he refuses to distinguish between nature and art (ibid.). "We do not want to copy nature, we do not want to reproduce, we want to produce like a plant that produces a fruit and not to reproduce. We want to produce directly and not through interpretation. As there is not the slightest trace of abstraction in this art, we call it: concrete art." (p. 70.) Note (ibid.) that such works should remain anonymous; they should remain unsigned in "the great studio of nature like clouds, mountains, seas, animals, men." Throughout the essays the same notion is reaffirmed: "Man behaves as if he had created the world and could play with it" (p. 35). Man "has broken away from nature. He thinks that he dominates nature. He thinks he is the measure of all things. Engendering in opposition to the laws of nature, man creates monstrosities." (p. 49.) In short, Arp wants art to be rooted in the productivity of nature in order to kill its ambition of being a creator, or re-creator, of nature. "Art is a fruit that grows in man, like a fruit on a plant, or a child in its mother's womb. But whereas the fruit of the plant, the fruit of the animal, the fruit in the mother's womb, assume autonomous and natural forms, art, the spiritual fruit of man, usually shows an absurd resemblance to the aspect of something else. . . . I love nature, but not its substitutes. Naturalist, illusionist art is a substitute for nature." (Pp. 50–51.)

39. Letter to Vollard, January 9, 1903 (*Correspondance*, p. 252). — Yet the same Cézanne had a photograph of Thomas Couture's *Roman Orgy* hanging on the wall of his studio (probably as an example of composition). He admired the craftsmanship of Meissonier (Bernard, *Souvenirs*, p. 29) and of Doré: "The great Doré has a stunning picture at the Salon" (*Correspondance*, p. 80). Precisely—Doré is an excellent example of a great maker of images, or of pictures, who was far from at his best when it came to painting.

things they liked to look at or things they would like to have seen. Nowadays, we are concerned with reality rather than with the merely visible; we thereby express our belief that the visible realm is no more than a 'special case' in relation to the cosmos, and that other truths have potentially greater weight. In our pictures, the visible appearances of things have a wider and more complex meaning, which often seems to contradict the rational experience of yesterday. We are striving for the essence that hides behind the fortuitous." [40] Such is indeed the intimate conviction more or less confusedly expressed in so many modern works of art. This visible world of ours is only one particular instance of what was, to its Creator, the inexhaustible realm of possible reality. There still remains more reality, either real for us to discover or possible for art to actualize. And to do so is the proper function of creative art. If he desires to attain this lofty end, an artist cannot submit his art to superficial appearances. [41] His place is not in the world of man, things, and images. It is "somewhat nearer to the heart of all creation than is usual. But still far from being near enough." [42]

40. "Creative Credo" (quoted in Grohmann, *Paul Klee*, p. 99).

41. The formula "abstract art" is so commonly accepted that there would be no point in opposing its use. Let us observe, however, that the abstract character of a large section of modern painting does not come from any preconceived intention of achieving abstraction. Its abstractiveness is a consequence, not a principle. What we call abstract art is the kind of art that "has attained to an act of creation set free by its very decision to renounce, in both spirit and will, the representation or interpretation of the forms of nature" (R. V. Gindertael, "L'Art 'abstrait': Nouvelle situation," in Robert Lebel, ed., *Premier Bilan de l'art actuel*, p. 35.) Gindertael's essay establishes with unsurpassable clarity of thought that to define the new style of painting by its "abstract" character is to mistake the effect for the cause. "The order between cause and effect has been inverted," so that what was but a consequence of a revolution in the exercise of artistic creation has been mistaken for this revolution itself. Gindertael has no less clearly warned of the peril that threatens "abstract art" if what has been the affirmation of the pure pictorial *act* is reduced to its first manifestation, the *fact* "abstractionism." Such an error would simply sterilize an artistic revolution whose consequences must not be arbitrarily limited.

42. Borrowed from the fragment of Paul Klee's *Journal* that was engraved on his tombstone: "I cannot be understood in purely earthly terms. For I can live as happily with the dead as with the unborn. Somewhat nearer to the heart of all creation than is usual. But still far from being near enough." (Grohmann, p. 95.) Cf. Klee, *Über die moderne Kunst*, p. 47: "Im Schosse der Natur . . ."—The spirit of renunciation implied in this notion of art clearly expresses itself in the following lines, also quoted by Grohmann (p. 95): "My light burns so white-hot that to most people it seems to lack warmth. So I shall not be loved by them; no sensuous link, however subtle, exists between them and me. I do not belong to the species but am a cosmic point of reference."

CHAPTER NINE

THE SIGNIFICANCE OF
MODERN PAINTING

BY THE "significance of modern painting" we mean all that the preceding considerations can suggest to a philosopher concerning the ultimate nature of reality. Such views of the mind are limited in a twofold way. First, they hang on the nature of the particular problem from which they are taken: only a limited number of determined questions can be asked about the world from the point of view of the art of painting. Next, such considerations are still more limited by the particular approach of the philosopher to this particular problem. The fact that the art of painting seems to have reached a critical point in its history can be said, in a sense, to dominate the discussion of the whole problem. An observer asking the same questions two centuries from now will find himself confronted with new forms of the same problem, even perhaps with new problems. Another observer living in our own times and asking the same questions would probably consider them in the light of different facts. But may we not hope that, in the last analysis, all these different approaches and all these differently formulated conclusions will ultimately point out a common truth?

The significance of modern painting is perhaps better seen when painting is compared with other arts, such as music, in which, because it consists of sounds only, imitation is practically impossible. Imitative music is immediately recognized for what it is. In the "Pastoral" Symphony, it occupies about the same place and fulfills the same function as that of certain "collages" in cubist paintings. In both cases the creative nature of art is emphasized by the insertion, in the musical piece or in the painting, of a fragment of reality. But even among what have often been called the "arts of design," there is at least one that has never been submitted to the servitude of imitation—namely, architecture. There is nothing in the material used by architects that is not likewise included in sculpture or painting. Solid materials, such as those used by sculptors, are assembled by architects in a certain order and according to certain proportions; architecture has lines, volumes, geometrical intelligibility immediately perceptible to sight, tone values due to the ceaselessly changing way in which light plays over the accidents of its surface; architecture can even make use of color if it chooses, and still architecture is not, has never been, and is not even now in danger of becoming an art of imitation.

Some painters, wholly unrelated to the nonimitational school, have clearly discerned this eminent dignity of architecture.[1] Their remarks give full meaning to the old tradition, mostly Greek in origin, that associated music with the birth of certain famous architectural masterpieces. And, indeed, in a sense architecture is a sort of solidified music. A building is like a stone symphony whose parts coexist in space instead of succeeding one another in time. In neither one of these two arts is there any direct imitation of nature. There are caves in nature, but there are no houses, still less temples, community centers, or commemorative buildings of any kind. True enough, architecture, too, has its own artistic limitations. Functional architecture, which comes under the heading of engineering rather than of the fine arts, is a perfectly legitimate and necessary type of architecture; there is hardly a building in which functional considerations do not play a determining part; only, to the extent that they do, architecture

1. *"On architecture.* It is itself the ideal, for everything in architecture is idealized by men. Even the straight line is man's invention; it exists nowhere in nature. . . . Architecture, unlike sculpture and painting, takes nothing directly from nature, and here it resembles the art of music—unless it be claimed that just as music recalls the noises of the outside world, so architecture echoes the dens of animals, the caves and the forest. But this is never direct imitation as we understand the word when we speak of the two arts that copy the exact forms to be found in nature." (*Journal of Eugène Delacroix,* p. 160 [September 20, 1852].)

pursues another end than beauty—that is to say, that quality which enables an object to please the eyes.

Since they are man-made realities without any model in nature, buildings can be considered so many additions to the world of natural objects. This is so true that one of the latest additions to the body of scientific disciplines, human geography, has often incorporated the study of human habitations in the general description of the face of the earth, which is geography. In beginning to build houses, man was simply continuing the natural process by which nature evolves animal shells. The process is different, and shells are usually more beautiful than houses, but, in both cases, the result is an increase in the number of existing beings, not the duplicating of some of them by a set of images whose only end is to be their imitations. There is therefore a possible use of lines, surfaces, and colors other than the imitational use that is still so often considered co-essential with painting.

Strangely enough, it seems that primitive arts exhibit the same lack of interest in the imitational reproduction of visual appearances. The reason usually given for this is that primitive artisans could not, and still cannot, achieve the perfect resemblance that is supposed to be the ideal of sculpture and painting. This is tantamount to saying that the *Iliad* and the *Odyssey* were written in verse because their authors could not have written them in prose. It does not take into consideration another possibility— that as soon as they undertake to create, men go straightway not to that which is more useful or more obvious, but to that which is noble, more beautiful, and therefore more important. It is more important to create a being whose justification is in itself than to turn out endless clever images of such beings. If it is a true painting, a simple still life creates a new pattern of plastic forms well calculated to please the eye. Images add nothing to existing reality; artistic creations do increase the sum total of the objects whose reality is as certain as their intelligibility.

[81]

An obvious fact should suffice to convince us all of this truth. The development of art history and art criticism parallels the admirable development of modern science. Neither art criticism nor science would exist if art and nature did not first provide them with an objective reality to study. Being comes before knowledge; because it is art, painting stands on the side of being.

This applies to the history of painting from the early Middle Ages to our own times. The unanimous admiration for Giotto expressed by practically all painters who ever wrote probably can be attributed to a felicitous blending of incipient imitation with a large proportion of the artistic creativity of Byzantine art. Up to Giotto, paintings continue to be, like human dwellings, so many products of the human power to add artifacts to the number of natural beings. Such artifacts are beings produced by nature through the agency of man, himself a product of nature. Petrarch and Laura never lived in Pistoia, but if an artist puts them there, they will eternally be passing before its cathedral. We beg to suggest that the art of painting always keeps faith with its own essence when, whatever its date, local origin, and style, it fulfills this creative function.[2]

[83]

But man has other functions to fulfill. Besides that of making, he also fulfills those of doing and knowing. This assertion, which probably sounds metaphysical to the ears of our contemporaries, would have been maintained as strictly biological by Aristotle, as indeed it is. Leaving aside the order of morality, which is that of doing, we can state as a bare fact that, if there were no men in the world of nature, reality would no more be aware of its own existence and of its own intelligibility than of its power to increase the sum total of beauty in the cosmos. It is now customary, in certain circles, to poke fun at the simplicity with which the Greeks, then the Christians, expressed their admiration for that peerless natural being, man, but this admiration was much more justified than the present tendency to vilify human nature by reducing it to the common

2. "Actually, plastic art is manifested in two principal tendencies, the 'realistic' and the 'abstract.' The first is viewed as an expression of our aesthetic feelings evoked by the appearance of nature and life. The latter is an abstract expression of color, form and space by means of more abstract and often geometric forms or planes; it does not follow nature's aspect and its intention is to create a new reality." (Piet Mondrian, "Liberation from Oppression in Art and Life," *Plastic Art and Pure Plastic Art*, p. 43.) The new reality at stake is what Mondrian calls "universal beauty" (universal, as liberated from the particular limiting forms); here again, the notion of creation in art excludes that of imitation (p. 50).

level of brute life. Even apart from any theological assumption, it remains a scientifically objective fact that, through man, and through him alone, nature finally achieved self-awareness. Science is the name for this outstanding achievement.

During the long episode that lasted from the end of the fifteenth century to the beginning of nonrepresentational art, painters, instead of remaining firmly established on the ground of nature, progressively or regressively shifted over to the ground of imitation, representation, and, in short, exchanged making for knowing. Imitation—that is, representation of reality as it appears to be—stands on the side of science or, to use a more modest word, knowledge. Reduced to its simplest expression, the function of modern art has been to restore painting to its primitive and true function, which is to continue through man the creative activity of nature. In so doing, modern painting has destroyed nothing and condemned nothing that belongs in any one of the legitimate activities of man; it has simply regained the clear awareness of its own nature and recovered its own place among the creative activities of man.[3]

The evolution of modern painting entails consequences that go beyond the boundaries of pure art. Because these consequences are philosophical in nature, no painter should be made responsible for them. As to philosophers, it is too easy to foresee that, even if they agreed to discuss these problems in the light of what precedes, each of them would draw a different set of conclusions from the same facts. We shall therefore content ourselves with pointing out the main lines of thought that, as far as we can

3. "This is an age in which the glories are shared by the money makers & the literary men. It is an age of money & an age of print. This is inevitable (vide *Game*, Dec. 1922, article 'Idiocy or Ill-Will') & one of the results is that the literary critic of works of art always seeks for and belauds only 'literary content' in such works &, where he finds none, weeps or howls. The painting of Giotto is admirable and the more remarkable because it is great painting in spite of his preoccupation with illustration or story telling. The painting of Cimabue is upon a higher plane, a more exalted plane, a plane more removed from representation & one upon which the painter finds himself face to face with God. It may well be maintained that the great Byzantine school deserves even greater honour for here was not simply one individual bathing in the vision of God but, as it seems, a whole people, & for several centuries, filled with the Holy Ghost. Their works are indeed the evidence— to the Jews a stumbling block, to the Gentiles foolishness, & to Mr. Chesterton & Sir William Orpen ugliness and dullness." (*Letters of Eric Gill*, pp. 179–80.)

see, would best agree with the suggestions made by painters themselves in those of their writings which we have read.

Starting from the last conclusion to which modern painters have led us, one seems to be well founded in saying that their common ambition is to bring art closer to nature than it seems to have been ever since, considering itself a sort of speculative approach to truth, it began to take sides with knowing against making. Many painters now tend to consider themselves natural forces sharing in the fecundity of nature and their works so many beings produced by nature through their own art. Everything invites them to adopt such an attitude—first of all, their recent rediscovery of the nonimitational character of painting qua painting, but also their increasing awareness of the biological affinities between the conception and birth of a painting and those of any living being. In Herbert Read's words: "Aesthetic activity is biological in its nature and functions."[4] If we remember that the life of man is that of an animal endowed with intellectual knowledge, we shall not fail to use the term "biological" in the fullness of its meaning. To make works of art is proper to man, and it differentiates human evolution from common animal evolution precisely because the life of an intellectual animal is essentially different from that of any other known species of living beings.

The peril that threatens this recent orientation in the field of aesthetics is precisely to forget that, if the study of intellectual life belongs to biology, as could be gathered from the study of Aristotle's treatise *On the Soul,* biology itself has to broaden its field to make room for the disci-

---

4. *The Philosophy of Modern Art*, p. 13. We apologize for borrowing this perfect formula without subscribing to all the consequences that it entails in the mind of its author. It is important, however, that two authors whose general philosophies are so different should meet on such an important point, and that they should do so on the strength of two distinct analyses of the meaning of modern art considered as a sort of collective experiment. We would willingly subscribe to the following sentence (pp. 13–14) : "There is no phase of art, from the palaeolithic cave-paintings to the latest developments of constructivism, that does not seem to be an illustration of the biological and teleological significance of the aesthetic activity in man." This view has been more fully developed in the Conway Memorial Lecture for 1951, given by the same author under the title of *Art and the Evolution of Man.* — By "constructivism," Read seems to mean the position maintained by Naum Gabo in "A Retrospective View of Constructive Art," included in *Three Lectures on Modern Art.*

plines that deal with the problems related to knowledge, action, and creation. In the present case, a deep difference separates the natural production of things and beings from the production of works of art by man. The fact that all artists designated it by the word "creation," which is borrowed from Christian theology, clearly shows that the biological process by virtue of which paintings come to be is somewhat different from the natural evolution of animals from their conception to their birth. The distinction of the two biological levels that has just been suggested finds here its necessary application.

In speaking of creation, no artist normally imagines himself a rival of the supreme being Paul Cézanne used to call *Deus Pater Omnipotens*. Some artists may have been tempted by pride, but few succumbed to the temptation. Yet the sole fact that such an illusion was at least possible proves that the making of works of art implies a feeling of power and of domination over matter analogous to those which religion attributed to God. We have noted several expressions of this creative exaltation written by various painters, but some of them have carried their observation deeper and attempted to say in what sense, although the formula could not be taken as literally true, they felt justified in describing their work as creation.

Seen from without, works of art are characterized by their amazing diversity. Civilizations, countries, schools, individual artists, all leave behind paintings recognizable by their styles and bearing the marks of their various origins. Seen from within—that is, from the point of view of their authors—these paintings are characterized by their imprevisibility. Naturally, history does not hesitate to explain how, and for what reasons, the art of painting has followed the evolution that it has taken. What has not yet been seen is a painter able to foretell the future evolution of his art or the probable development of his own career, or even, when he begins a new painting, what this particular work will look like after being completed. Unless we are mistaken, what the term "creation" expresses in the writings of artists is precisely that character of "novelty" which is so typical of artistic production. Far from proceeding with the mechanical previsibility of natural operations, whose effects are always more or less previsible and, as they say, determined, art is full of ignorances, uncertainties, and surprises for the artist himself, who sometimes sees his work docilely following his decisions, sometimes entering ways he had not foreseen.

These two characteristics of imprevisibility and liberty are the more remarkable in that, according to the unanimous consent of painters, nothing is more dangerous for them than to trust to luck. The kind of imprevisibility that characterizes the work of art is very different from that which attends chance. No true artist will leave anything to chance; only, when everything has been foreseen, prepared, and calculated, the creative painter still does not know what his work is going to be. What he has calculated is less his work than the way he is going to do it. An artist somewhat resembles a man who, before making a decision of vital importance, collects all the facts relevant to the case, weighs the various decisions that are possible, calculates their probable consequences, and still does not know how his will ultimately will decide. These are the classical moments of the philosophical description of a free act. Just as previsibility attends determination, imprevisibility attends liberty. The true meaning of the word "creation" in the writings of painters is practically the same as that of the word "liberty" when it is understood in this sense. As Eric Gill once said, the artist does not create *de nihilo*, but he does create *de novo*. This is so true that when we want to say of an artist that he has had his day, we simply say that he is unable to renew himself. A self-repeating artist has reached the end of his creative activity.[5]

Remarkably enough, the questions we ask about the probable future of a painter's career, or, for that matter, about the probable future of the art

5. "Plato's theory is right enough but does not go *all* the way. The word 'type' suggests one thing which is typical of many things. No doubt this is an important department of 'art'—the discovery of the *type*, the weeding out of the accidental & extraneous so that, as in a Hindu sculpture of a tree, all trees are resumed. But this job is only one department & not I think the *most* important—it is one of the arts but not the highest or most specifically artistic art so to say. The art which is art specifically & at its highest is that of pure creation—*de novo, ad hoc & ex nihilo*. This is God's art & not man's. But man, in the second degree, by virtue of 'free will' can create (not out of nothing but, *de novo & ad hoc*, out of what God has made). Thus he makes not types but *uniques*—things that represent nothing but themselves & of which there is & cannot be another example in the whole Universe of created beings." (*Letters of Eric Gill*, p. 235; cf. pp. 275–76.)

of painting in general, are similar to the questions an observer could have asked, many millenniums ago, concerning the probable development of life on the surface of the earth. Even now, confronted with the results of these millenniums of change, modern science does not find it too easy to explain how this change took place. The word "evolution" remains a symbol for a demonstrated explanation still to come. We simply do not know.[6] But if it is true that man is part and parcel of nature, and that artists are men, then their personal experience of artistic creativity should be able to unveil to us some of the secrets of the inventiveness of nature. Unless we decide that man is unrelated to the cosmos in which he lives, what happens in him must bear some relationship to what is happening to the whole of which he is a part. What happens in painters suggests the presence, at the origin of universal becoming, of an inner force of invention and creativity that, everywhere at work in the world of matter, achieves self-awareness in the mind of artists.

This approach to the cosmic problems discussed by scientists and philosophers is neglected by almost all philosophers. The reason for this is that philosophy itself is knowledge, and since knowledge must be true to exist, philosophical problems are usually related to the truth of certain propositions. Now, truth is the conformity of intellection with its object. Consequently, where there is no object, there is no truth. This consequence entails another one. If there are forces or energies in the world whose operations cause effects that are new in both existence and nature, philosophers feel naturally inclined to disregard them as irrelevant to their own discipline. In this, science in no way differs from philosophy. Always ready to account for works of art, and even for artists, once artists have already

6. Biological evolution is a fact; what still remains obscure are the limits of this fact as well as the reasons that make it different from mere change. There is, as biologists say, "orthogenesis"—that is, "the process by which a certain number of characteristics are modified in evolution in the same direction and according to a principle of increasing unity" (Jean-Paul Aron, "The Problem of Evolution," *Diogenes*, VII [1954], 94, n. 5). This is what remains to be accounted for—namely, the very fact, known to all those who ever considered the most elementary facts in embryogeny, and which Aristotle explained by the notion of final cause. — On the present scientific formulation of these problems, see L. Cuenot, *L'Évolution biologique.* His conclusions are summed up in Jean-Paul Aron, p. 96.

produced their works, science is unable to say anything sensible about the very act by which works of art are being produced by artists. Some painters have been so acutely aware of the opposition between the respective attitudes of artists and scientists toward reality that they expressed their dislike of scientists in somewhat crude terms.[7] But there is no opposition between art and science; there simply is a real distinction between their functions. The very possibility of science presupposes the existence of realities produced by art, or by a still higher power than that of artists and of art. By definition, science is not qualified to deal with what it presupposes. When science attempts to deal with what it itself naturally presupposes, it simply denies the existence of such problems or of such realities. The natural tendency of science and speculative philosophy is to consider their intellectual formulations of reality equivalent to reality itself. True enough, philosophers and scientists are well aware of the fact that they do not know everything; on the contrary, they often declare that what they know is little in comparison with what still remains to be known; but they also believe that what remains to be known will be found to be homogeneous in nature with what they already know.

If there are forces or energies in the world productive of novelty, the only discipline that can directly communicate with them is art, any art, provided only it keeps faith with its own essence, which is that of a creative activity in the order of formal being. When approached from the point of view of art, reality becomes very different from what it seems to be when seen from the point of view of speculation. It is being only to the extent that becoming is being. Art introduces us to a world of forms whose final completion is the outcome of a sort of biological growth.[8] But even this

7. See the comic hostility of Delacroix toward scientists in general, *Journal*, pp. 155–56 (May 6, 1852), quoted above, p. 138, n. 5.

8. Art imitates nature (Aristotle, *Physics*, II, 2, 194a, 21). This saying is usually understood in the sense that the works of art strive to imitate the visual appearance of the works of nature. This is not what it means in Aristotle; the art he has in mind is medicine, which works as nature does. As Thomas Aquinas understands it, this famous saying means that art is to its operations and its works in the same relationship as nature is to its own operations and its own works. The whole doctrine has been summarized as follows: "The origin of what is made by art is the human intellect, itself derived, as some sort of resemblance, from the divine intellect, which is the origin of natural things. Whence it neces-

is not quite true, for biological growth does not seem to have any choice, whereas artists are in quest of forms that only their own free choice is able to determine. Nor should we feel surprised to hear some of them describe their attitude as one of obedience to an "internal necessity," for, indeed, the long and ascetic preparation that precedes artistic creation has precisely for its object to eliminate the obstacles—perceptions, images, imitational urges, acquired habits, and even skill—that stand in the way of the new germinal form and impede its materialization. The internal necessity to which an artist must submit is not a necessity for his will. The internal necessity by which creative artists often feel bound is that of the very form to which their own free will chooses to give actual existence in a matter fittingly disposed to receive it. Other disciplines, such as, for instance, ethics, can introduce philosophers to the problems related to the freedom of doing; art is the only approach we have to the freedom of making.

This is to say that art invites philosophy to take into serious consideration problems for which philosophers exhibit little interest.[9] In Plato's doctrine, all questions related to existence as well as to the causes and origins of things are kept out of the domain of science properly so called and reserved for probable opinion, which expresses itself under the form of nar-

---

sarily follows that the operations of art imitate the operations of nature, and also that the products of art imitate the products of nature." Man looks at the way God does things in nature in order to learn, as a good pupil, how to do his own works; but the two domains remain distinct because the works of nature are no works of art. "If art had to make things of nature, it would operate as nature does. But, on the one hand, nature does not bring any work of art to completion; it simply prepares certain of their elements and places under the eyes of artists, so to speak, a model of the way to operate. On the other hand, art may well examine the products of nature; it even can make use of them in order to perform its own works, but it cannot produce the works of nature. Whence it appears that with respect to the things of nature, human reason does nothing more than to *know*; but with respect to works of art, human reason both *knows* and *makes* ["est et cognoscitiva et factiva"]. Thus, those among the human sciences which are about natural objects are speculative, whereas those which are about man made things are practical, and about operations carried in imitation of nature." (Thomas Aquinas, *In libros politicorum Aristotelis expositio*, Prooemium, 1–2 [ed. Spiazzi, p. 1].) — The doctrine is sometimes expressed in saying that art imitates nature in operation rather than in representation: "ars imitatur naturam in operando, non in repraesentando."

9. Our own views on this philosophical problem are to be found in *Being and Some Philosophers*.

ratives, or myths. Plato's *Timaeus* is the best example of such an approach to these problems. In the philosophy of Aristotle, on the contrary, there are no such things as myths, so all problems related to origins disappear at once. The world of Aristotle is eternal, indestructible, as well as uncreated, and all the fleeting beings that ceaselessly come to be and pass away are nothing more than temporary embodiments of their eternal and immutable species. Only the accidental is new in the world of Aristotle; it is no wonder, then, that when the time came for him to define art, he found nothing better to say about it than to reduce it to imitation. What else could he have done? Both philosophy and science are hostile to becoming, except, of course, to the becoming that brings nothing really new into the world and does not endanger previsibility.

Theology has often favored similar views, for the simple reason that, since they had to credit God with science, many theologians naturally conceived him by analogy with a perfect human scientist. But there were difficulties. The first one was that, since Aristotle had not had to solve any problem of origins, he had had no use for the notion of Ideas. It thus became imperative for theologians to supplement Aristotle with Plato. Now, this simply cannot be done. Philosophies just are not that way. One cannot possibly retain ninety-five per cent of Aristotle and add five per cent of Plato to it. If one does, the resulting mixture is plain incoherence. So theologians have had no other choice than to evolve their own notion of the creative power of God and of the way in which this power has been exercised. This has led them to two conclusions that, rather hard to reconcile from the point of view of man, must needs be actually reconciled, in fact, if there is a God. One of these conclusions is that, since the divine science must needs be perfect, the future of the universe must eternally remain an open book before the sight of God. The second one is that, since there are freedom and contingency in the universe, the perfect knowledge that God has of the future does not prevent contingency and freedom from playing their parts in the general history of the world. Various theological answers have been given to this essentially theological problem; the only point we are concerned with, as philosophers, is the fact that an exclusively speculative approach to the problem is bound to minimize the elements of novelty and natural imprevisibility which must be present in a world created by the free will of an all-powerful God. The reason for this assertion can be stated in a few words: if all effects resemble their causes, a freely created world must exhibit at least some traces of the free creative power of its Author.

This is the reason why, despite resemblances in terminologies, the created universe of Christian theologians has never been identical with the uncreated universe of Aristotle; but the same reason probably accounts for this other fact, that when modern artists undertook to investigate the nature of their own activity, they spontaneously resorted to the creationist terminology of Christian theologians. As often happens, while speculating in the light of its own principles, theology is here acting as a guiding star for philosophers considering the nature of the world as well as for artists considering the nature of art.

If there is such a thing as a divine art, it must be very different from our own. First of all, our own art never creates in the proper sense of the word. It does not create its matter; it does not even properly create its forms. Human art simply assembles the elements of composites that, once made, are possessed of their own forms for the sole reason that they *are*.[10] Moreover, if one can speak of God as of the supreme Artist, his art is certainly innocent of any groping and of any becoming due to what would be for him the incomplete previsibility of his own works. Unlike the Ideas of Plato, those of Christian theology are one with the very being of the Creator; unlike the Prime Mover of Aristotle, the Christian Creator of the world has Ideas of all things known by him and creatable by his power. For this very reason, nothing that happens can possibly be new in the sight of God. Yet, when all is said and done, the God of the Jews and of the Christians did create the universe, and if this was nothing new in him, it certainly was the beginning of all newness in the created world itself. According to Christian theology, creative power belongs to God alone, and the world of creation owns no parcel of it. But it does not take a divine power

10. Thomas Aquinas, *Summa theologiae*, I, 45, 5, 1st obj. and answer.

to achieve novelty in the communication of existence and in the forming of man-made beings. This is what artists do. It is what modern painting has done in the highest degree, and, be it for this reason only, it deserves the careful consideration of philosophers, even perhaps of theologians.

Metaphysicians and theologians usually say that, since effects resemble their causes, created beings resemble their Creator. Because his very essence is to be the pure act of being, the world created by God is, or exists. Because this existence of the world is due to the efficacy of the divine power acting as a cause, we see all the beings included in God's creation causing, acting, and operating in their diverse ways and according to their different natures. Things, Thomas Aquinas liked to say, imitate God in that they are and in that they are causes. Such are the painters, whose works add to the beauty of the world. Painters are the makers of new visual forms whose proper function is to make intelligibility perceptible to human sight.

This is the most solid ground there is for speaking of a religious art. In a created universe whatever exists is religious because it imitates God in its operations as well as in its being. If what precedes is true, art, too, is religious in its very essence, because to be creative is to imitate, in a finite and analogical way, the divine prerogative, exclusively reserved for HE WHO IS, of making things to be. Now, as has already been seen, to make things be and to make them beautiful are one and the same thing.[11] Each artist, then, while exerting his often anguished effort to add new types of beings to those which make up the world of nature, should be conscious of the resemblance between his finite art and the infinitely perfect efficacy of the divine power. All truly creative art is religious in its own right.

By the same token, the meaning of the words "Christian art" becomes at once apparent. The problem does not arise in connection with picturing conceived as an art distinct from painting properly so called. Some religions exclude images; others do not hesitate to appeal to them as to visual aids in the teaching of religious truth. Christianity has always done

---

11. The perfect formula is given by Eric Gill (*Beauty Looks After Herself*, p. 66): "Beauty—the word is a stumbling block. Do not let us stumble over it. Beauty is *the Splendour of Being*. The primary constituent of visible Being is Order."

so, the more willingly as, upholding the truth of the substantial unity of man, the Church has always associated, in both cult and prayer, the mind of man, his affectivity, and his activity. It seems therefore evident that picturing fulfills in Christian worship an important function, whose proper end is inscribed in its very nature and which cannot possibly reach this end without resorting to imitational art. The subject here is of primary importance, and nothing is more legitimate in it than to do what most creative artists would consider an abomination: to rely upon the subject more than upon the art as a source of emotion. In religious imagery, this is not only legitimate; it is necessarily required by its very end. He to whom a bare wooden cross does not suffice is perhaps not so wholly Christian as he should be; he who sees in a crucifix the thing of beauty it may well be, but nothing else, is not a Christian at all. The art of doing Christian pictures [84, 85] does not exclude the possibility of doing Christian paintings; by itself, however, it necessarily is representational art.[12]

This answer is but indirectly related to the problem of creative Christian art. On the contrary, the fact that all the main moments of human life have a religious significance lies at the very center of the question. Ever since the birth of Our Lord, the birth of every child is a nativity. There is, in a Christian universe made up of created beings, a direct invitation to artists to join in the praise of God by co-operating with his creative [86a, b] power and by increasing, to the extent that man can do so, the sum total of being and beauty in the world. This is the more instantly required when the works to be produced by human art are primarily destined to a specifically religious use. There then is an inner affinity between the intended end and the means to be employed to reach it. Religion can survive without art; it even survives in spite of the fact that its churches have largely

12. In his *Théories*, Denis strongly protested against the excesses of the "expression by the subject" in religious art. In 1896, he did not hesitate to write that, although a masterpiece, it was with Vinci's *Last Supper* that religious painting "entered the way to perdition." If he represents a subject endowed with an emotional value of its own, as was here the case, the painter does not act upon our emotions through his work, but through his subject. The way was then open to Munkácsy, Tissot, "and all that is worse in religious art." From then on, it was going to be the subject alone that, in religious painting, would invite to worship (pp. 41–42). This perhaps is the shortest definition of the art Philistine: "He does not look at the painting; he sees nothing but the subject."

become so many temples dedicated to the exhibition of industrialized ugliness and to the veneration of painted nonbeing. But when Christian artists
are called upon to celebrate the glory of God by co-operating, in their
modest human manner, with the work of creation, it becomes imperative that
their own works be things of beauty. Otherwise, these works would not truly
be, and the artists themselves would contribute nothing.

Philosophers, too, have something to learn from a careful examination
of art under all its forms. In the case of painting, we find ourselves enriched
with privileged information concerning the way physical beings come to
be. It would be somewhat naïve to imagine nature acting as an artist—
that is to say, as a man—but the fear of this kind of anthropomorphism
should not make us fall into another error, which consists in believing
that man is in himself a separate being, self-sufficient and wholly different
from the universe that includes him. The physical energies that move the
world of matter crop up, so to speak, in man's self-awareness of himself
as well as of his operations.

It is difficult for us, who are not sharing in their creative power, to
formulate inferences based upon what artists say. There would be no excuse
for taking such liberties if they themselves were not so often found struggling for words in an effort to go beyond the limits of their own personal
experience and to reach conclusions valid for all men. They do not all
use the same formulas, but the diversity of their language points out a
common truth for which perhaps there are no adequate words. The world
in which creative painters live appears to them, not at all as an obstacle,
but as something that must be transcended. Assuredly, for them as men,
[87]   the world of nature is the very same reality it is for us and that we share in
common with them, but for them as painters, it is not in the world of
nature that ultimate reality lies. They feel that there is still another reality
hidden behind the appearances of nature and that it is their own function
to discover it in order to express it, or, rather, to express it in order to
discover it; for, indeed, this metareality has to be made to be before being
made to be known. The constantly recurring opposition of painters of all
[88a]   schools to the literal imitation of nature finds its deepest justification in

JACQUELINE GILSON. Red and Green
1945. Hart House, Toronto

ALFRED RETH. Harmonie de matières
1951. Musée national d'art moderne, Paris

MAURICE DENIS. Petrarch and Laura
Private collection

PAUL GAUGUIN. The Yellow Christ
1889. Albright Art Gallery, Buffalo

GEORGES ROUAULT. Crucifixion
1925. Lithograph

85

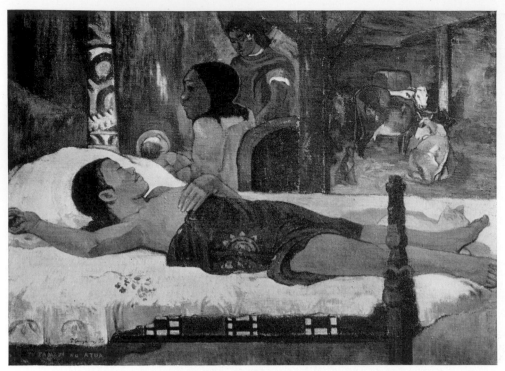

a. Paul Gauguin. Tahitian Nativity (Ne Tamari No Atua)
1896. Haus der Kunst, Munich

b. Maurice Denis. La Nativité de Jean-Paul
1895. Private collection

ROBERT DELAUNEY. Eiffel Tower
1910. Solomon R. Guggenheim Museum, New York

a. JUAN GRIS. The Open Window
1921. Private collection

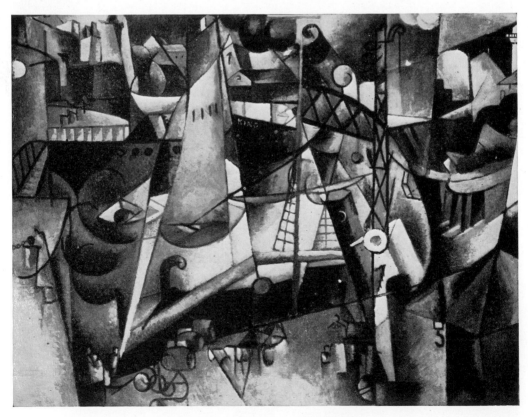

b. ALBERT GLEIZES. The Harbor
1912. Art Gallery of Toronto

this feeling. Nor is this conviction peculiar to painters alone. The "poetic principle" invoked by Edgar Allan Poe, which he simply calls "a sense of the Beautiful," seems to obey only one law—namely, not to be a mere repetition of the forms, the sounds, the odors of nature as well as of the common feelings with which they inspire all men.[13] When Poe says that "mere repetition is not poetry," he wholly agrees with the conviction expressed by so many painters that to initiate new realities, not to repeat already existing ones, is the proper end of the art of painting.

The universe in which painters live is therefore a still incomplete one. With a heart full of misgivings, the artist sees himself as one of those whom destiny has elected to enrich the world with new beings. Others before him have been honored with the same mission, and their works are there to witness their success in fulfilling it. But this is no reason he himself should evade his duty, for just as he could not have done the works of his predecessors, nobody else could possibly do the works he seems to be called upon to produce.

The force that will cause their existence is, first of all, an irresistible urge to paint probably akin to the fundamental forces that have given rise to the impressive procession of the vegetal and animal species since the first appearance of life upon earth. Despite its intensity, this force is neither a blind impulse nor a lucid progression toward a clearly seen goal. It could be more justly compared to the groping of primitive forms, if the forms of nature possessed an awareness of their own becoming. A sort of inner sense of direction, not always immune to error, seems to direct both nature and artists toward their respective goals, which are the perfecting of one more being of nature or one more work of art.[14]

13. *The Complete Tales and Poems*, p. 893.

14. See Eric Gill's letter to William Rothenstein, February 25, 1917 (in *Letters*, pp. 88–89) : "I am speaking only of the actual work—the paint or the stone—and not at all of its significance or meaning or value in the abstract, what it's 'worth to God,' but simply what it *is*. On the one side are e.g.: Giotto, etc.; Persian Rugs; Bricks & Iron Girders; Tools, Steam engines; Folk Song; Plain Song; Caligraphy [*sic*] ; Toys (not some few modern ones tho.) ; Animals; Men & Women physically regarded; Hair; Lines; String; Plaited Straw; Beer & so on. On the other are Velázquez, Rembrandt, etc. No, this second list is too difficult—what I wish to convey is that such things as I name in the 1st. list & such things as young children's drawings & the works of savages are themselves actually a

The most remarkable feature about this universe of creative artists is the particular relationship it reveals between being and intelligibility. The mechanically conceived universe of René Descartes, and all those which followed it to the end of the last century, were very different from the world in whose existence creative artists invite us to believe. Given a certain quantity of extended matter and the elementary laws of motion, Descartes could make bold to reconstruct a priori just such a universe as the one we live in. No artist ever lived in such a world. Not that there is less intelligibility in the universe of a modern painter than there was in the world of Descartes, but instead of preceding being, as it naturally does in a world for knowledge, intelligibility attends it and finds in it its very foundation [88b] in the world of intelligible qualities familiar to creative artists. It is a universe that is always trying to say more than has already been said, or, at least, to say it otherwise; but it does not yet know the sense of what it is about to say; the sense will be clear as soon as the words are found to say it. Yet there is surely going to be a sense; otherwise there would be no words. So also with paintings. All significant works of art, however much they may at first surprise the eye, the ear, or the mind, ultimately reveal the inner intelligibility without which they would not *be*. But it is in giving being to their works that painters themselves realize their intelligibility.

part of nature, organically one with nature and in no sense outside her—while, on the other hand, the work of Rembrandt & most moderns (the modern contribution—the renaissance) is not a part of nature but is apart from nature—is in fact an appreciation & a criticism of nature—a reviewing of nature as of something to be loved or hated. Good criticism is an excellent thing—why not? Well, it's no good trying to write all this—I wish we could meet & thrash it out." We intentionally preserve these last lines, as a symbol of the discouragement artists experience when they try to talk about art. Cf. the letter to Walter Shewring, March 28, 1933 (pp. 275–76), and to *The Friend,* July 14, 1933 (p. 277), where Gill forcibly restates his distinction between interpretative art and creative art— that is, "between the works which 'hold a mirror up to nature' and those which are themselves *part* of nature. It is clear that the characteristic works of post-Renaissance painters and sculptors are of the interpretative kind, while the works of the European and Indian middle ages and those of China, Mexico, Egypt and all 'primitive' and 'savage' peoples are of the other kind. They are 'natural' objects in the sense that they are the natural product of the kind of being that man is—a creature that needs things for use, who delights in making what he needs and who can only with difficulty be prevented from making things in such a way as that they please him when made."— Cf. Braque, *Le Jour et la nuit,* p. 13: "The painter does not strive to reconstitute an anecdote, but to constitute a pictorial fact."

However we may interpret them—and artists are not responsible for the reflections inspired by their art—the facts on which these remarks are founded should remain present in our mind, be it only as so many invitations to pursue the dialogue with the discoveries of modern art as eagerly as we do with the discoveries of modern science. It would be difficult to say which ones are the more important, not indeed in the order of practical life, where applied science reigns supreme, but in the disinterested order of philosophical speculation. A lifetime is not too long to understand the message of so many paintings waiting for us everywhere on the surface of the earth, but one cannot begin too soon to listen to what it says. Nor should one be afraid to embark on the somewhat strange adventures to which we are invited by some of these masterpieces. It is only too possible that some of them will always remain for us like those secret domains of which, in dreams, we vainly try to find the key. In such cases, we shall never know who was at fault, but the odds are on genius. He who sincerely exposes himself to creative art and agrees to share in its ventures will often be rewarded by the discovery, made in joy, that an endlessly increasing accumulation of beauty is, even now, in progress on this man-inhabited planet. As a still higher level, he will know the exhilarating feeling of finding himself in contact with the closest analogue there is, in human experience, to the creative power from which all the beauties of art as well as those of nature ultimately proceed. Its name is Being.

APPENDIX

After borrowing so much from the painters, it seems only just to let some of them speak for themselves. The following texts will make it possible for readers to hear the authentic voices of some artists selected among those whose reflections have seemed to us particularly inspiring. All of them are painters. Eric Gill is a sculptor with a personal experience of painting.

I.

JOSHUA REYNOLDS

i

LETTER TO "THE IDLER"

Numb. 79   Saturday, October 20, 1759

Sir,

Your acceptance of a former letter on Painting, gives me encouragement to offer a few more sketches on the same subject.

Amongst the Painters and the writers on Painting, there is one maxim universally admitted, and continually inculcated. *Imitate Nature,* is the invariable rule; but I know none who have explained in what manner this rule is to be understood; the consequence of which is, that everyone takes it in the most obvious sense,—that objects are represented naturally, when they have such relief that they seem real. It may appear strange, perhaps, to hear this sense of the rule disputed; but it must be considered, that if the excellency of a Painter consisted only in this kind of imitation, Painting must lose its rank, and be no longer considered as a liberal art, and sister to Poetry; this imitation being merely mechanical, in which the slowest intellect is always sure to succeed best; for the Painter of genius cannot stoop to drudgery, in which the understanding has no part; and what pretence has the art to claim kindred with Poetry, but by its power over the imagination? To this power the Painter of genius directs his aim; in this sense he studies Nature, and often arrives at his end, even by being unnatural, in the confined sense of the word.

The grand style of Painting requires this minute attention to be carefully avoided, and must be kept as separate from it as the style of Poetry from that of History. Poetical ornaments destroy that air of truth and plainness which ought to characterize history; but the very being of Poetry consists in departing from this plain narration, and adopting every ornament that will warm the imagination. To desire to see the excellencies of each style united, to mingle the Dutch with the Italian School, is to join contrarieties which cannot subsist together, and which destroy the efficacy of each other. The Italian attends only to the invariable, the great, and general ideas which are fixed and inherent in universal Nature; the Dutch, on the contrary, to literal truth and a minute exactness in the detail, as I may say, of Nature modified by accident. The attention to these petty peculiarities is the very cause of this naturalness so much admired in the Dutch pictures, which, if we suppose it to be a beauty, is certainly of a lower order, that ought to give place to a beauty of a superior kind, since one cannot be obtained but by departing from the other.

If my opinion were asked concerning the works of Michael Angelo, whether they would receive any advantage from possessing this mechanical merit, I should not scruple to say, they would lose, in a great measure, the effect which they now have on every mind susceptible of great and noble ideas. His works may be said to be all genius and soul; and why should they be loaded with heavy matter, which can only counteract his purpose by retarding the progress of the imagination?

If this opinion should be thought one of the wild extravagances of enthusiasm, I shall only say, that those who censure it are not conversant in the works of the great Masters. It is very difficult to determine the exact degree of enthusiasm that the arts of Painting and Poetry may admit. There may perhaps be too great an indulgence, as well as too great a restraint of imagination; and if the one produces incoherent monsters, the other produces what is full as bad, lifeless insipidity. An intimate knowledge of the passions, and good sense, but not common sense, must at last determine its limits. It has been thought, and I believe with reason, that Michael Angelo sometimes transgressed those limits; and I think I have seen figures by him, of which it was very difficult to determine, whether they were in the highest degree sublime or extremely ridiculous. Such faults may be said to be the ebullition, of Genius; but at least he had this merit, that he never was insipid; and whatever passion his works may excite, they will always escape contempt.

What I have had under consideration is the sublimest style, particularly that of Michael Angelo, the Homer of Painting. Other kinds may admit of this naturalness, which of the lowest kind is the chief merit; but in Painting, as in Poetry, the highest style has the least of common nature.

One may safely recommend a little more enthusiasm to the modern Painters; too much is certainly not the vice of the present age. The Italians seem to have been continually declining in this respect from the time of Michael Angelo to that of Carlo Maratti, and from thence to the very pathos of insipidity to which they are now sunk; so that there is no need of remarking, that where I mentioned the Italian Painters in opposition to the Dutch, I mean not the moderns, but the heads of the old Roman and Bolognian Schools; nor did I mean to include in my idea of an Italian Painter, the Venetian School, which may be said to be the Dutch part of the Italian Genius.

I have only to add a word of advice to the Painters,—that however excellent they may be in painting naturally, they would not flatter themselves very much upon it; and to the Connoisseurs, that when they see a cat or a fiddle painted so finely, that, as the phrase is, *it looks as if you could take it up*, they would not for that reason immediately compare the Painter to Raffaelle and Michael Angelo.

—*The Works of Sir Joshua Reynolds,*
II, 229–34

ii

LETTER TO "THE IDLER"

Numb. 82   Saturday, November 10, 1759
　　Sir,

Discoursing in my last letter on the different practice of the Italian and Dutch Painters, I observed that "the Italian Painter attends only to the invariable, the great, and general ideas, which are fixed and inherent in universal nature."

I was led into the subject of this letter by endeavouring to fix the original cause of this conduct of the Italian Masters. If it can be proved that by this choice they selected the most beautiful part of the creation, it will shew how much their principles are founded on reason, and, at the same time, discover the origin of our ideas of beauty.

I suppose it will be easily granted, that no man can judge whether any animal be beautiful in its kind, or deformed, who has seen only one of that species; this is as conclusive in regard to the human figure; so that if a man, born blind, were to recover his sight, and the most beautiful woman were brought before him, he could not determine whether she was handsome or not; nor if the most beautiful and most deformed were produced, could he any better determine to which he should give the preference, having seen only those two. To distinguish beauty, then, implies the having seen many individuals of that species. If it is asked, how is more skill acquired by the observation of greater numbers? I answer, that, in consequence of having seen many, the power is acquired, even without seeking after it, of distinguishing between accidental blemishes and excrescences which are continually varying the surface of nature's works, and the invariable general form which Nature most frequently produces, and always seems to intend in her productions.

Thus amongst the blades of grass or leaves of the same tree, though no two can be found exactly alike, the general form is invariable: A Naturalist, before he chose one as a sample, would examine many; since if he took the first that occurred, it might have, by accident or otherwise, such a form as that it would scarce be known to belong to that species; he selects, as the Painter does, the most beautiful, that is, the most general form of nature.

Every species of the animal as well as the vegetable creation may be said to have a fixed or determinate form, towards which Nature is continually inclining, like various lines terminating in the centre; or it may be compared to pendulums vibrating in different directions over one central point: and as they all cross the centre, though only one passes through any other point, so it will be found that perfect beauty is oftener produced by nature than deformity; I do not mean than deformity in general, but than any one kind of deformity. To instance in a particular part of a feature; the line that forms a ridge of the nose is beautiful when it is straight; this then is the central form, which is oftener found than either concave, convex, or any other irregular form that shall be proposed. As we are then more accustomed to beauty than deformity, we may conclude that to be the reason why we approve and admire it, as we approve and admire customs and fashions of dress for no other reason than that we are used to them; so that though habit and custom cannot be said to be the cause of beauty, it is certainly the cause of our liking it: and I have no doubt but that if we were more used to deformity than beauty, deformity would then lose the idea now annexed to it, and take that of beauty; as if the whole world should agree, that *yes* and *no* should change their meaning; *yes* would then deny, and *no* would affirm.

Whoever undertakes to proceed further in this argument, and endeavours to fix a general criterion of beauty respecting different species, or to shew why one species is more beautiful than another, it will be required from him first to prove that one species is really more beautiful than another. That we prefer one to the other, and with very good reason, will be readily granted; but it does not follow from thence that we think it a more beautiful form; for we have no criterion of form by which to determine our judgment. He who says a swan is more beautiful than a dove, means little more than that he has more pleasure in seeing a swan than a dove, either from the stateliness of its motions, or its being a more rare bird; and he who gives the preference to the dove, does it from some association of ideas of innocence which he always annexes to the dove; but if he pretends to defend the preference he gives to one or the other by endeavouring to prove that this more beautiful form proceeds from a particular gradation of magnitude, undulation of a curve, or direction of a line, or whatever other conceit of his imagination he shall fix on, as a criterion of form, he will be continually contradicting himself, and find at last that the great Mother of Nature will not be subjected to such narrow rules. Among the various reasons why we prefer one part of her works to another, the most general, I believe, is habit and custom; custom makes, in a certain sense, white black, and black white. . . . We, indeed, say, that the form and colour of the European is preferable to that of the Ethiopian; but I know of no other reason we have for it, but that we are more accustomed to it. . . .

The black and white nations must, in respect of beauty, be considered as of different kinds, at least as different species of the same kind; from one of which to the other, as I have observed, no inference can be drawn.

Novelty is said to be one of the causes of beauty. That novelty is a very sufficient reason why we should admire, is not denied; but because it is uncommon, it is therefore beautiful? The beauty that is produced by colour, as when we prefer one bird to another, though of the same form, on account of its colour, has nothing to do with the argument which reaches only to form. I have here considered the word Beauty as being properly applied to form alone. There is a necessity of fixing this confined sense; for there can be no argument, if the sense of the word is extended to everything that is approved. A rose may as well be said to be beautiful, because it has a fine smell, as a bird because of its colour. When we apply the word Beauty, we do not mean always by it a more beautiful form, but something valuable on account of its rarity, usefulness, colour, or any other property. A horse is said to be a beautiful animal; but had a horse as few good qualities as a tortoise, I do not imagine that he would be deemed beautiful.

A fitness to the end proposed, is said to be another cause of beauty; but supposing we were proper judges of what form is the most proper in an animal to constitute strength or swiftness, we always determine concerning its beauty, before we exert our understanding to judge of its fitness.

From what has been said, it may be inferred, that the works of Nature, if we compare one species with another, are all equally beautiful, and that preference is given from custom or some association of ideas: and that, in creatures of the same species, beauty is the medium or centre of all its various forms.

To conclude, then, by way of corollary: if it has been proved that the Painter, by attending to the invariable and general ideas of Nature, produce beauty, he must, by regarding minute particularities, and accidental discriminations, deviate from the universal rule, and pollute his canvass with deformity.

—*The Works of Sir Joshua Reynolds,*
II, 235–43

iii

A facility in composing,—a lively, and what is called a masterly, handling of the chalk or pencil, are, it must be confessed, captivating qualities to young minds, and become of course the object of their ambition. They endeavour to imitate these dazzling excellences, which they will find no great labour in attaining. After much time spent in these frivolous pursuits, the difficulty will be to retreat; but it will be then too late; and there is scarce an instance of return to scrupulous labour, after the mind has been debauched and deceived by this fallacious mastery.

By this useless industry they are excluded from all power of advancing in real excellence. Whilst boys, they are arrived at their utmost perfection: they have taken the shadow for the substance; and make the mechanical felicity the chief excellence of the art, which is only an ornament, and of the merit of which few but painters themselves are judges.

This seems to me to be one of the most dangerous sources of corruption; and I speak of it from experience, not as an error which may possibly happen, but which has actually infected all foreign Academies. The directors were probably pleased with this premature dexterity in their pupils, and praised their dispatch at the expense of their correctness.

But young men have not only this frivolous ambition of being thought masters of execution, inciting them on one hand, but also their natural sloth tempting them on the other. They are terrified at the prospect before them, of the toil required to attain exactness. The impetuosity of youth is disgusted at the slow approaches of a regular siege, and desires, from mere impatience of labour, to take the citadel by storm. They wish to find some shorter path to excellence, and hope to obtain the reward of eminence by other means than those which the indispensable rules of Art have prescribed. They must, therefore, be told again and again, that labour is the only price of solid fame, and that, whatever their force of genius may be, there is no easy method of becoming a good Painter.

When we read the lives of the most eminent Painters, every page informs us, that no part of their time was spent in dissipation. Even an increase of fame served only to augment their industry. To be convinced with what persevering assiduity they pursued their studies, we need only reflect on their method of proceeding in their most celebrated works. When they conceived a subject, they first made a variety of sketches; then a finished drawing of the whole; after that a more correct drawing of every separate part,—heads, hands, feet, and pieces of drapery; they then painted the picture, and after all retouched it from the life. The pictures, thus wrought with such pains, now appear like the effect of enchantment, and as if some mighty Genius had struck them off at a blow.

But, whilst diligence is thus recommended to the Students, the Visitors will take care that their diligence be effectual; that it be well directed, and employed on the proper object. A Student is not always advancing because he is employed; he must apply his strength to that part of the Art where the real difficulties lie; to that part which distinguishes it as a liberal Art; and not by mistaken industry lose his time in that which is merely ornamental. The Students, instead of vying with each other which shall have the readiest hand, should be taught to contend who shall have the purest and most correct outline; instead of striving which shall produce the brightest tint, or, curiously trifling, shall give the gloss of stuffs so as to appear real, let their ambition be directed to contend, which shall dispose his drapery in the most graceful folds, which shall give the most grace and dignity to the human figure.

I must beg leave to submit one thing more to the consideration of the Visitors, which appears to me a matter of very great consequence, and the omission of which I think a principal defect in the method of education pursued in all the Academies I have ever visited. The error I mean is, that the Students never draw exactly from the living models which they have before them. It is not, indeed, their intention; nor are they directed to do it. Their drawings resemble the model only in the attitude. They change the form according to their vague and uncertain ideas of beauty, and make a drawing rather of what they think the figure ought to be, than of what it appears. I have thought this the obstacle that has stopped the progress of many young men of real genius; and I very much doubt whether a habit of drawing correctly what we see, will not give a proportionable power of drawing correctly what we imagine. He who endeavours to copy nicely the figure before him, not only acquires a habit of exactness and precision, but is continually advancing in his knowledge of the human figure; and though he seems to superficial observers to make a slower progress, he will be found at least capable of adding (without running into capricious wildness) that grace and beauty, which is necessary to be given to his more finished works, and which cannot be got by the moderns, as it was not acquired by the ancients, but by an attentive and well compared study of the human form.

—*The Works of Sir Joshua Reynolds,*
I, 13–18

II.

EUGÈNE DELACROIX

i

The type of emotion peculiar to painting is, so to speak, tangible; poetry and music cannot give rise to it. In painting you enjoy the actual representation of objects as though you were really seeing them and at the same time you are warmed and carried away by the meaning which these images contain for the mind. The figures and objects in the picture, which to one part of your intelligence seem to be the actual things themselves, are like a solid bridge to support your imagination as it probes the deep, mysterious emotions, of which these forms are, so to speak, the hieroglyph, but a hieroglyph far more eloquent than any cold representation, the mere equivalent of a printed symbol. In this sense the art of painting is sublime if you compare it with the art of writing wherein the thought reaches the mind only by means of printed letters arranged in a given order. It is a far more complicated art, if you like, since the symbol is nothing and the thought appears to be everything, but it is a thousand times more expressive when you consider that independently of idea, the visible sign, the eloquent hieroglyph itself which has no value for the mind in the work of an author, becomes in the painter's hands a source of the most intense pleasure—that pleasure which we gain from seeing beauty, proportion, contrast, and harmony of colour in the things around us, in everything which our eyes love to contemplate in the outside world, and which is the satisfaction of one of the profoundest needs of our nature.

Many people will think the art of writing superior to painting precisely because of this simpler means of expression. Such people have never taken pleasure in considering a hand, an arm, or a torso from the antique or by Puget; they appreciate sculpture even less than they do paint-ing, and are strangely mistaken if they imagine that when they have written down the words *foot* or *hand* they have inspired me with an emotion com-parable to what I feel when I see a beautiful foot or a beautiful hand. The arts are not algebra, where abbreviation of the figures contributes to the success of the problem. To be successful in the arts is not a matter of summarizing but of amplifying where it is possible, and of prolonging the sensation by every means. What is the theatre but clear evidence of man's need to experience the greatest possible number of emotions at once? It brings together all the arts in order that the effect of each may be en-hanced. Miming, costume, and the beauty of the actor enhance the effect of words that are spoken or sung, and the representation of the scene where the action takes place adds still further to all these different impressions.

What I have been saying about the *power of painting* now becomes clear. If it has to record but a single moment it is capable of concentrating the *effect* of that moment. The painter is far more master of what he wants to express than the poet or musician who are in the hands of interpreters; even though his memory may have a smaller range to work on, he produces an effect that is a perfect unity and one which is capable of giving complete satisfaction. Moreover, the painter's work does not suffer so much from variations in the manner in which it is understood in different periods. Fashions change, and the bias of the moment may cause a different value to be set upon his work, but ultimately it is always the same, it remains what the artist intended it to be, whereas this cannot be said of the art of the theatre, which has to pass through the hands of in-terpreters. When the artist's mind is not there to guide the actors or singers the performance no longer corresponds to his original intention; the accent disappears, and with it, the most subtle part of the work is lost. Happy in-deed is the author whose work is not mutilated, an insult to which he is exposed even during his lifetime. Even the change of an actor alters the whole character of a work.

—*The Journal of Eugène Delacroix*, pp. 200–201 (October 20, 1853)

ii

Wednesday, 20 April [*1853*]

To Princess Marcelline's [Czartoriska] house. Arrived in time to hear some of the music. Found Mme Potocka there, looking extremely handsome. Came home with Grzymala; we talked of Chopin. He said that Chopin's improvisations were far more daring than his finished compositions. They probably take the place of the sketch for a picture compared with the finished work. No! one does not spoil a painting by finishing! Perhaps there may be less scope for imagination once the work has been sketched out. You receive a different impression from a building under construction where the details are not yet shown, than from the same building when it has received its full complement of ornamentation and finish. It is the same with ruins, which appear all the more impressive because of the missing portions; their details are worn away or defaced and, as with buildings under construction, you see only rudiments and vague suggestions of mouldings and ornamentation. A finished building encloses the imagination within a circle and prevents it from straying beyond its limits. Perhaps the only reason why the sketch for a work gives so much pleasure is that each beholder can finish it as he chooses. Artists gifted with very strong feeling, when they consider and admire even a great work, are apt to criticize it not only for the faults it actually possesses, but also for the way in which it differs from their own feeling. When Correggio made his famous remark: "*Anch' io son pittore,*" he meant, "This is a fine painting, but I should have put something into it that is not here." Thus an artist does not spoil a picture by finishing it, but when he abandons the vagueness of the sketch he reveals his personality more fully, thereby displaying the full scope of his talent, but also its limitations.

iii

Thursday, 21 April [*1853*]

. . . The same evening: the Mozart trio for viola, piano and clarinet; I delighted in some passages, but the rest seemed to me monotonous. When I say that works like this can give only a few moments' pleasure I certainly do not mean that the fault always lies in the work, and, where Mozart is concerned, I am sure that I am the one to blame. In the first place, some forms have become antiquated; they have been hackneyed and spoiled by the composers who came after him, a thing that is bound to destroy the freshness of any work. Indeed, it is astonishing that some parts should have contrived to remain so delightful after such a long time (time moves fast with artistic fashions), and after so much good and bad music has been based on this enchanting model. Another reason why a work by Mozart does not grip us with the feeling of sheer novelty that we find in Beethoven or Weber is that, in the first place, the latter are our contemporaries, and in the second, they have not the perfection of their illustrious predecessor. This is exactly the effect which I was discussing on the preceding page —the effect of the sketch compared with that of the finished work; the ruins of a great building, for example, or its rudimentary stages, compared with the same building at its completion. Mozart is superior to all others in the art of carrying his ideas through to their conclusion. The beauties of Racine do not shine beside the great writers who sometimes lapse into bad taste or spoil their effects; yet this seeming lack of brilliance in the poet and the musician is the very quality that consecrates them for ever in the admiration of their fellow-men and raises them to the greatest heights.

After such men (or on a level with them if you prefer) come those whose works actually show considerable lapses, defects which perhaps render them unequal, but do not detract from the impression they produce, except in so far as certain parts are only relatively successful. Rubens is full of such lapses or hasty work. The superb "Flagellation" at Antwerp, for instance, with the ridiculous executioners; also the "Martyrdom of St. Peter" in Cologne, which has the same drawback—the principal figure admirable, and all the others bad.

—*The Journal of Eugène Delacroix*, pp. 173–74

iv

23 April [*1854*]

Took up the "Clorinde" again; I think that I have arrived at an entirely different effect reverting to the original idea, which I had gradually been losing. Unfortunately, it often happens that either the execution, or some difficulty, or even some quite minor consideration, causes one to deviate from the original intention. The first idea, the sketch—the egg or the embryo of the idea, so to speak—is nearly always far from complete; everything is there, if you like, but this everything has to be released, which simply means joining up the various parts. The precise quality that renders the sketch the highest expression of the idea is not the suppression of details, but their subordination to the great sweeping lines that come before everything else in making the impression. The greatest difficulty therefore, when it comes to tackling the picture, is this subordination of details which, nevertheless, make up the composition and are the very warp and weft of the picture itself.

If I am not mistaken, even the greatest artists have had tremendous struggles in overcoming this, the most serious difficulty of all. Here, it becomes even more obvious that the disadvantage of giving too much interest to details by grace of charm in execution is that at a later stage you bitterly regret having to sacrifice them when they spoil the whole effect. This is where the specialists in light and witty touches, those people who go in for expressive heads and brilliant torsos, meet with defeat where they are accustomed to triumph. A picture built up bit by bit with pieces of *patchwork*, each separate piece carefully finished and neatly placed beside the rest, will look like a masterpiece and the very height of skill as long as it is unfinished; as long, that is to say, as the ground is not covered, for to painters who complete every detail as they place it on the canvas, finishing means covering the whole of that canvas. As you watch a work of this type proceeding so smoothly, and those details that seem all the more interesting because you have nothing else to admire, you involuntarily feel a rather empty astonishment, but when the last touch has been added, when the architect of this agglomeration of separate details has placed the topmost pinnacle of his motley edifice in position and has said his final word, you see nothing but blanks or overcrowding, an assemblage without order of any kind. The interest given to each separate object is lost in the general confusion, and an execution that seemed precise and suitable becomes dryness itself because of the total absence of *sacrifices*. Can we expect from this almost accidental putting together of details that have no essential connexion, that swift keen impression, that original sketch giving the impression of an ideal, which the artist is supposed to have glimpsed or fixed in the first moment of his inspiration? With the great masters, the sketch is no dream or remote vision; it is something much more than a collection of scarcely distinguishable outlines. Great artists alone are clear about what they set out to do, and what is so hard for them is to keep to the first pure expression throughout the execution of the work, whether this be prolonged or rapid. Can a mediocre artist, wholly occupied with questions of technique, ever achieve this result by means of a highly skillful handling of details which obscure the idea instead of bringing it to light? It is unbelievable how vague the majority of artists are about the elementary rules of composition. Why indeed should they worry over the problem of retaining through their *execution* an idea which they never even possessed?

—*The Journal of Eugène Delacroix*, pp. 224–25

III.

JUAN GRIS

NOTES ON MY PAINTING

The world from which I draw the elements of reality is not visual but imaginative.

Though the way of looking at the world and the concentration on certain of its aspects—that is to say, the aesthetic—has varied from period to period, the relationship of one coloured form to another—that is to say, the technique—has always, so to speak, remained fixed. I therefore believe that my technique is classical, for I have learnt it from the masters of the past.

It would almost be true to state that, with rare exceptions, the method of work has always been inductive. The elements of a concrete reality have been rendered pictorial, a given subject has been made into a picture.

My method of work is exactly the opposite. It is deductive. It is not picture "X" which manages to correspond with my subject, but subject "X" which manages to correspond with my picture.

I call this a deductive method because the pictorial relationships between the coloured forms suggest to me certain private relationships between the elements of an imaginary reality. The mathematics of picture-making leads me to the physics of representation. The quality or the dimensions of a form or a colour suggest to me the appellation or the adjective for an object. Hence, I never know in advance the appearance of the object represented. If I particularise pictorial relationships to the point of representing objects, it is in order that the spectator shall not do so for himself, and in order to prevent the combination of coloured forms suggesting to him a reality which I have not intended.

Now painting is foreseeing—foreseeing what will happen to the general effect of a picture by the introduction of some particular form or some particular colour, and foreseeing what sort of reality will be suggested to the spectator. It is, then, by being my own spectator that I extract the subject from my picture.

I do not know if one can give to this aesthetic, this technique and this method, the name of Cubism. Anyway, I make no claim to represent any particular sort of appearance, be it Cubist or naturalistic.

It is the appearance of the work as a whole which is its culmination, for this aspect is unknown to me. My subject, obviously, modifies the pictorial relationships without destroying or changing them. But it does not modify them any more than a numerical relationship is modified by the multiplication of both quantities by the same figure.

Therefore I would say that a subject painted by myself is simply a modification of pre-existing pictorial relationships. Nor do I know until the work is completed just what modification it is, which gives it its character.

Quoted from Daniel-Henry Kahnweiler, *Juan Gris, His Life and Work* (tr. Douglas Cooper), Appendix A, No. 4, pp. 138–39

IV.

ERIC GILL

In his book on *Christianity and Art,* Eric Gill proceeds to eliminate misunderstandings about the nature of art. The first one is: "That a Work of Art is essentially an imitation of something in nature." To which he opposes his own view that "Upon the contrary, a work of art is essentially an original creation" (p. 22). In developing this point, Gill remarks that "Man by his free will is capable of original creation, and a work of art is such by reason of its original form" (p. 24). At this point, a footnote directs the reader to an appendix, which we are here reproducing in full.

ESSAY IN AID OF A GRAMMAR OF PRACTICAL AESTHETICS

There are three possible qualities in a work of art. These three qualities are mimicry, literary content, and original form. Every work of art must have one or other of these three in one degree or another. By "mimicry" I mean what is called representation, i.e. likeness to something existing in Nature. By "literary content" I mean that in the work which expresses the story or anecdote it relates, that is to say, its literary significance apart from its significance as a representation of something. These two qualities are, I suppose, readily understood. Everybody is able to judge as to the degree of likeness to something which artists achieve in their work; also everybody is able to understand the notion that by means of representation it is possible to tell a story or express an idea.

It is the third quality, which I have called "original form," which is the most difficult to define, and yet it is original form that is especially the artist's business, whether he be painter, poet or potter. For an artist is not so called because he has the ability, in paint, words or clay, to make things which shall resemble things seen in Nature; if it were so any kind of imitation would rightly be called a work of art, which is absurd. Neither is a man an artist because he has the ability to present in paint, words, or clay some matter of fact or even of fiction, for were that so every spoken sentence would be a work of art, which again is absurd. It is not that a spoken sentence cannot be a work of art, nor is it that an imitation of something seen in Nature cannot be a work of art; but it is not likeness in the one case or presentation of fact in the other which makes it so. For otherwise, as we have said, all imitations and all statements would be works of art, which is absurd. The quality which makes a work of art is a quality independent of, though not necessarily divorced from, representation or literary content, and it is this quality which I have called original form.

By original form, then, I mean that quality in the thing made which owes its origin directly to the workman or artist, and is not either an imitation of something seen or an idea given to him by another person. For instance, if a man paints a picture of a bird because he has been asked to do so, the fact that his picture represents a bird is a fact for which he can claim no originality for two reasons. First of all, because somebody asked him to paint a bird, and secondly, because a bird is something he has seen and not something he has invented.

Again, if a man be asked to paint a picture representing two cocks fighting, the picture, when done, will have the quality of mimicry in so far as the objects shown are like cocks, and in so far as their attitude suggests fighting; and it will also have literary content in so far as by means of this representation the painter has conveyed to the mind of the spectator the facts incidental to the sport of cock-fighting.

Examples may be multiplied to any extent and be made more simple or more elaborate. For instance, a man may paint a picture of the

Deluge, and in such a picture there might be a very great amount of mimicry according to the number of figures and realistic treatment of rain and so on. Such a picture would have what is called literary content in so far as it conveys to the mind of the spectator not merely the vision of rain falling and people drowning, but, by the arrangement of the people or their dress or by the expression of their faces, or by some other means, first, that the incident portrayed was that recorded in the book of Genesis, and second, the theological and moral aspects of the situation.

Mimicry knows no bounds, and literary content, whether philosophical or merely anecdotal, is also possible to an almost unlimited extent: but in neither mimicry nor literary content is there anything for which the artist or workman is himself responsible, qua artist or workman. The mimicry is necessitated by the subject given or chosen; the literary content is given or chosen by the customer who orders the picture or, if it is given or chosen by the workman, it is given or chosen by him as if he were his own customer ordering it. But the actual manner of laying on the paint, the shape or grouping of the parts, are matters for which he is responsible as a workman, and are not things given or chosen by a customer. Therefore, it is clear that there is in every work of man this third thing which is especially the business of the workman, which is done by him at his own initiative, and which can only be done to order where the servile conditions of modern commercialism and the factory prevail.

I am not here concerned with the problems arising out of modern servile conditions: I am only concerned with the analysis of a work of art, not with the conditions under which works of art are produced.

It is necessary to make it clear that by the words "works of art" I mean the widest possible range of objects. Any work of man may be a work of art, and when men are free (not necessarily economically free, but free in the sense of being responsible for the form and quality of the work they do) practically everything made is a work of art. That is to say that everything in such periods contains at least the one quality which I have called original form.

Not everything made has the quality of mimicry; not every-thing made is like something else. A chair is not generally like anything but a chair; chairs made to look like fallen trees are obviously absurd, though many people like them because they think they look well in a gar-den. But though almost anything may be made to look like something not itself, it is clear that this quality of mimicry is not essential. We are sat-isfied with chairs even if they only fulfil the one merely material object of their existence—that of supporting our bodies—and do not by their shape either imitate some other object or tell us some story.

Not everything made has the quality called literary content. Not everything tells a story, although by a figure of speech we may say that we can see a story in everything. Thus a blood-stained knife picked up on the road may tell a story, but that is only a figure of speech, for it is clear that the knife itself has not necessarily that quality called literary content.

But everything made by free workmen has the quality of orig-inal form, that is to say, it has a form for which the maker is responsible.

The matter becomes considerably more difficult, apparently, when we deal with those things which, like pictures, sculptures, poems or music, have commonly, as far as the people who buy them are concerned, the qualities of mimicry and literary content. People have ceased to re-gard pictures, for instance, in the same way as they regard chairs, that is, as furniture. They think of them as things having no intrinsic purpose and no quality whatever but that of being like something or telling some story; and although people are quite ready to appreciate the form of chairs and tables—that is, the original form and not merely the form determined by the use of such objects—they are quite unable to view pictures in the same dispassionate way, and are even inclined to deny that anything besides mimicry or story-telling is either possible or desirable in painting or sculp-ture. In music it is quite clear that neither mimicry nor literary content are regarded as essential, for except in so called "programme" music there is neither. We are quite capable of appreciating a tune for its own sake, even though it be quite unlike the song of any bird or any other natural noise, and even though it have no story to tell. But in the matter of poetry, sculpture or painting we appear to be unable even to imagine what value there can be apart from representation or story-telling.

Yet if we consider the works of the past, those which we are at such pains to preserve in our museums and picture galleries, we shall, if we consider them critically, see very easily that as representations they are generally inferior to the work of most modern art-school students, and as story-tellers they are outdone by any modern novelist or photographer. If they are worth preserving at all, and a modern manufacturer may well doubt it, it must be on account of some other quality, some quality independent of time and place, unless we are prepared to assert that our museums have a merely historical interest as showing the kind of things our half-civilized ancestors had to make do with. But historical sense is not of universal importance. The comparative study of religions is of little value compared with the possession of religion, and the study of past manners is unimportant compared with the possession of our own. It is interesting to know that such and such a thing was made in France in the thirteenth century (e.g. the ivory Madonna and Child in the British Museum), but it is more important to have the thing itself, wherever or whenever it was made, provided that we deem it good.

Now, apart from this historical value, the only value of the things in our museums is intrinsic. In shape or colour or arrangement there is something about them that is of God, godly. And as God reduced chaos to order, so men in past times have given the quality of order to the things they made.

The thing, then, that I have called "original form" is essentially a matter of order, it is the "splendor formae" of St Thomas, it is the shining out of Being, it is the thing called beauty. And to achieve it men must will it, and to will it they must be free. The free man is responsible for what he does, but for the work of the slave another is responsible. That is the whole difference between the modern workman and his counterpart of past times. The modern workman is not responsible for doing anything but what he is told. The modern industrial system needs tools, not artists, and a century of industrialism has destroyed in the workman the very memory of artistry. With this destruction it has come about that beauty has ceased to be the common quality of things made, for under the factory system, with its concomitant machine production, no man can be held responsible; and therefore to conscience, which is essential to the production of things of beauty, no appeal is made. The only thing which is considered is the satisfaction of the consumer, the buyer. Thus not only workmen but the whole world is degraded. Artists become fewer and fewer and more and more eccentric, and the appreciation of art becomes the special province of the connoisseur.

—*Christianity and Art*, pp. 36–42 (reprinted in *Art-Nonsense and Other Essays*, pp. 250 56)

V.

AMÉDÉE OZENFANT

CREATE!

A need: an anguish, a restlessness, a buzzing: something is deeply moved in us: there is an uneasy disturbing throbbing: we feel the need to create. And that that need shall be realised, that a stray limb shall be grasped and dragged to the light, we must explore ourselves.

A diver's effort, descending or rising again from the sea bottom, must be made: an alternation of somnambulism and clairvoyance. Then everything fades out, the thread breaks. Gazing deep into ourselves, we seek again to make the circuit. By degrees, from the mist of the unconscious, there issue elements that are all but definite: we hook something relevant to us, but tenaciously it resists. And, surrounding all these fragments, there is night. Those summits which, half waking, we have seen surge forth, grow clearer. We unveil, or rather we image: to image is to give form to our dreams.

Our lucidity can, then, lend itself to help adjust the scattered fragments. The act of composition lies in finding the means of rendering perceptible such imaginings: objectivising. But will mankind succeed in crossing that bridge? Have his elaborations universal interest? Judgment must decide. It is a good thing to have an assured technic, but a keyboard must be ready.

The art of composition is the disposing of inspiration on such a keyboard.

We must not sow seed in our fields until we know that it is no weed we are sowing. Every work of art is determined from the first gesture, for every portion of it must depend on every other: the same thread must weave it throughout, each element must complement the next. Not all our ideas are worth-while or fecund. Too often we believe there will be plenty of time to deal with difficulties when they arise in the course of the work itself, but that is a grave error. The work must issue from the conception that lies behind it, as normally and fatally as a creature which comes to birth, must all its life, develop along the lines of the initial impulse.

And when, after protracted discipline, the creative effort can be envisaged in all completeness, then make the draft. From that moment no fundamental change can take place: it is either good or bad. But the attempt must be followed through and realised as completely as possible. That is what I mean by a draft.

Then carry the work out in final form, perfecting always. And here will intervene the craftsmen's conscience. Perfect; but do not overdo!

In this manner conception and realisation will bring to birth works of art which will not call to mind forceps, but instead, climb naturally like rockets, the laws of whose trajectories exist before ever they are fired.

We can no longer accept those works of art which are full of bits and pieces and afterthoughts: painful as a bad presentation extracted limb by limb and sewn up afterwards: books badly conceived, vacillating thoughts. What we want is the finest work, bearing witness to the meditation that conceived it. Execution is but the fine realisation of a conception ripened in advance. The work should be the most precise approximation to how it was conceived.

In art the decisions are always "on points." How unfortunate that the best works cannot "knock out" the worst!

—*Foundations of Modern Art*, pp. 299–300

BIBLIOGRAPHY

BIBLIOGRAPHY

This bibliography includes all the books actually cited in this work. A small number of titles, not cited but in mind during the composition of this book, have been added as a tribute of gratitude to their authors. Knowing from experience how difficult it sometimes is to locate certain books, I have mentioned the names of publishing firms when, having had the book in hand, this useful information was available. This will be found to be the rule, and there will be exceedingly few exceptions.

ADDISON [JOSEPH], STEELE [RICHARD], *et al. The Spectator.* Edited by G. G. Smith. 4 vols. London: J. M. Dent, 1930–34. (Everyman's Library, Nos. 164–67.)

ALAZARD, JEAN. *Le Portrait florentin de Botticelli à Bronzino.* Paris: H. Laurens, 1924. (First published as a doctoral thesis under the title *Essai sur l'évolution du portrait peint à Florence de Botticelli à Bronzino.*)

AMAURY-DUVAL [EUGÈNE-EMMANUEL PINEU-DUVAL]. *L'Atelier d'Ingres.* 5th edn., Paris: G. Crès, 1924.

APOLLINAIRE, GUILLAUME. *The Cubist Painters: Aesthetic Meditations.* Translated by Lionel Abel. New York: Wittenborn, Schultz, 1949. (The Documents of Modern Art.)

ARBER, AGNES. *The Mind and the Eye: A Study of the Biologist's Standpoint.* Cambridge University Press, 1954.

———. *The Natural Philosophy of Plant Forms.* Cambridge University Press, 1950.

ARISTOTLE. *The Basic Works of Aristotle.* Edited, with an introduction, by Richard McKeon. New York: Random House, 1941.

———. *Aristotelis Ethica Nicomachea,* recognovit F. Susemihl. Revised edition by Otto Apelt. Leipzig: B. G. Teubner, 1903.

ARON, JEAN-PAUL. "The Problem of Evolution," *Diogenes* (Chicago), VII (1954), 90–103.

ARP, JEAN (or HANS). *On My Way: Poetry and Essays. 1912–1947.* New York: Wittenborn, Schultz, 1948. (The Documents of Modern Art.)

AUGUSTINE, ST. *S. Aureli Augustini Confessionum* libri tredecim post Pium Knoell iteratis curis edidit Martinus Skutella. Leipzig: B. G. Teubner, 1934.

————. *Confessions*. Translated, with a preface, by Edward Bouverie Pusey and with a foreword by A. H. Armstrong. New York: E. P. Dutton, 1907 (last reprinted 1953). (Everyman's Library, No. 200A.)

BACHELARD, GASTON. *La Terre et les rêveries du repos*. Paris: J. Corti, 1948.

BALTRUŠAITIS, JURGIS. *Anamorphoses ou Perspectives curieuses*. Paris: O. Perrin, 1955.

BARAZZETTI, SUZANNE. *Maurice Denis, 25 novembre 1870–13 novembre 1943*. With a preface by Robert Rey. Paris: B. Grasset, 1945.

BARR, ALFRED H., JR., ed. *Masters of Modern Art*. New York: Museum of Modern Art, 1954.

BASCH, VICTOR. *Titien*. 2nd edn., Paris: Albin Michel, 1926.

BATAILLE, GEORGES. *Lascaux; or, The Birth of Art*. Translated by Austryn Wainhouse. Geneva: Skira, 1955.

BATTAGLIA, FELICE. "Forme naturalistiche e forme estetiche," *Convivium* (Turin), n.s., V (Sept.–Oct., 1954), 513–33.

BAUDELAIRE, CHARLES. *The Mirror of Art: Critical Studies*. Translated and edited, with notes and illustrations, by Jonathan Mayne. London: Phaidon Press, 1955.

BAZAINE, JEAN. *Notes sur la peinture d'aujourd'hui*. 2nd edn., Paris: Éditions du Seuil, 1953.

BAZIN, GERMAIN. *La Crépuscule des images*. Paris: Gallimard, 1946.

BEHRMAN, S. N. *Duveen*. New York: Random House, 1952.

BERENSON, BERNARD. *Aesthetics and History*. Garden City, N. Y.: Doubleday, 1954. (Anchor Books.)

BERGSON, HENRI. *La Pensée et le mouvant*. 22nd edn., Paris: Presses universitaires de France, 1946.

BERNARD, ÉMILE. *Souvenirs sur Paul Cézanne, et lettres*. Paris: À la Rénovation esthétique [1920].

BLANC, CHARLES. *Grammaire des arts du dessin: architecture, sculpture, peinture*. 7th edn., Paris: H. Laurens, 1888.

BODKIN, THOMAS. *The Approach to Painting*. London: Collins, 1945.

BOETHIUS, ANICIUS MANLIUS SEVERINUS. *De Trinitate*. In: H. F. Stewart and E. K. Rand, trs. *Theological Tractates*. New York: Macmillan, 1918. (Loeb Classical Library.)

BOULDING, KENNETH. *The Image*. Ann Arbor: University of Michigan Press, 1956.

BRADLEY, MORTON C., JR. *The Treatment of Pictures*. Cambridge, Mass.: Art Technology, 1950.

BRAQUE, GEORGES. *Le Jour et la nuit: Cahiers, 1917–1952*. Paris: Gallimard, 1952.

BRETON, JULES. *Nos Peintres du siècle*. Paris: Société d'éditions artistiques [189–].

————. *La Vie d'un artiste: Art et nature*. 2nd edn., Paris: Lemerre, 1890.

BROCKWELL, MAURICE W. *The Pseudo-Arnolfini Portrait: A Case of Mistaken Identity*. London: Chatto & Windus, 1952.

BRU, CHARLES-PIERRE. *Esthétique de l'abstraction: Essai sur le problème actuel de la peinture*. Toulouse: Privat, 1955.

BURCKHARDT, JAKOB. *Recollections of Rubens*. Edited by H. Gerson. London: Phaidon Press, 1950.

BURNET, JOHN. Explanatory notes to *The Discourses of Sir Joshua Reynolds*. See under REYNOLDS, SIR JOSHUA.

CAIRNS, HUNTINGTON, ed. *The Limits of Art: Poetry and Prose Chosen by Ancient and Modern Critics*. New York: Pantheon Books, 1948. (Bollingen Series XII.)

CARCO, FRANCIS. *L'Ami des peintres: Souvenirs*. Paris: Gallimard, 1953.

CASSOU, JEAN. *Situation de l'art moderne*. Paris: Les Éditions de Minuit, 1950.

CELLINI, BENVENUTO. *The Life of Benvenuto Cellini, Written by Himself*. Edited by John Pope Hennessey. London: Phaidon Press, 1949.

CÉZANNE, PAUL. *Paul Cézanne: Correspondance*. Collected, with notes and a preface, by John Rewald. Paris: B. Grasset, 1937.

CHASSÉ, CHARLES. *Gauguin et le groupe de Pont-Aven: Documents inédits*. Paris: H. Floury, 1921.

CLERICI, FABRIZIO. "The Grand Illusion: Some Considerations of Perspective, Illusionism and Trompe-l'œil," *Art News Annual* (New York), XXIII (1954), 98–178.

COLQUHOUN, NORMAN. *Paint Your Own Pictures: A Guide for Those Who Would Like to Paint But Do Not Know How to Begin, Discussing the Materials Needed, Their Preparation, and the Handling of Paint*. 2nd edn., Harmondsworth and Baltimore: Penguin Books, 1954.

CONSTABLE, JOHN. *Memoirs of the Life of John Constable*. See LESLIE, C. R.

COURTHION, PIERRE. "Le Temps libre et enchaîné," *XXᵉ Siècle* (Paris), n.s., V (June, 1955), 37–40.

COUTURE, THOMAS. *Méthode et entretiens d'atelier*. Paris, 1868. (*Conversations on Art Methods*. Translated by S. E. Stewart. New York, 1879.)

CUENOT, L. *Évolution biologique*. Paris: Masson, 1951.

DANTZIG, M. M. VAN. In: *True or False?* [Catalogue of] an exhibition organized . . . by the Stedelijk Museum in Amsterdam (Holland), circulated in the U. S. A. by the Corning Glass Center, 1953–54 season. n.p., 1953. (See pp. 6–10.)

DEBIDOUR, VICTOR-HENRI, *et al.* (Bernard Champigneulle, Henri Charlier, Michel Florisoone, Joseph Paramelle, Pie-Raymond Régamey, Paul Romane-Musculus). *Problèmes de l'art sacré*. Paris: Le Nouveau portique, 1951.

DEGAS, EDGAR. *Lettres de Degas*. Collected, with notes, by Marcel Guérin, and a preface by Daniel Halévy. Paris: B. Grasset, 1945.

DELACROIX, EUGÈNE. *Correspondance générale d'Eugène Delacroix*. Edited by André Joubin. 5 vols. Paris: Plon, 1936–38.

———. *Journal de Eugène Delacroix*. Edited by André Joubin. 3 vols. Paris: Plon, 1950.

———. *The Journal of Eugène Delacroix*. A selection edited, with introduction, by Hubert Wellington, translated by Lucy Norton. London: Phaidon Press, 1951.

———. *Œuvres littéraires*. 2 vols. Paris: G. Crès, 1923. (Bibliothèque dionysienne.)

DEMEURE, FERNAND. *Les Impostures de l'art.* Paris: F. Chambriand, 1951.

DENIS, MAURICE. *Charmes et leçons de l'Italie.* Paris: A. Colin, 1933.

————. Fragments of a "Journal" in the Catalogue for the *Exposition Maurice Denis (1870–1943).* Paris: Musée d'art moderne, 1945.

————. *Nouvelles Théories sur l'art moderne, sur l'art sacré (1914–1921).* Paris: L. Rouart & J. Watelin, 1922.

————. *Sérusier, sa vie, son œuvre.* In SÉRUSIER, PAUL, q.v.

————. *Théories (1890–1910): Du symbolisme et de Gauguin vers un nouvel ordre classique.* 4th edn., Paris: L. Rouart & J. Watelin, 1920. (Includes the famous article of 1890, "Définition du néo-traditionnisme.")

————. See also BARAZZETTI, SUZANNE.

DEWEY, JOHN. *Art as Experience.* New York: Minton, Balch, 1934.

————. *Intelligence in the Modern World: John Dewey's Philosophy.* Edited, with an introduction, by Joseph Ratner. New York: Random House, 1939. (Modern Library.)

DIDEROT, DENIS. "Essai sur la peinture," in: *Œuvres.* Edited by André Billy. Paris: Gallimard, 1946. (Bibliothèque de la Pléiade.)

DORIVAL, BERNARD. *Les Étapes de la peinture française contemporaine.* 3 vols. Paris: Gallimard—vol. I, 19th edn., 1943; vol. II, 18th edn., 1944; vol. III, 18th edn., 1946. (Vol. IV, the plates, has not yet been published.)

DUFRENNE, MIKEL. *Phénoménologie de l'expérience esthétique.* 2 vols. Paris: Presses universitaires de France, 1953.

DUFRESNOY, CHARLES-ALPHONSE. *The Art of Painting.* Translated into English verse by William Mason, with annotations by Sir Joshua Reynolds, in *The Works of Sir Joshua Reynolds* (see under REYNOLDS, SIR JOSHUA), III, 3–92 (includes Latin text of poem along with the English translation).

ERGMANN, RAOUL. "The Chances of a Dialogue: Berenson and Malraux," *Diogenes* (Chicago), VII (1954), 68–89.

ESTIENNE, CHARLES. *L'Art abstrait est-il académique?* Paris: Éditions de Beaune, 1941.

FLAHIFF, GEORGE B. "Commentaries on a Way of the Cross," *Liturgical Arts* (New York), XX (Aug., 1952), 112, 121–22.

FOCILLON, HENRI. *Hokousai.* Paris: F. Alcan [1914].

————. *Vie des formes.* Paris: E. Leroux, 1934. (The 2nd edn.—Paris: F. Alcan, 1939—includes an addition: "L'Éloge de la main.") (*The Life of Forms in Art.* Translated by Charles B. Hogan and George Kubler. London: Oxford University Press, 1942. 2nd edn., enlarged, New York: Wittenborn, Schultz, 1948.)

FONTAINAS, ANDRÉ. *Histoire de la peinture française au vingtième siècle.* Paris: Mercure de France, 1906.

FONTAINE, ANDRÉ. *Les Doctrines d'art en France, peintres, amateurs, critiques, de Poussin à Diderot.* Paris: Librairie Renouard–H. Laurens, 1909.

FRANCASTEL, PIERRE. "L'Expérience figurative et le temps," *XXᵉ Siècle* (Paris), n.s., V (June, 1955), 41–48.

FRANKFURTER, ALFRED M. "The Gentle Art of Faking," *Art News* (New York), LII (Feb., 1954), 16–19, 66–67.

FROMENTIN, EUGÈNE. *Dominique.* Translated by Edward Marsh. London: Cresset Press, 1948.

———. *The Masters of Past Time: Dutch and Flemish Painting from Van Eyck to Rembrandt.* Translated by Andrew Boyle, edited by H. Gerson. London: Phaidon Press, 1948.

GABO, NAUM. "A Retrospective View of Constructive Art," in: J. J. Sweeney, Katherine Dreier, and Naum Gabo. *Three Lectures on Modern Art.* New York: Philosophical Library, 1949.

GAERTNER, JOHANNES A. "Art as the Function of an Audience," *Daedalus* (Boston), LXXXVI, No. 1 (1955), 80–93.

GAUGUIN, PAUL. *The Intimate Journals of Paul Gauguin.* Translated by Van Wyck Brooks, with a preface by Émile Gauguin. Melbourne, London, and Toronto: William Heinemann, 1952. (First pub. in a limited edn., 1921.)

———. *Lettres de Gauguin à sa femme et à ses amis.* Collected, with notes and a preface, by Maurice Malingue. Paris: B. Grasset, 1946.

———. *Lettres de Paul Gauguin à Georges-Daniel de Monfreid.* With an *hommage* by Victor Segalen. Paris: G. Crès, 1918. (Reprinted Paris: Plon, 1930.)

GHYKA, MATILA C. *Le Nombre d'or: Rites et rythmes pythagoriciens dans le développement de la civilisation occidentale.* With a letter of Paul Valéry. 2 vols. Paris: Gallimard, 1931 (9th edn., 1952).

GIDE, ANDRÉ. *Journal (1889–1939).* Paris: Gallimard, 1948. (Bibliothèque de la Pléiade.)

———. *Journal II. Écrits intimes.* Paris: Gallimard, 1954. (Bibliothèque de la Pléiade.)

GILL, ERIC. *Art-Nonsense and Other Essays.* London: Cassell and Francis Walterson, 1929.

———. *Autobiography.* London: Jonathan Cape, 1940.

———. *Beauty Looks After Herself.* London: Sheed & Ward, 1933.

———. *Christianity and Art.* Capel-y-ffin, Abergavenny: Francis Walterson, 1927. (Reprinted in *Art-Nonsense*, pp. 216–49.)

———. *Letters of Eric Gill.* Edited by Walter Shewring. London: Jonathan Cape, 1947.

———. *Work and Property, &c.* London: J. M. Dent, 1937.

GILLET, LOUIS. "Visites au musées de Province: III. Aix-en-Provence," *Revue des deux mondes* (Paris), 8th per., XI (Sept. 15, 1932), 315–44.

GILSON, ÉTIENNE. "Art et métaphysique," *Revue de métaphysique et de morale* (Paris), XXIII, No. 1bis (Jan., 1916), 243–67.

———. *Being and Some Philosophers.* 2nd edn., Toronto: Pontifical Institute of Mediaeval Studies, 1952.

———. *L'École des muses.* Paris: J. Vrin, 1951.

———. *Introduction à l'étude de saint Augustin.* 2nd edn., Paris: J. Vrin, 1943.

————. *Le Thomisme.* 5th edn., Paris: J. Vrin, 1948.

GILSON, JACQUELINE. "Stations of the Cross, Saint Basil's Seminary, Toronto, Canada: Fourteen Plates," *Liturgical Arts* (New York), XX (1952), 116–17.

————. See also FLAHIFF, GEORGE B.; McCARTHY, PEARL.

GINDERTAEL, R. V. "L'Art 'abstrait': Nouvelle situation," in: LEBEL, ROBERT, ed., *Premier Bilan de l'art actuel,* q.v., pp. 35–39.

GLEIZES, ALBERT, and METZINGER, JEAN. *Du Cubisme.* Paris: E. Figuière, 1912.

GOETHE, JOHANN WOLFGANG VON. *Zur Farbenlehre* (1810), in: *Sämtliche Werke,* XXVIII. Stuttgart and Tübingen, 1851. (*Theory of Colours.* Translated by Sir Charles Lock Eastlake. London, 1840.)

GOGH, VINCENT VAN. *Lettres de Vincent van Gogh à son frère Théo.* Translated (into French) by Georges Philippart, with a biographical introduction by Charles Terrasse. Paris: B. Grasset, 1937.

————. *Lettres de van Gogh à van Rappard.* Translated (into French) by L. Roelandt. Paris: B. Grasset, 1950.

GOLDWATER, ROBERT, and TREVES, MARCO, eds. *Artists on Art, from the XIV to the XX Century.* Rev. edn., New York: Pantheon Books, 1947.

GOODHART-RENDEL, HENRY STUART. *Fine Art.* Oxford: Clarendon Press, 1934. (As quoted by OSBORNE, HAROLD, q.v.)

GRIS, JUAN. See KAHNWEILER, DANIEL-HENRY.

GROHMANN, WILL. *Paul Klee.* New York: H. N. Abrams [1954].

GUIGNARD, JACQUES. "Maurice Denis et l'art du livre," *Le Portique* (Paris), IV (1946), 48–71.

HAHN, HARRY J. *The Rape of La Belle.* With an introduction by Thomas Hart Benton. Kansas City: Frank Glenn Publishing Co., 1946.

HAYDON, BENJAMIN ROBERT. *The Autobiography and Journals of Benjamin Robert Haydon (1786–1846).* Edited, with an introduction by Malcolm Elwin. London: Macdonald, 1950.

HERSCH, JEANNE. *L'Être et la forme.* Neuchâtel: Les Éditions de la Baconnière, 1946.

HESS, THOMAS B. "Artists/Writers: an Impure Excursion," *Art News* (New York), LIV (Dec., 1955), 26–29, 59–60.

HOURTICQ, LOUIS. *L'Amateur de peinture.* 2nd edn., Paris: H. Floury, 1926.

————. *La Jeunesse de Titien.* Paris: Hachette, 1919.

HUIZINGA, JOHAN. *The Waning of the Middle Ages: A Study of the Forms of Life, Thought and Art in France and the Netherlands in the XIVth and XVth Centuries.* Translated by F. Hopman. Garden City, N. Y.: Doubleday, 1954. (Anchor Books.)

HUYGHE, RENÉ. *Les Contemporains.* New edn., Paris: P. Tisné, 1949.

————. "Simple Histoire de 2414 faux Corots," *L'Amour de l'art* (Paris), XI (Feb., 1936), 73–76.

INGRES, JEAN-AUGUSTE-DOMINIQUE. *Ingres raconté par lui-même et par ses amis.* 2 vols. Vésenaz-Geneva: Pierre Cailler, 1947–48.

————. See also WILDENSTEIN, GEORGES.

ISNARD, GUY. *Les Pirates de la peinture.* Paris: Flammarion, 1955.

JAMOT, PAUL. *Dunoyer de Segonzac.* Paris: H. Floury, 1929.

JOHN, AUGUSTUS. *Chiaroscuro: Fragments of Autobiography.* New York: Pellegrini & Cudahy, 1952.

JOHN OF ST. THOMAS. *The Material Logic of John of St. Thomas: Basic Treatises.* Translated by Yves R. Simon, John J. Glanville, G. Donald Hollenhorst, with a preface by Jacques Maritain. University of Chicago Press, 1955.

JOUFFROY, ALAIN. "Pour 1.250 francs on peut se procurer les chefs-d'œuvre de la peinture," *Arts* (Paris), DIV (Feb. 23–Mar. 1, 1955), 14.

JOYCE, JAMES. *A Portrait of the Artist as a Young Man.* New York: W. B. Huebsch, 1916. (Also a Signet Book, No. 664. 5th printing, New York: New American Library, 1953.)

KAHNWEILER, DANIEL-HENRY. *Juan Gris: sa vie, son œuvre, ses écrits.* 5th edn., Paris: Gallimard, 1946. (*Juan Gris, His Life and Work.* Translated by Douglas Cooper. New York: Curt Valentin, 1947.)

————. *The Rise of Cubism.* Translated by Henry Aronson. New York: Wittenborn, Schultz, 1949. (The Documents of Modern Art.) (The German original, *Der Weg zum Kubismus*, written in 1915, was first pub. Munich: Delphin-Verlag, 1920.)

KANDINSKY, WASSILY. *Concerning the Spiritual in Art, and Painting in Particular.* New York: Wittenborn, Schultz, 1947. (The Documents of Modern Art.)

KEATS, JOHN. *The Letters of John Keats.* Edited by Maurice Buxton Forman. 4th edn. (with revisions and additional letters), New York: Oxford University Press, 1952.

KECK, CAROLINE K. *How to Take Care of Your Pictures: A Primer of Practical Information.* New York: Museum of Modern Art and Brooklyn Museum, 1954.

KLEE, PAUL. In: *Schöpferische Konfession* [an anthology of artists' writings]. (Tribüne der Kunst und Zeit, edited by K. Edschmid, XIII.) Berlin: E. Reiss, 1920. (Klee's contribution, pp. 28–40. Excerpts translated in GROHMANN, WILL, q.v.)

————. *Über die moderne Kunst.* Bern-Bümpliz: Benteli, 1945. (*On Modern Art.* Translated by Paul Findlay, with an introduction by Herbert Read. London: Faber & Faber, 1948. Excerpts translated in GROHMANN, q.v.)

KLEIN, ADRIAN BERNARD. *Colour-Music: The Art of Light.* London: Lockwood, 1926.

————. "Colour-Music," *The Encyclopaedia Britannica*, 14th edn., VI, 64–65.

KRESTOVSKY, LYDIE. *La Laideur dans l'art à travers les âges.* Paris: Éditions du Seuil, 1947.

LALO, CHARLES. "Classification structurale des beaux-arts," in: Lalo *et al. Formes de l'art, Formes de l'esprit.* Paris: Presses universitaires de France, 1951.

LAMING, ANNETTE, and EMPERAIRE, JOSÉ. *L'Art préhistorique: peintures, gravures et sculptures rupestres.* Paris: Braun, 1951.

LAPOUJADE, RENÉ. *Les Mécanismes de la fascination.* With a preface by Jean Hippolyte. Paris: Éditions du Seuil, 1955.

LEBEL, ROBERT, ed. *Premier Bilan de l'art actuel* (*1937–1953*). Paris: Le Soleil noir. Positions (Nos. III and IV), 1953.

LEONARDO DA VINCI. *The Notebooks of Leonardo da Vinci.* Arranged, rendered into English and introduced by Edward MacCurdy. 2 vols. London: Jonathan Cape, 1938 (5th edn., 1948).

LESLIE, C. R. *Memoirs of the Life of John Constable.* Edited by Jonathan Mayne. London: Phaidon Press, 1951.

LHOTE, ANDRÉ. *De la Palette à l'écritoire.* Paris: Éditions Corrêa, 1946.

——. *La Peinture, le cœur et l'esprit.* Paris: Denoël et Steele, 1933.

——. *Traité de la figure.* Paris: H. Floury, 1950.

——. *Traité du paysage.* 3rd edn., Paris: H. Floury, 1946. (*Treatise on Landscape Painting.* Translated by W. J. Strachan. London: A. Zwemmer, 1950.)

MAGNY, CLAUDE-EDMONDE. "Malraux le fascinateur," *Esprit* (Paris), CXLIX (Oct., 1948), 513–34.

MALRAUX, ANDRÉ. *Le Musée imaginaire de la sculpture mondiale.* 3 vols. Paris: Gallimard, 1952–54.

——. *The Voices of Silence.* Translated by Stuart Gilbert. New York: Doubleday, 1953.

MARITAIN, JACQUES. *Creative Intuition in Art and Poetry.* (The A. W. Mellon Lectures in the Fine Arts, 1952.) New York: Pantheon Books, 1953. (Bollingen Series XXXV: 1.)

MAROGER, JACQUES. *The Secret Formulas and Techniques of the Masters.* Translated by Eleanor Beckham. New York and London: Studio Publications, 1948.

McCARTHY, PEARL. "Jacqueline Gilson," *Arts et pensée* (Montreal), XIV (Nov.–Dec., 1953), 53–54.

McLUHAN, HERBERT M. *The Mechanical Bride: Folklore of Industrial Man.* New York: Vanguard Press, 1951.

MEIER-GRAEFE, JULIUS. *Vincent van Gogh.* 4th edn., Munich: R. Piper, 1918.

MIRIMONDE, A. P. DE. *Pour mieux comprendre la peinture.* Paris: F. Nathan, 1953.

MONDRIAN, PIET. *Plastic Art and Pure Plastic Art* (*1937*) *and Other Essays* (*1941–1943*). With a preface by Robert Motherwell. New York: Wittenborn, Schultz, 1945 (3rd edn., 1951). (The Documents of Modern Art.)

MORGAN, CHARLES. *Sparkenbroke.* 5th edn., London: Macmillan, 1950.

MOTHERWELL, ROBERT. See MONDRIAN, PIET, *Plastic Art.*

MOUTON, JEAN. *Suite à la peinture.* Paris: Flaize, 1952.

MUNRO, THOMAS. *The Arts and Their Interrelations.* 2nd printing, New York: Liberal Arts Press, 1950.

——. "The Concept of Beauty in the Philosophy of Naturalism," *Revue internationale de philosophie* (Brussels), XXXI (1955), 33–77.

——. "Form and Value in the Arts: A Functional Approach," *The Journal of*

Aesthetics and Art Criticism (Baltimore), XIII (Mar., 1955), 316–41.

———— and GRIMES, JANE. *Educational Work at the Cleveland Museum of Art.* 2nd edn., Cleveland Museum of Art, 1952.

NADEAU, MAURICE. *Histoire du surréalisme.* Paris: Éditions du Seuil, 1945.

NAHM, MILTON C., ed. *Selections from Early Greek Philosophy.* New York: F. S. Crofts, 1934.

NEWTON, ISAAC. *New Theory About Light and Colours.* 1672.

ORLANDI, PELLEGRINO ANTONIO. *Abecedario Pittorico.* 1719. (As quoted by CLERICI, FABRIZIO, q.v.)

OROZCO, JOSÉ CLEMENTE. "Orozco 'Explains,' " *Bulletin of the Museum of Modern Art* (New York), 4, VII (Aug., 1940).

————. See also BARR, ALFRED H., JR.

OSBORNE, HAROLD. *Theory of Beauty: An Introduction to Aesthetics.* London: Routledge & Kegan Paul, 1952.

OZENFANT, AMÉDÉE. *Foundations of Modern Art.* Translated by John Rodker. New American edn., New York: Dover Publications, 1952. (First French edn., 1928.)

PANOFSKY, ERWIN. *Meaning in the Visual Arts: Papers in and on Art History.* Garden City, N. Y.: Doubleday, 1955. (Anchor Books.)

PAREYSON, LUIGI. "Contemplation du beau et production des formes," *Revue internationale de philosophie* (Brussels), XXXI (1955), 16–32.

PIA, PASCAL. "Derain au musée," *Arts* (Paris), XDXCIII (Dec. 8–14, 1954), 14.

PICON, GAËTAN. *Introduction à une esthétique de la littérature.* Paris: Gallimard, 1953.

————. "Rigueurs d'un pluralisme esthétique," *Critique* (Paris), X (1954), 864–77.

PISSARRO, CAMILLE. *Camille Pissarro: Letters to His Son Lucien.* Edited by John Rewald with the assistance of Lucien Pissarro. New York: Pantheon Books, 1943.

PLANET, LOUIS DE. *Souvenirs de travaux de peinture avec M. Delacroix.* Edited by André Joubin. Paris: A. Colin, 1929.

PLATO, *The Dialogues of Plato.* Translated by Benjamin Jowett. 5 vols. 3rd edn., New York, 1892.

————. *Phaedrus, Ion, Gorgias, and Symposium, with Passages from The Republic and Laws.* Translated, with introduction and prefatory notes, by Lane Cooper. New York: Oxford University Press, 1938.

POE, EDGAR ALLAN. *The Complete Tales and Poems of Edgar Allan Poe.* With an introduction by Hervey Allen. New York: Random House, 1938. (Modern Library.)

POPE, ARTHUR. *The Language of Drawing and Painting.* Cambridge, Mass.: Harvard University Press, 1949.

PORTMANN, ADOLF. *Animal Forms and Patterns: Studies of Appearances of Animals.* Translated by Hella Czech. London: Faber & Faber, 1951.

POUSSIN, NICOLAS. *Lettres de Poussin.* Edited by Pierre du Colombier. Paris: La Cité des livres, 1929.

RAMUZ, CHARLES-FERDINAND. *Questions.* Paris: B. Grasset, 1936.

READ, HERBERT. *Art and the Evolution of Man.* (Conway Memorial Lecture.) London: Freedom Press, 1951.

——. *The Meaning of Art.* Rev. edn., Harmondsworth and Baltimore: Penguin Books, 1951. (Pelican Books.)

——. *The Philosophy of Modern Art: Collected Essays.* London: Faber & Faber, 1952.

REDON, ODILON. *À soi-même: Journal (1867–1916). Notes sur la vie, l'art et les artistes.* With an introduction by Jacques Morland. Paris: H. Floury, 1922.

REVERDY, PIERRE. *Le Gant de crin.* Paris: Plon, 1927.

REWALD, JOHN. "Modern Fakes of Modern Pictures," *Art News* (New York), LII (Mar., 1953), 16–21, 46–49.

REYNOLDS, SIR JOSHUA. *The Discourses of Sir Joshua Reynolds.* Illustrated by explanatory notes and plates by John Burnet. London, 1842.

——. *The Works of Sir Joshua Reynolds; Containing His Discourses, Idlers, A Journey to Flanders and Holland, and His Commentary on Du Fresnoy's Art of Painting,* to which is prefixed an account of the life and writings of the author by Edmond Malone. 3 vols. 4th edn., London, 1809.

RIMINGTON, ALEXANDER WALLACE. *Colour Music: The Art of Mobile Colour.* New York: F. A. Stokes, 1911.

ROGER-MARX, CLAUDE. *Vuillard: His Life and Work.* Translated by E. B. d'Auvergne. New York: Éditions de la Maison française, 1946.

ROSENBERG, LÉONCE. *Cubisme et tradition.* Paris: Éditions de "L'Effort moderne," 1920. (Reprint of the preface to a catalogue of French paintings at Geneva, Feb., 1920.)

RUYER, RAYMOND. "L'Esprit et l'œil," *Critique* (Paris), XI (1955), 161–71.

SAINTE-LAGUË, ANDRÉ. *Le Monde des formes.* Paris: A. Fayard, 1948.

SAINT-SAËNS, MARC. "Le Carton et la création dans la tapisserie," in Lalo *et al., Formes de l'art* (see LALO, CHARLES).

SAND, GEORGE. "Lettre à Eugène Delacroix, 27 juillet, 1855," *Nouvelle Nouvelle Revue française* (Paris), I (1953), 573–74.

SARTRE, JEAN-PAUL. *L'Imaginaire: psychologie phénoménologique de l'imagination.* Paris: Gallimard, 1948.

SERTILLANGES, ANDRÉ-DOMINIQUE. *Art et apologétique.* 2nd edn., Paris: Bloud, 1909.

SÉRUSIER, PAUL. *ABC de la peinture, suivi d'une étude sur la vie et l'œuvre de Paul Sérusier par Maurice Denis.* Paris: H. Floury, 1942.

SEUPHOR, MICHEL [FERDINAND-LOUIS BERCKELAERS]. *L'Art abstrait, ses origines, ses premiers maîtres.* Paris: Maeght, 1949.

——. "Matière à discussion," *XXᵉ Siècle,* n.s., V (June, 1955), 9–14.

SEVERINI, GINO. "L'Intuition futuriste du dynamisme plastique," *XXᵉ Siècle* (Paris), n.s., V (June, 1955), 49–52.

SIGNAC, PAUL. *D'Eugène Delacroix au néo-impressionnisme.* 4th edn., Paris: H. Floury, 1939.

SILVESTRE, THÉOPHILE. *Eugène Delacroix: Documents nouveaux.* Paris: Michel Lévy, 1867.

————. *Les Artistes français.* 2 vols. Paris: G. Crès, 1926. (Bibliothèque dionysienne.)

SLONIMSKY, NICOLAS. *Lexicon of Musical Invective.* New York: Coleman-Ross, 1953.

SOURIAU, ÉTIENNE. *La Correspondance des arts: eléments d'esthétique comparée.* Paris: Flammarion, 1947.

————. *Les Différents Modes d'existence.* Paris: Presses universitaires de France, 1942.

————. "L'Insertion temporelle de l'œuvre d'art," in Lalo *et al., Formes de l'art* (see LALO, CHARLES).

STECHOW, WOLFGANG. "Optics and Opulence: A Brilliant View of Dutch Painting," *Art News* (New York), LIII (Nov., 1954), 18–25, 74–75.

STEIN, GERTRUDE. *Picasso.* New York: B. T. Batsford, 1948.

STITES, RAYMOND S. *The Arts and Man.* New York: Whittlesey House, McGraw-Hill, 1940.

STOKES, ADRIAN. *Colour and Form.* London: Faber & Faber, 1950.

SWEENEY, JAMES JOHNSON. "Miro," *Art News Annual* (New York), XIII (1954), 58–81, 185–88.

TABARANT, ADOLPHE. *Manet et ses œuvres.* Paris: Gallimard, 1947.

TAINE, HIPPOLYTE. *Philosophie de l'art.* 2 vols. 16th edn., Paris: Hachette, 1918.

TAPIÉ [DE CÉLEYRAN], MICHEL. "Fautrier Paints a Picture," *Art News* (New York), LIV (Dec., 1955), 30–33, 63.

————. "Messages sans étiquettes," *XXᵉ Siècle* (Paris), n.s., V (June, 1955), 17–24.

THOMAS AQUINAS, ST. *Basic Writings of St. Thomas Aquinas.* Edited and annotated, with an introduction, by Anton C. Pegis. 2 vols. New York: Random House, 1945.

————. *In Aristotelis libros De sensu et sensato, De memoria et reminiscentia commentarium.* Edited by Raymundo M. Spiazzi. 3rd edn., Turin and Rome: Marietti, 1949.

————. *In decem libros Ethicorum Aristotelis ad Nicomachum expositio.* Edited by Raymundo M. Spiazzi. Turin and Rome: Marietti, 1949.

————. *In libros politicorum Aristotelis expositio.* Edited by Raymundo M. Spiazzi: Marietti, 1951.

————. "Quaestiones disputatae de virtutibus in communi," in: *Quaestiones disputatae.* Edited by Raymundo M. Spiazzi. 8th edn., Turin and Rome: Marietti, 1949. (II, 707–52.)

————. *Sancti Thomae Aquinatis Summa theologica . . .* cura et studio Collegii Provinciae Tolosanae . . . apud S. Maximinum. 6 vols. Paris: A. Blot, 1926–35.

TRILLING, LIONEL. *The Liberal Imagination: Essays on Literature and Society.* Garden City, N. Y.: Doubleday, 1953. (Anchor Books.)

————. *The Opposing Self: Nine Essays in Criticism.* New York: Viking Press, 1955.

UNESCO. "The Care of Paintings," *Museum* (Paris), III (1950), 2, 3; IV (1951), 1.

VALÉRY, PAUL. *Degas. Danse. Dessin.* Paris: Gallimard, 1938.

————. "Le Problème des musées," in: *Pièces sur l'art.* Paris: Gallimard, 1934. (pp. 93–99.)

VASARI, GIORGIO. *The Lives of the Painters, Sculptors and Architects.* Translated by A. B. Hinds. 4 vols. London: J. M. Dent, 1927. (Everyman's Library, Nos. 784–87.)

————. *Le Opere di Giorgio Vasari, pittore e architetto aretino.* 2 vols. Florence, 1832–38. ("Introduzione alle tre arti del disegno, cioè architettura, scultura e pittura" is in I, 17–51.)

————. *Vasari on Technique: Being the Introduction to the Three Arts of Design, Architecture, Sculpture and Painting, Prefixed to the Lives.* Translated by Louisa S. Maclehose, edited with an introduction and notes by G. Baldwin Brown. London: J. M. Dent, 1907.

VENTURI, LIONELLO. *History of Art Criticism.* Translated by Charles Marriott. New York: E. P. Dutton, 1936.

VLAMINCK, MAURICE DE. *Portraits avant décès.* Paris: Flammarion, 1943.

VOLLARD, AMBROISE. *En écoutant Cézanne, Degas, Renoir.* Paris: B. Grasset, 1938.

Webster's Collegiate Dictionary. 5th edn., Springfield, Mass.: G. and C. Merriam Co., 1936.

WERTH, LÉON. *La Peinture et la mode: quarante ans après Cézanne.* Paris: B. Grasset, 1945.

WILDENSTEIN, GEORGES. *Ingres.* London: Phaidon Press, 1954.

WITTGENS, FERNANDA. "Leonardo's *Last Supper* Resurrected" (introduction by Bernard Berenson), *Art News Annual* (New York), XXIV (1955), 28–52.

WITTLIN, ALMA S. *The Museum, Its History and Its Tasks in Education.* London: Routledge & Kegan Paul, 1949.

WORMSER, HENRI, and DURAND, LÉOPOLD. *Introduction à la peinture moderne.* Paris: Studio Raber, 1945.

INDEX

INDEX

A

abstract, and concrete, 34, 155, 200, 201, 202, 203

abstract art, 123 & *n*, 250, 253, 256 & *n*, 257, 258–59 & *n*, 269 & *n*–70, 280*n*, 284*n*

academicism, 30, 44, 168, 201, 202–03, 229*n*, 246*n*

Académie des Beaux-Arts, *see* Paris

academies, art, 201, 203

accidents, to paintings, 91, 93*n*

accuracy, and truth, 155*n*

action, and movement, 24*n*–25*n*; and painting, 21–25, 26, 28, 287

Adam, 154 & *n*

Addison, Joseph, 93*n*

addition, and becoming, 107

Adrianople, 144*n*

advertisement, 262, 276

Aeschylus, *Eumenides*, 219*n*

aesthetics, 120; and education, 64, 66, 68, 72, 90–91; and painting, 11–28, 53*n*, 78, 82, 113, 131 & *n*, 177, 207–40, 286 & *n*

Aëtius, *De placitis philosophorum*, quoted, 270

Africa, art of, 49; music of, 51*n*

aging, of paintings, 93 & *n*–96

air, and octahedron, 270

Aix-en-Provence: Museum, 141

Alazard, Jean, 86*n*

Albright Art Gallery, *see* Buffalo

allegory, painting and, 145, 146, 148*n*–49*n*, 244

Allnutt, John, 92–93

Altamira, 17, 49, 151, 166

Amaury-Duval (Eugène-Emmanuel Pineau-Duval), 15*n*, 66–67 & *n*, 163, 164*n*, 220*n*; Circé, Countess of, portrait of, 67

Amico di Sandro, 77*n*

Amiens (Derain), *Pl. 36*

Amsterdam: Rijksmuseum, *Pls. 12, 60a*; Stedelijk Museum, 89*n*

Analysis of Beauty, The (Hogarth), 194–95

André, Albert, 85*n*

anecdotes, 142, 298*n*, 320

Angel of the Annunciation (Schongauer), *Pl. 38*

Angelico, Fra (Giovanni da Fiesole), 160*n*

Angélique (Ingres), 220*n*

Angelus, The (Millet), 98 & *n*

animals, 26; and color, 52

Annunciation, The (5th cent.), *Pl. 22*

Annunciation (Lorenzetti), 243*n*

Annunciation with Two Saints (Martini), 243*n*

Anquetin, Louis, 56*n*, 57

anthropomorphism, 109, 296

antiquity, art of, 98*n*, 201 & *n*, 202*n*; of paintings, 82

Antonello da Messina, *St. Jerome in His Study, Pl. 68*

Antwerp, 315

Apollo, 202*n*

Apotheosis of Alexander the Great (Colonna & Mitelli), 247*n*

Apotheosis of St. Ignatius, The (Pozzo), 247*n*, *Pl. 69*

Apotheosis of Napoleon I, The (Ingres), 220*n*

appearance, visual, and art, 123 & *n*, 270–71, 277, 280, 283; and geometry, 254 & *n*–55

applause, 42 & *n*

apprehension, and pleasure, 180–87, 210, 212

Arab Horses Fighting in a Stable (Delacroix), 21, *Pl. 4b*

Arber, Agnes, 156*n*

archaeology, and art, 81, 82, 232

348INDEX

Bru, Charles-Pierre, 265*n*
Brueghel, Pieter, the Elder, 120, 148,
259*n; Harvesters,* 148; *Journey to
Emmaus, The,* Pl. *41*
Brunschvicg, Léon, 214*n*
Buffalo: Albright Art Gallery, *Pl. 84*
buildings, 282–83; art in, 234, 235
Bülow, Hans von, 37
Burckhardt, Jakob, 85*n*
Burnet, John, 26*n;* quoted, 98*n,* 168*n,*
183*n,* 202*n*
business, and art, 64–65 & *n,* 68, 71, 72,
207
buyers, of paintings, 92–93, 275–76
Bywater, Ingram, 134*n*
Byzantine art, 62, 232, 242, 284, 285*n*

C

Caillebotte, Gustave, 276
Callcott, Sir Augustus, 92
Camoin, Charles, 139*n*
Canaletto (Antonio Canal), 171*n*
canvas, 12, 109, 114; deterioration of,
99*n*
cardboard, 12, 122*n*
Carnegie Institute, *see* Pittsburgh
Carpaccio, Vittore, 192, 236, 258; *Legend
of St. Ursula, The,* 192; *St. Stephen
Disputing with the Doctors,* Pl. *66*
Cassatt, Mary, *Boating Party, The,* Pl. *77*
Castel, Louis, 50*n*
categories, 273*n*
causality, of form, 134–74; material,
and art, 54–64, 121; natural and
artistic, 112–13
cause/cause, and effect, 120 & *n,* 134,
289 & *n,* 293, 294; Prime, 120 & *n*
Cavé, Mme, 128*n*
cave paintings, 17, 49, 55, 151, 166
Cazalis, Henri, 278*n*
ceilings, painted, 70
Cézanne, Paul, 43*n,* 51*n,* 58*n,* 68, 71*n,*
94, 138–39 & *n,* 140 & *n,* 141, 143,
150, 151, 160*n,* 163 & *n,* 185 & *n,* 186*n,*
189*n,* 190, 218*n,* 220*n,* 253,
254 & *n*–55 & *n,* 256*n,* 267, 270, 276,
279 & *n,* 281; quoted, 139*n,* 221*n,* 226,
249*n,* 254 & *n,* 279 & *n*
chalks, 61 & *n*
Chambray, Roland Fréart de Chantelou,
Sieur de, 179*n,* 190 & *n*

chance, and art, 288
change, in aesthetic experience, 18–19;
in art, 218*n;* and being, 74–75, 95, 96
Chantelou, *see* Chambray
charcoal, 61 & *n*
Chardin, Jean-Baptiste-Siméon, 26;
Grace, Pl. *78b; Silver Cup, The,*
Pl. *14b*
chemistry, and painting, 51–54
Cherubini, Maria Luigi Carlo Zenobio
Salvatore, 14*n*
Chesterton, G. K., 239*n,* 285*n*
Chevreul, Michel Eugène, 49
chiaroscuro, 171*n*
children, art of, 38 & *n*
China, art of, 62, 232, 298*n*
Chirico, Giorgio di, 81*n*
Chocquet, Victor, 276
Chopin, Frédéric-François, 37, 219*n,*
314; Delacroix's portrait of, 46*n,* Pl.
17b
Christ, Nativity of, 142
Christ on the Cross (Giovanetti), *Pl. 1*
Christ on the Cross (Prud'hon), 57*n*
Christ on the Lake of Gennesaret
(Delacroix), 142, *Pl. 51b*
Christ on the Sea of Galilee (Delacroix),
Pl. 51c
Christianity, and art, 62, 141 & *n,* 239*n,*
261*n*–62*n,* 268, 293, 294–96; and
creation, 119–21, 150*n*
churches, art in, 262*n,* 295–96; paintings
of, 27, 28
Cimabue, Giovanni (Cenni di Pepo),
42*n,* 242, 285*n*
Circé, Countess of, portrait of
(Amaury-Duval), 67
Circus, The (Seurat), 21–22, *Pl. 5*
cities, paintings of, 27
claritas, 193 & *n*–94
classicism, 139*n,* 140, 201
Claude Lorrain, 26*n*
clavilux, 50*n*
clay, 107
cleaning, of paintings, 96
Clerici, Fabrizio, 247*n;* quoted, 246*n*
Cleveland: Museum of Art, 148, *Pl. 55*
Clorinde (Delacroix), 316
Cocq, Captain, 263
Cocteau, Jean, quoted, 264
cognition, 115, 116, 178, 179, 180, 194